THE HUNDRED DAYS

EDITH SAUNDERS

THE
HUNDRED
DAYS

W · W · NORTON & COMPANY · INC·

NEW YORK

COPYRIGHT © 1964 BY EDITH SAUNDERS

Library of Congress Catalog Card No. 64-20417

PRINTED IN THE UNITED STATES OF AMERICA

CONTENTS

ILLUSTRATIONS

MAPS

ACKNOWLEDGEMENTS

I wish to thank all who have helped me in the writing of this book. They include knowledgeable friends who have most kindly read the book in manuscript, my son who has spent so much time on the proofs, and many keepers and librarians, among whom I would like to mention Miss A. Scott Elliot, of the Royal Library, Windsor Castle, Mr. A. Taylor, lately of the Royal United Services Museum, and the late Major J. P. Kaestlin, M.B.E., M.A., formerly librarian of the Woolwich Military Academy. It is impossible to acknowledge adequately my debt to the London Library whose organization is so perfectly fitted to the needs of the writer, and whose staff are so unfailingly helpful. Finally, I am indeed grateful to Major P. P. R. de Burgh, R.H.A., in command of G (Mercer's troop) Parachute Battery, and to Captain D. J. Budd, M.B.E., R.H.A., for allowing me access to the Battery papers and providing the portrait of the great man who commanded G Troop at Waterloo, General (then Captain) Cavalié Mercer.

I am grateful to J. M. Dent & Sons Ltd. and E. P. Dutton & Co. Inc. for material from the Everyman's Library edition of Fanny Burney's *Diary* selected and edited by Lewis Gibbs.

THE HUNDRED DAYS

1

Napoleon's return from Elba in 1815 was the most daring feat of his career. With a small band of adventurous men he landed on the coast of France, from which he had been exiled less than a year previously, and against all probability marched from Cannes to Paris, beginning the journey as an outlaw and ending triumphantly in his former position of Emperor of the French. Such an enterprise required surpassing energy and full presence of mind. Long marches had to be made and hostile forces met; men had to be adroitly handled, proclamations had to be written and printed and speeches delivered. Napoleon conducted all with a victorious facility, winning the population over to him wherever he appeared and showing himself as the master of every event. It is not surprising that the majority of Europeans, amazed by such a brilliant *tour de force*, believed that he had returned to stay and that it was useless to contend with such a powerful genius. Yet only three months later, this man, the great Napoleon, was to conduct the Waterloo campaign in an entirely different fashion, making mistake upon mistake as though with a mind bemused. Scarcely does the same man seem to be acting; and it appears as though the Fates swept him back to power, removing all difficulties from his path and presenting favourable coincidences at every turn, only to show in greater relief the nemesis he had prepared for himself during the past twenty years. Supremely assured, he resumed his sway as Emperor, the man whom others honoured and acclaimed. But no sooner had he reached this position than the tide turned against him; and the history of the next three months, in which his most strenuous endeavours could bring about nothing except the reverse of what he willed, suggests that far from having consciously produced the events and victories of his successful days he was, in common with all men who make history, driven by forces beyond his control.

The month of March 1815 opened with prospects of an enduring peace in Europe. The long war with France in which England had been involved for more than twenty years had been brought to an end the previous spring, and the Emperor Napoleon, roundly defeated, had been obliged to abdicate and exchange the great Empire he had conquered for the sovereignty of the small island of Elba off the coast of Italy. In his place there now reigned his most Christian Majesty Louis XVIII, elderly and unambitious, whose main wish was to live on good terms with the great Powers to whom he owed his return to the throne of France. A treaty of 'Peace and Amity', too, had been signed a few weeks previously by Great Britain and the United States of America, between whom a state of war had subsisted since 1812. A most blessed calm had succeeded the widely extended tempest which had raged so furiously since the outbreak of the French Revolution, and it seemed that nothing was needed now but patience and industry to bring about the recovery of the nations.

In Vienna, monarchs and diplomats had been assembled since September for a general settlement of the tangled affairs of Europe. It was a conference of dynasts, seeking for an equilibrium on which to base future diplomacy with a view to maintaining their houses in security, free from revolution and war. The affairs of lesser men were hardly considered (apart from the matter of slavery, about which England was much concerned); however, peace was certainly the first necessity of the times, and it might at least be hoped that improved conditions for mankind in general would soon follow its firm establishment.

A basis for peace had been hard to find, although it was so greatly desired, and there had been some critical moments at the Vienna Congress when war seemed about to break out anew among the wearied and impoverished nations. It had been easy for the Allies to agree among themselves when they were bound together by the aim of defeating Napoleon; but now that this danger was over they were disunited by the separate interests they felt driven to pursue, and their councils had been stormy. The question that had most divided them was that of the fate of Poland. The Tsar, Alexander I, supported by Frederick William III, King of Prussia, had wished to create a united Poland under his own auspices; he had been sharply opposed by Francis I, Emperor of Austria, and Castlereagh, the plenipotentiary of Great Britain. The flames of discord had been fanned vigorously by Talleyrand, representative of Louis XVIII, who hoped to improve the status of France by siding with Great Britain and Austria. Eventually Alexander and Frederick William had made such warlike threats that Talleyrand was able to prevail upon Castlereagh and Metternich, the Minister of the Emperor of Austria, to sign a secret treaty of alliance between Great Britain, Austria and France against Russia and Prussia.

This secret treaty had been signed on 3 January 1815. It certainly served to re-establish the influence of France, and it must have been with great satisfaction that Talleyrand wrote to Louis XVIII: 'The Coalition is dissolved. France is no longer isolated in Europe.'

Secret though the treaty was, Alexander heard of it almost at once; and since neither he nor the King of Prussia really desired to bring about another general European war, the crisis vanished almost overnight. Castlereagh wrote to the English Prime Minister, Lord Liverpool: 'The alarm of war is over.' Argument continued in a more sober fashion, and early in February a compromise was agreed upon by the Powers and put into treaty form.

It was on 3 February, the day on which the compromise was accepted, that the Duke of Wellington arrived in Vienna to take the place of Lord Castlereagh who, as Leader of the House of Commons, had to return home to answer the criticisms being levelled against him in Parliament. After introducing Wellington to the members of the Congress and Viennese society, Castlereagh left the city on 14 February to face the strictures of the Opposition who charged him with being a party to reaction.

Argument continued, but guns were mercifully kept silent. In Vienna, the Duke caught a violent cold and found the drawing-rooms airless and overheated. In his position, however, he could not avoid social gatherings, and he put up with hot rooms and the adulation he received as the genius of the Peninsular War with dignity and composure. A controlled man, he seemed to be scarcely touched by the outer aspects of the moment.

When once the danger of renewed war was over, the members of the Congress had settled down to their normal routine of conferences and lavish entertainments. The problems still remaining presented difficulties but no particular danger; the question of Italy

3

had been thrashed out simultaneously with that of Poland and its fate was by now decided upon; other major problems had also been dealt with, and by the beginning of March the wider issues were settled and committees had to work only on details and small affairs. For a moment men had waited breathlessly in a nightmare of dread, expecting war to break out again; but now the tension was over, spring was approaching, and the visitors in the Austrian capital gave themselves up with joyful relief to the balls, banquets and other social events which made the Congress an extravagant festival. The palaces of the Emperor, the great houses of Metternich and Schwarzenberg, resounded with music and laughter every evening and shone with flowers and jewels in the light of thousands of wax candles. That any event could now set all the armed forces of Europe in motion again was unthinkable.

Great, therefore, was the astonishment and still greater the indignation when it was learnt early in March that Napoleon, after enduring his banishment with seeming resignation for nearly a year, had suddenly left the island of Elba to re-enter high politics. The famous 'hundred days' had begun. Our ancestors, however, had no way of knowing that such a term was set to their ordeal. The probability that faced them was a resumption of war which, if fortune once again favoured Napoleon, would bring him allies and might well prove endless. Only three years ago Napoleon had been the master of Europe; his prestige was immense, and his singular name could hardly be heard without the association of fear and the belief that things impossible to other men were possible to him. Suddenly Vienna was a changed city. Groups collected in the streets awaiting news and discussing rumours. What was Napoleon's intention? people asked one another. What steps were being taken by the Powers?

The Duke of Wellington was the first to hear the news in Vienna; it came in a letter from Lord Burghersh in Florence, saying that Napoleon had sailed from Elba to an unknown destination. The Austrian Minister Metternich received a similar message about the same time from the Austrian Consul General at Genoa. It ran as follows:

The English Commissioner Campbell has just entered the harbour enquiring whether anyone had seen Napoleon at Genoa, in view of the fact that he had disappeared from the island of Elba. The answer being in the negative, the English frigate without further delay put to sea.

Metternich records in his memoirs that he opened his letter from Genoa early in the morning of 7 March and hastened with it to the Emperor Francis. Francis sent him immediately to the Tsar and the King of Prussia with the message that he, Francis, was ready to order his army to march back to France. Metternich writes:

At a quarter past eight I was with the Emperor Alexander, who dismissed me with similar words to those of the Emperor Francis. At half past eight I received an identical declaration from King Frederick William III. At nine o'clock I was at my home again, where I had directed Field-Marshal Prince Schwarzenberg to meet me. At ten o'clock the Ministers of the four Powers came at my request. At the same hour adjutants were already on their way, in all directions, to order the armies who were returning home to halt.

Thus war was decided on in less than an hour.

Talleyrand was also asked to join the meeting of the four Ministers referred to above, and he was the first to arrive. If there were men in Europe who were willing to wait and hear what Napoleon had to say for himself before striking him down, Metternich and Talleyrand were not of their number. Both had long detested him, and they had exerted themselves far too strenuously and successfully in the diplomacy of the Congress not to be infuriated by this threat of seeing their work undone. Metternich was more pessimistic than Talleyrand who did not think Napoleon would risk landing in France where, on his way down to Elba the previous spring, he had been execrated in the southern Departments. 'He will land on some part of the Italian coast,' Talleyrand said, 'and then fling himself into Switzerland.'

'He will go straight to Paris,' Metternich replied.

The idea of setting Napoleon up as the sovereign of Elba had been Alexander's; Metternich had been obliged to consent to the scheme in view of the Tsar's immense power, although he protested that it was highly dangerous. The Tsar had replied that Napoleon had agreed to live from now on aloof from the affairs of the Continent, and that it would be insulting to doubt the word of a soldier and a sovereign. The Tsar was acting in accordance with the eighteenth-century code of limited warfare; but Metternich did not trust Napoleon who owed so much of his success to the opportunities that code had given him of stealing a march on other men. He told the Tsar he would sign the treaty according Napoleon his kingdom, but warned him it would bring the Allies back to the battle-field in less than two years.[1]

The Duke of Wellington also thought that Napoleon would make for Paris, and news arrived in a day or two showing that he and Metternich were right. Napoleon had landed on the French coast not far from Cannes with his small personal army of about 1,100 men. All was quiet in this region; mules, horses and supplies of food had been purchased at Cannes and Napoleon and his following had then set off northwards, presumably towards the capital. The date of their landing was 1 March, and they had taken the mountainous route to Grenoble at midnight.

The news travelled as rapidly as was possible in those times. It reached Marseilles on the 3rd and Lyons by the morning of the 5th. Transmitted by semaphore from this city to Paris, it reached the capital in the course of the same day. Louis XVIII, more astonished than alarmed, was somewhat at a loss at first as to what measures he should take. He felt it was important to keep the population in ignorance as long as possible so as to avoid public excitement, and apart from a few of his ministers no one but members of the royal family was told of the event.

Believing he had done his best for France since the restoration, the King imagined that the great majority of his subjects would support him, despite the state of unrest prevailing. He ruled constitutionally and had given the country peace and liberty. His government had been faced with the usual troubles of a country defeated in war; France was frustrated and disorganized and there was a huge financial deficit. The peace treaty had caused widespread dissatisfaction, although the Allies had been generous in their treatment of the nation at their mercy. France was left with its pre-Napoleonic frontier, the frontier of 1792, and the loss of Belgium and the left bank of the Rhine was keenly felt and even regarded as a grievance. Moreover, the old revolutionary animosities were still alive;

[1] Metternich, *Mémoires*, Vol. I, pp. 240-1.

the royalists, now that they were back in power, were often intract-
able, bigoted and vindictive, though in this they did not take after
their king who was a man of moderation and sublime patience; they
found ample encouragement, however, in the attitude of the
Comte d'Artois, brother of the King, and other reactionary princes
of the ruling house. In general, the returned *émigrés* were hated, and
the country was divided into factions which were always capable
of rending one another. The army above all was dissatisfied and
there had been various conspiracies among Bonapartist officers
to overthrow the régime. But the King believed these troubles would
pass and that the country would eventually settle down. What
could any government give France that was better than the Charter
he himself guaranteed? Bonapartists and Jacobins were allowed
positions of importance; the prefects and judges of the Empire had
been retained in office; the maintenance of the revolutionary land
settlements was guaranteed; men could live in security, without
fear of arbitrary acts of injustice. What alternative did Napoleon
offer? Could he do more? The King and his circle did not at first
believe that the deposed Emperor would obtain a following; but
they could see that the situation had its dangers and that immediate
steps must be taken.

Marshal Soult, Minister of War, greatly embarrassed by the
reappearance of the Emperor whom he had long served, took
energetic measures. He proposed to put 30,000 men into the southern
provinces; the Comte d'Artois would command them, assisted by
his sons the Duc d'Angoulême and the Duc de Berry and further
aided by three Marshals of France, Macdonald, Gouvion Saint-Cyr
and Ney. The Comte d'Artois left Paris for Lyons on the evening
of the 5th.

Napoleon's former Minister of Police, Fouché, who always had
means of knowing what was going on, learnt of Napoleon's landing
almost as soon as did the King. Fouché was at this time involved in a
Bonapartist military plot, the aim of which was to establish a
regency for Napoleon's son. He did not welcome the news; his
scheming was for personal power as member of a regency, and he
had no wish to see Napoleon himself back on the throne. With his
usual resourcefulness he decided to precipitate the revolt, intending
to turn events to his own profit whether Napoleon's venture

succeeded or failed. He accordingly sent messengers off to Lille where troops were ready to march on Paris and seize the Palace of the Tuileries; but the revolt was to come to nothing. A mere handful of men under General Lefebvre-Desnouettes marched as far as Fontainebleau, but they failed to arouse the least response and, completely discouraged, soon abandoned the attempt. This fiasco suggests that the country would indeed have settled down, as Louis expected, had Napoleon not returned.

Napoleon and his company had continued their march northwards. By dawn on 2 March they were in Grasse where a hurried meal was prepared while the local population looked on with no more than a mild interest. At eight in the morning the march was resumed. The road they had followed from Cannes ended at Grasse, and for the next sixty miles they had to take a mountain path, high and snow-covered, at times leading past precipices. The artillery and a carriage requisitioned at Cannes had to be abandoned; the treasure was loaded on to mules and the company walked in single file. Those provided with horses had to walk beside their mounts, and Napoleon himself went on foot. The route was difficult and more than once he stumbled and fell into the snow. Once after doing so he paused to take a rest in a solitary hut occupied by an aged woman and a few cows.

'Well,' Napoleon said to the old woman as he warmed himself at her fire, 'what news is there from Paris?'

She looked at him in surprise. How should she know what was going on in Paris? The short, heavy man in his plain grey overcoat might as well ask her what was happening in China.

'You don't know what the King is doing, then?' Napoleon asked.

'The King?' the woman replied, looking still more puzzled. 'You mean the Emperor. The Emperor Napoleon rules in Paris.'

She had heard nothing of the great events of the last year or two, and Napoleon turned to one of his companions, General Drouot, as they left the hut and said:

'Well, Drouot, what is the use, after all, of struggling to impose our names upon the world?'[1]

He did not, however, retrace his steps after this sage reflection.

[1] Thiers, *Histoire de l'Empire*, Vol. IV, p. 351.

The long journey continued; the sun set and the party marched onwards until, twelve hours after leaving Grasse, they reached the hamlet of Seranon where they spent the night. In twenty hours they had covered over thirty miles without meeting any opposition; they had, indeed, seen very few people, for the route they were taking was almost deserted at this time of year. The simple inhabitants of the mountain villages were not disposed to resist the arrival of hundreds of armed men, though the mayor of Seranon sent a messenger off to the authorities of Castellane, informing them that the 'Emperor Bonaparte' was in his commune with an army. At Castellane Napoleon and his soldiers arrived during the following morning and were well received; they obtained large supplies of bread, meat and wine, and Napoleon promised the sub-prefect promotion as soon as he reached Paris. It was snowing and the march became still more difficult. A mule carrying cases of money fell from the narrow path into a ravine and was killed; nearly two thousand gold coins were lost in a stream and in the crevices of rocks. The party reached Barrème late at night having advanced another twenty-nine miles during the day. In the course of the next two days they continued along icy roads, crossing the river Durance and arriving at Gap on the evening of the 5th; here they were welcomed by a rejoicing population who had illumined the buildings in their honour. The further north they went the more friendly the people grew.

By now they were nearing Grenoble, centre of the 7th military division, where General Marchand was in command. News of Napoleon's approach had reached the town, and the General was preparing to arrest him in his course, though with many misgivings since the majority of the men in the barracks had remained faithful to the fallen ruler and the townspeople, apart from the nobility and the clergy, shared their views. Having put the town in a state of defence, General Marchand now sent out an infantry battalion under royalist officers to meet the former Emperor, and the decisive moment came when these troops held a pass at Laffray and the men from Elba came in sight.

Napoleon must have known that he would have to face a crisis such as this some time in the course of his journey, and he was ready for it. Ordering his men to halt and reverse their arms, he marched calmly forward towards the troops from Grenoble whose officers, though aware of their disloyalty, were now commanding them to fire. 'Soldiers of the 5th', he cried, 'do you recognize me?' Hundreds of voices responded and, throwing open his coat, he invited them to shoot their Emperor if they would. Smiling, confident, he walked up to them; the soldiers lowered their muskets and broke into loud cries of '*Vive l'Empereur.*' Hastening forward with outstretched hands, he greeted them as well loved friends. The battalion commander handed over his sword, and Napoleon shook hands with him and then allowed him to ride away.[1] Shortly afterwards, Colonel Labédoyère, carried away by the emotions of the hour, pranced from the town at the head of a tumultuous infantry regiment which he led over to Napoleon. After this, Grenoble fell inevitably into Napoleon's hands, while the royalists hastened from the district. He had ceased to be a mere rebel and felt himself a prince once more.

Napoleon took possession of the town on the evening of 7 March, the day when Metternich conferred with the monarchs and plenipotentiaries in Vienna and war was decided on in less than an hour. In a week he had marched two hundred miles, and not a shot had been fired. The citizens of Grenoble received him with clamorous rejoicing, and that night he held a reception at his hotel and addressed army officers, the mayor and municipal authorities, showing himself at the window from time to time to the cheering crowds outside.

He talked eloquently and modestly of his reasons for returning and his plans for the future. He had had ten quiet months in which to reflect on the past, he said, and to seek for its lessons. The animosity which had been poured upon him, far from irritating him, had been instructive; he now saw what France really needed and he would endeavour to obtain it for her. Peace and liberty were the imperative needs of the hour, and his conduct would be entirely ruled by these necessities. He would respect the Treaty of Paris as the basis of his policy. He had no doubts at all about maintaining peace; he had already communicated his views and intentions to his father-in-

---

[1] In addressing the battalion which had just come over to him, Napoleon was by no means truthful. It was not ambition that had brought him back, he said. Leading members of the Paris government had been in touch with him at Elba, and he had the support of the three chief Powers of Europe. (This information was given in the deposition of the battalion commander, Lessard, in February 1816 when an enquiry was being made as to General Marchand's conduct in March 1815. See Chuquet, *Lettres de 1815.* pp. 96-7.)

law, the Emperor Francis, and he had reason to hope this would assure him the support of Austria. He was about to send a further despatch to Vienna via Turin, and he was counting on the arrival in France of his wife and son in the near future.

With regard to his internal policy, Napoleon entered into the controversies of the time. Since the return of Louis XVIII, the peasants had been fearful of losing the advantages brought to them by the revolution, particularly those amongst them who had bought land confiscated from the aristocracy. Their fears regarding their property had little justification, but it was natural that they should feel apprehension on this score now that the despoiled nobles were returned from exile and were free to voice their complaints. The army, too, had reason for discontent, for when peace was restored lack of funds had made a large reduction in the naval and military establishments unavoidable. Moreover, the famous Imperial Guard of Napoleon had been slighted by Louis who had established a bodyguard of 6,000 nobles and other gentlemen, most of whom had been living abroad for twenty years or so. Among these gentlemen were such soldiers as General d'Arblay, whom Fanny Burney had married when he was a penniless exile in England. A position in the King's army gave Monsieur d'Arblay a little status at last, and enabled him to live with his wife, who herself was not very well off, in a condition of modest ease in Paris. But to help his 'poor *émigrés*', as he called them, Louis could do no other in an impoverished country than neglect the favourites of the previous régime. Thus it was that many soldiers had been dismissed or placed on half-pay; moreover, the Treasury could not always provide even half-pay, so that there was much distress among deserving military men. Finally, the clergy, by preaching a return to the old uncritical submission to Church and Crown, exasperated the large numbers who had learnt liberal ideas under the revolution.

Napoleon assured his audience at Grenoble that he had come to defend the interests of the peasants, to save the army from humiliation, and to ensure the preservation of all that had been gained for the people by the revolution. The Bourbons were incapable of governing France; the revolution had changed the country, and its new interests could be understood and protected only by a modern government which had arisen out of the new ideas. In such a fashion his own house had risen up; and now he had come back to prepare the way for his son. His son would be the true representative of the new France, and he was here to make ready his reign. Even if he had not returned, he said, the Bourbons would eventually have fallen in the midst of the disorders they were bound to provoke; whereas he, on the contrary, by giving security to new interests and by satisfying the spirit of liberty, would safeguard the country from future disturbances by suppressing their cause. He himself would shortly propose the revision of the Imperial constitution, so that there should emerge from it a genuinely representative monarchy, the sole form of government worthy of a nation as enlightened as France.

He spoke with dignity and simplicity, made excuses for the mistakes of Louis XVIII, and kept any words of criticism for his own past alone. He skilfully identified the rights of his dynasty with the rights of the nation, and he spoke principally of his son, indicating that he had reappeared upon French soil with the sole desire to place on the head of a child the crown of a peaceful, free and prosperous nation.

There is no reason to suppose that he was insincere at the moment of speaking, or to doubt that this had been the substance of his aspirations during his better hours of thought in Elba. Those who listened to him were deeply and favourably impressed, as well they might be; for if all were to be as he said, no wiser and better man could come forward to lead the country. Yet these avowed aims and intentions, however sincerely spoken they might be, had no workable reality. At that moment, in full triumph and vigour, after a good dinner, surrounded by converts such as Labédoyère in all the emotional glow of their apostasy, he spoke from the highest and best of his conceptions of himself and his duty. But this conception belonged only to one of his ever-changing moods and required for its duration a world of people in agreement with him, and a perpetuation of his present frame of mind.

On the following day Napoleon reviewed the troops assembled in Grenoble, 7,000 in all. Overnight these men had brought out the tri-colour cockades which they had never thrown away and now wore them in place of the white emblem of the Bourbons. A surge of joy and enthusiasm ran through their ranks and their acclamations shook the heavens. To their delight, they learnt that they were to march forthwith to Lyons in advance of their Emperor who would join them later and ride at their head as they entered the city. After that, they would march to Paris. They would fight any who opposed them, but the probability was that their enthusiasm would prove contagious when other troops were encountered and that Napoleon would be welcomed wherever he appeared.

The force Napoleon had now gathered was indeed small compared with the entire army which the government had to set against him; but he had within him the premonition of success. He felt that all would yield and give way to his will; the army would turn to him as one man; the Bourbons would retire into exile, the unwanted *émigrés* with them. And, indeed, such was to be his experience.

When his soldiers had marched away from Grenoble, he returned to his hotel where he wrote to his wife, Marie Louise, who was in Vienna with their son, the little 'King of Rome'. He told her of his successful entry into Grenoble, and assured her of his certainty of being welcomed in Paris. He urged her to rejoin him there with their son, and to assure her father, the Emperor Francis, of his desire for peace and good relations. A courier rode off openly with the letter by way of Mont Cenis, so that the idea should be given that communication had been established between himself and the court of Austria.

The following day, 9 March, Napoleon rode off, surrounded by his retinue from Elba, to catch up the troops on their way to Lyons.

By this time the whole population of France had heard the great news which could not long be hidden. The royalists were naturally much incensed and the Bonapartists delighted. The peasants and the working classes of the large towns welcomed the news, except in certain districts with royalist sympathies. In the ranks of the army there was intense excitement and every sign that discipline would be hard to maintain. Tradesmen and the professional classes, however, were scarcely less annoyed than the royalists. Although most of them disliked the Bourbons, they much preferred them to a régime likely to bring on an endless series of wars. The Bourbons now perforce ruled constitutionally, and the more thoughtful members of society hoped as time went on to build up an increasing opposition to the King in the Chamber of Deputies, and so gradually produce a truly democratic and modern government. Such would have been a better way out of the country's difficulties than a return to power of an emperor who had made himself intolerable to every foreign government.

At first it was thought that Napoleon would quickly be killed or captured. A proclamation had been issued on the 7th, forbidding any Frenchman to aid or adhere to him, and calling on those through whose districts he passed to capture him, dead or alive. If taken alive he was to be delivered up forthwith to the military authorities who, in consequence of his armed entry into France, would treat him as a malefactor and an outlaw, and punish him with immediate execution. But when it was learnt that the troops of Grenoble had gone over to him, men began to fear that it would be no easy task to suppress him.

The King and his Ministers knew they had cause to fear disloyalty in the army which for so many years had served Napoleon. They could rely upon the marshals, however; Napoleon's reign had been brought to an end by an insurrection of his marshals who would therefore scarcely wish him back again. Macdonald, an excellent soldier, had followed the princes to Lyons; Ney was in Paris, on his way from his country home to Besançon where he was in command of the 6th division, garrisoned in that town. Ney's reputation was legendary. If anyone could ensure the devotion of the ordinary soldier, he was the man, for he had proved himself time and again to be, as he was popularly called, 'the bravest of the brave', and he was the hero of every private in the army.

Having been ordered to Besançon, Ney had decided to call first on Marshal Soult in Paris, and he had arrived in the capital on 7 March. There he heard for the first time of Napoleon's landing on French soil. He avowed himself so shocked by the event, and appeared so indignant and alarmed, that the King was delighted and reassured.

The royalists had in mind the events of a year ago at the time of Napoleon's fall. Even with the victorious Allies in occupation of Paris, Napoleon would have carried on the war to the last extremity had he not been firmly opposed by his marshals. Marshal Marmont had settled the matter by taking over a whole army corps to the enemy, after which Napoleon had been forced to admit himself defeated. Napoleon's negotiations with the enemy in Paris, had been conducted by Marshals Macdonald and Ney and the Minister Caulaincourt, and while Macdonald and Caulaincourt were discreet and dignified Ney had criticized Napoleon very freely.

Ney was a lively and talkative man who habitually behaved as if slightly intoxicated. The thoughts of the moment, which another would keep to himself, flowed out aloud so that everyone knew exactly what he was thinking and judged him accordingly. In the presence of the Tsar Alexander, he had talked of the dangers of Napoleon's militarism, urging that he should be forced to abdicate; subsequently, when Napoleon, being persuaded that it was inevitable, had signed the act of abdication, Ney had boasted among the royalists of the part he had played in compelling him to take this course. As a result, he was generally regarded in society as a man who had failed in loyalty and respect to the ruler who had loaded him with riches and honours.

Napoleon was well aware of his conduct, and if he should now succeed in winning his way back to power, Ney would have nothing to expect but disgrace.

Summoned before the King, Ney was emphatic in his protestations of fidelity to the royal cause, and in a moment of bravado he declared he would bring Napoleon to Paris in an iron cage, a phrase that was soon being repeated all over the capital. Such words were not much to the taste of Louis who, after his marshal had left, remarked that he would not care to be presented with such a bird; none the less, the court circle was greatly encouraged by Ney's fiery zeal and confident that all would now be well.

Michel Ney was born in 1769, so that he was now forty-six years old, the same age as Napoleon and the Duke of Wellington. The son of a tradesman, he began life as a clerk to an attorney. But he had no taste for office life and at the age of nineteen he joined the army as a private.

His career was brilliantly successful and he enjoyed it to the full as he played his adventurous part in the revolutionary wars and steadily rose in rank. He was a tall, powerfully built man with auburn hair and bright blue eyes; though hot-tempered at times, he was essentially good-natured and jovial. His tastes were simple; he was honest and without guile, and his brilliant capacities as a soldier had been enhanced by good luck and fearlessness. By the time he was thirty he was a General of Division, and Napoleon's attention had been drawn to him after the capaign of Hohenlinden in which he distinguished himself. In 1801 Napoleon, being established now as First Consul, had made him his Inspector-General of Cavalry, and Joséphine had arranged a match for him with a friend of her daughter Hortense. Napoleon settled a huge income on him and successively gave him the titles of Duc d'Elchingen and Prince de la Moskowa. When the Empire was proclaimed Ney was made a Marshal, and soon after was invested with the insignia of a Grand Officer of the Legion of Honour.

This rapid advancement was not enjoyed, however, without some deterioration of character. While he became an increasingly able soldier and leader of men, Ney grew very difficult as a colleague, and during the war in Spain he had quarrelled violently with Masséna and Soult; he tended to be suspicious and easily took offence.

He had surpassed himself in bravery during the Russian campaign, and had Napoleon paid attention to his warnings the disasters of the retreat might have been avoided. Ney had urged Napoleon not to advance far into Russia in view of the rigours of the winter climate; but Napoleon had, as usual, gone his own way with his habitual conviction that all would turn out as he wished; he had led his unfortunate soldiers to Moscow, and had lingered there week after week until winter suddenly came, and his army, obliged to retreat, was caught in the snow and ice.

During the retreat from Moscow, Ney had commanded the rearguard and had distinguished himself by his endurance and power to impart courage to others. Obliged to keep in contact with the enemy so that the main body of the army could retreat unmolested, he and his men had little hope of survival. Day after day, hungry and thinly clad, they tramped across the icy plains, shelterless among enemies, with nothing to eat but their horses as they died. Starving, frost-bitten, the dwindling band struggled on week after week, enduring blizzards and frozen nights. For everyone whose courage was sinking Ney found words that consoled and cheered; he seemed to be in touch with some inexhaustible spring of inward strength, enabling him to pass unharmed through the nightmare, regardless of himself and concerned only to give help to his companions.

Nearly three months after the retreat began, he brought the survivors safely into Prussia. No one recognized the swaggering Marshal Ney; he was red-eyed, emaciated and in rags. But like the fighting cock of Epictetus, though battered he was triumphant.

The experience had its effect. As a young man he had believed ardently in the justice of the battles he was fighting; but now he had doubts and suspected that Napoleon was to blame for keeping Europe perpetually at war. But he was not allowed any rest for he had to serve Napoleon in the campaign of 1813, and then in the campaign of France. He contributed powerfully to the victories of Bautzen, Lutzen and Dresden; he fought heroically and was wounded at the terrible battle of Leipzig. By January 1814 he had recovered and joined the army again. Napoleon, although his fortunes were now on the decline, still envisaged a long series of battles with zest and confidence that his luck would turn. On his behalf, Ney fought furiously at Brienne, Rothière, Troyes, Champ-Aubert, Château-Thierry, Montmirail, Vauchamp, Craonne, Laon and Arcis-sur-Aube. Then came the fall of Paris, and with the Tsar and the King of Prussia in the capital, Ney felt, in common with other marshals, that the time had come to capitulate. Napoleon demanded a last battle, but the French marshals refused to fight it.

A mood of exasperation had come over Ney at the end. He was one of those men who are by nature fond of a fight and who turn their excess of energy to the pursuit of danger and excitement; but, Napoleon apart, such men come at last to have their fill. Such a stage Ney had reached in the spring of 1814, and he had been thankful to witness Napoleon's departure into exile while a less active personality took possession of the throne of France.

Ney now rode off to join his troops at Besançon, and such was the general confidence in his ability as a soldier that the spirits of the royalists rose considerably. Fanny Burney received an encouraging note from her husband who, as a member of the King's bodyguard, was unable to leave the Palace of the Tuileries during these anxious times. 'We have better news,' General d'Arblay wrote. 'I cannot enter into details, but set your mind at rest. . . .'

This news, [says Fanny Burney] hung upon the departure of Marshal Ney to meet Buonaparte and stop his progress, with the memorable words uttered publicly to the King, that he would bring him to Paris in an iron cage. The King at this time positively announced and protested that he would never abandon his throne nor quit Paris.

When Marshal Macdonald arrived at Lyons he found the Comte d'Artois already in the town with the Duc d'Orléans; they were in a state of consternation, as there was little doubt that Lyons would follow the example of Grenoble. News of Napoleon's successful advance was filling the population with high enthusiasm, and the troops garrisoned in the town made no attempt to hide their Bonapartist sympathies. Napoleon had always been popular in Lyons, for he had enriched the city by opening up the whole Continent to its trade. Only the nobility were ready to resist him; but how were they to induce the soldiers to fight for them? The princes regretted having come, for their presence would make the loss of Lyons the more serious. It appeared that to lead the local troops against Napoleon was to present them to him, while to retire before him, taking the troops with them, was to give him the whole region. Such was the dilemma which the princes placed before Marshal Macdonald.

The Marshal did not recommend evacuation until it became essential, but proposed to cut the bridges of the Rhône and to hold a review of the troops in which the royal cause would be put to them as persuasively as possible. Since it was calculated that Napoleon would reach the town the following day, he ordered the immediate destruction of the bridges and summoned the commanding officers of the local regiments to a meeting. He found the officers prepared to obey him, though in many cases only from a sense of duty; they were unanimous in their view that the troops were ready to revolt in favour of Napoleon.

The weather of the following morning, 10 March, did not help the Marshal when he reviewed the troops in the Place Bellecour. The ceremony took place in torrential rain, and the men were no doubt too wet and cold to take an interest in his warnings. If Napoleon were allowed to come back, he said, they would have all Europe against them, more united, more powerful, and more exasperated than ever. He spoke with feeling, and at the end of his discourse raised his sword and cried 'Long live the King!' There was no response. Even when the Comte d'Artois arrived and they were ordered to acclaim him the soldiers remained silent. Nothing was to be heard but the rain driving down on to the cobbled roadway.

The princes now had no alternative but to retire, leaving the Marshal to await events and improvise as best he could. The bridges had not been destroyed, for the townspeople would not allow it, nor had they been barricaded. Marshal Macdonald personally directed the obstruction of the bridges and ordered trenches to be dug. The soldiers were now cheerful in the knowledge that Napoleon was drawing near. As the Marshal was watching his trench-diggers, one of them called out to him: 'Come, now, Marshal, you're a brave man and you've spent your life with us, not with these *émigrés*. You'd do better to lead us to our Emperor who's on the way and would receive you with open arms!' There was no possibility of punishing such familiarity; it reflected the mood of all present, and Marshal Macdonald remained silent.

Napoleon arrived in the outskirts of Lyons late in the afternoon. He was travelling at his ease in an open carriage which, as he neared the city, moved at a walking pace amidst the local country folk assembled on the main road to acclaim him. Everywhere were cries of 'Long live the Emperor!' interspersed with 'Down with the nobles! Down with the priests!' And at every village he was obliged to stop while its mayor harangued him with compliments and a simplified version of the prevailing political aspirations.

He was preceded by an advance guard against which Macdonald sent out a detachment of dragoons from Lyons. The opponents met at the suburb of Guillotière, but instead of opening fire the dragoons greeted the arriving troops with cries of 'Long live the Emperor!' Mingling together, the soldiers of both sides now paraded about the suburb exchanging congratulations, while their excitement spread to the townspeople who had turned out in strength to rejoice with them and lead them to the bridge that was being blocked under the eye of Marshal Macdonald.

The Marshal saw their approach and ordered two battalions to follow him to the bridge; but the frenzy of the approaching troops spread irresistibly to his own following, and his men, ignoring their officers who rode ahead with raised swords, at once set to work to remove the barricades and clear the way for their hero, Napoleon. Their greatest desire now was to see the Marshal join forces with Napoleon, and, indeed, they tried to seize him and lead him to Napoleon by force; he was obliged to turn and gallop through

Lyons with his aides-de-camp, only narrowly escaping the pursuing men.

While Macdonald returned to Paris, Napoleon entered Lyons. He came as a master recovering his own domains. He took up his abode at the Archbishop's palace and received the civil and legal authorities of the town who hastened to congratulate him. Here his language was decidedly more imperial than it had been at Grenoble. At Grenoble he had announced himself as the lieutenant of his son, arrived to prepare the way for his liberal rule by correcting abuses in the government. Now that he was in possession of the important city of Lyons and was hailed Emperor by the soldiers, he assumed his former dignity as a matter of course.

The following day he reviewed his troops, now 12,000 strong, and then returned to the palace to make a variety of decrees and pronouncements. These were high-handed to say the least, and were prefixed with the words 'Napoleon, by the Grace of God and the Constitutions of the Empire, Emperor of the French.' He issued a decree by which he declared all changes made during his absence in the administration, both civil and military, to be null and void; the military establishment of the King was suppressed; the goods and chattels of the Bourbon princes sequestered; the nobility and feudal titles abolished; the emigrants who had entered France with the King banished, and the Chambers of Peers and Deputies dissolved. His own reign was to be founded on a constitution formed with the consent of the people, and he ordered the electoral colleges of the Empire to assemble in Paris in the course of May ensuing to celebrate this new order of things at a festival to be called the *Champ de Mai*, and to be held in the parade ground of the Champ de Mars. At this festival there would take place the coronation of the Empress Marie Louise and the King of Rome.

While Napoleon was thus disposing the future, Louis XVIII, unable to hide the facts any longer, was making public all the available news. In the course of the day a report was made to the Chamber of Peers in which the whole progress of Napoleon from the time of his landing was related as far as it was known.

Such, gentlemen, [the report ended] is the true position in which France is now placed. Buonaparte, who landed with 1,100 men, makes rapid progress. We do not know exactly to what extent defections have increased his band; but these defections cannot be doubted when we find Grenoble occupied, and the second city of the kingdom ready to fall and probably in the hands of the enemy. Numerous emissaries from Buonaparte repair to our regiments; some of them are already in our ranks. It is feared that many misled men will yield to their insinuations, and this fear alone enfeebles our means of defence.

During the day the King dismissed his Minister for War, Marshal Soult, replacing him by General Clarke, Duc de Feltre. Though Soult had had nothing to do with Napoleon's return, many of the royalists detested him and suspected him of treason; they put such pressure on the King that he was obliged to turn him out of office.

By 12 March the fall of Lyons was known in Paris. The Duc de Berry was given command of the Army of Paris, 40,000 strong, and Marshal Macdonald was made his Chief of Staff. The hopes of the royalists now rested on Marshal Ney at Besançon. He alone could arrest Napoleon's progress, and fortunately he was well placed for a flank attack. He was now marching to Lons le Saulnier, and the capital waited anxiously for news of battle. Up and down the Paris streets young royalists paraded, waving flags and endeavouring to muster recruits. 'To arms!' they cried. 'Rise against the usurper, the tyrant, who is bringing back war and despotism.'

2

*Napoleon's relations with Marie Louise; Defection of Marshal Ney;
Fall of Louis XVIII*

The news of Napoleon's return was made public later in London than
in Paris and Vienna. *The Times*, always inclined to view Continental
politics as a kind of third-rate melodrama, announced the great
event on Saturday, 11 March.

> Early yesterday morning we received by express from Dover the
> important but lamentable intelligence of a civil war having again
> been kindled in France by that wretch Buonaparte, whose life was so
> impoliticly spared by the Allied Sovereigns. It now appears that the
> hypocritical villain, who, at the time of his cowardly abdication,
> affected an aversion to the shedding of blood in a civil warfare, had
> been employed during the whole time during his residence at Elba,
> in carrying on secret and treasonable intrigues with the tools of his
> former crimes in France. . . .

For England, the resumption of war was exceedingly onerous; but
it was regarded by Lord Liverpool's government as inescapable
should Napoleon manage to seize power. On the 12th, Castlereagh
wrote to Wellington, authorizing him to act as he thought fit.
'The Prince Regent,' he said, 'relying entirely upon your Grace's
zeal and judgement, leaves it to you, without further orders, either to
remain at Vienna or to put yourself at the head of the army in
Flanders.'

The Opposition Whigs were preparing to demand that possibilities for preserving the peace with Napoleon should be explored;
but, had they known it, the die was cast and every effort they might
now make was futile. What could be done, when the powerful
Metternich, who for long years had patiently worked to gain his
present influence over emperors and kings, had resolved upon war?
When Talleyrand, who had made such strenuous efforts to bring
France back on equal terms among the monarchies of Europe, saw
his work threatened? When Alexander, deeply offended that his
magnanimous terms had not been appreciated, was bent on teaching

Napoleon a lesson? When the Emperor Francis wanted to be rid of the son-in-law who had forced his way into his family in the arrogant days of high success? When the King of Prussia, when Hardenberg, when Blücher, found it intolerable to be faced with the Emperor who had insulted and humiliated them so often? Everyone in Vienna had shivered when war had seemed to loom in sight over the Polish question, but no one in Vienna thought appeasement with Napoleon possible. In such an atmosphere Wellington could not consider peace with a restored Empire; Castlereagh, moreover, was working for a balance of power in Europe which was entirely opposed to Napoleon's system, and it might be assumed that a restoration of the Empire would sooner or later bring about the ruin of Britain, even if it kept the peace. The truth was that no one actively concerned with the Vienna negotiations was prepared to endure a return to power by Napoleon; war had been decided upon, as Metternich said, in less than an hour, and the English Opposition, reasonable and humane though their views might be, had no chance of persuading anyone in power to their way of thinking.

Moreover, up and down the country, ordinary Englishmen reacted with that superstitious horror of Boney, the Corsican Ogre, inculcated during the long years of war; the feeling was that the nation had struggled in and out of season to bring the tyrant down, and that they had not so sacrificed themselves only to tolerate him in the end.

News that Grenoble had fallen to Napoleon reached Vienna on the 12th. For a few days the city had been comparatively calm, the first shock having given way to hopes that Napoleon might soon meet with resistance. Now there could be no further doubts as to the possibility of his succeeding. The leading members of the Congress at once assembled, and Prince Talleyrand produced a solemn declaration in the course of the day. Talleyrand was filled with a lively rage; his diplomacy was being undone, and he foresaw himself left without office. The declaration reflected his displeasure. Based upon that of Louis XVIII, its purpose was to frighten the French into refusing to hand themselves over to Napoleon; he wished there to be no doubt in their minds that a revival of the Empire meant war.

By breaking the convention which established him in the island of Elba, said the declaration, Napoleon had destroyed the only legal title on which his existence depended. By appearing in France with projects of confusion and disorder, he had deprived himself of the protection of the law and had manifested to the world at large that there could be neither peace nor truce with him. 'The Powers consequently declare that Napoleon Buonaparte has placed himself without the pale of civil and social relations, and that as an enemy and disturber of the tranquillity of the world, he has rendered himself liable to public indictment.' The declaration, continuing in this vein, made clear the determination of the sovereigns to unite their efforts and employ all their means to destroy him should the French nation allow him to re-establish himself at their head.

The sovereigns and plenipotentiaries, or at least some among them, felt a certain hesitation about signing a document so insulting to Napoleon and perhaps distressing to his wife, Marie Louise, the daughter of their host. But Metternich had foreseen this possibility, and even as Talleyrand was preparing to produce his declaration he had prevailed upon Marie Louise, through the medium of Count Neipperg, to write him a letter which should give all concerned an easy mind on this score. This letter he now produced; it was an official declaration that Marie Louise had had no knowledge of her husband's intention to leave Elba, and that she placed herself under the protection of the Powers. From this it was evident that she disavowed her husband's present aims; the sovereigns and representatives of the eight Powers accordingly felt free to sign Talleyrand's document. Had Marie Louise taken Napoleon's side, avowed her intention of rejoining him, and raised her voice in conviction that he would wish to keep the peace, it would have been difficult for the statesmen to denounce him as an outlaw, a public enemy to be executed out of hand when caught.

Napoleon's hopes on leaving Elba cannot be appreciated without consideration of his relations with Marie Louise. Their correspondence at the time of his first abdication and banishment to Elba shows how devoted his second wife was to him at the time of his fall in 1814, and how justified he was in counting upon her help when he decided to make the attempt to return to power.[1]

[1] See *Marie-Louise et Napoléon, 1813-14. Lettres inédites de l'Impératrice avec les résponses déjà connues de Napoléon de la même époque. Réunies et commentées par C. F*

Nothing is more curious than the story of Napoleon's second marriage, which took place in 1810. Austria, defeated and helpless, had been faced with an ultimatum from France demanding the hand of the eighteen-year-old Grand Duchess Marie Louise; and her father, the Emperor Francis I, had sacrificed her for the sake of obtaining peace for his country. Marie Louise had grown up in fear of France, where her great-aunt, Marie Antoinette, had lost her head on the scaffold, and in terror of Napoleon, the enemy of her country. The ordeal of leaving her home and her friends to marry a man of forty whom she had never seen, and had been taught to think of as a foe, was certainly formidable. Yet the unexpected had happened; Napoleon had attracted her; he had done all in his power to please her and the marriage had turned out happily. Relieved and thankful to find that she was treated with every consideration, and interested in the powerful ruler who was so indulgent to herself but so greatly feared by others, Marie Louise had responded with affection. Napoleon on his part had not only been much attracted to his new wife – she was a young and, in his eyes at least, an exceedingly beautiful girl – but had approved of her in every way and felt at ease with her when once he came to know her. She was unassuming, innocent and sincere, and he esteemed her greatly on that account. Her letters show her to have been a normal, intelligent girl, genuinely fond of him and won over to his cause. She had few social graces, but rather seemed born to lead a quiet family life among those she loved. Napoleon took such a liking to her that he altered his way of living for her sake; he became more domesticated, he was punctual for meals. He not only enjoyed talking to her but often relied on her judgement. He trusted her absolutely and told her all his plans, even, on one occasion at least, his proposed military manoeuvres in the midst of war. Marie Louise had fallen under the spell he exercised on so many of those who knew him; and being lonely in Paris, away from her family and friends, she came to rely greatly on him, wanting him with her every moment of the day. Napoleon changed;

Palmstierna, Secrétaire particulier de S.M. le roi de Suède. 1955. The letters which Napoleon received from Marie Louise during his absence in 1813 and 1814 (127 in number) were entrusted by him to his brother Joseph after Waterloo. Being obliged to leave Europe for America, Joseph deposited the letters, with other papers, with his sister-in-law, Désirée Bernadotte, later Queen of Sweden. The letters have remained ever since in the Bernadotte Archives at Stockholm, and it is only recently that they have become accessible to scholars.

on many occasions he neglected affairs of State in order to keep her company.

It was not long, indeed, before the foreign affairs of France began to go amiss; and the divorced Josephine, looking on, could say once again that it was she who had brought Bonaparte his luck and that without her he was lost.

Eventually the happy marriage was interrupted by political disasters, and soon the Empire collapsed. Napoleon had seen Marie Lousie for the last time in January 1814 when he left her to join the army. Their parting had been affectionate, and Marie Louise had written regularly to her husband, always showing an ardent desire to be with him again. When he was defeated, she made every effort to join him at Fontainebleau; but her father and the diplomats of the Coalition contrived to prevent her doing so, and she was per-suaded to go to Vienna with her three-year-old son, the King of Rome. To Vienna she went in May, regarding this as a temporary measure, and continuing to send to Napoleon affectionate letters in which impatience to join him was the dominant note. Napoleon was banished to Elba; but no suggestion had ever been made that he would be separated from his wife and son.

Exile in Elba had appeared a pleasing prospect to Marie Louise, and tolerable enough to Napoleon himself during the weeks when he believed his wife and son would join him. In their letters they referred to Elba as their 'island of repose', a desirable haven after the troubled life they had been leading. But eventually their letters were intercepted and everything possible was done to influence Marie Louise's mind and reverse her opinion of her husband. This was Metternich's work, a part of his long, silent and unseen struggle against Napoleon.

At first there seemed to be no possibility of changing Marie Louise, for she was perfectly sincere in her attachment to Napoleon and absorbed by the desire to join him in Elba. Sad and lonely without him, she could scarcely wait to set off. Again and again, however, specious political reasons were produced to persuade her that it was necessary to remain in Austria a little longer; and when once Napoleon was in Elba few of his letters reached her. She had brought her French suite with her from Paris, and no objection was raised to their remaining with her although all of them were

Bonapartists; nor was any suggestion made that she was to be kept apart from her husband. Much was done, however, to bring to her notice the charges Austria had against Napoleon, the miseries of war and his guilt as a power seeker.

At the end of June she set off for a long holiday at Aix-les-Bains on the pretext that this was necessary for her health. She hoped to go from Aix to the Duchy of Parma, promised to her by Alexander as compensation for the loss of her position as Empress; there she would be conveniently placed to join Napoleon in Elba. She believed she was free and could please herself; she was, in fact, a prisoner, although she travelled with friends and chosen servants. Her custodian was an Austrian adviser whose apparent duty was to manage her household and generally assist her. That someone appointed by the court of Austria should accompany her was perfectly natural; what she did not know was that his main task was to keep an eye on her movements, to prevent communication with Elba and, above all, to make sure she did not set off to join her husband. Her father had first designed Prince Esterhazy for the position, an old man who would have limited himself to the duties of surveillance. But Metternich suggested a more able candidate, General Count Adalbert de Neipperg, a distinguished soldier and a man of cultured tastes and unusual charm of manner. The Count, who was over forty years of age, had a strong attraction for women, despite the loss of an eye in battle which caused him to wear a black bandage. He had recently obtained a divorce in order to marry his mistress, Mme Thérèse Pola. The provision of this adviser for Marie Louise was Metternich's culminating stroke in his unremitting and patient struggle against Napoleon. 'Neipperg,' says Marie Louise's French secretary, Meneval, in his memoirs, 'was given the mission of making the Empress forget France and consequently the Emperor'. Neipperg, indeed, was allowed to understand that he would be saving everyone a great deal of trouble if he were able to console Marie Louise for the absence of her husband. Such a diplomatic mission was well within his powers; and though quiet and unnoticed it was enough to sway the course of history.

At Aix, Marie Louise took remedial baths, went out riding and walking, and spent the evenings working on tapestry for a suite of furniture for Napoleon's study. When Napoleon's birthday,

15 August, drew near, she sent him a lock of her hair, secretly employing as messenger a servant of Joseph Bonaparte; Joseph was living in Switzerland and was in touch with her, ready to assist her when he could.

Napoleon for his part was preparing rooms for his wife in his villa at San Martino. Artists were working on a painted ceiling in the salon, and he himself had chosen the subject which would remind them both in happier days of their long separation. It showed two doves, divided by clouds but attached by lengths of ribbon whose knots tightened the further they flew apart. It represented constancy.[1] Napoleon talked much of his wife, feeling certain that she would join him as soon as she was able to do so; but he complained bitterly of the interception of their letters. Late in July, having been long without news, he sent emissaries from Elba to Aix with messages urging Marie Louise to join him at once. She replied immediately, explaining her difficulties. By now she realized that she was being watched, not only by Austria but by Russia and France. An emissary of Louise XVIII had orders to arrest her if she tried to reach Elba, she wrote. However, she was ready to overcome all obstacles and hoped to be with Napoleon in the near future. 'I am very sad,' she added, 'not to be with you already in your happy island, which would be heaven to me.'

Her letter did not reach Napoleon. The officer carrying it was arrested and searched. Marie Louise had been given away by a lady-in-waiting. When it had been read in Vienna, Marie Louise was requested to give her word that she would not undertake the journey to Elba without her father's consent. The Emperor Francis also desired her to be back in Vienna by the beginning of October. She was told that before she could take possession of the Duchy of Parma the Congress would have to make the necessary settlements, and her presence in Vienna would be essential. Being devoted to her father, she submitted to his will, though hoping to join Napoleon after the Congress ended.

Having spent two months in Aix, she passed the month of September in touring Switzerland with Count Neipperg as her guide. Throughout this time the Count had been quiet and discreet and had created a favourable impression by his tact and courtesy.

[1] *Marie-Louise et Napoléon*, pp. 269-72.

During the tour of Switzerland, which he organized in an agreeable fashion, Marie Louise spent much time with him. His charm of manner, his extensive knowledge of European affairs and his love of the arts made him a congenial companion. Marie Louise was an earnest young woman, eager to improve her mind, and she learnt much from him. As well as being lively and amusing, he was a sympathetic and understanding listener, and her own troubled situation seemed less of a burden to her when she talked to him about it. Not least of his attractions was that, like Marie Louise herself, he was an excellent musician. Napoleon had no ear for music, yet made a habit of singing to himself, always out of tune. Neipperg now found that he had won the confidence and admiration of Marie Louise, and this was all he needed for the completion of his mission. C. F. Palmstierna writes:

> In the course of her excursions in Switzerland, often alone with Neipperg . . . Marie-Louise arrived on 24 September at the Chapel of William Tell. A storm forced her to stay for the night at an inn, the *Soleil d'Or*. There she became Neipperg's mistress.[1]

At the beginning of October Marie Louise reached Vienna where she settled down in the Palace of Schönbrunn. Infatuated now by Count Neipperg, she became a willing listener to those who assured her that, having made a diplomatic marriage for the sake of her country, she had done all that was expected of her as an Austrian princess and need no longer feel herself bound to Napoleon.

When Alexander I generously allowed Napoleon sovereignty over the agreeable little kingdom of Elba, he had no thought of separating him from his wife, nor had he any strong aversion to a regency for the King of Rome. It was Metternich, with his influence over Francis I, who had made up his mind that Marie Louise should be detained in Austria and kept within her father's power. Metternich well understood the dynastic Europe he served and was deeply concerned to patch it up after the disrupting effects of the French Revolution and the Napoleonic wars; but what did he gain by the Neipperg intrigue? There can be no doubt he thought it would be for the eventual good of Europe; it could easily be foreseen that if the King of Rome were brought up in Elba under his father's eye he would in time become a pretender to the French

[1] *Marie-Louise et Napoléon*, p. 276.

throne. In 1815, with the Bourbons re-established on the throne of France, this must have seemed a serious threat to future peace. But looking back it appears that it might have been wiser to take the risk of allowing Marie Louise to go to Elba when she wished to do so. The King of Rome, brought up as the grandson of the Emperor of Austria, under the influence of his peace-loving mother, would hardly have grown into the military adventurer that entirely different circumstances had made of his father. Moreover, the harsh measures which ruined the life of this young prince did not prevent his cousin, Napoleon III, from forcing a second Empire on France later in the century. It seems obvious, too, that Napoleon would scarcely remain quietly in Elba if denied the company of the wife and child he loved, and even denied all news of them.

In Vienna, Marie Louise spent a happy winter; Neipperg continued his office in her household, she ceased writing to Napoleon and passed on the letters he sent her unopened to her father. While the Congress danced and wrangled she lived quietly, occupying herself with lessons in music, painting and Italian. Thankful that she had not to participate in royal entertainments, she enjoyed the constant presence of the Count with whom she could look forward to a long and delightful association, her reward for deserting Napoleon.

Napoleon could know nothing of this flagrant infidelity. When Marie Louise's letters ceased to reach him, he concluded that his enemies had decided to separate him from his wife and son, but he did not suspect that Marie Louise had changed, or that she was capable of doing so. He had always trusted her goodness and sincerity, and to the end of his life he was never heard to express a doubt concerning her.

Without Marie Louise and his son, without the income promised him by the Powers for his expenses in the island (which Louis XVIII obstinately neglected to pay), he had reason for discontent and leisure for plotting, and it is scarcely surprising that, on learning of the widespread unrest in France under the Bourbons, he decided to make an attempt to return to power. In doing this he counted on the energy and co-operation of Marie Louise. He believed that as soon as she heard of his arrival in France she would do her utmost to further his plans. She had always been zealous and active in trying to promote their joint interests, and he envisaged her warmly taking his part in Vienna and preparing to join him. She would impress upon her father the wisdom of preserving peace; the Emperor Francis, who was accustomed to changing his policy, could change it once again. She had, too, a powerful friend in the Tsar who had always been kind to her and did not care overmuch for Louis XVIII. Napoleon had some grounds for thinking that if he gave assurance of his peaceful intentions, backed by his wife, whom everyone knew to hold war in abhorrence, he stood a chance of coming to terms with the Powers, provided he could show that France welcomed him back with unanimity. Marie Louise's repudiation of him was a stroke of ill fortune for which he had not bargained.

Marie Louise learnt of the return from Elba with consternation, and probably with terror. She had more reason now than almost any other European to view with alarm the great event of the day. In her new love, she had turned against Napoleon altogether; on no account could she wish him success in his venture. Under the guidance of Count Neipperg, she willingly wrote the letter asked for by Metternich; it was placed upon the conference table, and the sovereigns and plenipotentiaries signed Talleyrand's manifesto the following day, 13 March. Count Neipperg was rewarded for thus influencing the former Empress by being made her *maréchal de cour*, a title giving him the privilege of riding with her in her carriage.[1] 'I will not set foot in that horrible country France again for anything in the world,' said Marie Louise at this time.

Napoleon, therefore, was banned as an outlaw, and the proclamation taken to Strasbourg and distributed along the length of the French frontiers. Its publication was followed by immediate preparations for war.

Napoleon left Lyons on the 13th, having again written to Marie Louise, telling her of his continued success and once more urging her to rejoin him. He told her he had resolved to make his entry into Paris on the 20th, the birthday of their son. Leaving early in the morning, and travelling through a country which had prospered during his reign and was still favourable to him, Napoleon reached Mâcon by the evening and was accorded a delirious welcome. All was as he wished; it appeared that he was being swept back to power by the will of the people. However, Marshal Ney stood in his path, determined to force a battle.

[1] Houssaye, *1815*, Vol. I, p. 456.

Ney had arrived at Lons-le-Saulnier to learn that Lyons had fallen. Bonapartism was sweeping across the district like a tidal wave and the local troops scarcely hid their delight at the Emperor's return. The royalists welcomed Ney eagerly, but appeared almost to have lost hope. Ney reassured them and showed confidence in victory and a convincing zeal for the royal cause, despite the news that arrived from hour to hour. He was told of insurrection in first one and then another of the regiments stationed in the region; and when he was awaiting the arrival of a battalion bringing artillery from Chalons, he was informed that the men had decided instead to take their guns to Napoleon. Ney's manner remained firm; he called on the officers under him to remember their duty to the King; if necessary, he said, he himself would fire the first shot in the battle; the troops, he felt sure, would follow his lead.

Napoleon, well informed of all that was taking place in France, knew that his old friend and favourite, Ney, had been sent to attack him and that a critical moment had been reached in his hazardous enterprise. It was necessary to make a supreme effort to avoid a conflict. Full success depended upon his reaching the capital without a shot having been fired, so that he could face the world as having returned by the will of the people. Knowing Ney's impulsive character, he believed it would be possible to undermine his loyalty to the King and sway him to the opposite side. Ney's greatest fault was a lack of judgement in worldly affairs; he was a great man in his profession, great in meeting adversity; but he was not a shrewd nor even a sensible man in society. It was only necessary to make a sufficiently dramatic appeal and he would lose his head. With his close companion, Bertrand, Napoleon laid his plans. Several old soldiers of fanatical enthusiasm were sent off to act as agents among the troops under Ney, inciting them to prepare to join the Emperor; they were followed by messengers with letters for Ney from Bertrand and Napoleon. Bertrand's letter, written under Napoleon's instruction, if not dictated by him, described the brilliance of Napoleon's successes and said that the welcome accorded by the whole of France was overwhelming. Victory was assured, whatever action might be taken against Napoleon; if Ney insisted upon fighting he would be responsible before the whole country for civil war and bloodshed. Ney was urged, or rather ordered, to bring his troops over to Napoleon, and separate instructions for the march were enclosed. In addition the emissaries brought with them a proclamation for Ney to read to his troops. Already printed, it was complete even to Ney's signature.[1]

Napoleon's brief letter was as follows:

My Cousin,
My Chief-of-Staff is sending you your orders. I do not doubt that the moment you learnt of my arrival at Lyons you placed your troops under the tri-colour flag. Execute Bertrand's orders and join me at Chalon. I shall receive you as after the battle of the Moskowa.

This letter is a model of Napoleon's skill in bending others to his will. His self-confidence is absolute; he disdains all explanation and self-justification, knowing that they will only encourage argument and doubt; he is magnanimous, showing with an economy of words that Ney's support now will wipe out all the discord there has been between them and restore their friendship at its best.

The messengers sent by Napoleon reached Ney in the early hours of the 14th. They were officers of the Guard whom the Marshal knew well; later, he generously refused to reveal their names. They repeated all that Bertrand said in his letter and more. They told him that the tri-colour flag was flying over every town in France; that the King had already left Paris; that Europe was in favour of the revival of the Empire; that Marie Louise and the Imperial Prince were returning to France from Vienna; that the British naval forces in the Mediterranean had had orders to allow Napoleon's crossing from Elba to the French coast.[2]

With the greatest enthusiasm these officers of the Guard poured out their story to Marshal Ney, possibly believing all they said. By the wildest exaggeration, and by expressing their master's hopes as if they were certainties, they did everything possible to ensure that what they claimed had already happened would in fact take place.

Napoleon had judged accurately. Ney had no capacity for doubting the convictions of these specious emissaries. He had been driven into a political trap and could not extricate himself. Like a man

[1] Chuquet, *Lettres de 1815*, p. 233. Houssaye, *1815*, Vol. I, p. 312. Houssaye, while expressing doubts as to the authorship of the proclamation, shows that Napoleon was not incapable of signing documents with the names of others.

[2] Chuquet's *Lettres de 1815* shows the use Napoleon made on his journey of the pretence that he had an understanding with the Powers.

hypnotized, he felt compelled to obey the orders sent to him. At every moment news reaching him from surrounding towns and villages confirmed the overwhelming nature of Napoleon's success. From his generals of division, de Bourmont and Lecourbe, he obtained no help. Both hated Napoleon but were afraid of taking a firm stand in the dangerous situation. Informed that Ney had decided to go over to the enemy, they made some protest but were ready to look on passively while he plunged rashly into the greatest folly of his life.

During the morning he made his preparations for a march to join Napoleon; and at 10.30 a.m., having paraded his troops, he read aloud the proclamation which was to become notorious in history and for which he was to pay with his life.[1]

'Soldiers!' he began in a firm and loud voice, 'The cause of the Bourbons is for ever lost. The legitimate dynasty, chosen by France, is about to re-ascend the throne. It is the Emperor Napoleon, our sovereign, who has the right henceforth to rule over our beautiful country . . .'

Among his staff officers there was silence and surprise, but the soldiers broke their ranks in transports of enthusiasm to surround the Marshal as they shouted their approval.

When the ceremony ended, royalist officers left Ney to retire to Paris. 'Monsieur,' said one of them, breaking his sword, 'you should have forewarned us of your intention, and not have left us to be the witnesses of such a spectacle.' But the views of the few who preferred to serve the King now counted for nothing, and preparations for the reunion with Napoleon went forward with all assurance.

Napoleon, having continued his triumphal march through Chalon, Autun and Avallon, reached Auxerre on the 17th; everywhere he treated the friendly populace with the gracious affability of a man who believes he is entirely at their service. Ney reached Auxerre the following day; he was brought into Napoleon's presence and greeted him with tears in his eyes. The meeting was melodramatic enough to please even the most sentimental. Napoleon had every reason to feel satisfied with Ney who had had it in his power to ruin his plans. With the additional troops now brought to him he had 20,000 men and sixty guns. He felt he was perfectly safe.

Leaving Auxerre on 19 March, he arrived with his army in the

---

[1] Ney was tried and sentenced to death under the restored monarchy at the end of the year.

Forest of Fontainebleau late that night and reached the château in the early hours of the 20th. Here, eleven months before, he had been forced to abdicate. Now, free and exultant, he felt himself once more the master of events.

The effect of Ney's defection was immense everywhere; no one now knew what the future held; the fall of Louis XVIII appeared inevitable and with it the renewal of an era of warfare.

> Whatever may be the case in France, [*The Times* wrote] there certainly is not a man, woman or child in the British empire who would not sincerely desire that France should enjoy the paternal government of the virtuous Louis, rather than that she should be enslaved by the traitor and rebel Buonaparte. The temporary success of that monster, and the fatal consequences which it threatens to all Europe, have indeed confounded and alarmed most of us. We see crime bursting from its just degradation, and insolently trampling on freedom and justice. We see that peace which seemed to promise so many blessings suddenly ravished from us, and the most terrific and tempestuous clouds at once enveloping prospects which seemed laughing with delight. It is natural that these awful changes should disquiet the most settled minds. It is natural that anxiety should make us listen to every breath of rumour, and mould it into an imaginary voice, and hear in the inarticulate sounds of the tempest denunciations of woe to ourselves and our posterity. . . . The first enormous blunder was in not hanging Buonaparte. . . . The next piece of folly was placing him in Elba, to be always at hand for a rebellion.

News of Ney's defection had reached Louis XVIII on the 17th. The infirm old man sighed. 'Is there no more honour?' he said. And despite his previous assurances, which, however, had rested on his confidence in Ney, he began preparations to leave the capital. He had foreseen a civil war, but he now realized there were not to be two sides to this question. Napoleon, even before he had landed in France, had written a proclamation to the French army in which were the words: 'Victory will advance at full speed. The eagle, with the national colours, will fly from steeple to steeple right to the towers of Notre Dame.' The words had hypnotized the country; as if a god were on the way with manifold blessings, the soldiers and the people exulted. There was little for the King to do but bow before the approaching storm. Fanny Burney writes:

The next day, the 18th of March, all hope disappeared. From north, from south, from east, from west, alarm took the field, danger flashed its lightnings, and contention growled its thunders: yet in Paris there was no rising, no disturbance, no confusion – all was taciturn suspense, dark dismay, or sullen passiveness. The dread necessity which had reduced the King, Louis XVIII, to be placed on his throne by foreigners, would have annihilated all enthusiasm and loyalty, if any had been left by the long underminings of revolutionary principles.

I now come to the detail of one of the most dreadful days of my existence, the 19th of March 1815, the last which preceded the triumphant return of Buonaparte to the capital of France. Little, on its opening, did I imagine that return so near, or believe it would be brought about without even any attempted resistance. General d'Arblay, more in the way of immediate intelligence, and more able to judge of its result, was deeply affected by the most gloomy prognostics. He came home at about six in the morning, harassed, worn, almost wasted with fatigue, and yet more with a baleful view of all around him, and with a sense of wounded military honour in the inertia which seemed to paralyse all effort to save the King and his cause. He had spent two nights following armed on guard, one at the Tuileries, in his duty of Garde du Corps to the King; the other on duty as artillery captain at the barracks. He went to bed for a few hours; and then, after a wretched breakfast, in which he briefly narrated the state of things he had witnessed and his apprehensions, he conjured me, in the most solemn and earnest manner, to yield to the necessity of the times, and consent to quit Paris with Madame d'Hénin, should she ultimately decide to depart.

We knelt together in short but fervent prayer to heaven for each other's preservation, and then separated. At the door he turned back, and with a smile which, though forced, had inexpressible sweetness, he half-gaily exclaimed: '*Vive le Roi!*' I instantly caught his wish that we should part with apparent cheerfulness, and re-echoed his words – and then he darted from my sight.

This had passed in an ante-room; but I then retired to my bed-chamber, where, all effort over, I remained for some minutes abandoned to an affliction nearly allied to despair, though rescued from it by fervent devotion.

But an idea then started into my mind that yet again I might behold him. I ran to a window which looked upon the inward courtyard. There, indeed, behold him I did, but oh! with what anguish! Just mounting his war-horse, a noble animal of which he was singularly fond, but which at this moment I viewed with acutest terror, for it seemed loaded with pistols, and equipped completely for immediate service on the field of battle; while Deprez, the groom, prepared to mount another, and our cabriolet was filled with baggage and implements of war.

General d'Arblay rode off to the Palace of the Tuileries where all was confusion and uncertainty. Three possibilities had been put before the King. The first was that he should fortify his palace and remain there with his bodyguard, refusing to leave it and thus putting Napoleon under the necessity of besieging and bombarding the place in the midst of universal indignation. Louis refused to take this proposition seriously, replying that such a solution was as antiquated in spirit as any of the ideas for which his poor *émigrés* were blamed. The second was that he should go to the royalist regions of the west of France, where the Duc and Duchesse d'Angoulême still held out in a country which had always been loyal to the Bourbons. But the King preferred the third proposal, which was that he should retire to Lille and cross the frontier into Belgium if necessary. Very probably, he thought, this course would lead him back to his English retreat, Hartwell, where he had enjoyed six tranquil years while more warlike men were fighting their battles. It was arranged, therefore, that he should leave Paris later in the day, unless events meanwhile took a turn for the better.

Remembering the fate of his brother, Louis XVI, when he attempted to leave Paris, the King drove out in the afternoon to test the temper of the people and judge whether he would be permitted to leave. The crowds were quiet and even friendly, frequently calling out '*Vive le Roi*!' He reviewed the Household troops in the Champ de Mars, then returned to his palace where orderly crowds were assembled. Nowhere had he seen any sign of hostility. News had come, however, that the troops round Melun were in revolt and were waiting to join Napoleon as soon as he reached the district. Night fell, the hours passed and icy rain began to come down in sheets. The crowds returned home and the courtyards and gardens of the palace were left empty and silent.

Inside the palace all was equally sombre. General d'Arblay sent off a note to his wife who read it with a sinking heart. '*Ma chère amie*, all is lost! I cannot give you any details, but for heaven's sake leave, and the sooner the better. *A la vie et à la mort*, A. d'A.' When would she see him again? It seemed certain to Fanny Burney that the King's forces would now engage in some furious battle and that her husband was lost. She went to the house of the Princesse d'Hénin who, soon after her arrival, received a note from Comte Lally Tollendal, sent by a confidential servant, announcing that Napoleon was within a few hours' march of Paris. 'He begged her to hasten off and said he would follow in his cabriolet when he had made certain arrangements and could gain some information as to the motions of the King.'

So Fanny Burney took flight in the heavy *berline* of Mme d'Hénin which clattered from the courtyard into the cobbled streets, drawn by four horses, between ten and eleven that night.

At the same time, six gilded coaches were drawn up outside the *pavillon de Flore* of the Palace of the Tuileries, and inside the building a confused crowd of courtiers, officers and citizens under arms surged about the vestibule, pale and anxious. Young pages with torches waited to escort the royal family to the waiting vehicles; servants stood ready to open the great doors. And now the King appeared, leaning on the arm of his favourite, the Duc de Blacas, and followed by a group of princes. Gouty and infirm, he walked with difficulty, but he looked round at the assembled crowds with his habitual benevolence, bowing in acknowledgement of their respectful greetings. His expression was calm and patient; there was nothing new to him in the present situation, for events had driven him from place to place since he was a very young man, often enough in rough weather when travelling was difficult. He wore an aura of majesty, which shone through his personal inadequacy; and his courtiers, many of them in tears, fell on their knees as he passed. Ardent Catholics and royalists, they saw in Louis the representative of higher powers making for harmony on earth; but it was a system of thought that was passing away, and to the world in general Louis was only a tedious old man with gout. As he descended the flight of steps towards the door, the prostrated crowd of subjects blocked his way. 'My children,' he said, 'I am deeply touched by your devotion; but spare me, I lack strength.' And they moved aside so that he could pass. The doors swung open letting in a wind which blew the torch flames horizontally, and Louis stepped outside.

The rain fell in torrents, the pages held their torches aloft, and the King climbed slowly and laboriously into his coach. And now he drove off through empty streets, towards St Denis, followed by his family and personal friends.

The Emperor Napoleon was free to resume his reign, and he entered Paris, according to plan, the following day, March 20, the fourth birthday of the King of Rome.

The Bourbon flag still flew over the palace on the morning of the 20th; but news of the King's flight quickly spread through the capital and the former dignitaries of the Empire took possession of the building. With them came hundreds of officers whose first concern was to take down the white flag and hoist the tri-colour. It was Monday, the weather was cold and wet, and there was no sign of excitement or enthusiasm in the streets. Those sections of the community most likely to welcome Napoleon's return were at work; the leisured classes, unless they were Bonapartists, kept to their homes. There was no repetition in the capital of provincial enthusiasm; everyone dreaded disorder and foreign opposition. When the sun set, the streets were deserted.

Thousands of soldiers, however, had assembled in the Carroussel courtyard, behind the palace, while thousands more were on their way to meet the approaching Emperor and join his escort. Napoleon was coming from Fontainebleau, riding in a carriage with his former Minister, Caulaincourt, who had hastened to welcome him. At Villejuif the majority of the troops brought to the district for the defence of Paris had gone over to him, and their officers added to his now considerable escort. Progress was slow, and night had fallen before he reached the capital.

Though the streets were empty, the dense mass of enthusiastic soldiers round the palace gave him a resounding welcome. In the palace itself, the ex-Queen Hortense, now its mistress, stood with other ladies of the Bonaparte clan ready to receive him, while most of his former ministers were near at hand. As his carriage drew up, soldiers flung themselves upon it and even under its wheels in a frenzy of idolatry. Tearing open the doors, they seized their hero and carried him aloft into his palace while thousands of military voices acclaimed him. As in the later days of Imperial Rome it was the soldiers who chose the emperor.

3

Napoleon's reign resumed; Hostility of the Powers; War between Austria and Joachim Murat; Secret Mission to Vienna

Napoleon was able to form his government immediately, since most of the Ministers who had previously served him were ready to take office again. Maret, Duc de Bassano, resumed the post of Secretary of State, Fouché that of Minister of Police, Gaudin that of Minister of Finance. Cambacérès became Minister of Justice, and Caulaincourt, after showing some hesitation, agreed to become Minister for Foreign Affairs. There were two important new appointments. Carnot became Minister of the Interior, and Marshal Davout Minister for War.

L'Empire, c'est la paix, the refrain of his nephew, Louis Napoleon Bonaparte, when he was seeking power later in the century, was equally the theme of Napoleon's public utterances in March 1815. But his words to Davout were very different. However much he hoped that his seizure of power would be tolerated abroad, he realized that war was almost inevitable. He had left Elba with the conviction that peace with Austria at least could be maintained; but even this might now be doubted in view of Talleyrand's proclamation, which by this time he had seen. He conferred with his Minister for War on the morning of the 21st and put before him a scheme of military preparation. Already the Belgian campaign was taking shape in his mind; if war should come it would give him the opportunity of seizing the country which he much desired to win back for France. He calculated that the Allies would not be ready to attack him before the middle of July at the earliest; a large part of England's best troops were in America, the Russian armies were in Poland; Austria, if she decided to fight, would be greatly hampered by the troubled state of Italy, where his sole ally, his brother-in-law Joachim Murat, King of Naples, could create a diversion. He intended to divide his enemies, and hoped hostilities could be postponed until the early autumn by which time he believed he could have 800,000 men under arms.

Shortly after his conference with Davout he called to the Tuileries several generals who had served him well in the past and who, all only in their forties, were likely to give good service in the coming campaign where they might earn the rank of marshal by their victories. These were Drouet d'Erlon, Reille, Gérard, Rapp and Lobau. Drouet d'Erlon was asked to form the 1st Corps which would be stationed round about Lille; Reille was given the 2nd Corps in the region of Valenciennes; the 4th Corps, to be established in the region of Metz, went to Gérard; Rapp was given the 5th corps, with Strasbourg as its centre; and Lobau the 6th, stationed in and around Paris. In the course of April, the 3rd Corps was to be given to General Vandamme. Napoleon planned to operate from Maubeuge, to which point these six army corps would march in due course as rapidly and as inconspicuously as possible. For the moment they were named *corps d'observation*, to conceal their warlike intention. A seventh and an eighth corps were to be formed later to guard the south and west frontiers.

Napoleon would have liked to introduce conscription immediately. He wrote to Davout on 26 March: 'To think that the army can be recruited other than by conscription is an idea devoid of sense. Moreover, I believe I have enough authority over the nation to make it understand this.'[1] But he was to discover that he did not command the authority that his journey from Elba, amidst cheering crowds, had seemed to promise him. Louis XVIII's most popular measure had been the abolition of conscription, and Napoleon was assured that the nation would not endure its revival. He must rely on the regular army and on volunteers.

Napoleon realized as soon as he reached Paris that the atmosphere was not such as it had been in the provinces. He had been given a welcome of the utmost enthusiasm at the Tuileries, but only by the military men and Bonapartist place-seekers. The citizens of Paris had not participated. In the coming weeks he was to learn that enthusiasm in Paris came mainly from idle, thoughtless sightseers in search of entertainment, and from dangerous street crowds athirst for excitement and violence. The steady, hard-working sections of the population were either against him or indifferent; the legal profession in particular was hostile.

[1] Houssaye, *1815*, Vol. II, p. 14.

On his journey from Cannes to Paris he had responded to the spirit of the crowds, and had presented himself as the soldier of the revolution. He wished to be less the sovereign of France, he had said, than the first of its citizens. He had returned to deliver the country from the slavery which the priests and nobles wished to impose upon it.[1] But there was no sincerity in this, except in so far as he intended to keep everyone in order, and he now sought to speak a language more in keeping with his claim to a place among the dynasts.

Revolutionary feeling was strong, and had been intensified by the King's flight. 'I find the hatred of the priests and the nobles is as widespread and as violent as at the beginning of the revolution,' Napoleon said. One day shortly after his arrival, when he was out riding in the Faubourg St Germain, he found himself surrounded by furious crowds who raised their fists menacingly at the nearby houses of the aristocracy and looked to him for leadership. They found him, however, severe and disapproving. 'An imprudent word,' he said later, 'or even an expression of indecision on my face, and all would have been sacked.' Napoleon's sense of order and discipline allowed him no sympathy with unruly crowds. He was proud, too, of his own descent from noble Italian families, and took pleasure in reinstating his palace prefects, pages, heralds and all that made for the etiquette of monarchy.

Louis XVIII entered Belgium to find the people in a state of alarm. It was generally believed there that Napoleon would immediately occupy the country which the French army thirsted to conquer anew.[2] English and Hanoverian troops were hastily assembling along the frontiers and preparations for defence were everywhere being made.[3] There were many in Europe who thought that Napoleon would strike immediately and enter Brussels within a few days, and some of his followers urged him to take this course. He could hardly do so, however, if he hoped to come to terms with the Allies. Moreover, although the frontier regions of France were all in Bonapartist hands and his position was apparently strong, the regions of Marseilles and Bordeaux were in revolt against him. There were

[1] Houssaye, *1815*, Vol. I, pp. 486–9
[2] Hobhouse, *Letters from Paris*, p. 17.
[3] These troops were present to ensure that order was kept while the kingdom newly created by the Allies settled down.

disorders to suppress at home before he could begin a foreign war.

On 28 March the Allies renewed the Treaty of Chaumont whereby Great Britain, Russia, Austria and Prussia bound themselves to employ all their resources to work together for the common end, which was the removal of Napoleon from power. The four nations were each to provide 150,000 men, though Great Britain, with much of her army making the homeward journey from the United States, would compensate for her inability to put so many in the field by subsidizing her Allies.

The full extent of Napoleon's success was not yet known in Vienna, nor had the diplomats any notion that he was to confront them as a reformed character. They were not, indeed, concerned with anything but his past. Napoleon had a complex personality; now one side, now another would take over, and it is conceivable that in March 1815 he was potentially the peaceful and liberal character he had professed himself to be on leaving Elba, ready to live on terms of equality with other rulers. The previous April his brother Joseph had urged him to abolish conscription and put an end to war, assuring him that France wanted peace and a liberal constitution.[1] The advice had come too late, since Napoleon was then on the point of abdicating; but the spirit of constitutional liberalism was very much alive in Europe, and he had it in mind to offer France, now that he had returned, a certain measure of freedom. He had therefore come back talking of peace and liberalism, and it may be that a sympathetic reception of his promises would have strengthened his good resolutions – the result of his better moods – and encouraged him to keep his word. But there was to be no sympathetic reception outside France, not even the least intention of listening to anything he said. He was not to be allowed to repent, even if he sincerely wished to do so. Talleyrand and Metternich had had to be silent many a time in the face of his arrogance and his insults; now they wished not to see him repent, but only to see him punished.

Certainly it is not easy to believe that, had Europe taken him at his word and given him the opportunity, he would not have waited his time and won back his old advantages as occasions presented themselves. It can be said for Napoleon, however, that he

[1] Joseph Bonaparte, *Mémoires et Correspondance du Roi Joseph*, Vol. X, pp. 222-3.

made some show of liberalism during the hundred days, for he abolished the censorship of the Press on 25 March. The following day he reaffirmed his promise to give France a liberal constitution, and three days later he abolished the slave trade, an action calculated to touch the English if anything could.

But England was to have no time to consider such gestures, for the diplomats had already assessed the situation and troops were everywhere on the move. Wellington wrote to Castlereagh on the 26th, giving his opinion that the only chance of peace lay in renouncing the Allied conquests as far as the Rhine at least, 'and our chance then depends upon his moderation'.[1] It was the firm belief of those in responsible places that Napoleon would never rest without winning back the Rhine frontier, so dear to French diplomacy. He was to meet with almost universal mistrust, to find Europe ready to endure any hardship rather than submit to his domination.

The first to feel the effect of this attitude was the son he glorified, the King of Rome. Napoleon had planned to arrive in Paris on his son's fourth birthday, and he had succeeded in doing so. In terms of power-seeking, the birthday was perhaps a notable one; in human terms it was desolate. It was on this day, 20 March, that the child was taken from the woman in whose care he had been since birth, Mme de Montesquiou, who loved him as if he were her own. He called her 'Maman Quiou' and knew no other mother, for Marie Louise had not been intimately connected with his upbringing and had acquired little feeling for him.

When news came of the return from Elba, some of Marie Louise's French servants had been heard crying enthusiastically, 'Vive l'Empereur!' This could hardly be allowed, and Count Neipperg, less genial among the servants than in the salon, had threatened to hang any one of them who ventured to repeat the cry. Before long, the whole of Marie Louise's French suite had been escorted to the frontier, apart from M. Meneval, her secretary, whom she particularly asked to be allowed to keep with her. At the same time the little King of Rome was taken under the protection of his grandfather, the Emperor Francis, and removed to the Hofburg where he was to live the remainder of his short life as a State prisoner. A rumour that an attempt was to be made to abduct him was the

[1] Wellington, *Dispatches*, Vol. XII, p. 280.

pretext for this action, and *Maman Quiou* was taken from him as being likely to influence his mind in favour of his father. Abruptly separated from everyone he knew and taken to the gloomy Hofburg with its massive walls and iron gates, the child was confused and frightened and did little but weep for many days. Abandoned by Marie Louise, who was fully occupied with Count Neipperg, he was kept in rooms guarded day and night and looked after by strangers. He had been a gay, friendly child, but overnight he changed completely. It is not surprising that he eventually contracted tuberculosis. His life was to be as short as that of the nameless thousands of young Europeans whose days his father felt he had every right to cut short.

'A man such as I am is not much concerned over the lives of a million men,' Napoleon had said to Metternich in 1813. And it had been his boast at the height of his power that he had a hundred thousand men and ten million francs to spend every year.[1]

Marshal Ney had reached Paris on the 23rd and had been sent off immediately on a mission to the northern frontier region. He was one of the *commissaires extraordinaires* being sent to the provinces to inspire confidence and counteract the effects of the declaration signed by the Powers on the 13th. 'My instructions,' he says, 'carried the express order to announce everywhere that the Emperor would not and could not resort to war, having agreed not to do so in talks concluded in the island of Elba between himself, England and Austria; that the Empress Marie Louise and the King of Rome were to remain in Vienna as hostages until he had given France a liberal constitution and fulfilled the conditions of the treaty, after which they would join him in Paris.'[2] Ney had been taken in by such statements himself at Besançon, and no doubt believed that the reports he was ordered to spread were true. But things looked different in Paris where Caulaincourt, as Napoleon's Minister for Foreign Affairs, was granting all the ambassadors, at their own request, facilities for returning to their countries.

Meantime, Napoleon's brothers, Louis excepted, lost no time in hastening to Paris from their various places of exile. Joseph arrived

[1] Metternich, *Mémoires*, Vol. I. pp. 151-2. Baron Thiébault, *Mémoires*, Vol. 5, p. 342. '*Où était le temps où il pouvait se vanter d'avoir cent mille hommes et cent millions dépenser par an?*'
[2] Charras, *Histoire de la Campagne de 1815*, p. 12, note.

from Switzerland a day or two after Napoleon had established himself in the Tuileries. Jérôme was coming from Trieste by way of Italy, and Lucien had crossed the French frontier; both were in Paris by the beginning of April.

Before leaving Switzerland, Joseph had written to his brother-in-law Murat, King of Naples, urging him to assist Napoleon by all the means at his disposal. He was to do what he could to detach Austria from the Coalition, but at the same time put himself at the head of his army and march to the Alps. It was an ambiguous letter which was to cause much trouble.

Joachim Murat alone, of the crowned Bonaparte family, had kept his throne. He had been left in the somewhat precarious enjoyment of his kingdom by the Allies in return for assistance given to them against Napoleon in 1814; but he was well aware that the Allies had for some time been seeking means to rid themselves of him. Before leaving Elba, Napoleon had sent a messenger to the court of Naples, announcing his intention of returning to power, and requesting Murat to send a confidential agent to Vienna assuring Austria of his peaceful disposition. At the same time, Murat was requested to hold his army in readiness to fight. If war broke out between France and the Allies, Murat would be there to create a diversion.

Murat, however, preferred to assure both Austria and Great Britain that he had had no knowledge of his brother-in-law's plan to leave Elba, and that he would remain loyal to the Allied Powers. Eventually, on hearing that Napoleon was making successful progress through France, he called his people to arms and marched northwards. He established himself at Ancona on 19 March and professed to have mobilized his troops in order to assist the Austrians if necessary. But with such a man there was every reason to suspect that he was playing a double game.

Jérôme Bonaparte, having disembarked on the coast of Italy about twenty miles north of Ancona, had unexpectedly run into his brother-in-law, King Joachim, surrounded by Neapolitan troops. When asked what he was doing in this part of the country, Joachim replied: 'I am making war on Austria.' The following day Joachim received Joseph's letter urging him to march to the Alps. Jérôme continued on his way to France; Joachim pressed forward in the ensuing days and attacked the Austrians at Cesena, where they retired before him. Charras quotes a letter written by Murat during the month of June 1815 in which he says: 'King Joseph wrote to me: "The Emperor has ordered me to write and tell you to move rapidly on the Alps."'[1] It therefore seems possible that Napoleon wished to create an immediate diversion in Italy, though it is more likely that he hoped to make use of Murat's forces later in the event of war and that the recommendation to march to the Alps came only from Joseph. However that may be, Joachim Murat published a manifesto on 31 March, calling on all Italians to rise and fight for the unity and freedom of their country, of which he proclaimed himself the king. The result was a declaration of war upon him by Austria. Thus Europe was sliding down again into the confusion from which she had been so painfully raised in the past few months.

Marie Louise now found herself obliged to part with Count Neipperg, who was ordered to the scene of war. Everything in her extraordinary life appeared to grow more and more involved, for she could not be certain now even of obtaining the Duchy of Parma, other powerful claimants to the territory having recently come forward. The news of her husband's successes, too, was highly alarming.

Soon there came news of Murat's successes also. The Austrian outposts were retreating before him; on 2 April he entered Bologna, and on the 4th he arrived at Modena, while two of his generals took possession of Ferrara and Florence. But long and reassuring letters came from Count Neipperg; as soon as the Austrians had assembled in force the picture would be very different, and one would then see what would become of the adventurer Murat.

The days of Murat's success were indeed numbered; he could hardly prevail against the Austrian army without the help of France. But for the moment his triumphs appeared to the world in general to be the offshoot of Napoleon's sudden return to power. It looked as though the march from Elba was to be followed by a great wave of events in favour of Napoleon and the Bonaparte family. The prevailing feeling in Europe was that Napoleon was invincible. He appeared to have some unaccountable power which preserved him from all that was unpropitious.

[1] Charras, *Histoire de la Campagne de 1815*, p. 16.

47

This widespread superstition, which made Europeans regard Napoleon with awe as either divine or diabolical, is well shown in a letter sent by Catherine of Wurtembourg at this time to her husband, Jérôme Bonaparte:

All that M. de Gaye [an ambassador from Napoleon] tells me of the march of the Emperor and his rapid progress through France is stamped with the marvellous. Never has anything like it been seen! What a genius! What a man! One is almost tempted to say he is a god! Not one drop of blood spilled! His mere presence has achieved everything, has electrified everything, has brought about the miracle. Those who were the most faithful, the most devoted to the Bourbons have been unable to resist him. What grandeur of soul he shows! What moderation![1]

So his admirers looked on, amazed and fascinated, investing him with special powers and virtues and blaming his enemies for any discord or danger in Europe. Napoleon could do no wrong. And those who feared him despaired of seeing him fall a second time.

The popular conviction of his immunity, however, was not shared by the diplomats of Vienna, nor even by his own ministers and generals. The diplomats had experienced such great relief in being rid of him since his abdication that they were resolved not to show any of that indecision or spirit of compromise which he had so often taken advantage of in the past. Their resolution had been indicated in the proclamation of 13 March and the renewal of the Treaty of Chaumont, and it caused Caulaincourt great anxiety. Although he consented to act as Minister for Foreign Affairs, Caulaincourt regarded Napoleon's enterprise as folly and foresaw for France a shipwreck so violent that there would be scarcely a plank left to hold on to. 'What will be the outcome of this terrible war he is bringing back in his train?' he said to Pasquier. 'The generals themselves are afraid, even the most resolute of them. . . .' Fouché, who had none of Caulaincourt's devotion to Napoleon but had joined the Ministry to be at hand for what he considered useful action, also spoke of Napoleon's madness and believed he would inevitably be destroyed. 'It will all be up with him in less than four months,' was his opinion at the end of March.[2]

[1] Jérôme Bonaparte, *Mémoires et Correspondance du Roi Jérôme*, Vol. VII, pp. 33-4.
[2] Pasquier, *Mémoires*, Vol. III, pp. 170-1; 177-9.

Caulaincourt, having been unable to persuade the foreign embassies to remain in Paris, sought an interview with the Austrian ambassador and Russian chargé d'affaires, giving the former a letter to take to Marie Louise and the latter a copy of the secret treaty of 3 January, signed by Great Britain, France and Austria against Russia and Prussia. This document had been thoughtlessly left behind by Louis XVIII's Minister Jaucourt. In addition, the Russian chargé d'affaires took with him a letter from the ex-Queen Hortense to the Tsar, with whom she was on friendly terms; this letter, written according to Napoleon's instructions, assured the Tsar that the Emperor of the French desired to become once more the friend and ally of Russia.

By far the most urgent of Napoleon's desires was to welcome home his wife and son who were to adorn the *Champ de Mai*. Still ardently hoping to re-establish friendly relations with he Austrian court, he wrote to the Emperor Francis on 1 April:

> My sole aim will be to consolidate the throne ... so that I may leave it one day, standing upon unshakeable foundations, to the child whom your Majesty has surrounded with his paternal kindness. A durable peace being an essential necessity for this deeply desired end, nothing is nearer to my heart than the wish to maintain it with all the Powers, but above all with your Majesty. I hope that the Empress will come by way of Strasbourg, orders having been given for her reception on this route in my realm. I know your Majesty's principles too well not to feel every confidence that you will be most eager, whatever the trend of your policy may be, to do everything possible to accelerate the reunion of a wife with her husband, a son with his father.[1]

To all the governments, Caulaincourt sent a formal announcement that Napoleon was back in power, and Napoleon himself addressed a letter to the various sovereigns, assuring them of his peaceful intentions. Napoleon's letter to the Prince Regent, which he wrote with his own hand, was sent on 4 April and was accompanied by Caulaincourt's notification and a covering letter. Caulaincourt wrote at length, assuring Castlereagh that the French people were unanimous in their joy and their loyalty to the returned Emperor. The Emperor ruled by the overwhelming will of the people, and he would keep the peace. But the Regent sent back Napoleon's letter

[1] Napoleon, *Correspondance*, Vol. II, pp. 60-1.

unopened, and Castlereagh replied to Caulaincourt with the following note:

Downing Street,
April 8 1815.

Sir,

I have been honoured with two letters from your Excellency bearing the date the fourth inst. from Paris, one of them covering a letter addressed to his Royal Highness the Prince Regent.

I am to acquaint your Excellency, that the Prince Regent has declined receiving the letter addressed to him, and has, at the same time, given me his orders to transmit the letters addressed by your Excellency to me, to Vienna, for the information and consideration of the Allied Sovereigns and Plenipotentiaries there assembled.

I am etc.
Castlereagh.

On the Continent, Napoleon's couriers were all stopped at the frontiers and their letters seized and taken to Vienna. Every attempt at diplomacy was useless. Alexander paid no attention to the secret treaty; Francis ignored his son-in-law's respectful overtures; Marie Louise shivered at the thought of seeing her husband again and sheltered behind the powerful dynasts; kings and reigning dukes refused even to read the letters sent to them. Apart from the Bonapartists, no one outside France believed in Napoleon's protestations except certain Englishmen moving in Whig or Radical circles, and these last came in for much abuse and ridicule from their fellow countrymen. There was, for instance, a caricature by Cruikshank, entitled 'General Nap turned Methodist preacher', which showed Napoleon delivering a sermon, and which was dedicated to Sam Whitbread.[1] Talleyrand observed that Napoleon had become a wolf in sheep's clothing, and this expressed the almost universal opinion.

Good relations with Austria, and if possible with Russia, were so desirable that Napoleon attempted various secret missions in the hope of making contact with his wife, his father-in-law and others who were refusing open negotiations with him. To be in touch with his wife was the first necessity; after that he desired nothing so much as to win back the services of Talleyrand, of whom he said at this

[1] Fox's successor in the Commons and leader of the Mountain, most active of the three Whig groups.

time: 'His knowledge of the world and of our age, his familiarity with cabinets and peoples, are unequalled.'[1] M. de Montrond and M. de Flahaut were the first emissaries sent, both leaving Paris at the beginning of April. M. de Montrond took with him a letter from Napoleon to Marie Louise and various letters from Caulaincourt; M. de Flahaut carried letters from Napoleon to Marie Louise and the Emperors of Austria and Russia. Lucien Bonaparte, who came to Paris early in April, left soon afterwards on a special mission to the Swiss frontier where he was to endeavour to make contact with the court of Austria and obtain information through spies and agents.[2] Flahaut was stopped at Stuttgart, his letters were seized and he was sent back to France; Lucien Bonaparte was no more successful. But M. de Montrond, a man with an exceptional capacity for political intrigues, reached Vienna without difficulty.

Comte Casimir de Montrond was an adherent of Talleyrand whom Napoleon had once imprisoned in the fortress of Ham as an enemy of the State. M. de Montrond, *âme damnée*, had no scruples about serving his former persecutor, providing he was suitably rewarded. M. de Jaucourt, in Ghent with King Louis, soon came to hear about the impending mission, and he wrote informing Talleyrand that M. de Montrond had been promised an income of 200,000 francs if he succeeded in undermining Talleyrand's loyalty to the Bourbons.[3] This, if Jaucourt was correctly informed, is some measure of the wealth Napoleon must have been ready to bestow upon Talleyrand himself in order to win back his services.

Besides being authorized to offer terms to Talleyrand and to certain other Frenchmen in Vienna, M. de Montrond was instructed to get in touch with Meneval, who was still there with Marie Louise. If possible, he was to gain an audience with Marie Louise herself and offer her facilities for leaving Vienna secretly with her son. Ample credit was provided for this enterprise, and M. de Montrond set off in the guise of an abbé, furnished with a passport from the Papal States.[4]

[1] Mollien, Comte. *Mémoires d'un Ministre du Trésor Public*, Vol. II, p. 439

[2] Jung, *Lucien Bonaparte et ses Mémoires, 1775-1840*, Vol. III, pp. 242, 246-51. Piétri, François, *Lucien Bonaparte*, pp. 291-2.

[3] Talleyrand, *Correspondance inédite du Prince Talleyrand et du Roi Louis XVIII pendant le Congrès de Vienne*, p. 511. Caulaincourt, *Mémoires*, Vol. I, p. 189. Lacour-Gayet, *Talleyrand*, Vol. II, p. 439.

[4] Thiers, *Histoire de l'Empire*, Vol. IV, p. 406. Caulaincourt, *Mémoires*, Vol. I, p. 190.

Having reached Vienna, his first visit was to Prince Talleyrand. He was not long in discovering that Talleyrand's animosity towards Napoleon was now unshakeable. 'Read the declaration of 13 March,' he said. 'It does not contain a word with which I disagree.' Napoleon's emissary saw that all attempts to persuade Talleyrand would be useless, and he wisely refrained from making further overtures. From Talleyrand he went to the other great diplomats in Vienna to learn their views and point out to them the strength and unity of France, and the inadvisability of reopening the conflict. It was useless. Nesselrode said: 'No peace with Bonaparte'. Metternich was equally inflexible.[1]

It was most difficult to gain access to the palace of Schönbrunn, but M. de Montrond presented himself as a keen amateur of flowers and was allowed to visit the gardens. The Austrian police were vigilant, but no suspicion was aroused by the tactful emissary. M. de Montrond contrived an interview with M. de Meneval, and gave him the letter from Napoleon to Marie Louise, as well as other letters from Paris. He told Meneval that if Marie Louise cared to trust him, he would undertake to get her away with her son to Strasbourg, and that he would guarantee the success of the enterprise. Meneval had to disillusion him in his belief that Marie Louise was anxious to rejoin her husband. Marie Louise, he told his visitor, had no wish to return to France; she would not now even consider a Regency, the idea of which was as repugnant to her as to the sovereigns of Vienna. Her sole interest lay in the future promised to her by the Powers; and, in her aspirations for the future, her son did not occupy the only place. M. de Montrond did not pursue the matter. At a later interview with Meneval he was given letters to take back to Paris. But there was not one from Marie Louise among them. Her secretary had deemed it wise to burn Napoleon's letter to his wife. Had he given it to her she would have passed it on unread to the Emperor Francis.

So M. de Montrond set off on his return journey. He had been unable to achieve anything of use to Napoleon, apart from learning the exact nature of the attitudes of Marie Louise and the diplomats in Vienna.

[1] Talleyrand, *Correspondance avec Louis XVIII . . .*, pp. 380-1.

4

Life in the Capital; News of Marie Louise; A visit to Malmaison

In Paris, Napoleon continued his military preparations and took measures to suppress resistance in the south and west of France where many districts were faithful to the King. The Duc d'Angoulême was still in the country, arousing the royalists to civil war, and he was now following in the path of Napoleon's triumphant progress from Elba which had been almost denuded of troops. The Duke was approaching Lyons where the royalists among the population were consequently taking courage and had even ventured lately to call out '*Vive le roi!*' in the streets. General Grouchy had been sent to Lyons to deal with the situation and had displayed much energy, placing the city in a state of siege and arming local volunteers. He was soon to force the Duke to fall back towards the south.

Assisted by his brother Joseph, Napoleon was trying to win over all men of reputation and ability to his cause. Men whom he had always profoundly disliked were now flattered; he wished to impress foreign governments with the spectacle of a capital in which all those of merit and distinction were firmly on his side. Many, unable to resist his blandishments, now lent their names to his cause, persuading themselves that it was their patriotic duty to do so. Others, however, had no difficulty in withstanding his advances. Marshal Macdonald, for instance, whom he would much have liked to bring round, regarded his return as a dangerous adventure and would have nothing to do with it.

Among those won over was Benjamin Constant, whom Napoleon invited to prepare the promised liberal constitution. La Fayette, too, was sought out and offered a peerage. This the renowned general refused, but he agreed to leave his country retreat and take his place in the Chamber of Deputies when it should assemble. Napoleon and Joseph, it transpired, would have done better to have left La Fayette to the rural pursuits he had chosen to follow for many years past, for he was to be instrumental in bringing about the second abdication.

La Fayette records in his memoirs that, although Parisians were dejected and worried at the time of Napoleon's arrival, crowds collected round the palace in the days following, sharing the enthusiasm of the soldiers and eager to acclaim *le petit caporal*, or *père la violette* as he was rather unsuitably named by some of his devotees. There were, indeed, many signs of popular rejoicing during the first weeks of Napoleon's return. Shouts of '*Vive l'Empereur!*' mingled with the singing of Napleonic hymns; caricatures were displayed in the shops, pouring ridicule and insult on the Bourbons and glorifying Napoleon. Only a year ago the caricatures had ridiculed Napoleon, as they would again when 'the hundred days' were over; but in its hour Napoleon's ascendancy appeared unchangeable to the Parisians.

The soldiers were enthusiastic to the point of insubordination. Having brought Napoleon back to power, they believed he was under their special protection and felt that anything was permitted to them provided they cried '*Vive l'Empereur*' often enough. Throughout Napoleon's journey from Elba to Paris, the hierarchy of the army had been largely ignored, men of lower rank often imposing their will on those above them and being praised for so doing. The conviction that the lower ranks could give orders still prevailed; it was felt that the Emperor trusted them, while he could not trust the Marshals of France, and that this state of affairs gave them certain rights.

On one occasion, when Napoleon was inspecting his troops at a review, the Dragoons of the line took it upon themselves to step forward and cross their swords above his head. To retain his popularity he accepted such gestures with apparent pleasure, just as he accepted the homage of the crowds who gathered outside the Palace of the Tuileries, shouting for him until he appeared on the balcony.

It was the hour of the army, or at least of those vociferous and enthusiastic soldiers who set the tone. Ever since Napoleon's abdication, the rumour had been circulating round the barracks that he would return; and here he was, back again because he was greater than all other men and no one could get the better of him. The fanatical soldier would not admit that his idol had ever been defeated. The disaster of 1812 was the fault of the weather; the disaster of 1814 was the result of treason; Napoleon made no mistakes.[1]

[1] Houssaye, *1815*, Vol. II, p. 75.

On 2 April the Imperial Guard gave a great banquet to the troops who had marched with Napoleon from Grenoble and Lyons, and to those members of the National Guard who had been on duty at the Tuileries on the evening of his arrival. 15,000 soldiers and militiamen sat down at their tables in the Champ de Mars while over 1,000 officers dined near by in the *École Militaire*. Toasts followed one another, the health of the Emperor, the Empress and the King of Rome was drunk. Then, under the influence of the freely flowing wine, the officers with unanimous inspiration jumped to their feet, crossed their swords over the tables and swore they would die for their country. So much for the peace promised by Napoleon to Europe! Then a voice was raised: 'To the column!' And a long, unruly procession made its way from the Champ de Mars to the Place Vendôme where stood the column erected to Napoleon's victories; at the head of the procession a bust of the Emperor was carried aloft like a relic, while drums rolled and a band played the *Marseillaise*. Arrived at their destination, the officers placed the bust before the column while the inhabitants of the square hastened to illumine their windows with lanterns and candles. The owners of those houses where lights were slow to appear were reminded of their patriotic duties by the rattle of stones against their windows.[1]

The fact that the Marshals of France had nearly all served the King faithfully and had disobeyed Napoleon's orders even after 20 March, had done much to destroy discipline in the army. The rank and file had become mistrustful, and there were demonstrations and complaints against officers who had appeared fully satisfied with the rule of Louis XVIII, even though they were now willing to serve under Napoleon. There was a strong tendency to suspect that officers of the grade of colonel and upwards were not genuinely loyal to the Emperor. Officers of high rank still wielded real authority only if they had encouraged their men to go over to Napoleon before the King had left Paris.

In the theatres the audiences clamoured to hear such tunes as '*Veillons au salut de l'Empire*'; Mlle George, a former mistress of Napoleon, received tremendous applause at the *Théâtre Français*. And when the Emperor himself appeared there one night he was acclaimed with delirious enthusiasm. His demeanour was unassuming,

[1] Houssaye, *1815*, Vol. I, pp. 525-6.

however, and he slipped away hurriedly at the end of the play before the audience had a chance to renew its applause.

Rumours of a most reassuring nature flew about the capital, always seeming to come from reliable sources. Thus the Baron de Thiébault was assured that Marie Louise was already on her way to France with her son, and that she came with the blessings of Austria and the approval of all the Powers.[1] Many who were hesitating went over to the Emperor on the strength of such rumours, anxious to have their place in society before the arrival of the Empress.

Only the presence of Marie Louise and the Imperial Prince was needed to complete the happiness of the Bonapartists, and they told one another that she was already in Strasbourg.

Marie Louise, practising at her clavichord and her easel, kept Paris as far from her mind as possible. Her thoughts went only to Count Neipperg who was now preparing to take the offensive against King Joachim.

There was to be no compromise with the King of Naples. 'If we do not destroy Murat, and that immediately,' said the Duke of Wellington in a letter to Castlereagh, 'he will save Buonaparte.'

The Powers in Vienna had not yet decided on the details of their plan of campaign, but their general intention was to send three great columns of men into France simultaneously, aiming at Paris; Russia and Austria would enter from the east (Austria having first defeated Murat); the Prussians would drive down from the Rhine; the Anglo-Hanoverian troops and those of the Low Countries would move across the Belgian frontier, led by the Duke.

The citizens of the Austrian capital, who had hitherto watched the members of the Congress amusing themselves, who had seen them riding in their decorated coaches to balls and banquets and had even been regaled in January with the spectacle of sovereigns driving their own sleighs, were now entertained by continual military reviews and the strains of martial music. The Duke of Wellington had left to take command of the armies in the Low Countries, but the Tsar Alexander was to be seen daily in the Prater, clad in an Austrian uniform, taking the salute from the regiments passing on their way to war.

[1] Thiébault, *Mémoires*, Vol. V, pp. 299–300.

The Duke of Wellington had reached Brussels on 4 April; he knew the town well for as a boy he had lived there for two years. Born three months before Napoleon, in 1769, he had spent the years 1781 to 1784 at Eton. His mother had then taken him to Brussels where his education was continued by a private tutor. At the age of seventeen he had gone to a French military academy at Angers, and in the following year, 1787, had begun his military career in the British army.

The situation in the Low Countries was hazardous, and there would have been no chance of resisting Napoleon successfully if he had immediately marched to Brussels. Blücher, who was to join forces with Wellington, was still in Berlin; few English troops were available, and such forces as there were, were thinly spread over a great area. The Duke took stock of the position and wrote to Blücher's Chief-of-Staff, General Gneisenau, on the 5th to tell him what his resources were and to suggest that the Prussian army should assemble with his own in front of Brussels, being placed without loss of time along the Meuse and quartered between Charleroi, Namur and Huy. Reports as to the situation, number and intention of the enemy were extremely vague, he said, but it appeared to him that the Allies should be prepared to resist a sudden blow which Napoleon might be tempted to make at any moment.

To Earl Bathurst, Secretary of State for Foreign Affairs, he wrote the following day, expressing his concern that more was not being done in England to meet the emergency. The troops available were a mixed lot, and those from Britain were sadly insufficient to maintain their country's reputation on the Continent.

In England, soldiers were on the alert, awaiting orders to embark for the Continent. Many a homeless young man who had dreaded the reduction of the army to a peace-time establishment felt relief at the prospect of being needed still and looked forward to a campaign abroad, particularly as the weather was fine. But although the available regiments were ready, and were highly efficient, lethargy hung over those in authority, and Wellington's patience was to be greatly tried in the weeks to come.

Outside military circles, the resumption of war was regarded with horror, yet nearly everyone felt it to be unavoidable. 'England wears a melancholy air,' Hobhouse had written on 23 March. 'All is to be done over again; we have lived in vain for twenty-five years, we are bankrupt as it were of power, and must recommence our struggle for life. I foresee everything bad . . .'[1]

On 7 April a message from the Prince Regent was debated in the House of Commons. His Majesty's land and sea forces were to be augmented, and the Regent deemed it incumbent upon him to enter into immediate communication with his Majesty's Allies for the purpose of acting in unity with them for the safeguarding of Europe. Sir Francis Burdett[2] declared it his conviction that Bonaparte was the choice of the French nation and that any attempt to re-establish the Bourbons would be unjust and hopeless. He feared a war of which no man could see the termination. Mr Samuel Whitbread blamed the Duke of Wellington for having signed Talleyrand's declaration of 13 March, and moved an amendment to the address imploring the Prince Regent 'that he would be graciously pleased to exert his most strenuous endeavours to secure to this country the continuance of peace,' so long as it could be honourably maintained. But this motion was rejected, and it was clear from Lord Castlereagh's reply to speeches from both sides of the House that the English cabinet was committed to war. Since Napoleon was without good faith, he said, and acted from self-interest alone, the principle of power and not reliance upon his word must settle the question. War was inevitably approaching and soldiers were already being sent across the Channel into Belgium.

On the day following the debate in Parliament a troop of horse artillery stationed at Colchester received orders to march forthwith to Harwich and there embark for Ostende: 'An order,' says General Cavalié Mercer, at that time their captain and a man of thirty-two, 'received with unfeigned joy by officers and men, all eager to plunge into danger and bloodshed, all hoping to obtain glory and distinction.' The war was opening, with French soldiers thirsting for revenge after their recent defeat, and English soldiers bent upon teaching Boney, the Corsican Ogre, a lesson he would not forget.

Three weeks had now elapsed since Napoleon had taken possession

---

[1] Lord Broughton, *Recollections of a Long Life*, Vol. I, p. 221.
[2] A Radical M.P. who in 1810 had made his name by leading an agitation against the Speaker and the House of Commons – long an opponent of the war with France.

of Paris, and the sharp decline in his fortunes was about to show itself. So far he had been sustained by the elation of success; but now he was beginning to feel the strain of mounting difficulties both at home and abroad. He felt himself hampered by those in power about him; they were all ambitious men with no more taste for a servile place than he had himself. Formerly they had bowed to his will for the sake of the fortunes he bestowed on them; now they had him to some extent at their mercy and therefore watched him closely lest he should again get the better of them. They showed more interest in maintaining their liberty of action than in safeguarding the State which they had put in danger by consenting to his return.

Napoleon was aware by now that he could only hold his throne by fighting a war. Decrees were issued on 9 and 10 April calling up army men on furlough and the National Guard.[1] Though conscription was not at present allowed him, he was awaiting his time and was determined to call up the 1815 class as soon as the country was sufficiently alarmed by the menace from abroad. That moment could not fail to arrive. Not one of the monarchs to whom he had sent such amiable messages had deigned to receive his letters. His enemies had placed an invisible barrier round his frontiers and would hold no communication with him. Lucien Bonaparte had been unable to deliver his letters to the Emperor Francis and other important persons, and M. de Montrond was back in Paris with news of the failure of his mission.

M. de Montrond had brought back letters from the faithful Meneval. In a long communication to the Minister Caulaincourt, Meneval described the signs of military preparation in Vienna and the animosity of the Tsar who, it was said, had 'sworn on the Bible not to put down his arms while the Emperor Napoleon was the master of France'.

Napoleon's chance of coming to terms with Austria had depended on the loyalty of Marie Louise, and Meneval – feeling it essential that Caulaincourt should be fully informed – now explained how the Empress had been led to a complete reversal of feeling. He did

---

[1] All men between the ages of twenty and sixty were liable to serve with the National Guard. They were not trained as an offensive force, but could be used to man fortresses and frontier posts. There were about 200,000 enlisted at this time, and Carnot, Minister of the Interior, estimated that the number could be brought up to 2,500,000 in case of need. (See Houssaye, *1815*, Vol. II, p. 8.)

not, however, refer to her attachment to Count Neipperg. 'I beg you,' he wrote, 'to make such use of this information as your caution suggests. I dread the effect it may have on the Emperor.' But Caulaincourt had no chance to spare his master's feelings, for Napoleon, who had anxiously awaited the arrival of these important letters from Vienna, insisted upon reading the originals. Meneval wrote:

I do not know when the Empress will go to France. I have no way of foreseeing what may happen; the cabinet is far from being in favour of such a thing at the moment; the Empress's mind has been so worked upon that she only envisages a return to France with dread; every possible means has been employed for the last six months to alienate her from the Emperor. During all that time I have not been allowed to receive any order from her lest she should arouse the suspicions of the arbiters of the Congress by her confidence in *the Emperor's man*. When by chance I have been able to say a word to her I have urged her to remain neutral and not to sign anything. But pressure has been put on her to make a declaration saying the intentions of the Emperor were unknown to her, to put herself under the protection of her father and the allies, and to ask for the crown of Parma. General Neipperg, who is accredited to her by the Austrian Ministry, and who has obtained a great influence over her mind, has left for Italy. He has left with her a Mme de Mitrowsky, destined to be the governess of the young prince.

Last Sunday I dined alone with the Empress. Her Majesty said to me afterwards that an act of Congress had just been signed ensuring her the Duchy of Parma, the administration of which would be left for the time being to Austria who would pay her 100,000 francs a month; that she had not been able to obtain the inheritance of the Duchy for her son; that the son of the Queen of Etruria would be the heir; but that she would obtain for her son the fiefs of the Archduke Ferdinand of Tuscany in Bohemia, amounting to about 600,000 in revenues; that she had made up her mind irrevocably never to return to the Emperor. Questioned as to the motive of such a strange resolution, she gave various reasons which I ventured to demolish, after which she declared that not having shared the Emperor's exile, she could not now join him in a prosperity to which she had not contributed.

Marie Louise, Meneval explained, had promised her father not to open any communication from Napoleon; she kept this promise strictly and went even further, for she refused even to think in any way but that suggested by her present advisers. Meneval's letter continued:

> While waiting for the chaotic situation to clear up, I talk of the happiness the Emperor's return has brought to France, the impatience with which she is awaited there, the Emperor's desire to see her again, etc. etc.; but I have to be cautious, because this subject of conversation displeases her. We must leave everything to time and the moderation of the Emperor. Circumspect though I am, I am the object of an ignoble espionage. A cloud of informers hover round me and comment on my gestures, my movements and my expression. I fear I shall not be kept here much longer; I feel the need to breathe a different air, to see you all again; my health is very much shaken. It is only the Empress and her son who enjoy brilliant health. The Empress has become very plump; the Prince Imperial is an angel of beauty, strength and sweetness; Mme de Montesquiou weeps for him every day.[1]

This was the first precise information Napoleon had had about his wife's inconstancy. He had, however, suspected the truth from Austria's attitude towards him, realizing that by this time her family would have done much to bring her round to their own way of thinking. Yet even now he did not believe that she had ceased to care for him. For the moment, however, there was nothing to be done and he must wait upon events. There was talk among his advisers of seizing a royal hostage and offering him in exchange for his wife or son; but Napoleon valued his reputation and did not wish to give his enemies grounds for accusing him of barbarism.

He was, however, momentarily tempted to take this course, the opportunity offering itself at this time. The Duc d'Angoulême had met with reverses and his Chief-of-Staff had signed a capitulation on his behalf with General Gilly on 8 April, whereby he agreed to disband his army and leave the country from the port of Cette. Grouchy, on being informed of this, thought it wiser to refer to Paris for confirmation of the treaty, and he held the Duke a prisoner meanwhile. Grouchy's message was brought to the Tuileries on the morning of 11 April. Napoleon had thoughts of keeping the Duke as a hostage; but after some discussion he accepted the advice of the

---

[1] Meneval, *Napoléon et Marie Louise*, II, pp. 386-94, 401.

Duc de Bassano who maintained that the capitulation should be honoured.[1]

We know from the memoirs of Hortense that, as night fell on this day, 11 April, Napoleon's thoughts went to his first wife, Joséphine, who had died at Malmaison the previous May while he was in Elba, and that he made a sudden decision to visit her home the following morning.

Malmaison was now the property of Joséphine's two children by her first marriage, Hortense and Eugène. Neither, however, had been there since the time of their mother's death, and the house was abandoned to a few servants and caretakers. Hortense was much surprised to receive a message from her step-father at ten o'clock that evening saying that he wished to visit the place the next day and would like her to accompany him.

Hortense, who had been deeply attached to her mother, felt she could not trust herself to revisit Malmaison for the first time in the presence of Napoleon and his suite, so she decided to drive out immediately and spend the night there. If Hortense was dismayed, her *maître d'hôtel*, a M. Bazinet, was still more agitated, according to the account of Hortense's lady-in-waiting, Mlle Cochelet. A luncheon for the Emperor at eleven the next morning, and in the depths of the country! He threw up his hands in consternation and hastened off to arouse drowsy servants preparing for their night's rest, while his mistress set off in her travelling coach to Malmaison.

It was long after midnight when Hortense reached her house and roused its sleeping inhabitants. Old servants were alarmed when the silence was disturbed, and then delighted when they saw that 'Mlle Hortense' had arrived; rooms were hurriedly made ready, Joséphine's last days were recalled, and many tears were shed.

Napoleon left Paris at 7 a.m. the following day and reached Malmaison at nine o'clock. He, too, was in a sad and thoughtful frame of mind. With Hortense at his side he strolled round the gardens which were silent and beautiful on this spring day. They were the creation of Joséphine, who had spent much time among her gardeners, making these acres a paradise of ordered beauty. Rare trees and plants brought from the corners of the earth surrounded the wide lawns; classical statues and ornaments were reflected in

[1] Houssaye, *1815*, Vol. I, pp. 411-28.

glassy water; cascades and fountains varied the scene. In the meandering river swans both black and white were moving about, and willow trees, of pale but vivid green, bent gracefully round the Temple of Love where thousands of spring flowers bloomed.

Seeing the bright gardens after so long an absence, and after so many terrible events, Napoleon could scarcely believe he was not back in the happier days when this was his home. At every turn of the winding paths he felt that Joséphine must come in sight, dressed in one of the translucent muslin masterpieces of her couturier, Leroy. 'How it all brings her back to me,' he said to Hortense. 'I cannot persuade myself that she's no longer here.'[1] He could not help realizing, as he looked back on the past few years, how events had immediately taken a disastrous turn for him when he divorced the woman who had been so devoted to him, who had had her faults, indeed, but had been so true a friend.

Joséphine had brought good fortune to Napoleon; to her influence he owed the command of the Italian campaign which had given him the opportunity to rise to fame. Tactful and kind-hearted, always urging him in the direction of moderation, she had had the happiest effect on his career. He had divorced her out of ambition, in order to ally himself with the reigning house of Austria and found a dynasty. Marie Louise had been an excellent wife in her turn, yet all had gone wrong politically almost from the moment he married her. She had been loyal and conscientious, but the union had not been lucky and he regretted it, regretted his repudiation of Joséphine. He had admitted to Metternich in 1813 that his marriage to Marie Louise had been a mistake. Now that Joséphine had gone for ever and unexpected difficulties were arising on all sides, he could not help feeling that his fortunes had fled with her.

The gardens had not changed, except that they had increased in beauty from year to year. But their owners had changed completely in a brief time. What had gone wrong? What had brought about so sad an alteration in their affairs, which had begun so brilliantly? How was it that his love for Joséphine, so exalted when he married her, had faded so that he had come to divorce her? And how had his first great work for France, his restoration of her fortunes, his bringing of order out of the revolutionary chaos, led

---

[1] Hortense Bonaparte, *Mémoires de la reine Hortense*. Vol. II, p. 358.

imperceptibly to ambitions which ruined the country? He had taken up his work as the ruler of France from the highest motives and ideals; he had never consciously deviated from his path; yet within a very few years he had in some inexplicable way reversed his direction and was walking not towards but away from his goal. His aim had been human progress, his goal an ordered, happy and prosperous society in Europe; he had begun by doing all that was calculated to bring it about, yet unseen influences had driven him off his course and set everything awry.

It seemed no time at all since the days of the Consulate when he and his family were carefree, young and lighthearted. On these lawns Napoleon had raced about with furious energy, playing Prisoner's Base and Blind Man's Buff. But then he was the hero of France and the friend of Europe, a victor in wars he had not brought about and had hastened to end. He had not then taken possession of the throne nor crowned his brothers, he had not seen himself as master of the world.

He walked about in a melancholy silence speaking only now and then of Joséphine. Hortense, in her black silk dress, could not keep back her tears and could find nothing consoling to say.

Now it was eleven o'clock and they sat down with their ladies and gentlemen-in-waiting to the luncheon prepared by M. Bazinet. No doubt M. Bazinet had performed wonders, and one may imagine him triumphant but exhausted, for Mlle Cochelet records that such an occasion was a day of battle for him. But he and his assistants alone obtained satisfaction from the fine repast, for the meal was little noticed by those round the table. Napoleon was preoccupied and conversation lagged. Hortense had no appetite; she and Napoleon were almost silent, and if they did not speak others would scarcely venture to do so. It was a melancholy occasion, and those present had leisure to wonder what the future held.

When the meal was over the picture gallery was visited and Napoleon asked Hortense to make him a small copy of a portrait of Joséphine that he particularly liked. He wanted to have it with him as a talisman when he set off on his campaign.[1] Then a short drive was taken round the grounds, and on returning the Imperial party found the mayor and the curé had arrived to pay their respects;

[1] Thiers, *Histoire de l'Empire*, Vol. IV, p. 496.

they had come with a long address which they had no doubt spent the morning in composing. Napoleon replied graciously and promised to assist the commune to acquire a drinking fountain which he knew they needed.

When the mayor and the curé had left, Napoleon went alone to the room where Joséphine had died and remained there for some time. It had been left unchanged; richly and elaborately furnished, it was hung with scarlet and gold silk and was engulfed in a deep silence.

Early in the afternoon the visitors drove back to Paris where they found the Comte de Flahaut, one of Napoleon's aides-de-camp, who had just returned from the frontier after failing to reach Vienna with the messages he was carrying. The conversation continued on the serious note of the morning, everyone being aware that there was now no hope of avoiding an immediate war.[1]

The following day a report by Caulaincourt appeared in the *Moniteur* explaining his failure to enter into negotiations with any country in Europe. At the same time it was made known that decrees had been issued on the 9th and 10th calling up army men on leave and the National Guard. This news was a shock to the general public who had been led to believe that Napoleon had an understanding with the Powers, and government stocks fell sharply.

The French had reason to feel apprehensive, for the Allies were planning to invade their country in the near future. In Italy the Austrians had now taken the offensive and King Joachim Murat was in retreat, although this news had not yet reached Paris. Wellington's general scheme at this time was that operations should begin on the Allied right; the troops under his own command should move over the Belgian frontier simultaneously with the Prussians; the Allied Austrian and Bavarian army would follow, moving in by way of the Upper Rhine, the Russian army coming in from the east as a third great wave. Later on, when Napoleon had placed his army almost entirely on the Belgian frontier, Wellington was to change his plan and suggest that the great invasion should begin on the left of the Allied line, on the eastern side of France where there would be little resistance. But Napoleon himself was to strike before the Allied plans were completed.

[1] *Mémoires de la Reine Hortense*, Vol, II, pp. 360-1

5

Captain Mercer's troop lands at Ostende; Napoleon and the Liberal Constitution; Mercer at Strytem; Defeat of Murat

British soldiers were now crossing the Channel, and on the 13th Captain Mercer disembarked at Ostende with his troop. He was an excellent soldier who was to play a fine though unrewarded part in the battle of Waterloo. Unlike Wellington who destroyed his violin in his youth in order to attend more closely to his military career, Mercer took paints and brushes with him on his campaigns and spent his leisure time in sketching. He also kept a diary from day to day during the campaign of 1815 which gives a good idea of the life of the average soldier, as well as a brilliant picture of the Low Countries seen through the eyes of a man of keen awareness.

Mercer's diary describes how the *Salus*, the transport ship which took his troop abroad, ran in on the beach along with other vessels from which men and horses were landing. 'What a scene!' he writes. 'What hallooing, shouting, vociferating and plunging'. The *Salus* was at once boarded by an officious naval transport officer with a gang of sailors whom he ordered to throw horses and saddlery into the water. Thinking much of his own importance and authority, and nothing of the war in which his country was engaged, he brushed aside Captain Mercer's protests and was ready to throw even the ammunition into the sea. 'I can't help it, Sir,' he said as horses plunged unhappily into the cold water. 'The Duke's orders are positive that no delay is to take place in landing the troops as they arrive, and the ships sent back again.'

'The scramble and confusion that ensued baffle all description,' says Mercer. 'Bundles of harness went over the side in rapid succession, as well as horses. In vain we urged the loss and damage that must accrue from such a proceeding. "Can't help it – no business of mine – Duke's orders are positive," etc., etc., was our only answer.' Parties of men had to be sent overboard to collect and carry things ashore and to catch and secure the frightened horses while Mercer struggled to save the rest of his equipment. 'It was not without difficulty,' he

66

says, 'that I succeeded at last in impressing upon Captain Hill the necessity of leaving our guns and ammunition wagons etc. on board for the night – otherwise his furious zeal would have turned all out to stand on the wet sand or be washed away.'

It was evening by the time the men had disembarked, had gathered together the shivering horses and dragged the saddlery from the sea. They were wet, cold and tired, and no arrangements had been made for their reception; neither food nor shelter awaited them. No doubt this was the kind of treatment English soldiers had met with from 1066 onwards when driven forth to fight their country's battles, and no one was to raise any protest until Crimean days. And as for Captain Hill, while wars last he will always be in evidence.

Mercer rode off to look for shelter for the night while his men and horses waited patiently. He heard at length of some empty sheds outside the town, and returned to the beach as the light was fading.

And a most miserable scene of confusion I there found. Our saddles, harness, baggage, etc., were still strewed about the sand, and these the flood which was now making, threatened soon to submerge. *Pour surcroît de malheur* the rain came down in torrents, and a storm, which had been brewing up the whole afternoon, now burst over us most furiously. . . . Our people meantime, blinded by the lightning, had borrowed some lanterns from the ship, and were busily employed searching for the numerous articles still missing. . . . At length, having collected as many of our things as was possible, and saddled our horses (some two or three of which had escaped altogether), we began our march for the sheds a little after midnight, with a farrier and another dismounted man carrying lanterns at the head of our column.

The rain continued to pour down, and among other hazards was a flimsy bridge, which collapsed, hurling men and horses into the ditch below. The roads were deep in mud and so slippery that horses fell at every moment; the lanterns, too, were frequently extinguished. It was not until two in the morning that the sheds were found. Fortunately they were large and dry and contained a quantity of hay and straw. Thankfully the tired and hungry men took possession of them. Mercer writes:

All our enjoyments are the effect of contrast. It would be considered miserable enough to be obliged to pass the night under such equivocal shelter as these sheds afforded, and that, too, in wet clothes; yet did we now, after twelve hours of harassing work and exposure to the weather, look upon them as palaces, and, having cared for our poor beasts as far as circumstances would permit, proceeded to prepare for that repose so necessary and so longed for.

Mercer was already lying down on some hay when he received a message from the local miller's wife, offering hospitality for the night to himself and his officers.

Thither, therefore, we repaired; and being ushered into the kitchen, quite a pattern of neatness, found the good woman and one of her men already busy making a fire and preparing coffee – unlooked-for luxury! To this kindness she added the offer of two beds, which were eagerly and thankfully accepted by Lieutenants Ingleby and Bull. For my part, I preferred not pulling off my wet clothes and putting them on again in the morning, and therefore declined. Spite of our fatigue, we were all so refreshed by the coffee, that a pleasant hour was passed chatting to our kind hostess and joking with her man, Coché, a sort of good-humoured, half-witted Caliban. At last sleep began to weigh heavily on our eyelids. The lady retired to her chamber, Coché hid himself somewhere, and, sinking back in our old-fashioned, high-backed chairs, we were soon unconscious of everything.

The morning of the 14th was fine and the air filled with the song of birds. The soldiers rose, returned to their ship where they carefully disembarked their guns and carriages, then went to the commissariat for an issue of rations. They were kept waiting for four hours and Mercer had time to inspect his troop, whose appearance he found 'vexatious in the extreme'.

Our noble horses, yesterday morning so sleek and spirited, now stood with drooping heads and rough staring coats, plainly indicating the mischief they had sustained in being taken from a hot hold, plunged into cold water, and then exposed for more than seven hours on an open beach to such a tempest of wind and rain as that we experienced last night. . . . As for our men, they looked jaded, their clothes all soiled with mud and wet, their sabres rusty, and the bear-skins of their helmets flattened down by the rain. Still, however, they displayed the same spirit and alacrity which has always been a characteristic of the horse-artillery, more particularly of G Troop.

Soon, indeed, the troop, having eaten, was riding off cheerfully towards Bruges, and by the 15th they were all in the best of spirits. They had been billeted overnight in the village of Ghistel where their hosts had been kind. 'The novelty amused them, and everyone had some tale to relate of last night's adventure.' As they entered Bruges and heard its carillons they were reconciled to their lot.

On this same day, 15 April, Michel Ney, Prince of the Moskowa, returned to Paris, having accomplished the task Napoleon had set him three weeks before. He soon realized from the gossips of the capital that his boastful promise to Louis, made as he was setting off to oppose Napoleon, was not forgotten but had provided one of the best stories of the hour. Although most of the Bonapartists had themselves changed sides, all of them professed to despise him for the part he had played. Ney could not hold his tongue, could not refrain from showing off. In order no doubt to amuse someone, he had said at Dijon on his way to Paris: 'I congratulated myself on having forced the Emperor to abdicate, and now here I am having to serve him again!'[1] Nothing could have been more dangerous in times of political unrest; he was a man to whom all minds would turn when a scapegoat was required. The latest joke at his expense was the word that went round the salons, '*Il faut être né(y) pour ça.*' Napoleon himself had heard of Ney's indiscretions and his manner was now distant. Disconcerted, Ney retired to his country seat and nothing was heard of him for several weeks. If only he had remained there!

Napoleon now changed his place of residence from the Palace of the Tuileries to the Elysée. Since Marie Louise and his son had not returned a normal court life was impossible, and he forsook the large palace until better days should come, using it only for receptions and the religious services he was punctilious in attending at this time. Besides preparing his army, he was now fortifying Paris and provisioning the frontier fortressses.

General Grouchy had been given the rank of marshal for his work in terminating the Duc d'Angoulême's opposition in the south. Of the marshals Napoleon had formerly created, few, if any, now had confidence in him. Berthier, his Chief-of-Staff in every successful campaign, had followed Louis XVIII into exile. Macdonald,

---

[1] Houssaye, *1815*, Vol. II, p. 52.

Gouvion Saint-Cyr and Masséna were living in retirement. Others served him uneasily, aware of the risk they ran. In general it could be said that the highest ranking officers were the least satisfied by the revival of the Empire; Napoleon trusted most those officers who were closely connected with the rank and file. He dismissed many from the higher ranks, and forebade former emigrants to remain in the service.

In the generals he had chosen to lead his various army corps, he had a group of able men. General Drouet d'Erlon had fought at Iéna and Friedland and had served Soult and Masséna well in Spain; General Reille was a veteran of the Italian campaign; he had commanded a division of the Guards at Wagram, and at the end of 1812 had been Commander-in-Chief of the army of Portugal; General Gérard, one of the heroes of the Russian campaign, had commanded an army corps during the campaign of France; Vandamme, Rapp and Lobau were equally experienced and vigorous leaders. Yet, though they were loyal and reliable, they were less optimistic about the outcome of the war than were men of lower rank; they were better informed about the political situation in Europe, and they were of the small circle who knew that Napoleon was capable of making disastrous mistakes.

Men on leave were gradually rejoining their regiments. The response to the call-up of the National Guard varied from one region to another. In at least half the country the men joined up with a good heart, often buying their own arms and uniform. But in some districts the measure was greatly disliked and many men contrived to evade service; in Brittany and the Vendée, where royalist risings threatened to break out anew, it was thought wiser not to call them up at all.

Though Paris remained calm, fear of war and invasion was causing discontent almost throughout France, and there were riots and disorders in many districts. A thousand tri-colour flags were pulled down during the month of April, many of them from church steeples, for the clergy had no love for Napoleon. Government notices were torn from walls and a bust of the Emperor was smashed in Poitiers. In Amiens a notice was printed and circulated among men liable to be called up for service with the National Guard: 'Who recalled Bonaparte? The army. Then let the army defend him.

His enemies are our friends. Do not arm us to defend a man thrown up from hell'.[1] During a review of the National Guard at Saint-Omer, one of the militiamen seized the flag and trampled it underfoot; the Commander, fearing a riot, dared do no more than confine the culprit for a few hours in the police station. In many places blood was shed. Marseilles was particularly dangerous at this time. Its trade was ruined, the port was idle and the poor threatened with starvation. Napoleon was detested in this great town, and the National Guard were favourable to Louis XVIII. A patrol of these Guards fired one evening on a group of army officers whom they heard shouting 'Vive l'Empereur!'; on another occasion a café was stoned when army officers were seen sitting there. In many towns of the south and west great animosity was shown even to the ordinary soldiers of the regular army. Many an unhappy young man, conscientiously obeying the call to rejoin the army, found himself being stoned or otherwise maltreated, the wretched beginning of evil days culminating in Waterloo.[2]

Paris had by now lost its enthusiasm, its air of excitement. Shopkeepers anticipated ruin, unless they happened to sell arms or saddlery, and there was deep disappointment over the continued absence of the Empress and her son. The humble man in the street, who counted for nothing and had to take what came, began to see that once more the politicians had swindled him, had lied to him and claimed his support by idle words; but, since it was better to laugh than to weep, he amused himself with sly remarks and comic songs, many of them about the plight of the man whose wife refused to come back to him.

The prolonged absence of Marie Louise and the King of Rome could only suggest to the French that their Emperor's position was irregular and insecure. Napoleon himself, despite the discouraging news brought from Vienna by M. de Montrond, had not given up all hope of their return and continued his attempts to negotiate in secret. Caulaincourt discovered a willing emissary in the person of the Baron de Stassart who had formerly been in the service of Marie Louise and was now attached to the court of her father. The Baron, who was in Paris and about to return to Vienna, set off on 17 April with letters to the Emperor Francis and Metternich. Writing to

[1] Houssaye, *1815*, Vol. II, p. 10.   [2] Houssaye, *1815*, Vol. I, pp. 512-22.

Francis, Napoleon again asked for the return of his wife or, failing that, at least the return of his son who could not, he thought, legitimately be kept from him. The Baron was not able to deliver the letters, however; on reaching Lintz he was made to give them up and they were placed on the conference table of the Congress.[1]

Stassart was followed a week or two later by M. de Saint Léon, designated by Fouché who gave him a letter to Metternich, pleading the cause of Napoleon. Fouché is supposed also to have employed him on a secret scheme of his own in favour of the Duc d'Orléans. Caulaincourt gave the new emissary letters to Metternich and Talleyrand, urging them to rely entirely upon all he said. What Saint Léon had been instructed to say is indicated in a letter written by Napoleon to Caulaincourt on 22 April: 'I authorize you to have assurances given to the Prince de Bénévant [Talleyrand] that his property will be restored if he behaves as a Frenchman and renders me certain services. M. de Saint Léon may also enter into an engagement with M. de Metternich of from one to ten millions if Austria will withdraw from the Coalition and pursue a policy more in conformity with her real interests and the family ties which unite her to me.'[2] Saint Léon succeeded in reaching Vienna and was accorded interviews with Metternich and Talleyrand; but nothing was achieved. The two diplomats did not respond to Napoleon's overtures, and M. de Saint Léon returned with nothing more than a friendly personal letter from Talleyrand to Caulaincourt.

It was at this time, the end of April, that Napoleon discovered that Fouché was in secret communication with Metternich, their aim being to find a means of avoiding war by forcing Napoleon to abdicate and make way for a more acceptable form of government. Fouché had taken office under Napoleon in the belief that Europe would soon bring him down; if the unexpected happened and Napoleon prevailed, then Fouché, being in office, would be ready to profit from the circumstances; but if Napoleon fell, he could come forward as the indispensable friend of the succeeding government, whose triumph he would have helped to bring about. Catching him red-handed, Napoleon would much have liked to have had him

[1] Caulaincourt, *Mémoires*, Vol. I, pp. 190-1. Thiers, *Histoire de l'Empire*, Vol. IV, p. 460.

[2] Caulaincourt, *Mémoires*, Vol. I, pp. 191-3.

placed under arrest; he refrained, however, fearing to confirm the public suspicion that all was not well. Long afterwards, he expressed regret that he had not had Fouché executed.

Even more serious was further news from Meneval which reached him in the last week of April. Shortly after the Comte de Montrond had left Vienna, M. de Meneval had come to the conclusion that it was his duty to let Napoleon's real friends in Paris know the whole truth regarding Marie Louise's conduct, although it was painful to have to speak of it. Napoleon's position was dangerous, and he felt it was necessary that he should realize there was no hope of the Empress's return, and consequently no hope of Austrian support. He contrived to send a letter to the Comte de Lavalette, *Ministre des Postes*, and this was shown to the Emperor.

Meneval wrote, says Lavalette in his memoirs, that it was useless to count on the Empress. She did not hide her hatred for the Emperor, and she approved of every measure taken against him. It was useless to think of a reunion, for if the question was brought up she would raise every difficulty. Finally, said Meneval, it was impossible for him any longer to hide his indignation at seeing the Empress entirely given up to Count Neipperg, not even taking the trouble to conceal her taste for this man who had taken possession of her mind just as surely as he had of her person.

'This sad discovery did the Emperor a great deal of harm,' says Lavalette.[1] It was an end of his belief in success. From then onwards his moods of optimism were to alternate with a black pessimism that clouded his mind more and more frequently. There can have been little wrong with his health when he made his daring journey from Elba to Paris, but now the symptoms of various maladies to which he was subject began to show themselves in an alarming fashion. And yet he was to remain rashly over-confident in the organizing of the war. When he was in good spirits he shared the general view of the Continent, that he was certain to prevail in Belgium.

Captain Mercer's troop had reached Ghent where Louis XVIII and his court resided. One of the duties of the troop was to provide the King with a guard of honour. Mercer writes:

[1] Lavalette, *Mémoires*, Vol. II, p. 146.

Our subalterns were very well pleased with this arrangement, for the duty was nothing. They found an excellent table, and passed their time very agreeably with the young men of the *garde du corps*, some of whom were always in attendance. Many of these were mere boys, and the ante-room of his most Christian Majesty frequently exhibited bolstering matches and other amusements savouring strongly of the boarding school. The royal stud was in the barrack stables, and consisted principally of grey horses, eighteen or twenty of which had been purchased at a sale of *cast horses* from the Scots Greys.

The Bourbons were much in evidence in the ancient and picturesque old city which was crowded with troops. One of the amusements of G Troop was to watch the Duc de Berry's travelling carriage pass by; the postilions of this prince, in their glazed hats and plaited queues, their closely fitting jackets and enormous jackboots, wielded their whips with amazing dexterity, flourishing them over their heads, swinging them to the right and left at varying speeds and filling the air with a sound like barbaric music.

Mercer and his officers made friends with many of the officers of Louis XVIII's household, and the political situation was often discussed. Nothing was known of the position of the French army, nor of Wellington's plans, but regiments were arriving daily from England, halting for a night and then passing on again without knowing their destination.

Even Louis XVIII's officers shared the prevailing European conviction that no one could beat Napoleon. They much admired the British troops when they saw them passing through Ghent, but believed they would be overcome by Napoleon and his Grand Army in the approaching conflict.

On the 25th the troop was again on the march and in the evening arrived at St Gille. Here Mercer was billeted on the *juge de paix* and his wife, while the men and horses were dispersed among neighbouring farms. This was a country that had long been in possession of the French and was said to favour Napoleon; yet the English soldiers were given the kindest welcome in the village. Before dining in his own billet, Mercer visited his men who were scattered by threes and fours amongst the farm-houses:

With these good and simple people I found them quite at home. In most homes I found them seated at dinner with the family – at all they had been invited so to do; and everywhere the greatest good humour and the best possible understanding prevailed between the host and guests.

The horses were equally well cared for and were in stables of clean straw, their racks and mangers filled with clover. The farmers were pleased to have the army horses on the premises because the dung they provided was so valuable in the cultivation of their land. Everywhere in this friendly country even the most humble cottages shone with cleanliness. Meals were usually eaten in a kitchen furnished with a table and benches and hung with highly polished brass pots and pans; in the sitting-room there would be old-fashioned chairs and a heavy oak table; the windows were invariably hung with brilliantly white curtains, while prints of saints adorned the walls and wax fruit the mantelpiece, and a crucifix was certain to be in some prominent position. And all round, the fields were richly fertile with the rising crops: wheat, hops, buckwheat, clover, flax, all of superb quality – the result of endless care and labour.

The *juge de paix* and his wife had no doubt that the English would be forced to take to their ships the moment Napoleon chose to appear; they were well disposed to the French and looked forward to the return of a certain colonel who had formerly been billeted on them. None the less, visitors made an agreeable interlude if they were pleasant people, and the English guests were treated with hospitable kindness.

Now the troop was again to move on in the direction of Brussels; the wife of the *juge de paix* shed tears as she embraced Mercer and wished him well, and her Flemish cook wept over his groom. Mercer writes:

> Most of the peasants on whom our men had been billeted, accompanied them to the parade, and it was interesting to witness the kindness with which they shook hands at parting. . . . And yet these were Napoleonists, according to our *juge*. For my part, I believe they were utterly indifferent as to whether they lived under the rule of Napoleon or the house of Orange, so long as their agricultural labours were not interrupted.

Marshal Prince Blücher had arrived in the Low Countries to take command of the Prussian army, and the Duke of Wellington sent him a letter of welcome in which he informed him that the frontier was quiet although the number of French generals and staff officers had recently increased at Valenciennes.

The Duke, who was in constant correspondence with kings, princes and ministers and was overwhelmed with tasks of diplomacy and organization, was at the same time putting the towns of the Low Countries in a good defensive state and studying the lie of the land with a view to possible battles. Everyone in Europe with a position of authority seemed to need his advice, and in addition he was showered with requests from men who wished to serve on his staff or who had relatives to recommend in that capacity.

In his letters and despatches there are frequent references to the staff officers being sent to him from England, usually by the Prince Regent, and whom he scarcely knew how to employ. Sometimes he would dismiss a batch of them and write home explaining that he had far too many inexperienced young gentlemen to assist him; but the Regent paid scant attention and continued to appoint his own candidates while the Duke waited in vain for the good British infantry, the horses and guns he so urgently needed. He did not complain, but prepared to make the best possible use of what was available. All the same, he allowed himself to show something of his feelings in a letter sent to Lieut.-General Lord Stewart on 8 May:

> I have got an infamous army, very weak and ill equipped, and a very inexperienced Staff. In my opinion they are doing nothing in England. . . . They have not raised a man; they have not called out the Militia either in England or Ireland; are unable to send me anything; and they have not sent a message to Parliament about the money. The war spirit is therefore evaporating as I am informed.

England, indeed, was still arguing about the war as if it were a matter for debate, and it was the fashion among her wealthy subjects to visit Brussels. Brussels was overflowing with visitors, officers' wives among them, all of whom were enjoying the lively social life of the town.

Yet Brussels stood in imminent danger, for there were signs now that Napoleon was actively preparing to invade Belgium. On the 9th the Duke wrote to Lieut.-Colonel Sir Henry Hardinge, who was attached to Blücher's staff, 'There appears no doubt that the enemy's forces are collected at Maubeuge and Valenciennes, principally the former. The communication was put an end to yesterday, and it was said Buonaparte was at Condé. I was told at Ghent that he was to leave Paris on this day.'[1]

Napoleon, meanwhile, was still gathering his forces. While England in its peaceful unity moved slowly and attempted little, France was a hive of industry despite its deep-seated strife and the fact that civil war was already breaking out anew in the south and west. Arsenals and factories were working at full pressure; horses were being bought and requisitioned in thousands, while Wellington struggled to obtain a few hundred; armourers had been called up by decree at the end of March and were everywhere hard at work, while small arms were even being purchased from enemy countries and were arriving hidden in barges from Belgium and the Rhineland.[2] Saddlers and shoemakers were all fully employed, and so were tailors. Louis XVIII, who had hoped to see no more of war, had so neglected the army, apart from a few favoured regiments, that uniforms were shabby and sometimes even ragged; everything had to be renewed.

Napoleon gave much thought to the Imperial Guard which had long been the pride of the nation. It had been drastically reduced in the past year but he now added new regiments and generally raised its strength, so that by the time he set off on his campaign its numbers had reached 20,755. The battalion from Elba was included in the Old Guard; the Young Guard was now mainly formed of re-enlisted men and volunteers, while for the Middle Guard men were recruited from the *Gendarmerie* and the regiments of the line. The Imperial Guard, which was to be under Marshal Mortier, was a body of excellently trained men of good record and physique, unsurpassed in zeal and courage.

All that had to do with the reorganization of the army was stimulating to Napoleon; but the formation of a liberal constitution was irksome and he felt himself hampered at every turn by the demands and opinions of other people. Even at Elba he had been the undisputed master of his domain and had done exactly as he pleased. He saw, however, that the devolution of power was a necessity in present circumstances, and he had resigned himself.

[1] Wellington, *Dispatches*, Vol. XII, p. 368.   [2] Houssaye, *1815*, Vol. II, p. 18.

The new constitution, worked out for him by Benjamin Constant, was not essentially different from that by which Louis XVIII ruled, being based on that of England with a House of Representatives and a House of Peers. Napoleon objected to one thing only in the new constitution; it was presented to him as a new system, having no relation to his previous reign. 'You are depriving me of my past,' he said to Benjamin Constant. 'What have you done with my eleven years' reign? I suppose I have some right to it? This new constitution must be attached to the old; thus it will have the sanction of glory.'

Benjamin Constant, gratified that his liberal system of laws was being accepted so readily, was pleased to give way on this minor point, however little entitled the Emperor might be to claim that his old dictatorship was glorious or worthy of alliance with a just constitution. The new constitution was named, therefore, the *Acte additionnel aux Constitutions de l'Empire*.

This *Acte additionnel* had been read to the Ministers and the Council of State on 23 April, and for a moment Napoleon had shown his real feelings. It was noticed that the new laws, though certainly liberal, would still permit him to confiscate the property of his political adversaries, and he was asked to consent to the abolition of this privilege. He cried indignantly.

You are driving me into a way that is not my own. I am being weakened and put in chains. France seeks me and can no longer find me. Public feeling was at first excellent, and now it is execrable. France is asking what has become of the old arm of the Emperor, the arm she needs to subdue Europe. Why talk to me of goodness, abstract justice and natural laws? The first law is necessity; the first justice is public safety. I am asked to allow the men I have loaded with wealth to make use of their fortunes for plotting against me abroad. This may not be, it shall not be. When peace is established, we will see. To each day its difficulties, to each circumstance its law, to everyone his own nature. It is not my nature to be an angel. Gentlemen, I repeat, the old arm of the Emperor must be found again and must be seen.

The Ministers gave way, aware that if they did not do so they might see him tear up the constitution and resort to his power over the army and the masses in order to impose his will.

This, however, was his only protest against the restraints being put upon him, and the text of the *Acte additionnel* was published in the *Moniteur*. At the same time Frenchmen were called on to vote upon it on the registers to be provided in every commune. The result of the voting was to be announced at the forthcoming *Champ de Mai*.

Napoleon accepted the liberal role, but, as his outburst before his Ministers had shown, he felt himself handicapped at a dangerous moment. His old military successes had been made possible by his power to command instant obedience from other men. He had inspired fear, and thus he had had strength and power; now he was scarcely more formidable than any other man in France.

The situation was indeed irrational. A group of ambitious politicians had come forward to serve Napoleon, and they were now primarily concerned to limit his power and force him to play an unfamiliar role. As he said, he was not an angel. If the men about him wanted to be ruled by a good man, they should have looked for a good man and not have consented to Napoleon. If it was indeed Napoleon they wanted, then they should have let him be himself; he was a military dictator and as such he might well have won the victories that would have kept them all in office.

Captain Mercer and his troop were now in the village of Strytem, not far from Ninove where Lord Uxbridge, Commander of the Cavalry, had his headquarters. The rolling countryside abounded in rich and flourishing crops interspersed with dark woods and shining streams. The Captain and his officers had taken possession of an ancient château whose owners had left it long unoccupied; it was dilapidated and chilling, yet majestic with its ancestral portraits and its tapestries many centuries old. On arrival, the soldiers had been appalled by the forbidding aspect of the place. Captain Mercer writes:

Some of our people could not refrain from grumbling. 'By the Lord, gentlemen,' said old Lieutenant Ingleby, 'you ought to think yourselves very fortunate in getting such a quarter. In the Peninsula the Duke himself would have thought so, and was often glad to get a good roof over his head.' The grumblers were ashamed and we heard no more of it. A large salon in the left wing we chose as our mess-room, and the other officers established themselves upstairs. Fires were soon lighted above and below; servants running up and down; all was life and movement, and the old place had not been so gay for years before.

The old house was soon made comfortable, and excellent meals accompanied by good wines were served under the auspices of a certain Karl who had been made the major-domo of the establishment.

This Karl, as interesting a character as any taking part in the campaign, was a gifted but poor and homeless young European of eighteen or nineteen who had found no better opening in life than to be a servant. Captain Mercer does not tell us his country of origin, though his character indicates that he may have been a Rhinelander. His last master had been the French general, Vandamme, whom he had accompanied to Moscow. After the retreat, Vandamme had abandoned him in Saxony with long arrears of wages due to him. Karl had therefore set off on foot towards France in his green livery with red cuffs and collar and his glazed, cockaded hat, and he was still in search of a master when he happened to meet Captain Mercer's troop. He offered himself as a paragon among valets; he could speak several languages, cook, dress hair and do a thousand and one other things. Most useful of all, he said, was the talent he had acquired from being so long with the French army, that of 'discovering and appropriating' the resources of any country where fortune might place him. His appearance and manner were so attractive that one of the lieutenants at once engaged him. Captain Mercer writes:

> So henceforth he became one of us, and soon a general favourite; for although he had sounded his own trumpet, he had in nowise exaggerated his qualifications, nor even told us all, for in addition he was the merriest and most kind-hearted creature I ever met with. He had an inexhaustible fund of stories and songs, and sang beautifully, and in a most sweet and melodious voice; was an admirable mimic, and amongst other things mimicked so well two flutes, that one day, at Strytem, sitting smoking my cigar on the parapet of the bridge, I actually made sure two people were playing a duet in the kitchen; but upon going thither, found only Karl, who, seated on a table, was warbling out a favourite waltz, like a robin on the housetop.

On their first evening at Strytem, the mayor had arrived with a deputation to read an address of welcome. Clad in their best suits –

cotton jackets, velveteen breeches, striped cotton stockings, buckled shoes and large plush hats – the mayor and his companions showed by their demeanour that the men of the Low Countries were not without experience in the matter of foreign occupations and invading armies. He was doing no more, he told the English officers, than expressing the sentiments of the whole commune when he assured them that the arrival of the brave English had filled the local population with a most lively joy. A stream of compliments followed, after which the mayor went on to deplore the poverty of the commune and to express his despair that Milor Wellington should have sent his brave soldiers to a place so unworthy of them, so incapable of providing them with the amenities they so richly merited – and this, too, when all the surrounding districts abounded in wealthy, populous villages fully adequate to lodge them all comfortably and supply every need. The people of Strytem, he said, plundered and oppressed by the Prussians for several months the previous year, were ruined and quite incapable of supplying the rations now demanded.

It was in vain. Captain Mercer and his troop were not to be persuaded to ride off elsewhere; and, indeed, every village round about was rapidly filling with cavalry troops awaiting the orders of Lord Uxbridge. Gradually the soldiers settled down among the local people happily enough; Strytem turned out to be less impoverished than its mayor had suggested and in fact abounded in good things – 'the finest milk, eggs and butter I ever saw in my life, and in profusion,' Mercer says. 'During our whole stay at Strytem there was never any difference – always abundance.' The peasants prospered, the reward of their unremitting industry. The clover on this fertile soil, the main food for the horses at that time of year, was so thick as to give the impression one might walk on it without sinking to the ground. 'But to me the height attained by the rye was most astonishing,' says Mercer. 'In one field which I rode through nearly every day it was as high as my head, when mounted on my little horse Cossack, about $14\frac{3}{4}$ hands high, so that it could not have been less than seven or eight feet, the ears remarkably full and looking well.' The weather was warm and sunny, with a good soaking shower from time to time; wherever one looked there was wealth in the form of food for the future.

In the long, light evenings, the soldiers would join the peasants in a cabaret near the church and spend a few hours drinking and chatting. 'It is a curious fact,' says Captain Mercer, 'that upon enquiry of the sergeant-major how they could understand each other, he replied that the Yorkshire, Lancashire and Lincolnshire men, who spoke very broad, could make themselves understood pretty well, and in like manner could comprehend the Flemish of their boon companions'. Occasionally a quarrel would break out, due, no doubt, to the local habit of drinking gin, which Captain Mercer describes as 'a villanous kind of spirit', sold very cheaply. 'Though our men were really fine fellows, and generally very steady soldiers, yet, like other Englishmen, they could not resist a social glass nor avoid its consequences; and, indeed, if excuse it be, they were in a measure driven to the use of this pernicious spirit by the execrable quality of all the beer in the country, which more resembled a mixture of cow-dung and water than anything else.'

On the whole, the people of Strytem had little to complain of, though Karl was inclined to take liberties in his belief that a soldier helped himself; but plundering was forbidden by the Duke of Wellington and supplies were normally paid for. The soldiers were well behaved, and under good officers did comparatively little harm as they rode about the fields which, in so many districts, were being needlessly trampled down by the troops.

One of the characters of Strytem was the *garde champêtre*, an old French soldier who acted as the local policeman and was a firm ally of the English soldiers in any fracas that might take place between them and the peasants. When the Low Countries were a part of his empire, Napoleon had placed a *garde champêtre* in every village to exercise surveillance. They were usually retired men from the *grande armée*, and they were still in office, following their leisurely calling undisturbed by falling empires and changing dynasties. The one in Strytem had served under Marshal Suchet and had lost two fingers in battle. He wore a leather cocked hat and a green uniform adorned with large copper buttons decorated with the Imperial eagle of France, and he carried a javelin as a badge of office. On one occasion he learnt that a local peasant had struck a gunner of the English troop, not without provocation since he had caught the man plundering his garden. The peasant complained to Captain Mercer who went to investigate, taking the *garde champêtre* with him as the best the village could offer as a representative of law and order. But the old French soldier fell into transports of rage and promptly gave the unhappy peasant a sound thrashing, '*Quoi! Un vil paysan frapper un militaire? Ah, que cela me révolte! Sacré cochon!*'

There was little work to be done, and life passed by agreeably for the whole troop; even drill became rare in the month of May. 'So completely is the whole of this country (not occupied by wood) under tillage, that it was long after our arrival at Strytem ere we discovered a spot on which we could even draw out the troop, much less exercise it.' In fact the long and sunny days were so enjoyable that no one wished to see an end to them. The officers explored the countryside or spent their time in Brussels, according to their temperament. Those who visited Brussels would return in the evening with the latest military information; no one had the least idea what lay ahead, but there was much talk now of a possible invasion by Napoleon's army. Mercer writes:

Whilst our army thus revelled in luxury in this fine country, that of the enemy, we understood, was concentrating on our frontier, preparatory to the grand blow which was to drive us into the sea. To meet the threatened invasion, it was generally understood in the army that the Duke had made choice of two positions in the neighbourhood of Brussels – the one a little beyond the village of Waterloo, the other at Hal, the point where the roads from Ath and Mons unite. In one or other of these, it was said, he intended to await the attack, according as the enemy might advance. Frequently, attended only by an orderly dragoon, he would visit these positions, studying them deeply, and most probably forming plans for their occupation and defence. In confirmation, too, of the reports that the French army would shortly advance, we about this time received an order to divest ourselves of all superfluous baggage, and were given to understand that, in case of passing the frontier, the army must be prepared to forego all shelter but what would be carried with it, since the operations were to be of the most active nature.

The Duke, still very short of supplies, was patiently building up as good an army as was possible with what he had. 'For an action in Belgium,' he had written on 3 May, 'I can now put 70,000 men into the field, and Blücher 80,000; so that I hope we should give a good account even of Buonaparte.'

The Allies were helped at this time by the defeat of Murat who had been routed by the Austrian army. A terrible battle had been fought at Tolentino on 2 and 3 May, and the Neapolitans had left on the field 4,000 dead and wounded as well as their guns and their supplies. Now Murat was flying southwards, his army in dissolution. He reached Naples only to see to his wife's escape with their children, and then to leave himself the following day, disguised as a sailor.

On the same day, 19 May, Wellington wrote to Lord Uxbridge:

I have a most formidable account of the French cavalry. They have now 16,000 *grosse cavalerie*, of which 6,000 are *cuirassiers*. They are getting horses to mount 42,000 cavalry, heavy and light. It is reported that Murat has fled from Italy by sea; and by other reports it appears that he has arrived at Paris. He will probably command them.

Murat, one of the most famous leaders of cavalry living, would have liked nothing better than to redeem his failures in Italy by leading Napoleon's newly formed regiments to victory in Belgium. Arrived on the southern coast of France, he hastened to send a message to his Imperial brother-in-law offering his services. But he was coldly rebuffed and told to remain where he was.

6

Deterioration of Napoleon's energies; Military plans; The
Champ de Mai

M. de Meneval had decided to return to France. Although the
Empress Marie Louise wished him to remain with her, and invariably
treated him with kindness and consideration, he felt it was no longer
possible to serve a mistress whose conduct so profoundly shocked
him. He believed that Marie Louise was responsible for the dangerous
and practically hopeless situation in which Napoleon was now
placed, and in this he was to some extent right, for she alone linked
him to the dynasts and she alone could have reconciled them to him.
Placid, amiable and filled with rosy dreams of her own future,
Marie Lousie spent the days in writing interminable letters to her
lover, Count Neipperg, who found time while chasing Murat down
Italy to send lengthy replies by every courier.

Before leaving Vienna Meneval called at the Hofburg to take his
leave of the Imperial Prince. He found the child completely changed,
silent and mistrustful of everyone about him; precociously intelligent as he was, the little boy remembered well his father and his life
in Paris, and realized that all had gone wrong for him and that he
was among his father's enemies. It was a sad parting, for Meneval
was the last of his friends.

As he journeyed homewards, Meneval met with great enthusiasm
for the Emperor in north-eastern France where the people were
optimistic about the approaching war. From General Lecourbe,
however, he received anxious enquiries as to whether there was
any hope of avoiding a conflict. He reached Paris in the middle of
May and was cordially welcomed by Napoleon who spent many
hours with him in the gardens of the Elysée, closely questioning him
and listening attentively to his replies.

Napoleon's manner was sad and resigned, Meneval says. He
writes in his memoirs:

> I no longer found him animated by that conviction of success which
> had formerly given him such assurance. It seemed that the faith in his

fortunes which had inspired him to plan the bold enterprise of returning from the island of Elba, and which had sustained him during his
march across France, had abandoned him when he entered Paris.
He felt he was no longer supported with that ardent and devoted zeal
to which he had been accustomed, but that he was hampered by the
restraints that had been imposed upon him.

Outside the Elysée, Meneval found that the general concern was
to know the date of the Empress's return, for it was still widely
believed that she would eventually rejoin the Emperor with the
King of Rome. To the many questions he was asked concerning her
he had to give an evasive reply.[1]

Lucien Bonaparte was also back in Paris. His relations with
Napoleon had been stormy in the past, and for many years he had
been living abroad under the shadow of his Imperial brother's
displeasure. He had married the widow of an exchange broker, an
unequal match Napoleon regarded as the height of folly and an act of
insubordination since it upset his own political system. Lucien
had been invited to repudiate his attractive wife for the insipid and
plain Queen of Etruria and so take his place as a vassal of France;
refusing to do so, he had retired to Italy in 1804 after a bitter quarrel
with Napoleon and had played no part in the splendours of the
Empire. He enjoyed the rank of prince, but this had been bestowed
upon him by Pius VII.

After his brother's fall, however, he had sought a reconciliation,
and on learning of the return from Elba he had come back to France
in the hope of being able to serve the cause of his family. On his
return from the Swiss frontier, Napoleon received him most affably,
gave him the rank of Imperial Prince, bestowed the ribbon of the
Legion of Honour upon him and presented him with the Palais-
Royal as his town house; in fact Napoleon lavished upon him the
high favours he had always enjoyed handing out to his family and
friends in good moments. But the days passed, the enthusiasm of the
meeting wore off and he fell into his old inclination to disagree with
Lucien. It was not possible for these two headstrong brothers to
live long on peaceful terms.

Lucien, who had seen almost nothing of his brother since his best
days, soon realized that Napoleon was much altered and was not

[1] Meneval, *Mémoires*, pp. 325-7.

equal to the situation in which he had placed himself. With the refusal of Marie Louise to join him and so mitigate the wrath of the Powers against him, what could he do? Lucien saw, as Meneval did, that he was no longer confident of success and that his difficulties were overwhelming him.

The most alarming aspect of the situation was Napoleon's state of health. At times he would appear normal, cheerful and well; but then he would have a painful and prolonged attack caused by a disease of the kidneys of which the first symptoms had shown themselves after the disasters of the Russian campaign. During these crises he fell into a state of prostration and deep depression from which he could not rouse himself. Contractions of the stomach and a spasmodic cough also tormented him, and at times he had difficulty in remaining awake during the day and would be found dozing. He was in no fit state to lead the nation, still less to set off on a campaign, and Lucien urged him to abdicate.

He did not immediately reject this wise advice, leaving Lucien with the impression that he was thinking it over. But optimism and energy would return when he recovered from his attacks, and with them the determination to hold on to his position. Lucien was a man who could enjoy private life; Napoleon still loved power and could not bear to give it up. He prepared for the *Champ de Mai*, now postponed until 1 June, and gave much thought to the setting which was to reflect his theatrical taste. He planned to appear at the summit of a pyramidal edifice in his Imperial robes, with his brothers standing near by in costumes of white silk and velvet; the dignitaries of Church and State, equally resplendent, would take their appointed places between himself and ground level, the humble plane of the troops and the common multitude. Lucien records that he protested against the order to appear in white and proposed instead to wear the uniform of the National Guard, whereupon Napoleon gave him a disagreeable smile. 'Yes,' he said, 'in the hope of creating more effect in your uniform than I as Emperor, I suppose.'[1] Napoleon's tendency to bicker was marked at this time, and Lucien, after some unavailing argument, resigned himself for the sake of peace to the embarrassing fancy costume.

The idea that Napoleon might once again abdicate soon spread

[1] Jung, *Lucien Bonaparte et ses Mémoires, 1775-1840*, p. 265.

among the politicians; 'And as,' says Viel-Castel, 'men had grown very daring in his presence since his misfortunes had despoiled him of his former prestige, those who knew him most intimately broached the subject openly, appealing to his patriotism. They pointed out to him in every possible way that his presence was the sole cause of war, and that it would be an act worthy of him to give peace to France, and to ensure by sacrificing himself the continuance of his dynasty.' Even the Press, since it was now free, discussed the matter without reserve.[1] But Napoleon was unable to listen to such a suggestion with an open mind; his strongest desire was to be at the head of a great nation, and it was all too easy for him to reverse the situation and to believe, not that France was indispensable to him, but that he was indispensable to France. He therefore made a virtue of remaining in the position he had so brilliantly won back, even though he had many a premonition of failure.

15,000 volunteers had now joined the army, and 25,000 retired soldiers had responded to an invitation to return to arms. Napoleon's attempts to reintroduce conscription had not yet met with success. The Council of State, jealous of its power, had to be consulted and refused to consent to the calling up even of the 1815 class. Since he had called up this class in advance of their time in 1813 and 20,000 of them had fought in his last campaign, he felt he had every right to claim them. In all, they would provide him with 120,000 additional soldiers. He now suggested, avoiding the word 'conscript', that the young men should be called up as part of the National Guard and thence directed into the army proper. When the Council of State refused its consent it occurred to him to claim that the 1815 class were, in fact, men on leave, since they had already served. To this the Council of State could find no answer, and Davout was therefore able to issue orders recalling them. Happily for these young men, Napoleon was to fall before they were ready for service and they were destined to live out their lives in an era of peace.

Far from suspecting at the end of May that his days of power were numbered, Napoleon counted on using his conscripts later in the year and had calculated that by 1 October his army would number 800,000 men.[2] For the moment his active army numbered 291,249

---

[1] Viel-Castel, *Histoire de la Restauration*, Vol. III, p. 114.
[2] Houssaye, *1815*, Vol. II, pp. 14-16, 39.

men, and the Army of the North, that part of it which he was able to spare for the Belgian campaign, consisted of 124,139 men. Wellington had assessed the situation well when he wrote earlier in the month: 'I reckon the force with which Buonaparte can attack this country at 110,000 men.[1]

Napoleon was drawing up his plan of campaign in full detail. The basic scheme was that he was to march headlong into the midst of the Allied armies in Belgium, striking them where the two commands met on the road from Charleroi to Brussels and driving them apart. There was apparently no secrecy about the matter, for the English Radical, Hobhouse, who was in Paris at this time, says in a letter written on 29 May:

Visiting an aide-de-camp of the Emperor, I found him mapping in detail the country on the Belgian frontier, and was asked by him whether a separation of the Prussian and English armies, and a rapid march upon Brussels, would not surprise our politicians in England. 'We can beat Blücher first, and then,' he added with a smile, 'we shall try your Wellington. No one doubts the undaunted bravery of English soldiers, but the loss of 20,000 men would make the people of London look a little pale. You are rather sparing of your own blood, though I cannot say that you care about that of your friends.'

Mr Hobhouse appears to have found these remarks acceptable, and the following day he was able to watch Napoleon reviewing the Imperial Guard on the eve of the ceremony of the *Champ de Mai*. Napoleon, he says in his letter of 31 May, was standing in the shade of the Palace of the Tuileries; the regiments were passing by in the warm sunlight, and Napoleon suddenly moved forward to place himself in the sun also, 'evidently,' Hobhouse says, 'because he observed that he alone was protected from the heat'.

Napoleon, in fact, born in Ajaccio, loved warmth and felt the cold exceedingly; nor was he much inclined to give thought to other people's feelings. It is highly probable that he stepped forward to enjoy the sunshine. His admirers, however, liked to ascribe high-minded motives to his least movement, and were ready to marvel over a supposed act of courtesy which would have been little noticed in another.

[1] Wellington, *Dispatches*, Vol. XII, p. 372.

Soon after, Hobhouse records, Napoleon was to be seen marching a few paces with the soldiers as they filed past. And now a regiment presented arms and he, 'seeing a grenadier with a petition in his hand, stopped before him, took the paper, talked for two minutes to him, and ended by pulling the man's nose. A little afterwards a colonel came running up to him with some news, which he communicated with a laugh, the Emperor raised himself on tiptoe, and interrupted him by giving him a sound box on the ear, with which the officer went away smiling and shewing his cheek, which was red with the blow.'

Hobhouse was assured by a French officer who was with him that such 'friendly flaps' were not uncommon, and he was told of other instances. 'These manners may appear gross and vulgar,' he says, 'but certainly they have succeeded completely with the French soldiery; for both on the present occasion and at other reviews, I have remarked an enthusiasm, an affection, a delight apparent in the countenances of the troops at the sight of their general, which no parent can command in the midst of his family.'

1 June, the day of the *Champ de Mai*, dawned fair and cloudless, and at an early hour the troops were taking their places on the parade-ground outside the *École Militaire*. The *Acte additionnel* was to be solemnly inaugurated and the Imperial standards, surmounted by brass eagles, were to be distributed to the troops. On this morning the result of the plebiscite was published in the *Journal de l'Empire*, showing that 1,288,257 citizens had voted for and 4,802 against the new constitution. However, more than 5,000,000 citizens had been entitled to vote; and many had felt disinclined to give up half a day's work in order to go to a voting centre, while others, fearing reprisals, had been unwilling to inscribe their names on a register on a political issue when once more the future was to be settled by the lottery of war.

Between the centre of Paris and the *École Militaire* the streets were thronged with spectators on their way to the ceremony. At ten o'clock, members of the Imperial court and the government began to take their places on the stands; cardinals and bishops arrived, the electoral delegates and visitors of importance were looking for their seats. Flags flapped lazily in the warm air, while 50,000 soldiers assembled on the parade-ground, their helmets and bayonets flashing in the sunlight; and on all sides the Paris crowds were pouring into the spaces reserved for them.

A salvo of a hundred guns was to herald the Emperor's departure from the Tuileries, to be fired by a battery on the terrace of the palace. Nor was this all: the salute was to be echoed by five other batteries placed at the bridge of Iéna, the Invalides, the heights of Montmartre, the Château de Vincennes, and the *Champ de Mars* itself, the site of the ceremony. This meant that six hundred guns would be fired at every salute, and there were to be many of them throughout the day. The *Champ de Mai*, despite its disarming name, was a great military review, a sign of the progress and development of warfare which, in the eighteenth century, had been limited in Europe as if by common consent. War, once the concern of small professional armies, now involved whole nations, and Napoleon expected his subjects to show enthusiasm, to enjoy the sound of guns, and to think of themselves as belligerents.

The firing began at eleven o'clock, and soon scarlet-coated lancers were seen making their way down the gardens of the Tuileries, followed by mounted guardsmen and then by the Comte de Lobau, Governor of Paris, with his aides-de-camp. Mounted heralds followed, their violet tunics embroidered with golden eagles. After these came State carriages, each drawn by six horses and carrying Imperial princes and court dignitaries. Napoleon now emerged from the palace, clad like a pantomime king, and stepped into his decorated coronation coach with its floral paintings and gilding, its wide glass panels and top-heavy ornamental crown. Drawn by eight plumed, festooned white horses, the coach lumbered slowly off, accompanied by an escort of equerries and pages and followed by more troops.

The Emperor was out of humour, still under the shadow of the arguments he had been having with Lucien who had urged him to announce his abdication at today's ceremony. He professed to see in Lucien's advice nothing but ambition. Lucien, he told Joseph, the eldest of the Bonaparte brothers, was hoping to oust them all and get himself elected as regent for the King of Rome. '*Mais, abdiquer! pas si bête!*' he had snapped at the finish.[1]

Four marshals of France pranced in attendance alongside the

[1] Jung, *Lucien Bonaparte et ses Mémoires, 1775-1840*, p. 265.

91

windows of his coach, holding back their spirited chargers to the walking pace of the procession. Among them was Michel Ney, Prince de la Moskowa, who had come up from the country especially to take the place to which he was entitled on this great occasion.

'You here!' Napoleon had said irritably on catching sight of him. 'I thought you had emigrated.'

'I ought to have done so long ago,' said Ney who could never resist answering back.[1]

It was mid-day when the head of the procession approached the *École Militaire*. As it passed over the bridge of Iéna a new cannonade shook the city, while military bands blared forth, drums rolled, commands to present arms were roared across the parade-ground, and the crowds completed the pandemonium by their acclamations. On his arrival, Napoleon was greeted by deafening cries of *'Vive l'Empereur!'* from the troops. On one side of the field were 25,000 National Guards, on the other 25,000 soldiers from the Imperial Guard and the 6th Army Corps which was to leave for the Belgian frontier as soon as the ceremony ended. The most enthusiastic cries came from the regular soldiers whose devotion to the Emperor and misguided enthusiasm for battle now rose to new heights. Hypnotized by the flags and banners, the sunshine and their own imagination, they saw the impending conflict as a glorious episode which was to set the world in order and send their enemies flying. The enemy, whose absence was a gratifying aspect of this aggressive rally, was the figment of that deceptive dreamland where the sleeper wins all the battles and all the arguments with such ease and distinction.

A large erection had been fabricated for the occasion, adjoining the *École Militaire*, with an elevated platform for Napoleon and his suite and graded stands surrounding it. A throne and an altar had been set up, and there was a second stand, pyramidal in form, out on the parade-ground, from which the Emperor was to distribute the eagles later in the day. Pages and courtiers were taking their places on the steps beneath the throne when Napoleon reached the *École Militaire*, which he entered.

Guns still thundered when, a little later, he emerged from the

[1] Houssaye, *1815*, Vol. II, p. 53. Thiers, *Histoire de l'Empire*, Vol. IV, p. 486.

building surrounded by princes and nobles. Those seated on the stands – some thousands in number – rose with a shout as he walked towards the throne. He was now fully to be seen in his astonishing costume, and the acclamations quickly gave way to silence. Though the spectators were ready to cheer the Emperor as he advanced, says Henry Houssaye, their first impulse of enthusiasm was brief and they 'stopped short at the sight of the peculiar costumes of Napoleon and his brothers'.[1] Napoleon's suit was made of white satin, and his white shoes were trimmed with rosettes. From his shoulders hung a purple velvet mantle thickly embroidered in gold and lined with white ermine; on his head, says Hobhouse, was 'a black bonnet, shaded with plumes, and looped with a large diamond in front.' As for the brothers, Joseph, Lucien and Jérôme, 'they were caparisoned in fancy dresses of white taffety from head to foot; and, excepting the house of Austria, looked as ill as the princes of any legitimate house in Christendom.'[2]

The ceremony opened with the celebration of Mass, during which, says Hobhouse 'Napoleon was less occupied with his prayers than with an opera-glass, with which he was contemplating the assembly.' Hobhouse continues:

> The music ceased, the velvet altar was removed, and immediately a large body of men crowded from the area, and ascended the steps of the throne. These were the central deputation from the electors of the empire, chosen a few days before by selection from all the colleges. They filled the whole flight of steps and were introduced in a mass to the Emperor.

After one of the representatives had made a speech, the Arch-Chancellor, Cambacérès, announced the result of the voting and, to the rolling of drums and the flashing of raised swords, the herald-at-arms declared the acceptance of the constitution. Another salute of guns now thundered forth, and a small table furnished with pen and gold ink-stand was placed before Napoleon. Hobhouse's description goes on:

> The arch-chancellor laid the constitution on the table and handed the pen to Prince Joseph, who gave it to Napoleon. The Emperor quickly and carelessly put his name to the famous act at ten minutes

---

[1] Houssaye, *1815*, Vol. I, p. 601.
[2] Hobhouse, *Letters from Paris* . . . , Vol. I, pp. 407-8.

before two o'clock. The table was moved away; and then, opening a roll of paper, he addressed the immense concourse in a loud shrill voice, which at times made him audible even to the benches where we were placed. His opening words – *Empereur, consul, soldat, je tiens tout du peuple* – reached us distinctly.

In his reply to the delegates, Napoleon presented himself as the saviour of the nation. His abdication the previous year had been a sacrifice he had made in the interests of France, and his return from Elba was due to the threat to French rights. 'My indignation on seeing those sacred rights, acquired by twenty-five years of victory, misprized and thrown aside, the cry of injured honour, and the wishes of the people, have brought me back to this throne, dear to me because it is the guardian of independence, honour and the rights of the people.'

He had had every reason, he continued, to count on a long peace, and as he returned among his rejoicing people he was solely concerned to give them a constitution which should conform to their wishes. But, as he quickly found, the princes of Europe were determined to make war on France. 'They have in mind an enlargement of the kingdom of the Low Countries by the addition of all the fortified places of our northern frontier, and a settlement of the differences between them by means of dividing Lorraine and Alsace. It has therefore been necessary to prepare for war.'

All was presented as Napoleon chose to see it. Having recently declared with satisfaction that he was not an angel, he now took upon himself precisely that role – he was the blameless man, and evil was all on the side of the enemy. The enemies of France were 'foreign kings whom I raised to their thrones, or who owe to me the preservation of their crowns'; France was the victim of their aggression, and the circumstances were grave; but victory was assured provided the nation was united and determined. 'So long as the French people retain those feelings of love for me of which they have given me so many proofs, the fury of our enemies will be powerless.'

'Frenchmen,' Napoleon ended, 'my will is that of the people; my rights are their rights; my honour, my glory, my happiness are inseparable from the honour, the glory and the happiness of France.'

Loud applause followed, and the Bonapartists and army men

within hearing gave particularly hearty cries of approval. But among the more thoughtful civilians were many who felt dismayed. They had come hoping to hear that a solution to the troubles of the country had been found, and they had been given empty political phrases and the promise of war. Some of them had hoped for the announcement of good news from Vienna, of a settlement with Austria and the return of Marie Louise; others hoped that Napoleon would announce his abdication in favour of his son, thus saving them all by removing the sole cause of war.[1] He had won his way back by promising peace, but although he now knew that his rule meant war, he did not intend to withdraw from the position he had seized. On the contrary, he had just given proof that he intended to maintain his hold on the community, and that they must fight the whole of Europe for the privilege of keeping him at their head. It was well enough for the army, who were thirsting to seize Belgium and avenge themselves for past defeat; but the representatives of the voters, who now had to return to their provincial homes, thought ruefully of the prospects of failing trade, of invasion and conscription, for none of which Napoleon's honour and glory were much of a recompense.

Now an archbishop was kneeling respectfully before Napoleon, holding a Testament on which the Emperor swore to observe the constitution. But of what use was a constitution, however liberally expressed, when no man could protest that he wanted to live his life in peace? There were renewed cries of '*Vive l'Empereur!*, and a few ventured to raise their voices to cry '*Vive Marie Louise!*' This caused an embarrassed silence which was quickly broken by the soldiers within hearing who waved their swords, shouting '*Vive l'Impératrice! Vive le Roi de Rome! Nous irons les chercher!*'[2]

After the Te Deum had been solemnly chanted, Napoleon left his platform for the pyramidal stand prepared for his use during the distribution of the eagles. Drums rolled anew and guns fired with deafening crashes. High above the ground, the Emperor was enthroned among his marshals and courtiers who stood graded on the steps below him on all four sides of the stand. The scene,

---

[1] Houssaye, *1815*, Vol. I, p. 606.
[2] Thiers, *Histoire de l'Empire*, Vol. IV, p. 488. Hortense Bonaparte, *Mémoires de la Reine Hortense*, Vol. III, p. 12.

Hobhouse says, was more magnificent than any pen could describe.

> The monarch on his open throne, which seemed a glittering pyramid of eagles, the arms, and military habits, crowned by his own white plumes – an immense plain, as it were, of soldiers flanked with multitudes so innumerable that the sloping banks on each side presented but one mass of heads – the man – the occasion – all conspired to surprise us into a most unqualified, unphilosophical admiration of the whole spectacle before us; which was not diminished when the bayonets, and cuirasses, and helmets, flashing as far as we could see, and the flags of the lancers fluttering, and the music bursting from the plain, announced that the whole scene, far and near, began to move.[1]

The troops marched to and fro, and the eagles were paraded before the throne.

'I entrust to you the eagle and our national colours,' Napoleon was calling out. 'Swear that you will die in their defence!'

'We swear!'

'Soldiers of the Imperial Guard, swear you will surpass yourselves in the campaign which is about to open, and die to the last man rather than allow foreigners to come here and dictate to our country!'

'We swear! We swear!'

Back and forth the troops paraded in admirable order, the Imperial Guard marching from right to left and the others from left to right. Their united cries of '*Vive l'Empereur!*' made scarcely less noise than the guns and had little more meaning, for the sound was the outer reflection of an inner delusion which convinced them that Napoleon was no less than God, and that all his enemies were fiends to be put to the sword. Marching with such fine precision in their thousands to the rolling of drums and the roar of guns, they appeared to be a terrible and irresistible force. This was the calculated effect of the military review; it was designed to inspire confidence, and even Napoleon himself saw in it the promise of victory.

Lucien Bonaparte describes the scene as superb and intoxicating; but while his ambitious brother was lost in visions of triumph, he

[1] Hobhouse, *Letters from Paris* . . . , Vol. I, p. 413.

himself had other thoughts: 'What a fine moment it would have been for abdicating in favour of his son!' he said afterwards.[1]

Fouché was of the same opinion and said to Hortense during the ceremony, 'The Emperor has just lost a very good opportunity. I urged him to abdicate today. Had he done so, his son would reign and there would be no war.'[2]

During the grandiose parade of the eagles, the civil dignitaries and other spectators on the stands adjoining the *École Militaire* sat in their places in profound boredom, for the arrangement was such that they could see little of what was going on. All but the most insensitive were uneasy about the future, wearied by the interminable ceremony and deafened by gunfire. It was with relief that they eventually saw the Emperor descend from his pyramid and prepare to drive back to the Tuileries.

The *Champ de Mai* being over, there was little for Napoleon to do but set off on his campaign against Wellington and Blücher. Lucien Bonaparte records that he was in a poor state of health and delayed his departure for a few days in the hope of some improvement. He was in low spirits in the early days of June. News came that Berthier had died suddenly in Bavaria, and he sat long in silence, deeply oppressed. Berthier had been his Chief-of-Staff throughout his years of power and had been at his side in every victory; he had tried unsuccessfully to obtain his services once more, and instead he had appointed Marshal Soult as his Chief-of-Staff.

Napoleon appeared to be taking a last farewell of Paris on Sunday 4 June, which had been made a public holiday. There was a further distribution of eagles in the Louvre, and the people were regaled in a manner long since forgotten in Europe. Wine was free and flowed from thirty-six fountains in the Champs Elysées; twelve enormous buffets offered cold meats and other dishes to all comers; there were open-air orchestras, free performances at the theatres and entertainments by conjurors and tight-rope dancers. 'All the fooleries of Bartholomew Fair were let loose, gratis,' says Hobhouse. 'Not a melancholy nor an angry face was to be seen throughout the vast concourse thus celebrating, as it were, the eve of a day which

[1] Houssaye, *1815*, Vol. I, p. 607.
[2] Hortense Bonaparte, *Mémoires de la Reine Hortense*, Vol. III, p. 13.

must make widows and orphans of half the officiating crowd.'[1]

When night fell a concert was given for the public in front of the Palace of the Tuileries. The palace was illumined, and Napoleon with the princes of his family sat on the balcony listening and looking down on the vast but orderly crowds below in the gardens. It was a happy day; the sun had shone hour after hour and now the night was balmy. The Emperor, people were saying, had always had fine weather for his fêtes except on the eve of the disastrous Russian campaign;[2] the crowds were optimistic, and even thoughtful men hoped that some initial success might make negotiation possible.

As the concert ended, a firework display began in the Place de la Concorde. It included a set piece showing a ship at sea – the brig on which Napoleon had returned from Elba. Napoleon himself was portrayed, standing on deck, a bright star shining auspiciously over his head. As the crowds watched admiringly, their attention was diverted from the dim, small figure on the balcony. Indeed, he was fading from their lives. Their next fête day, for which they had but a month to wait, was to celebrate the return of the King, old Louis XVIII whose benevolent person was to be greeted with smiling faces.

[1] Hobhouse, *Letters from Paris* . . . , Vol. I, p. 445.
[2] Hobhouse, ibid., p. 448.

7

Military preparations; Opening of the French Parliament; Napoleon joins his Army; English and Prussian dispositions; Eve of the invasion

The French Army of the North was now concentrating in the region of Beaumont and Philippeville, between the rivers Meuse and Sambre, ready for the invasion of Belgium. Wellington and Blücher between them had to guard the entire Belgian frontier, and their line ran from Ostende as far as Liège, beyond which other Allied armies were assembling for the great assault on France when it should be ordered from Vienna. Wellington's army had reached the strength of 105,950 men, the army of Blücher numbered 124,000. Wellington held Brussels and the country to the west; Blücher occupied Charleroi and eastwards, and guarded the Charleroi-Brussels road. Napoleon meant to strike Charleroi and drive up between the two armies, as his aide-de-camp had told Hobhouse at the end of May. He hoped to throw the English and Prussians apart, each on their lines of retreat; and if the Prussians, whom he would encounter first, did not retire before him he would inflict an immediate defeat on them.

The Allied armies in Belgium outnumbered the French by nearly two to one. But the French army was better equipped, particularly with guns, and was more seasoned and experienced. Its enthusiasm and national spirit made it capable of a fine, united performance. Wellington's army, on the contrary, was a heterogeneous company of several races, varying much in quality and reliability. Too few of the Duke's Peninsular veterans were available to him, and a great many of the men under his command were unfitted for service in the field. The nominal strength of his army gave no true picture of its actual strength. The British field force formed about a third of the number. The King's German Legion, soldiers of great value, amounted to hardly more than 6,000, and there were about four times as many Hanoverians, mostly inexperienced recruits. The Dutch-Belgians, nearly as numerous as the British, were the weakest element of the army. Newly united under the house of Orange, they had little sympathy for one another and no enthusiasm for the cause they were called upon to support; those who had military experience had gained it as Napoleon's conscripts, and the rest were mostly untrained militia. Although they had no cause to desire a renewal of Napoleon's exacting control of their provinces, they were convinced that he would win the coming war and felt little inclined to resist him. The Brunswick troops were loyal, but the great majority were boys with scarcely any training. As for the Prussians, their national spirit was admirable and they were ready for every exertion. Towards Prussia Napoleon had been so ruthless in his days of success that to a man they preferred death to a new subservience to him. But a large proportion of the Prussian army consisted of inexperienced recruits; they were hampered, too, by exceeding poverty which made it difficult for them to maintain themselves. It seemed, then, that the well organized French army had good chances of an initial success. Napoleon was about to throw a powerful mass of devoted, well-armed soldiers at the centre of a greatly extended line. It was quite conceivable that he would succeed in breaking through and seizing Brussels.

Such a plan was typical Napoleonic strategy; a superior force was to be concentrated rapidly at the point where it could be most effectively used; feints would be made to draw attention from the point, and the attack would take the enemy by surprise. Secrecy was a necessary element of such a scheme; yet we can see from Hobhouse's letter of 29 May that French staff officers were not always discreet. If they talked to Hobhouse no doubt they talked to many another. Presumably Napoleon trusted to rumour and conflicting reports to counteract the passing on of information by men who could not hold their tongues.

It is clear from the despatches of the Duke of Wellington that the Allies were well informed as to what was taking place in France. With Louis XVIII and his ministers close at hand, in touch with their friends in Paris, it could not be otherwise. The reorganization and movements of the French army and the militia were closely watched and the state of the country was reported by reliable observers. It was known that Napoleon intended to join his main army on the northern frontier as soon as the *Champ de Mai* ceremony had taken place. 6 June was the date usually given for his departure for the front, and this, according to Lucien Bonaparte's memoirs, is about the time he would have left but for his illness. Troop movements on a large scale were noticed in the frontier region, and it remained to be seen where they were being massed. It was here that Napoleon's feints were successful. Demolition work on frontier roads and bridges gave the impression that he was only preparing for defence against the impending Allied invasion of France; reports were spread that large bodies of men were marching back into the interior.[1] He contrived with great skill to mask his intentions, using the militia to make conspicuous movements misleading to his adversaries. Among other ruses, knowing that Wellington would be exceedingly watchful of his line of retreat to the sea, he made movements suggesting a threat to the western end of the Allied line. Wellington himself says: 'the enemy . . . took a position in which his numbers could be concealed, his movements protected, and his designs supported by his formidable fortresses on the frontier, up to the last moment.'[2]

The French Army of the North was organized in seven bodies: the 1st, 2nd, 3rd, 4th and 6th Infantry Corps, the Imperial Guard, and the Reserve Cavalry. At the end of May it was still widely dispersed. The 1st Corps (d'Erlon) was at Lille; the 2nd (Reille) at Valenciennes; the 3rd (Vandamme) at Mézières; the 4th (Gérard) at Metz; the 6th (Lobau) at Laon; the Imperial Guard in the region of Paris; the Reserve Cavalry between Laon and Avesnes. The Imperial Guard was to be commanded by Marshal Mortier, and the Reserve Cavalry by Marshal Grouchy, though only the latter of the two marshals actually took part in the campaign.

Gérard, being furthest away from the point of concentration, was the first to move, leaving Metz on 6 June. Two days later the Imperial Guard left Compiègne, and in succession the different infantry and cavalry corps were set in motion and closed in upon the frontier. The movements of these 124,000[3] men were carried out with a remarkable degree of speed and efficiency; but there was one serious miscalculation in the otherwise impeccable massing of the army. 6 June was too late a date for Gérard to leave Metz, and his corps was to be behind time, causing dangerous delays in the opening phase of the campaign.

[1] Wellington, *Supplementary Despatches*, Vol. X, pp. 280, 290, 412-3, 430.
[2] Ibid., p. 518.   [3] Houssaye's figures.

The 5th Corps, under Rapp, was left at Strasbourg, guarding the north-eastern frontier. To guard his frontiers and keep order in La Vendée, where open insurrection had recently broken out, Napoleon deprived his Army of the North of 55,000 troops of the line,[1] an unjustifiably high figure, perhaps, since in any case it was impossible to defend French frontiers against an entirely hostile and armed Europe.

Before leaving Paris to join his army, Napoleon attended the opening of the new Parliament. The ceremony took place on the 7th, and among the peers were his brothers Joseph and Lucien, again clad in their white costumes. Napoleon, too, was in his robes of the *Champ de Mai*. He took his place on the throne and listened while both commoners and peers swore obedience to the constitution and loyalty to himself, which last oath was quickly to be broken. Then he rose and gave a short address which left little to be desired, since he avowed his limitations. 'Today my dearest wish is accomplished,' he said, 'for I now begin my reign as a constitutional monarch. Men in themselves cannot safeguard the future; institutions alone determine the destinies of nations.'

But he was ill and out of humour, and his tense, contracted features and lack of cordiality belied his words.[2] The representatives had already shown themselves to be captious and suspicious, concerned solely with their personal ambitions and political theories when both were dependent on victory in the coming war. In present circumstances, Napoleon and his soldiers alone, by their exertions, could safeguard the politicians, and he felt he should have been accorded dictatorial powers until the conflict was over. He must now count on a rapidly won victory which would renew the old enthusiasm of the nation and give him once more the power to keep lesser men in their places.

Four days later, the two Chambers presented their addresses in reply at the Palace of the Tuileries. It was Sunday, and Napoleon was to leave Paris to join the army that night. The representatives dwelt rather menacingly on their rights, and behind polite phrases there was evidence of mistrust on both sides. In the course of the same day, Napoleon gave orders that the Council of Ministers

[1] Grouard's figures.
[2] Houssaye, *1815*, Vol. I, p. 616.

should hold regular meetings under the presidency of his brother Joseph. Every question of importance was to be submitted to himself, for he would trust no one to govern in his absence. It was arranged that Davout, Minister for war, should appoint officers to leave Paris daily at a gallop, carrying despatches to the Imperial headquarters.

Another of Napoleon's acts on this day was to invite Ney to participate in his campaign. Hitherto there had been no question of giving him a command, and Ney had not ventured to ask for one. Now Napoleon relented, no doubt under the influence of one of those sudden impulses which he was in the habit of trusting. He sent a message to Davout: 'Call Ney and tell him to come to my head-quarters at Avesnes on the 13th if wishes to take part in the first battles.' It was not an order, but rather an intimation that he had forgiven Ney who could join him if he wished to do so. Ney, unable to see the advantage of remaining in private life after his extravagant avowals, now on one side and now on the other, accepted the offer with alacrity, hoping, no doubt, to redeem his reputation on the field. He set off immediately for the frontier but, no preparation having been made to include him in the army, he was obliged to travel by post as a civilian.

Having settled his affairs in Paris, Napoleon dined with his family and friends on this Sunday evening and showed himself to be in good spirits although, Lucien Bonaparte says, his health had not improved. After weeks of exhausting work and argument with politicians, he seemed to be relieved to be setting off at last on his campaign. Confidence had returned. Events at home were improv-ing, for the insurrection in the western districts had been suppressed, and the imminence of hostilities was producing an upsurge of patriotic feeling in the country. Gifts of money had recently been pouring in for the prosecution of the war, desertions from the army were becoming rare, and hostility to Napoleon himself was lost sight of in the general hatred of foreigners.

As he took leave of Mme Bertrand, who with her husband had been with him in Elba, he remarked: 'Well, Mme Bertrand, let us hope we shan't soon be regretting that we ever left Elba!'[1]

Though he jestingly hinted at the worst, he was certainly prepared for the best; for with his baggage, already sent off, were bales of

[1] Hortense Bonaparte, *Mémoires de la Reine Hortense*, Vol. III, p. 15.

proclamations to be displayed in Brussels the following week, dated from the Palace of Lacken where he intended to reside. They were worded as follows:

> Proclamation to the Belgians and Inhabitants of the left Bank of the Rhine.
>
> The ephemeral success of my Enemies detached you for a moment from my Empire; in my exile, upon a rock in the sea, I heard your complaint, the God of Battles has decided the fate of your beautiful provinces; Napoleon is among you; you are worthy to be Frenchmen; rise in mass, join my invincible phalanxes to exterminate the remainder of these barbarians, who are your enemies and mine; they fly with rage and despair in their hearts.
>
> At the Imperial Palace of Lacken, June 17 1815.
>
> (signed) NAPOLEON.[1]

With the great train of luggage there went also an immense treasure: a fortune in money and diamonds; gold plate for the Imperial table; eighty Arabian horses; a travelling library of about 800 volumes; the State coach with its eight white horses; and ceremonial dress, including an embroidered State mantle. There was also ample provision for the upkeep of Imperial dignity on the field of battle.

Napoleon left Paris at 3.30 a.m. on 12 June and slept that night at Laon. The following day he reached Avesnes where he dined with Ney and others and spent the night. On the 14th he reached Beaumont at the centre of the army. Everything was now ready for a blow at the enemy; the whole army with its equipment was to cross the frontier and the river Sambre the following day, and the first movements were to begin during the night. (See map, p. 306.)

Reports of intensified French activity had been reaching Wellington and Blücher for several days. On the evening of the 12th, Major-General Sir William Dörnberg, who commanded one of the cavalry regiments of Wellington's army and was in the region of Mons, wrote as follows to Lord Fitzroy Somerset:

> My Lord,
>
> A French gentleman, coming from Maubeuge to join the King, gives the following intelligence. The corps of General Reille is come

[1] *The Battle of Waterloo* (*Accounts and Official Documents*) pp. 125, 142-3.

yesterday to Maubeuge and vicinity. The head-quarters of the army are transferred from Laon to Avesnes, where a division of the Guards is to arrive today. Buonaparte is expected every minute, but nothing certain was known when he had left Paris, where it appears he was still on the 10th. Jerome Buonaparte is at Solre le Château. Soult passed through Maubeuge this morning, coming from Laon, but the gentleman did not know where he was gone to. He estimates the forces between Philippeville, Givet, Mézières, Guise and Maubeuge at more than 100,000 troops of the line. A very considerable corps of cavalry was reviewed at Hirson two days ago by Grouchy. The general opinion in the army is, that they will attack, and that the arrival of Buonaparte at Avesnes will be the signal for the beginning of hostilities.

The camp de Rousies was not yet armed.

> I have the honour to be, my Lord,
> Your most obedient humble servant,
> Dörnberg.

The Duke of Wellington sent a copy of this letter to Marshal Blücher; but on the 13th he said in a letter to Lord Lynedoch: 'We have reports of Buonaparte's joining the army and attacking us; but I have accounts from Paris of the 10th, on which day he was still there; and I judge from his speech to the Legislature that his departure was not likely to be immediate. I think we are now too strong for him here.' Gneisenau, too, had written on the 12th: 'The danger of an attack has almost vanished.' However, General Dörnberg wrote directly to Blücher on the 13th saying that he thought an attack was imminent, and this was followed by a similar warning from Pirch II, the Prussian general in command at Marchienne. Blücher now had news enough to cause him to act, and before noon on the 14th he had given orders for the drawing together of those divisions of his army which were posted at the more distant points.

Wellington made no move, except, as he says himself, 'for the assembly of the troops at their several alarm posts, till he should hear of the decided movement of the enemy'.[1]

A great part of Wellington's secret intelligence was conducted by

[1] Wellington, *Supplementary Despatches*, Vol. X, pp. 456, 524. Houssaye, *1815*, Vol. II, pp. 115-6. Wellington, *Dispatches*, Vol. XII, p. 462. Henderson, *Blücher*, pp. 281-2.

Major Colquhoun Grant who had performed extraordinary feats of espionage in Spain, although he made it a point of honour always to wear his uniform. Sir James McGrigor, in an appendix to his autobiography, quotes a memorandum written by Lieut.-General William Napier in 1857, concerning Grant. According to this, Grant sent definite news on the 15th of the outmarch of the French army. General Dörnberg had the task of ensuring the regular transmission of the reports of the many agents employed, and we are told that he 'mistook his position and fancied he was to judge of the importance and value of the reports; hence on receiving Grant's important letter he sent it back, saying that so far from convincing him that the Emperor was advancing for battle, it assured him of the contrary. Grant immediately conveyed the letter direct to the Duke but it only reached him on the field of Waterloo . . .' The letter was given to the Duke on 18 June at midday. 'Had it been received, as it ought to have been, two days before the battle,' the memorandum says, 'no surprise of the Allies could have happened, and the great battle would have been fought and won on the banks of the Sambre.'[1] This story has been accepted by some historians, and Dörnberg severely blamed. It would seem, however, from the letter to Fitzroy Somerset quoted above, that Dörnberg was alive to the signs of an impending clash, and that if Grant's letter reached him only on the 15th it was too late to alter the situation, since by then the French were crossing the Sambre; there is no reason why a despatch rider sent by Dörnberg should reach Brussels any sooner than the messengers who would be set off from other frontier regions during that day.

The mass of Wellington's troops were cantonned in the plains between the river Scheldt and the high road running through Charleroi and Brussels to Antwerp. The 1st Corps, commanded by the Prince of Orange, was on the left and therefore nearest to the Prussians, its headquarters being at Braine le Comte on the road from Mons to Brussels. The 2nd Corps, under Lieut.-General Lord Hill, had its headquarters at Ath, on the road from Lille to Brussels, beside the river Dender; it stretched out to the right as far as the river Lys, and to the left in the direction of Mons. The Cavalry, commanded by Lieut.-General the Earl of Uxbridge, was cantonned in the valley of the Dender with its headquarters at Gramont. The

---

[1] McGrigor, *Autobiography*, pp. 413-16.

Reserve, commanded by Wellington, was in and around Brussels, with one brigade in Ghent.

The Prussian army was organized in four corps, having their headquarters at Charleroi, Namur, Ciney and Liège. The 1st Corps, at Charleroi, would be encountered by the French as soon as they crossed the frontier; it was commanded by Lieut.-General Von Ziethen, and as well as Charleroi it occupied Thuin, Fontaine Levèque, Marchienne, Moustiers, Fleurus, Sombreffe and Gembloux. The 2nd Corps, at Namur, was under General Von Pirch I; the 3rd Corps, at Ciney, was commanded by Lieut.-General Von Thielemann; the 4th Corps, at Liège, was commanded by General Count Bülow.[1]

Wellington's forces were so placed as to protect the roads from Lille and Mons; Blücher's forces protected the Charleroi-Brussels high road and the eastern side of the country; and both armies, although on the defensive, thought of themselves principally as part of the great Allied line that was preparing to sweep forward very shortly into France.

The French army was to invade Belgium in three columns, and when night fell on 14 June it was placed as follows: the 1st and 2nd Corps were on the extreme left, Reille at Leers and d'Erlon behind him at Solre sur Sambre. In the centre, before and behind Beaumont, were the 3rd and 6th Corps, under Vandamme and Lobau respectively, and the Imperial Guard which was at the rear. On the right, stretched between Beaumont and Philippeville, were the four corps of Reserve Cavalry, and the 4th Corps, under Gérard. But Gérard's corps had not yet completed its march from Metz.

This army was one of the most complete and efficient which had ever assembled at that time. Houssaye says of it:

Impressionable, argumentative, undisciplined, suspicious of their leaders, agitated by the fear of treachery and therefore open to panic, they were yet seasoned warriors, animated by the love of fighting and inflamed by the longing for vengeance, capable of heroic efforts and furious onslaughts, and more spirited, more exalted, more ardent in combat than any republican or imperial army whatsoever. Never had Napoleon had at his disposal an instrument of war at once so formidable and so easily broken.

[1] See Appendix A for the numbers of these and Wellington's army corps.

The men now bivouacked for the night, lighting their fires in the ravines and reverse slopes of the land so that they would not be visible across the frontier. They sat in groups, talking; but although the army was dominated by a mass emotion of enthusiasm, there were those who felt uneasy and feared the worst. Many would have preferred to complete their careers peacefully under the Bourbons, although they remained with the army, having usually no other means of livelihood. The private soldier who ventured to differ from the majority would have fared ill; but the officers in their greater freedom spoke their minds. One of the generals was so pessimistic that a junior officer reproached him angrily. 'The die is cast,' he said, 'and you ought to play your part, not spread demoralization amongst us.'[1] And two or three days previously General Ruty, Commander-in-Chief of the Artillery, had said, 'Napoleon is irretrievably lost. Before long the King will be back, and then what will become of us? What a wretched army, refusing to fire a rifle shot three months ago!'[2]

Napoleon, on the other hand, had become surpassingly confident and the fears of his recent dark moods had vanished. He did not doubt that he would be dining at his ease in Brussels by the end of the week, nor that the Belgian people would rally to him as soon as he entered their country. He felt himself invincible, and most Europeans of the time, had they been privileged to view the whole situation as it was at this moment, would have believed him on the the eve of one of his gigantic victories. Blücher was twenty miles away, peacefully sleeping at his headquarters at Namur; Wellington was still further off in Brussels and appeared to be unaware of danger. The Duke had accepted an invitation to the Duchess of Richmond's ball in Brussels the following night, and so had most of his generals and staff officers. The combined Allied forces in Belgium were scattered over an area 100 miles in length and about forty in depth, skilfully placed, indeed, but unable to concentrate before Napoleon had had time to strike his first great blow. Liège, round which the 4th Prussian Corps was placed, was over fifty miles from Charleroi; Ciney, the headquarters of the 3rd Corps, was nearly twenty-five miles south-east of Namur.

[1] Houssaye, *1815*, Vol. II, p. 72.
[2] Pion de Loches, *Mes Campagnes*, p. 465.

Late that night, spies came in from Brussels, Namur and Charleroi, telling Napoleon that all was quiet; nothing was suspected.[1] Since the spies had left the Prussian camps, however, much had taken place.

It was Napoleon's custom to keep his intentions to himself, and the generals commanding the different army corps were not informed as to the strategic plan of operations which was to unfold the next day as they entered Belgium. There was no conference on the evening of the 14th at which Napoleon, treating them with the confidence they merited, might have told them what would be expected of them when they had moved their troops across the Sambre.[2] Instead, an order of movement was carried by messengers during the evening to the general officers concerned, giving them no more than a timetable for their various departures, and instructions as to the routes to be followed to the river Sambre, together with a multiplicity of inessential details and a repetition of phrases that required much time for the reading. The only real information that Napoleon gave in this movement order was that he was taking the army to the left side of the river and that he himself intended to be in Charleroi by mid-day.

This curious document, of unheard-of length and verbosity in view of the urgency of the moment, opens as follows:

'Tomorrow the 15th, at half past 2 in the morning, General Vandamme's light cavalry division will mount their horses and take the road to Charleroi. They will send out parties in all directions to reconnoitre the country and capture enemy posts; but each one of these parties will consist of at least fifty men. Before putting the division in motion, General Vandamme will make sure that it is provided with cartridges. . . .'

It would be odd, indeed, to launch an attack without cartridges! Grouchy was instructed to move three cavalry corps on Charleroi at the hours of five, six and seven. 'But Marshal Grouchy,' the order continued, 'will take care to move the cavalry along roads parallel to the principal route which the infantry column is taking, so as to avoid overcrowding, and also to enable his cavalry to keep in better order.'

[1] *Mémoires de Napoléon*, Vol. IX, p. 68.
[2] This subject is discussed by E. Lenient in *La Solution des Enigmes de Waterloo*, pp. 139-46.

'One would think' says E. Lenient in *La Solution des Enigmes de Waterloo*, 'that Grouchy had never executed a march in his life.'

As Chief-of-Staff, Marshal Soult presumably was responsible for this order; according to Houssaye Napoleon dictated it, but he would rely on Soult to see that his essential instructions of timing and movement reached the various generals promptly and in a reasonable form.

All the army but for the left column was to cross by the bridge at Charleroi, while the left (Reille and d'Erlon) was to advance from its positions at Solre and Leers up the right side of the river and cross at Marchienne, two or three miles west of Charleroi. Certain military critics have suggested that Napoleon should have taken his army over the Sambre rapidly on a wide front, making an enveloping movement to surround Ziethen's corps before it had time to withdraw eastwards to join the main body of the Prussian army. As it was, he had planned to take about 80,000 men over the bridge at Charleroi, not to mention 250 guns and masses of equipment. This movement would necessarily be slow. An early crossing at Châtelet and eastwards would have enabled the French to cut off the retreat of the Prussians. Gérard was indeed to be directed to Châtelet in the course of the 15th, but only as an afterthought, and long before he arrived there Ziethen had saved himself. This head-on approach that Napoleon had planned was to be typical of the whole brief campaign.

Napoleon intended to advance towards Sombreffe as soon as he had a large enough force across the river and destroy such of the Prussians as he found in the region; it may be that he hoped to take both Sombreffe and Quatre Bras in the course of the day, but about this one cannot be certain. Well informed by his friends and agents in Belgium, he knew exactly how Wellington's forces were disposed and how inferior an army he commanded. Underestimating Wellington, whom he affected to despise, he discounted the English altogether for the time being; and with little more respect for Blücher, whom he looked upon as a kind of bold and blustering sergeant, he misjudged the Prussians also, failing to realize how alert they were and how remarkable a capacity they had for forced marches. He believed, therefore, that he had time to spare.

The preliminary moves had been made. The Prussian army, with the exception of the distant 4th Corps, was watchful. As night fell on the 14th there was great animation in the advance posts of Ziethen's corps. It was in vain that the French lit their fires in concealed places, for the Prussians observed a reflected glow on the underside of the clouds. But General Ziethen did not depend on this observation to know that the French army was massed before him. Late that night, the Chief-of-Staff, General Gneisenau, acting on the many reports now reaching him, ordered a general concentration of the Prussian army, without disturbing Blücher's sleep.

While the French soldiers took their brief rest, the Prussian army was in the highest state of activity. Pirch I was moving the 2nd Corps from Namur to Sombreffe; Thielemann was moving from Ciney to Namur. Ziethen was preparing to concentrate at Fleurus. Only Bülow at Liège delayed his departure owing to a misunderstanding of the messages he received.

8

Entry of the French into Belgium; Ney in command of the left wing;
The right wing under Grouchy attacks the Prussians

Soldiers! This day is the anniversary of Marengo and of Friedland, which twice decided the destiny of Europe. Then, as after Austerlitz, as after Wagram, we were too generous! We believed in the protestations and the oaths of Princes whom we left on the throne! Now, however, coalesced among themselves, they would destroy the independence and the most sacred rights of France. They have commenced the most unjust of aggressions. Let us march, then, to meet them. Are they and we no longer the same men?

Soldiers, at Jena, against these same Prussians, now so arrogant, you were one against three, and at Montmirail one against six!

Let those among you who have been prisoners of the English, detail to you the hulks, and the frightful miseries which they suffered!

The Saxons, the Belgians, the Hanoverians, the soldiers of the Confederation of the Rhine, lament that they are compelled to lend their arms to the cause of Princes, the enemies of justice and of the rights of all nations; they know that this Coalition is insatiable! After having devoured twelve million Poles, twelve million Italians, one million Saxons, six million Belgians, it must devour the states of the second rank of Germany.

The madmen! A moment of prosperity blinds them. The oppression and humiliation of the French people are beyond their power. If they enter France, they will there find their tomb.

Soldiers! We have forced marches to make, battles to fight, dangers to encounter; but, with steadiness, victory will be ours – the rights, the honour, the happiness of the country will be re-conquered!

To every Frenchman of spirit, the moment has come to conquer or to perish.

Such were the words that rang out in the French camps in the early hours of Thursday, 15 June. With cries of enthusiasm, loudly acclaiming the Emperor, the soldiers responded and long before the sun rose the forward regiments were marching over the frontier. General Pajol, at the head of the centre column, mounted his horse at 2.30 a.m. and led off his cavalry. General Reille, on the left, began the advance of the 2nd Corps at three o'clock, and thereafter division upon division moved forward at half-hourly intervals according to the directions given in Napoleon's movement order.

There were, however, various delays. One occurred at the centre where the 3rd Corps, which should have begun its march at 3 a.m. was two or three hours behind time, no instructions having been received. The aide-de-camp carrying Napoleon's order to General Vandamme had fallen from his horse and broken a thigh; the accident having occurred in a lonely place, he lay helpless throughout the night and the message was not delivered. In the morning, therefore, Vandamme's thousands slept on until aroused by the troops due to follow them. A party of marines and sappers then went ahead, closely followed by Napoleon himself, while Vandamme did his utmost to make up for lost time.

Soult as Chief-of-Staff is blamed by Adolphe Thiers and his school for the non-arrival of Vandamme's instructions. Such a thing, they say, could never have happened in the days when Berthier was Chief-of-Staff and unfailingly made sure that the Emperor's messages arrived and were understood. But Colonel Chesney in his *Waterloo Lectures* has shown that this is mere legend and that the famous Berthier's staff work left much to be desired.

A more serious incident occurred on the right where Gérard's corps, having been late in assembling at Philippeville, could not leave until two hours after the appointed time and even then was subjected to further delay. The first division was under General de Bourmont, one of the royalist officers who had been with Ney when he went over to Napoleon. De Bourmont was riding well ahead of the column with his staff officers and a small escort. Presently he was seen to set off at a gallop with his staff officers, while the escort turned and brought back a letter for General Gérard. The letter gave the information that General de Bourmont and his companions had deserted and were on their way to join the King at Ghent.

The news spread rapidly and brought the troops to a halt. All was in confusion. The soldiers, whose bivouacs for weeks past had been centres of political argument, had long believed that some of the generals were in league with the King at Ghent; now they had sudden and startling proof that their suspicions had had foundation and that there was treachery in the air. General de Bourmont's desertion had no military significance, since the Prussians were by now fully aware of the approach of the French; but the event profoundly impressed the French soldiers and led to their belief later on that the Emperor had been betrayed, not beaten in a fair contest.

A curt order to the division to march on would have been useless in view of the prevailing lack of discipline. General Hulot, in command of one of the brigades, dealt with the crisis by assuring the troops of his own loyalty. Waving his sword aloft, he swore to join them in fighting the enemies of France to his last gasp. General Gérard himself rode at a gallop up and down the ranks, shouting encouragement. Finally, order was restored, but it was 7 a.m. by the time the division was on the march again and much valuable time had been lost.

Although the early hours had been misty, the sun now came out in full splendour, and the Imperial Guard, who brought up the rear of the fighting forces, began their advance in perfect weather. Captain Mauduit, who was with them, describes the beauty of the day and the joy of his companions as they proceeded further and further into an unknown and attractive countryside. Singing and laughter filled the air although the men had heavy loads to carry and the roads were rough. Never were soldiers so confident of success, so ready for every exertion. They saw about them woods and orchards, sunlit fields, bright streams and ancient villages. The effect was exhilarating and they went forward in good heart, believing their cause was just and convinced they were invincible.

By 10 a.m. General Reille held the right bank of the Sambre between Solre and Marchienne and had driven back the Prussian outposts on his side of the river. Drouet d'Erlon was following with the 1st Corps. The bridge of Marchienne was barricaded and defended by the Prussians, but it was carried after several atacks, and Reille's corps began the crossing while the Prussians fell back on Gilly and Fleurus.

Pajol had reached the Charleroi bridge at about the same time; but it was strongly defended by one of Pirch II's brigades. He attempted to carry it at a gallop, but the fire of the enemy was too heavy and he had to retire and await the arrival of the infantry. Vandamme should have followed him; but instead it was the Emperor himself who arrived about eleven o'clock with the sappers and marines. Also with him were the Young Guard, under Duhesme, which he had ordered forward by a side road on being informed of Vandamme's delay. The obstructions before the bridge were now cleared, and the Prussians, seeing themselves outnumbered, evacuated the town. The bridge was then crossed, and the French were in possession of Charleroi by noon. Reille had by this time begun his crossing at Marchienne, so that both banks of the river were held between the two places. But Gérard was still far away.

The Prussians were retiring north-eastwards; Steinmetz's division alone was in danger; having been stretched out as far westwards as Binche, it was now hastening to reach Gosselies before being cut off by the French. Pirch II's division was advancing up the Sombreffe road with orders to take up positions behind Gilly where it would make a stand to slow down the French. Blücher was hastening towards Sombreffe which was to be his headquarters.

Napoleon established himself in the house recently vacated by General Ziethen, the home of a M. Puissant which, during its brief occupation by his Majesty, was called 'the palace'[1] The house was at the lower end of the town, on the right side of the river, and the Imperial luncheon was served there. Napoleon, who never lingered over meals, was soon on his horse again, and had crossed the bridge by about 12.30.

General Pajol, having been instructed to pursue the Prussians, had taken his squadrons through Charleroi at a quick trot as far as a fork in the road just outside the town. Here he detached a regiment of hussars to reconnoitre to his left up the Brussels road while he continued with the rest of his forces up the Sombreffe road. This road is intersected at Sombreffe by the route from Nivelles to Namur, along which the English would have to come to the aid of the Prussians if Blücher decided to accept battle in this area. The Nivelles-Namur road traverses the Charleroi-Brussels highway at Quatre Bras, (see map p.116). Both these important points are about thirteen miles from Charleroi, and within the triangle they formed Napoleon would soon have his Army of the North assembled, favourably placed to keep the two enemies apart and make the swift drive up to Brussels that he had planned. Although he must have had all possibilities in mind, his actual expectation seems to have

[1] Lachouque, *Le Secret de Waterloo*, p. 53.

been that the Allies would not fight in this area. In his account of the campaign Baron Gourgaud, Napoleon's chief aide-de-camp, says: 'Napoleon supposed that Blücher would not have given battle in Ligny, nor the Duke of Wellington at Quatre Bras. Their armies ought to have united, and evacuated Belgium without loss, in order to wait for the arrival of the armies of Russia and Austria on the Meuse.'[1] It is true that he was hoping to strike so rapidly that he would spoil their plans and inflict a defeat upon each of them in turn; but he had firmly in mind the idea that they would retreat before him as he entered Belgium. Quatre Bras was the gateway of his own army to Brussels, not that of Wellington's army to a battlefield in the Charleroi region.

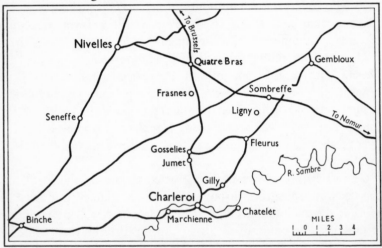

As he rode up the main street of Charleroi, he was acclaimed by the townspeople who were assembled to watch his historic arrival. Certainly he had his friends in the town, and the rest, the majority, presumably took the precaution of appearing pleased over what they were powerless to alter. He continued through the town with his staff officers, and dismounted somewhere to the south of the fork in the road where there was a small restaurant with a garden, called *La Belle Vue*. The road had risen steeply to this point and now afforded a view across the valley of the Sambre. There he sat down to

[1] Gourgaud, *The Campaign of 1815*, p. 121. This book, though appearing under Gourgaud's name, is regarded as Napoleon's work. It is the Emperor's first account of the campaign.

watch the advance of the Young Guard, which was following Pajol's forces.

As the soldiers approached and saw him, enthusiasm rose to the highest pitch. Many broke from their ranks to stroke his horse – Marengo or Désirée, both of which he had with him during the campaign. The Emperor saluted for a time, then fell back into a deep sleep despite the continuous acclamations and the rolling of drums. Sleep, which in youth he had easily controlled, now mastered him.

Some time after two o'clock he was awake again, receiving Baron Gourgaud, who had accompanied the hussars up the Brussels road and now came to say that Gosselies was strongly held by the Prussians. Although General Ziethen had ordered a retreat on Fleurus, he had reinforced Gosselies in order to hold back the French while General Steinmetz brought in his division, which had been stretched as far to the west as Binche.

On hearing this news, Napoleon ordered the light cavalry of the Guard, under General Lefebvre-Desnouettes, to proceed up the Brussels road, and sent a message to Reille instructing him to march on Gosselies and attack the enemy there. D'Erlon was to follow Reille and support him, while at the same time guarding Marchienne and sending a brigade in the direction of Mons. There was no mention of Quatre Bras.

By this time the cavalry corps of Exelmans had crossed the bridge, and Vandamme's corps was following. Napoleon ordered both up the Sombreffe road to support Pajol. Marshal Grouchy had already galloped on to Gilly to find out what was taking place and was on his way back to ask for orders.

Soult's despatch to d'Erlon had just been sent off when Marshal Ney arrived a little after three o'clock. There can be no doubt that his arrival at this juncture was unexpected. Ney had dined with Napoleon at Avesnes, and we do not know what took place between them; but it seems that at Avesnes Napoleon did not mind whether Ney participated in the war or not, since he had offered him no facilities for acquiring horses or advancing with the army. Ney had gone from Avesnes to Beaumont in a farmer's pony-trap; no accommodation awaited him, and he had slept in a room offered by one of the administrative generals. Nor were there horses anywhere for sale. The following morning, while Napoleon left the town at 2 a.m. and troops marched forward hour after hour, Ney had sought in vain for mounts for himself and his aide-de-camp. It was not until about 10 a.m. that he heard Mortier had been taken ill and found he was able to purchase horses from him. Marshal Mortier, Duke of Treviso, who had been given command of the Imperial Guard, had awoken on this fatal morning to discover himself incapacitated by sciatica and obliged to keep to his room.[1] Perhaps the ailment was unconsciously brought on by his deep misgivings as to Napoleon's chances of success; certainly it served to preserve Mortier from the fate of his colleagues, Marshals Soult, Ney and Grouchy, who were all to be turned into scapegoats by the zealous architects of the Napoleonic legend.

Ney, accompanied by his aide-de-camp, Colonel Heymès, left Beaumont at about 11 a.m. He found Napoleon at *La Belle Vue* with Marshal Soult at his side and other staff officers near by. Napoleon welcomed him graciously and, acting on impulse, put him in immediate command of the left wing of the army, which consisted of the 1st and 2nd Corps, under Reille and d'Erlon, the cavalry already sent up the Brussels road, and the heavy cavalry of Kellermann which was still on the other side of the river. Ney was to go immediately to Gosselies and take charge. Propaganda from St Helena asks us to believe that in the brief time which had elapsed since Napoleon had sent off Reille's and d'Erlon's instructions, he had suddenly become urgently concerned over Quatre Bras. Ney, it is said, was instructed to seize this point. He was to make a head-on attack on all that lay before him on the route from Gosselies to Brussels and to take up his position astride the road beyond Quatre Bras, stationing strong advance guards on the routes to Brussels, Namur and Nivelles.[2] Whether such an order would have been a wise one, is a point that has been much discussed since that summer afternoon of 1815. In the opinion of Thiers and many other historians it is clear that Quatre Bras should have been seized at once and that Napoleon could not have failed to order this to be done. But Charras and Grouard consider it would have been dangerous to

[1] Mortier was not replaced, but orders were passed through the deputy head of the General Staff of the Guard, Lieut.-General Drouot.
[2] *Mémoires de Napléon*, Vol. IX, p. 71.

throw Ney upon Quatre Bras while the Prussians still held Sombreffe. No mention had been made of Quatre Bras in the instructions to Reille and d'Erlon, and no mention of it was made in a further order sent to d'Erlon by the Chief-of-Staff after Ney had left to take up his command. It seems likely that Napoleon, following his usual practice of justifying himself at the expense of others, invented his order to Ney after the event.[1]

In all the discussion and research regarding this question of Napoleon's orders to Ney, in all the attempted reconstructions of the interview, one may look in vain for the least hint that Marshal Ney was given any information about the military situation. How much did he know? Presumably nothing, since it was Napoleon's method to keep the essential data to himself, giving orders but no explanations as to his plans and intentions. Yet Ney was now in command of a third of the army and was being sent off to act independently. About the general conception of the manœuvre, says Lenient, Ney, Marshal of the Empire and Commander-in-Chief of the left wing, was no better informed than the last and least infantryman.[2] His position was not easy; he did not know the names of the generals and colonels serving under him, nor the size of the regiments. It is not surprising that he acted with caution.

Marshal Grouchy arrived back from Gilly with information as Napoleon was taking leave of Ney. Ney rode off forthwith, accompanied by Heymès. Making his way up the Brussels road, he placed himself at the head of Reille's forces which were now arriving from Marchienne, and set about organizing the assault on Gosselies. The Prussians resolutely threw the French back and succeeded in holding them at bay until Steinmetz had collected his most distant men and brought them safely to the east of the Brussels road. They now abandoned the town and the French took possession.

The French now had the road to Brussels open before them, but they had the Prussians on their flank, for Steinmetz had retired no further than Heppignies. To the rear, at Gilly, were more Prussian forces. If he had indeed been commanded to march headlong on Quatre Bras, Ney evidently felt too uneasy about the order to carry it out and believed it was advisable to keep his wing of the army

[1] See Appendix B.
[2] Lenient, *La Solution des Enigmes de Waterloo*, p. 186.

close to that of Napoleon, rather than risk its being cut off by the Prussian army. He established three of Reille's divisions round about Gosselies, and sent the fourth north-eastwards to Mellet. He sent only the cavalry of the Guard, under General Lefebvre-Desnouettes and Colbert, up the Brussels road towards Quatre Bras. These two generals reached Frasnes at about five in the afternoon, and now for the first time the French came in contact with an outpost of Wellington's army. Frasnes was held by Major Norman with a battalion of Nassau troops and a Dutch battery of horse artillery. He was without instructions but had heard the firing at Gosselies and had made preparations to defend his post. He now made a firm stand against the French cavalry who were obliged to halt and send back a request for infantry; while waiting for this to arrive, Colbert took a party of lancers to reconnoitre to the right and rear of Frasnes. He went as far as Quatre Bras and found it unoccupied. The horsemen looked at the peaceful hamlet grouped about the crossroads, then wheeled round and returned to Frasnes. By this time a battalion of French infantry had arrived, and Major Norman was retreating up the road towards Quatre Bras where he eventually established himself in a wood just south of the crossroads. As he reached this point, Prince Bernard of Saxe-Weimar arrived there also, coming from Genappe.

For some time now the entire countryside had been in disorder and the unhappy farmers and peasants, in despair at finding themselves full in the path of war, were either in flight with all they could carry or were endeavouring to protect their homes, to the small extent that this was possible, from the hunger and passions of the French soldiery. Wounded Prussian soldiers were staggering about the northward-running lanes, and the forward posts of Wellington's army were aware that the French had invaded and threatened the Brussels road. The Dutch-Belgian generals stationed between Braine-le-Comte and Mons were all on the alert. General Baron de Perponcher was in command of the division in this area, and next in command under him were Major-General Count de Bylandt and Colonel Prince Bernard of Saxe-Weimar.

As the French entered Gosselies, Perponcher, who was in Nivelles, was preparing on his own initiative to hold them at Quatre Bras on the assumption that Wellington would be assembling his forces to join with those of Prussia by way of this point. About four o'clock he had sent a message ordering Prince Bernard of Saxe-Weimar, stationed at Genappe, to go at once to Quatre Bras. But Prince Bernard had not waited for the order; he was already marching to the crossroads with his force of 1,480 men. Thus Wellington was well served by his forward officers.

Prince Bernard was joined between 6.15 and 7 p.m. by three more battalions, sent down by Perponcher, and now had about 4,000 men and eight guns. Marshal Ney now rode up to reconnoitre the position. For some time he had heard gunfire in the direction of Gilly and knew that Napoleon was engaged in fighting the Prussians. He therefore drew back the small force which had followed Major Norman up the road and placed it at Frasnes for the night. At eight o'clock General Girard, commander of one of Reille's divisions, received an order from Napoleon to march from Gosselies to Wangenies, which is near to Fleurus. On their way, Girard's division exchanged shots with Steinmetz's troops in Heppignies.[1] Thus Ney had every evidence of danger on his right flank and was confirmed in his decision not to press forward along the Brussels road. Reille's troops, too, had been marching since 3 a.m. and had had to fight long at the river crossing and again at Gosselies; they were now exhausted.

Having given his orders for the night, Ney rode back to Gosselies where he dined and wrote a report to Napoleon.[2]

Soon after Ney had left him, Napoleon had ridden off with Grouchy up the Sombreffe road to Gilly. As they hastened along, they overtook the leading columns of Vandamme's infantry, now passing through Charleroi and up the Sombreffe road. Pirch II, on retreating from Charleroi, had placed his forces in the woods and hills behind Gilly. Blücher, being now at Sombreffe, was assembling his army rapidly, and already his second corps, under Pirch I, was within five miles of Prussian headquarters. Thielemann's corps was round about Namur, having left Ciney in the early morning. Blücher felt fully equal to meeting the French, and he had chosen his battleground some time beforehand in case the French should

[1] Houssaye, *1815*, Vol. II, p. 129, note 1.
[2] Houssaye, *1815*, Vol. II, p. 136, note 2. According to Colonel Heymès, Ney rode back to Charleroi that night and had a meal with Napoleon, remaining with him until 2 a.m. But this seems unlikely, since he sent a report. It seems probable that he would remain with the wing of which he was in command.

invade at Charleroi; it was at Ligny, a little to the north of Fleurus.

In Brussels, Baron Müffling, who had only learnt within the previous hour or two of the French invasion, assumed that Blücher would be preparing for battle and was endeavouring to learn how soon Wellington would march to his assistance.

Napoleon, however, believed that Ziethen's corps alone was in the region. Having verbally invested Grouchy with the command of the right wing of the army, he gave instructions for an attack. One of Vandamme's divisions was to approach the enemy from the front, while Grouchy took him in the flank with Exelman's dragoons. The Prussians were to be pursued as far as Sombreffe where Grouchy would consolidate his position.

Having given his orders, Napoleon returned to Charleroi, in order, says Houssaye, to hasten the arrival of Vandamme. This seems no adequate reason, since Vandamme was an energetic soldier who needed little urging. Moreover, Napoleon failed to inform Vandamme that he was now under Grouchy's orders, an omission almost certain to create difficulties.

Why did Napoleon so hurriedly leave this important scene of action? It was not in order to ride up the Brussels road to see for himself that Quatre Bras was taken, which was something he might well have done if that point had been as essential to him as he was later to make out. It was not much after 3.30 when he left Gilly, and there is no record of how he disposed of the next two hours.

During his absence, Soult had sent a despatch to Gérard, ordering him to change his direction and cross the Sambre at Châtelet. Gérard was to advance along the Fleurus road on Lambusart, and was to join in the attack on the Prussians if they were still in the region when he arrived.[1]

Grouchy had nothing to prove his new authority, and Vandamme, who had begun the day badly and was not in the best of humours, saw no reason to accept the orders he now gave. Napoleon's generals and marshals were haughty men, and an angry argument began. Two hours later, when Napoleon reappeared, the two generals had still not agreed over the combining of their attack. Furious at having heard no gunfire, the Emperor had galloped out from Charleroi to see what was going on. He now ordered Vandamme to make a

[1] Despatch quoted in the *Mémoires du Maréchal de Grouchy*, Vol. IV, p. 163.

head-on attack on the Prussians, still in position beyond Gilly. The attack was vigorously carried out under Napoleon's direction, but the Prussians broke off the engagement and retreated. Annoyed at seeing them escape him, Napoleon ordered General Letort to charge; but although heavy casualties were inflicted, the main body of the Prussians managed to retire in good order.

Having thus started the fighting, Napoleon now gave orders to Grouchy to continue the pursuit of the Prussians, to take Fleurus and then push on as far as Sombreffe.[1] Then once again he rode back to his headquarters in Charleroi, arriving there at 8 p.m. according to the army bulletin.

He had, however, still omitted to inform Vandamme that Grouchy was in command, and when in due course Grouchy sent instructions to Vandamme for the taking of Fleurus, the only reply he received was that Vandamme did not take orders from the commander of cavalry, and that his men, who were exhausted, were about to bivouac for the night. The cavalry could not act without the infantry, so that was an end to the matter and all firing ceased.

General Pajol spoke angrily of Vandamme in a report he sent to Grouchy at 10 p.m. 'It appears,' he said, 'that this general has taken it upon himself to do all that is contrary to war.' Yet Vandamme was an excellent soldier. His troops were probably exhausted, as he said; and he must have thought that, if it was necessary to continue the pursuit of the Prussians that night, Napoleon would be there in person to give instructions. No doubt he also felt some resentment that Grouchy had been made a marshal while he, who had deserved the honour for his outstanding services, had been persistently overlooked.

It does not appear from Napoleon's conduct that he had considered it essential to push the Prussians back with vigour in the course of this day. He felt, no doubt, that he was in an advantageous position and could await developments for a few hours. On reaching his headquarters, he took a meal and then retired to rest. His chief secretary, Baron Fain, wrote to Prince Joseph Bonaparte:

Monseigneur, it is nine in the evening. The Emperor, who has been on his horse since three this morning, has returned, exhausted. He has

[1] Houssaye, *1815*, Vol. II, pp. 123-4, note 1.

thrown himself on his bed for a few hours' rest. At midnight he will have to mount his horse again. His Majesty, being unable to write to your Highness, asks me to give you the following information:

The army has crossed the Sambre round Charleroi and placed its advance guards half way along the roads from Charleroi to Namur and Charleroi to Brussels. We have taken 1,500 prisoners and captured 6 pieces of cannon. Four Prussian regiments have been crushed. The Emperor has had few losses. . . .

It was an optimistic picture of the situation. The French had in fact killed, wounded or taken prisoner about 1,200 Prussians with small losses themselves. But the Prussians had no cause to feel dissatisfied that night. Ziethen's one corps had faced almost the whole of the French army, and he had collected his scattered forces and saved nearly all of them, while seriously delaying the French advance.

The French army bivouacked that night in the following positions: the 1st and 2nd Corps, between Marchienne and Frasnes, with Girard's division at Wangenies, near Fleurus; the cavalry corps of Pajol and Exelmans between Lambusart and Campinaire, with Vandamme's corps just behind them, round about Soleilmont; the infantry of the Guard between Gilly and Charleroi; the cavalry corps of Milhaud and Kellermann, and the 6th Infantry Corps, near Charleroi, but still on the far side of the Sambre; the 4th Corps, round about Châtelet, with only one division across the river.

Late at night, Napoleon rose to take a meal and read the reports, which included one sent in from Marshal Ney.

The report sent back to Paris that evening contained the words: 'The joy of the Belgians is not to be described.' However, while it is true that the Belgians did not wish to be united with Holland, to be conquered anew by Napoleon who had enslaved them in the past to fight his battles was no agreeable alternative. The arrival of the French army on Belgian soil was a disaster for the inhabitants and meant ruin for all who lay in its path. Most French soldiers gave themselves up to pillage and violence as a matter of course. For them the laws of normal civilized life were suspended; they were excited by the prospect of battle and lived as adventurers and gamblers. Moreover, they were obliged to fend for themselves and live on the land they overran; any who behaved with kindness and consideration no doubt had to go hungry. An Englishman who visited Belgium just after the battle of Waterloo says of the French soldier:

> When he should have acquired what would have enabled him to become an independent and useful member of society, he was dragged away, a mere boy, and chained to the car of the Imperial Moloch. Here his tastes were perverted to the abominations and degradations of his condition: his hopes were inseparably connected with the success of crime, the diffusion of slaughter, and the unbridled exercise of robbery; his feelings, in short, were poisoned in all their sources – and when thus rendered completely fit for his master, he might be considered in a state of almost hopeless reprobation.[1]

The process had been continually at work on the youth of France since the system of conscription had been devised, the writer says. It had suited Napoleon very well to have an army unfitted for normal life, for the men would endure any campaign rather than be let loose in their own country to starve. In France itself the army was as much of a scourge as elsewhere, and ever since the Directory it had been the aim of French governments to keep it abroad. General Dörnberg had written a few weeks previously: 'The requisitions the French make on the frontiers are enormous, not only in provisions and forage but also money, so that small villages are obliged to pay 5,000 or 6,000 francs.' And shortly before the invasion there had been rumours that the French troops were about to make incursions into Belgium to forage the villages and take off all the cattle.

Now that the campaign had begun, the Belgians were receiving scant mercy from the invaders who trampled down their crops, destroyed poultry and animals for food, rifled their homes and generally behaved as men to whom all is permitted. Only a consideration of the habits of the French army makes understandable the later savage conduct of the Belgian peasants towards the men fallen on the battlefield. The Belgians, as Captain Mercer's journal shows, were remarkably kind and hospitable in normal circumstances; but now they were being maddened by the treatment they received.[2]

[1] Scott, *Paris revisited in 1815*, p. 250.
[2] General Radet, the Provost Marshal, resigned on the 17th on the grounds that it was impossible to control the soldiers. Houssaye, *1815*, Vol. II, p. 80.

9

*In Brussels; Napoleon's orders on the 16th; The battle of Ligny opens;
Ney against Wellington at Quatre Bras; D'Erlon's false march*

As thousands of exhausted men fell asleep among the crops, as
Napoleon and his staff officers sat talking round their abundant
table in Charleroi, the Duke of Wellington drove off to the Duchess
of Richmond's ball in Brussels. Only at three o'clock in the afternoon
had he heard of the French invasion. The Prince of Orange, who had
come up from his headquarters to attend the ball, had brought him
news of the French attack on Thuin; and shortly after, Baron
Müffling, the Prussian *attaché* on Wellington's staff, came with a
report from Ziethen saying that Charleroi appeared to be threatened.
The Duke told Müffling that his troops would be ordered to their
concentration points, there to hold themselves in readiness to march
at the shortest notice; but the point of assembly could not be decided
upon until the French design was known.

During the evening Müffling received a despatch from Gneisenau,
sent off at noon, informing him that hostilities had opened, that the
Prussian army was concentrating at Sombreffe, covered by Ziethen's
corps, and that Blücher intended to fight a battle on the 16th. The
Duke, on being informed, issued further orders. The 1st Corps was
to assemble at Enghien, Brain-le-Comte and Nivelles; the 2nd at
Ath, Grammont and Sotteghem; the reserve (at present in and
around Brussels) was to be ready to move at a moment's notice;
the cavalry reserve was to assemble at Ninove.

Having done all that he thought immediately necessary, the Duke
went to the ball. He had encouraged the officers invited to this
function to attend, although commanders of divisions and brigades
were advised to leave early. Brussels abounded with friends and
agents of the Bonapartists, and an apparent preoccupation with
frivolities on the part of Allied staff officers would encourage
Napoleon in his belief that he had taken them by surprise.

Wellington has often been criticized for his hesitation in ordering
troops to the Charleroi area. To the last moment, indeed, he was

covering Mons, and he never deviated from his conviction that Napoleon would have done better to invade further to the west. As it was, Napoleon was striking the extreme right of the Prussian line, and the English were extended just behind and could support the Prussians easily. Thus he would have two armies upon him fairly quickly. In advancing by Mons up to Braine-le-Comte, he would have been certain of having only the English army to contend with when fighting his first battle. Napoleon's view was that if he attacked the right of the English[1] line he would drive the two armies together, whereas by invading at Charleroi he was driving up between them and would throw them apart. But could it not equally be said that he was running his head into a noose? Could not his enemies quickly fall upon him, from both sides, if he invaded at Charleroi?

Wellington arrived very late at the ball. Rumours of a crisis were circulating and general officers already leaving. Towards midnight he received a letter from General Dörnberg informing him that all the French had left the region of Mons for Charleroi. There seemed to be no doubt, then, that Napoleon was arriving by way of this last town and was attacking the extreme right of the Prussian line. Wellington therefore ordered the whole of his army to march on Quatre Bras, with the exception of the detachment at Hal.

Groups of men were hastening from the ballroom on which a chill had fallen; but the Duke remained to supper where the Prince of Orange proposed the health of the Prince Regent, to which he replied. Shortly afterwards he left and went home for a brief sleep while the Prince of Orange rode down the road to Quatre Bras.

The wax candles of the ballroom were snuffed out, while torches flared in the streets and squares. Drums rolled and bugles sounded; soldiers assembled and the regiments formed. Baggage wagons were loaded, artillery and commissariat trains were harnessed. Alarmed citizens leaned from their bedroom windows, and country wagons added a touch of incongruity to the scene as they arrived laden with strawberries, peas and potatoes for the market.

By four in the morning, as the sun was rising, the 42nd and 92nd Highland Regiments were marching down the Charleroi road to

---

[1] Although Wellington's army consisted of men of various nationalities, I use the word 'English', as was the contemporary custom, for the sake of simplicity.

the strains of their bagpipes; and about an hour later the Duke of
Wellington rode from the town, accompanied by the Duke of
Brunswick.

The Brunswick troops followed and were marching from the
town when Fanny Burney rose and went out to see what was taking
place. She had come to Brussels from Paris, and describes the sad
impression made on her by the vast numbers marching by in their
black battle dress.

> This gloomy hue gave an air so mournful to the procession, that,
> knowing its destination for battle, I contemplated it with an aching
> heart. On enquiry, I learned it was the army of Brunswick. How
> much deeper yet had been my heartache had I foreknown that nearly
> all those brave men, thus marching on in gallant though dark array,
> with their valiant royal chief at their head, the nephew of my own
> King, George the Third, were amongst the first destined victims
> to this dreadful contest, and that neither the chief, nor the greater part
> of his warlike associates, would, within a few short hours, breathe
> again the vital air!

She records that the people of Brussels looked on with indifference,
and no kind wishes followed the soldiers. She found it impossible
to decide whether the Belgians were for or against Napoleon,
although there was no doubt that they all expected him to win the
war. 'The opinion of both sides, alike with good will and with ill,'
was nearly universal that Bonaparte was invincible.'[1]

Napoleon himself, as if equally certain of his own invincibility,
took his time on this morning of the 16th. He was up early, making
his plans known to Soult, but his orders were late in going out and
he made no personal reconnaissance until midday, thus giving
Blücher invaluable time for bringing up Thielemann and Pirch I.

On the left wing and the right, his generals were up at dawn.
Grouchy was preparing to carry out the orders of the previous night
which Vandamme's opposition had interrupted. Ney was still
without orders. Skirmishing was taking place in front of Quatre
Bras where General Perponcher arrived at 5 a.m. with reinforcements. At seven the Prince of Orange reached the point with still
more troops. Ney was gathering information from his officers, and

[1] Fanny Burney, *Diary*, p. 386.

a message was sent to Napoleon reporting the arrival of forces from Wellington's army. Colonel Heymès was inspecting the regiments, noting their numbers and the names of the commanding officers. General Reille's troops were ready to march, and at about seven o'clock he went to ask Ney for his orders, but was told that Ney himself still awaited instructions from the Emperor. All Ney had so far received was a despatch from Soult, informing him that Kellermann was being sent to Gosselies and asking for information about the enemy on his front and the positions of the 1st and 2nd Corps.[1]

General Girard, who had taken one of Reille's divisions to Wangenies the previous evening, was observing the movements of the Prussians who were very active at this time.

Marshal Grouchy sent the following report to Napoleon at 5 a.m.:

> While making the rounds of my advance posts, I have caught sight of strong enemy columns moving in the direction of Brye, Saint-Amand and neighbouring villages. They appear to be emerging from the Namur road. General Girard, whose division on my left occupies higher ground than that on which my troops are placed, has also drawn my attention to the fact that Prussian troops are arriving at Point-du-Jour. At the moment I am assembling my troops in order to execute the movement towards Sombreffe ordered by your Majesty.
>
> Grouchy

At 6 a.m. Grouchy wrote again:

> I am warned by General Girard that the enemy continues to arrive in force by Sombreffe on the heights about the windmill of Brye.

This was a clear indication that Blücher was assembling his army to fight between Fleurus and Sombreffe if the French ventured that way; yet Napoleon, although he had originally hoped to join battle with the Prussians, had become convinced that they were retreating, and his convictions were too strong to be shaken by evidence from without. Houssaye writes: 'When the Emperor, back at Charleroi in the night, had considered the reports of Grouchy and Ney, he thought that the Allies, disconcerted by his unexpected

[1] This despatch is quoted in *Documents Inédits*, by J. M. Ney, p. 26. Ney's reply is timed 7 a.m.

aggression, were withdrawing towards their bases, the Prussians to the region of Liège and Maestricht, the Anglo-Belgians to the region of Antwerp.' His intention was to occupy Sombreffe and Gembloux; then, having cleared the area of Prussians, he would make a night march to Brussels. He did not change his plan, and Soult now sent out the orders he dictated.[1] Kellermann (Comte de Valmy) was directed on Gosselies; Drouot was ordered to send the Guard towards Fleurus; Vandamme and Gérard were to march on Sombreffe, and were at last formally notified that Grouchy was in command of the right wing of the army. Ney was to take up his position at Quatre Bras with six infantry divisions and Kellermann's cuirassiers, and was to send his two remaining infantry divisions to Genappe (north of Quatre Bras on the Brussels road) and Marbais respectively.

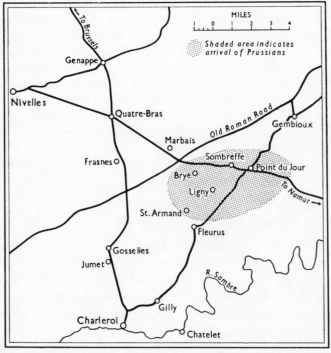

[1] The hour was not marked on Soult's orders, and Houssaye calculates that they must have been sent out between 7 a.m. and 8 a.m. (*1815*, Vol. II, pp. 136-8). But the orders to Ney had not reached Gosselies at 10 a.m., which suggests they were sent out after 8 a.m.

As the messengers hastened off with these instructions, Napoleon dictated his own personal despatches in which he explained his intentions more fully to Marshals Ney and Grouchy. The first of these was taken down by General Flahaut, and the second, the despatch to Grouchy, by General Labédoyère.

Ney rode up to Frasnes after conferring with Reille, leaving instructions that if orders came from Napoleon Reille was to put them into execution at once.[1] But it was not until 10 a.m. that the long-awaited orders arrived. These were not from Soult, but were contained in Napoleon's own despatch, carried by General Flahaut, which had arrived first.

By this time Reille had had information from Girard to the effect that the Prussians still held Fleurus and that they were arriving in great numbers by way of the Namur road. Since this indicated that Blücher was preparing to fight, Reille was surprised to find that Napoleon was ordering the left wing to march up to Quatre Bras and hold itself in readiness to march to Brussels that night. With the Prussians assembling in force about Fleurus, he would have expected to be called in that direction, and he felt too uneasy to carry out the Emperor's orders without further reference to Marshal Ney. He held his troops ready, instructed d'Erlon, who was waiting at Jumet, to be prepared to follow his movement, and sent a despatch to Ney with the information from Girard and a request for orders. At the same time he sent Girard's messenger on to Napoleon. General Flahaut continued on his way to Frasnes where he found Ney and gave him Napoleon's despatch at eleven o'clock.

There have been endless diatribes against Ney for his failure to seize Quatre Bras on the 15th or in the early hours of the 16th, in accordance with the order Napoleon claims to have given. But these accusations are not easily reconciled with the orders on Soult's register[2] nor with the despatch which Ney now read, which runs as follows:

[1] Information given in Reille's report of the movements of the 2nd Corps during the campaign, quoted in *Documents Inédits* by J. N. Ney, pp. 54-63.

[2] The despatch sent to Grouchy on the morning of the 16th contains these words: 'I have the honour to notify you that Marshal the Prince of the Moskowa is receiving orders to move with the 1st and 2nd Infantry Corps and the 3rd Cavalry Corps to the intersection of the roads named Trois Bras . . .' Since Ney was being ordered to Quatre Bras now, Napoleon presumably had not given him any urgent command to go there previously.

My cousin, my aide-de-camp, General Flahaut, brings you this letter. The Chief-of-Staff will have given you orders, but you will receive mine earlier, as my officers ride more quickly than his. You will receive the order of movement for the day, but I wish to write to you in detail, as it is of the greatest importance.

I am sending Marshal Grouchy with the 3rd and 4th Infantry Corps on Sombreffe; I am sending my Guard to Fleurus, where I shall be in person before mid-day. I shall attack the enemy there if I meet him, and I shall reconnoitre as far as Gembloux. Then, according to events, I shall make my decisions: perhaps at three this afternoon, perhaps this evening. My intention is that you shall be ready to march to Brussels immediately after I have made my decision. I shall support you with the Guard which will be at Fleurus or Sombreffe, and I should like to arrive at Brussels tomorrow morning. You should begin your march this evening if I make my decision early enough to be able to inform you of it by day, and cover three or four leagues this evening and be at Brussels at seven o'clock tomorrow morning.

You should therefore place your troops as follows:

1st Division, two leagues beyond Quatre Bras, if nothing prevents it; six infantry divisions round about Quatre Bras, and one division at Marbais so that I can call it to me at Sombreffe in case of need. This would not retard your march.

Count Valmy's corps, consisting of 3,000 cuirassiers, to be placed at the intersection of the old Roman road and the Brussels road, so that I can call on him in case of need. As soon as my decision is made you will order him to rejoin you.

I should like to have General Lefebvre-Desnouettes' division of the Guards with me, and I am sending you the two divisions of Count Valmy's corps to replace them. But as my project now stands, I prefer to place Count Valmy in such a way that I can recall him if I need him, rather than cause General Lefebvre-Desnouettes to make wasted marches (fausses marches), since it is probable that I shall decide this evening to march on Brussels with the Guard. However, cover Lefebvre's division with the cavalry divisions of d'Erlon and Reille, so as to spare the Guard; if there should be any skirmishing with the English, it is preferable that it should fall on the line rather than on the Guard.

For this campaign, I have made it a general principle to divide my army into two wings and a reserve. Your wing will consist of the four divisions of the 1st Corps, the four divisions of the 2nd Corps, two divisions of light cavalry, and two divisions of Count Valmy's corps. That cannot be much less than 45,000 to 50,000 men.

Marshal Grouchy will command the right wing with a force of about the same size.

The Guard will form the reserve, and I shall throw my weight on one wing or the other according to circumstances.

The Chief-of-Staff is giving precise orders to ensure that there is no difficulty with regard to obedience to your orders when you are detached; the corps commanders will take orders direct from me when I am present.

According to circumstances, I may reduce one or other wing to augment my reserve.

You will realize the importance I attach to the capture of Brussels. It could, moreover, give rise to far-reaching events, for such a rapid and unexpected movement will isolate the English army from Mons, Ostende, etc.

I wish your arrangements to be well made, so that the moment the order is given your light divisions can march rapidly and without obstacles on Brussels.

Napoleon.

It will be seen that this letter is not an order of battle. Napoleon is instructing Ney as to the best dispositions for a march on Brussels. He has Brussels in mind just as he had had Paris in mind on the journey up from Elba, with the same inward conviction that nothing can keep him from it. He anticipates no more than skirmishing with Wellington's army, and appears to forget his maps for the moment and imagines he will cut the English off from Mons and Ostende by his march on Brussels.

In his letter to Grouchy Napoleon gave orders that the right wing was to march at once on Sombreffe. The letter ends with the words: 'All the data I have shows that the Prussians are not able to oppose us with more than 40,000 men.'

Could Napoleon afford to adhere to his system of two wings and a reserve at this moment? Was it safe, after receiving clear information from Grouchy and Girard that the Prussians were assembling, to send off 50,000 men to Quatre Bras, instead of using his massed army to ensure the total defeat of the Prussians? In order to succeed, it was essential to fight the Prussians in the absence of the English. When once he was faced with the two enemy armies simultaneously the game could not be played at all. It therefore seems that he would have done better to have placed the left wing on the flank of the main army, keeping the whole under his own command and blocking the way to the English between Marbais and Frasnes. However, his plans were made on the assumption that he had no more than 40,000 Prussians to deal with, and that the English would make no serious effort to come forward; had that been the true position, it would have been reasonable to prepare at once for the march to Brussels.

Both Marshal Ney and Reille were uneasy about moving away from the main army and the assembling Prussians; but Ney, after reading Napoleon's despatch, decided to follow its instructions and sent orders to his generals accordingly.

Marshal Grouchy had taken possession of Fleurus during the morning, since the Prussians had evacuated it in the early hours; but he was unable to execute Napoleon's orders, for Ziethen's corps barred the way to Sombreffe. A battle would therefore have to be fought before Sombreffe could be reached, and for this he awaited the arrival of Gérard who was still bringing his troops across the river at Châtelet.

At 9.30, as Napoleon was preparing to leave Charleroi for Fleurus, a messenger had arrived from Frasnes to report the arrival of enemy troops at Quatre Bras. He had dictated a note to Ney, ordering him to destroy these troops and adding, 'Blücher was at Namur yesterday and it is hardly likely that he will have moved any troops to Quatre Bras. Thus you have nothing to concern yourself with except what comes from Brussels.'

Having thus brushed aside Wellington's army, Napoleon had ordered Lobau's corps to take up a position in front of Charleroi and had then ridden off towards Fleurus. As he was moving along the dusty roads, the Duke of Wellington arrived at Quatre Bras. All was quiet, and after inspecting the troops with the Prince of Orange, the Duke rode along the Namur road to discover how Blücher was faring.

Blücher had been at Brye since the earliest hours; from time to time he climbed up inside a windmill which afforded him an excellent view of the countryside and of the French troops round about Fleurus. He may well have been anxious, for as yet only his wearied 1st Corps was fully assembled for battle, and so far as he knew the entire French army was preparing to strike him at any moment. The 2nd Corps, though its regiments were successively arriving at the rear of Sombreffe, would not be ready for action until about mid-day, and the 3rd Corps was behind it. As for the 4th, it was now known that it could not reach Sombreffe that day but would be assembling in the evening at Hannut, about twenty-five miles away. As yet he had no news from Wellington, and he now requested Sir Henry Hardinge, the English attaché, to go to Quatre Bras in the hope of finding him there. Sir Henry Hardinge accordingly rode forth along the Namur road, on which he shortly met the Duke with his party.

It was a hot, glowing day and the Imperial escort marched in clouds of dust. Arriving at Fleurus at eleven o'clock, Napoleon received an excited ovation from the soldiers but was surprised to be met by Grouchy whom he had supposed by now to be well on his way to Sombreffe. The situation was explained to him with some difficulty, for he refused at first to believe in the massing of the Prussians.[1] He then made a tour of inspection. A mill was rapidly turned into an observation post for him and he climbed up, taking with him a local surveyor who was by chance to hand.

Before him stretched the setting of the battle he was about to direct. A broad, undulating plain sloped down to a valley through which a wide stream meandered, the Ligne. Straight ahead to the north was the village of Saint-Amand, on the Ligne; further back were the villages of Brye and Ligny, the latter standing on both sides of the stream. The countryside was scattered with villages and hamlets, all of them dominated by their church steeples and framed by woods and orchards; gold fields of wheat and maize extended as far as the eye could see, and the sky was without a cloud. To the north-east were Sombreffe and Gembloux; and barring the way to these stood the four divisions of Ziethen's corps. Napoleon could see them in part, assembled about and between the villages of Brye, Saint-Amand and Ligny. The main body of the corps was drawn up on high ground by the farm and windmill of Bussy between Ligny and Brye; this was the windmill Blücher was using. At mid-day, Napoleon could see nothing of the corps of Pirch I

[1] Charras, *Campagne de 1815*, p. 131, note 1.

and Thielemann, still mainly behind Sombreffe. At the far end of the plain was a row of elms, lining the Namur road along which Wellington was now riding.

The Duke of Wellington, whom Napoleon believed to be far away, was conversing with Sir Henry Hardinge, followed by Baron Müffling, the Duke of Brunswick, Count Dörnberg and a number of aides-de-camp. As they neared Brye, he surveyed the scene with his practised eye and asked how the Prussians were forming.

'In column, not in line,' said Sir Henry. 'The Prussian soldier, Blücher says, will not stand in line.'

'Then the artillery will play upon them, and they will be beaten damnably,' observed the Duke.

Napoleon would have liked to attack immediately, but learning that Gérard's corps had not arrived he decided to wait for it. Although he still thought he had only Ziethen's corps before him, he now realized by the extension of the Prussian line towards Wagnelée that Blücher must be counting on help from Wellington, and that the rest of the Prussian army was probably approaching.

Half the day had been lost. The infantry of the Guard which had escorted Napoleon from Fleurus stood lined up in the shadowless rye fields, facing Ligny. The heavy air was motionless and a blazing sun glared down on them while they waited for the battle to be joined. Others had been standing about since daybreak. It was not until one o'clock that the leading columns of Gérard's corps began to arrive.

The delays of the 4th Corps were most unfortunate for the French army. After being ordered the previous afternoon to change their direction, they had struggled with difficulty along narrow lanes and rough tracks, and only one division had managed to cross the bridge at Châtelet before nightfall. Had the crossing at Châtelet been organized at the outset, the 4th Corps would have been well in position for the impending battle at an early hour.[1]

Between one and two o'clock Napoleon disposed his troops, walking among them with a few staff officers. Wellington and Blücher watched him, according to Houssaye. If this is so, it must

---

[1] It might have been expected that, early on the 16th, Gérard would have carried out the instructions to march on Lambusart; but for some reason which is not clear he did not do this, but waited at Châtelet for further orders. These orders, informing him that he was under Grouchy's command and instructing him to march on Sombreffe, did not reach him until 9.30 a.m.

have been the Duke's first and only sight of his great adversary, unless he caught a glimpse of him through his glass two days later on the field of Waterloo. Wellington, anyway, was now up in the windmill at Bussy with Blücher, arranging to bring his forces forward to attack the French left, provided he himself was not attacked at Quatre Bras. At length the Duke left Ligny, though no doubt reluctantly since it was not every day that one could watch a Napoleon and a Blücher placing their pawns in position for battle.

As he was riding back to Quatre Bras, the Duke heard gunfire. Ney had opened his attack on the crossroads.

On receiving confirmation from Ney that Napoleon's orders were to be followed, Reille had moved up to a position before Quatre Bras with the divisions of Foy, Bachelu and Jérôme Bonaparte. Ney began the attack at about two o'clock. The crossroads were still held by Perponcher's division alone, and he did not anticipate any great difficulty in taking the point. He had no means of knowing the overall situation; and since Napoleon, with the essential data to hand, had told him he was marching to Brussels that night and had intimated that there was nothing to fear from such troops as might be sent down by Wellington, he had no reason to foresee difficulties. Bachelu's division made the first attack, and for a time it appeared that the crossroads would soon be seized. The farm of Piraumont was occupied and the Dutch-Belgian troops were slowly driven back. General Foy seized the farm of Gemioncourt, and by three o'clock Jérôme's division was attacking Pierrepont farm whose defenders were being forced back into the wood of Bossu. It was now that the Duke of Wellington arrived. The situation, he saw, was critical. The defence of Quatre Bras appeared to be collapsing rapidly.

Suddenly, however, events took a different turn. The Duke had scarcely had time to take in the situation when help arrived. A Dutch-Belgian cavalry brigade 1,000 strong came in from Nivelles, followed by the stalwart Sir Thomas Picton from Brussels with over 7,000 men. The troops ordered forward in the night from Brussels had been halted for a time at Waterloo; but the Duke had commanded them to resume their march after he had inspected Quatre Bras at 10 a.m. All was well, and although still outnumbered the Duke was confident now that he would hold his own.

As Wellington was taking leave of Blücher, Napoleon had been making up his mind to call Ney across to take the Prussians in the flank; his Chief-of-Staff had accordingly sent the following despatch to Marshal Ney at 2 p.m.

The Emperor has instructed me to inform you that the enemy has assembled a body of troops between Sombreffe and Brye, and that Marshal Grouchy is to attack them at 2.30 with the 3rd and 4th Corps.

His Majesty desires you also to attack the enemy before you and, after driving them back vigorously, to turn to your right so as to combine with us in encircling the body of troops above mentioned. But if this corps should be overcome first, his Majesty would manœuvre in your direction so as to hasten your operations in the same way.

Inform the Emperor at once of your dispositions and the situation on your front.

The carrying of urgent messages seems to have been conducted at a snail's pace by both sides in this famous campaign. News of the French attack on Thuin had been sent off to Brussels the previous day at 4 a.m. and had not arrived until 3 p.m., thus taking eleven hours to travel thirty-five miles; and now Napoleon's message from Fleurus was to take two hours to reach Marshal Ney at Quatre Bras. The message was sent in duplicate by two routes; and neither courier had much more than ten miles to ride.[1] At this rate, Napoleon would not obtain the information he asked for in the last sentence until 6 p.m.

The message shows that at two o'clock Napoleon had not realized how large a force he had before him, for he speaks only of a body of troops. But when Blücher made his final dispositions the 2nd and 3rd Prussian Corps were partly brought into view. Napoleon now saw that he had an army before him, and not merely Ziethen's corps. He regarded such a stand on Blücher's part as reckless folly and as a stroke of good fortune for himself. 'In three hours the outcome of the war may be decided,' he said to Gérard. 'If Ney executes my orders as he should, not a single Prussian gun will get away.'

Having, however, sent a third of his army to Quatre Bras,

[1] Lachouque, *Le Secret de Waterloo*, p. 139.

Napoleon was in fact outnumbered by the Prussians and his situation would have been extremely dangerous but for the mistake which kept Bülow's corps so far away. Blücher had present an army of 87,352 men and 224 guns; Napoleon's forces were 78,252 men and 242 guns, and these figures include Lobau's corps, the 6th, which was not used.[1] Napoleon appears to have thought that his left wing would still be available to him, whereas by sending it off to make a second and independent attack he had lost it for the time being, for there was no foreseeing how events would go on that side, and it was by no means certain that Ney would be able to follow his latest instructions. Napoleon's mistake lay basically in his attitude to Wellington, an attitude so contemptuous that he was unwilling to allow that the Duke could cause him any serious trouble.

Round Ligny, many thousands of men had long been waiting patiently in the heat of a summer day that grew more oppressive from hour to hour. It is reported that no one spoke, and it is easy to believe that the impending horror of the situation now silenced both sides. Not a leaf stirred. A heavy stillness lay over the country-side, disturbed only by the muffled, distant sound of gunfire at Quatre Bras. Between that battle-field and Ligny the ground rose, so that the sound was not loud; in the intervals between the firing the silence was tense.

The church bells now chimed the hour of three, their deep notes vibrating and lingering over the golden fields. As the sounds faded, the battle of Ligny began. Three cannon shots were fired in measured succession by the artillery of the Imperial Guard, for in those days Europeans were still in the habit of opening their battles with three beats as they opened theatrical performances.

On this signal, Vandamme launched an attack on Saint-Amand. On his left was Girard's division at Wagnelée, facing le Hameau de Saint-Amand; on the right Gérard's corps faced Ligny which it was about to assault. Grouchy, with his cavalry and an infantry division from Gérard's corps, faced the left wing of the Prussian army, nearer to Sombreffe.

General Lefol led his infantry division forward from Vandamme's corps; the men marched to the strains of a military band, preceded

[1] Figures given by Charras.

by skirmishers. They had no cover, no paths to march on, and their progress through corn standing four or five feet high was painfully slow. Prussian batteries soon drowned the martial music and dead and wounded men fell to the ground. The Prussians fired from the cottage windows of Saint-Amand, from behind walls and hedges, from the cemetery and from the church itself, mowing the French down as they approached. Driven on now by fear, by a wild urge to seize the shelter of their adversaries, the French infantry overcame the resistance of the dense and flourishing crops, and rushed forward in an agonized attempt to reach the village and escape from the open fields where they were such an easy target.

Further to the right, Gérard now sent forward two of his divisions, numbering about 10,000 men, to capture Ligny. The Prussians, under Generals Jagow and Henkel, were positioned behind the walls and hedges of the village, about 9,000 strong, with sixteen guns on each flank, silently awaiting the onslaught. With military airs and cries of 'Vive l'Empereur!' the attackers strove to keep up their spirits in the face of death. As they drew near, the Prussians opened fire. The French staggered before the blow, the dying and the wounded falling with cries and groans. Then perforce, they resumed their march until the Prussians were engaged at close quarters. Unable to penetrate the village they fell back, were re-formed by their officers and once more moved in to the attack. The Prussians stood firm, and again the French retired. They rallied and charged anew, fired on continually by the Prussian guns, while their own guns from the heights of Fleurus poured shells into Ligny. Here and there thatched roofs were set ablaze. Still the Prussians resolutely held their ground. But at last one of the French columns drove its way into the village, the men rushing towards the church to gain the protection of its walls. In the church square, however, they found themselves surrounded. From doors and windows, from behind tomb-stones, walls and trees, the Prussians effectively fired on them. Twenty French officers and 500 men fell almost at once, the rest escaping in disorder. But not for long; they were driven back again and again to take the village or die.

At Saint-Amand, Steinmetz was throwing back Lefol's infantry; but Vandamme sent another division forward and ordered Girard to attack Le Hameau de Saint-Amand. Grouchy had begun his attack on the Prussian left, at Boignée, Tongrinelle and Potriaux.

Napoleon, snuff-box in hand, watched the progress of the battle from his observation post on the heights of Fleurus. He soon saw that the Prussians were making a resolute stand and would be difficult to dislodge. It appears that he now realized he should have kept his army together instead of sending so large a part of it to Quatre Bras, for he instructed Soult to send the following order to Ney:

Monsieur le maréchal,

I wrote to you an hour ago to say that the Emperor would be attacking the enemy at half past two in the position he has taken between the villages of Saint-Amand and Brye. At this moment the engagement is very sharp. His Majesty orders me to say that you must manœuvre immediately so as to hem in the enemy's right and give him a good pounding in the rear. His army is lost if you act vigorously. The fate of France is in your hands. Do not hesitate an instant, therefore, to move as the Emperor orders, bearing on the heights of Brye and Saint-Amand so as to take part in a victory which may be decisive. The enemy has been caught *flagrante delicto* as he was seeking to join the English.

Duc de Dalmatie.

The register of the Chief-of-Staff shows that this message was sent out at 3.15. A duplicate was sent at 3.30, and at 3.30 also a message was sent to Lobau ordering him to bring the 6th Corps up to Fleurus. This was in answer to a message that had just come in from Lobau with news that Ney was faced with enemy forces numbering about 20,000 at Quatre Bras.[1] Realizing from this information that Ney might, after all, be unable to manœuvre at will, Napoleon decided to call up the 6th Corps which he would probably need.

On Soult's register no other message is entered at this time, an important point since some historians believe that Napoleon, after sending the 3.15 despatch to Ney, sent an order to d'Erlon, calling him across to the Ligny battlefield with the 1st Corps. Nothing Napoleon ever wrote or said indicates that he did such a thing, and it would have been hard indeed on Ney if he had deprived him of a

[1] Colonel Janin of the 6th Corps had been sent from Charleroi to Frasnes to gather information shortly before Napoleon left for Fleurus. (Houssaye, *1815*, Vol. II, pp. 143, 165-7. Lenient, *La Solution des Enigmes de Waterloo*, p. 274.)

whole army corps just as he learnt that he was in difficulties at Quatre Bras. D'Erlon was in fact to march towards Ligny, as will be seen, but it can scarcely have been by order of Napoleon.

At Quatre Bras both Marshal Ney and the Duke of Wellington were in the front line, well matched in valour and experience. Wellington's numbers were being increased by a constant stream of men moving to the crossroads, but Ney still had the advantage both in men and guns, although his infantry consisted of no more than three of Reille's divisions. The Brunswick corps which Fanny Burney had watched leaving Brussels now arrived, about 4,000 strong. But although they brought Wellington's forces up to 21,000 they were mostly untrained boys and they had no artillery. Fortunately, Picton's divison consisted of eight British and four Hanoverian battalions under Sir James Kempt and Sir Denis Pack, all of them troops of the finest quality. They fought gallantly throughout the afternoon, exposed to incessant fire from the French guns to which no adequate answer could be given. The Duke of Brunswick was killed and his troops routed; but while Foy and Jérôme drove the defenders out of the wood of Bossu and drew near the crossroads, Bachelu was thrown back by Kempt's brigade. Reille's cavalry rushed in to the assistance of Bachelu, but every attack was successfully resisted by the English.

A state of equilibrium was reached; Wellington waited for the arrival of further reinforcements to enable him to defeat the French, while Ney awaited d'Erlon's corps with which he hoped to carry the day.

Shortly before four o'clock, Napoleon's message of 2 p.m. reached Quatre Bras with the order that Ney was to push the enemy vigorously back and then wheel to the right and join the attack on the Prussians. To push back the enemy was just what Ney had been endeavouring to do for the past two hours, and for all he knew to the contrary it was he himself who was fighting the decisive battle of the day. Against Napoleon's expectations, Wellington was bringing his army down to Quatre Bras. England was the main enemy, the nation whose resolve to bring down Napoleon had never faltered, and to inflict a defeat upon the English at the outset of the campaign would indeed be a blow that must severely shake the coalition. But for the moment Ney could make no headway and must await the arrival of the 1st Corps, under d'Erlon, or perhaps the arrival of Napoleon himself. If Napoleon was engaged only against a single corps of Prussians, as the message indicated, Ney might hope for help from him in the course of the evening.

D'Erlon had concentrated his troops at Jumet that morning, and soon after mid-day had received Ney's order to advance to Frasnes; he had, however, been obliged to wait until Reille's corps had defiled, and this took a long time. When the battle opened, d'Erlon had only reached Gosselies where he was delayed for some time by false intelligence. Now, at four o'clock, he himself was quite close to the battle-field, for he had ridden ahead of his vanguard to announce to Ney the arrival of his corps. The centre of the corps was passing the Roman road, and the van was approaching Frasnes. It would not be long now before this body of over 20,000 men was available to join the attack on Quatre Bras. Unless, indeed, something extraordinary happened.

Unhappily for Ney, something extraordinary did happen. In d'Erlon's absence, his entire corps was ordered to change its direction and march over to the Ligny battlefield. The bearer of these instructions, which were given as coming from the Emperor, has never been conclusively identified, although d'Erlon, who should know better than anyone, says it was Labédoyère. Whoever it was, he succeeded perfectly in convincing the generals in charge of the 1st Corps that he was giving them a command direct from Napoleon, and after watching the leading columns turn off the Brussels road near the *Cabaret de l'Empereur*, he continued on his way to Frasnes in search of d'Erlon. He showed d'Erlon a pencilled note containing his orders, and explained that the 1st Corps was now on its way to Villers Perwin. He retained the note which, he said, had to be shown to Marshal Ney, and after that we hear no more of him. He vanishes from the scene.

D'Erlon unsuspectingly hastened off to the head of his troops, sending his Chief-of-Staff, General Delcambre, to Marshal Ney to explain what was taking place. This general, making his way up to Quatre Bras, found the roads much encumbered and his progress was slow. By the time he had sought out Ney it was about five o'clock. A critical moment had been reached. The Duke of Wellington was at this time receiving heavy reinforcements including the

Nassau contingent, two brigades of Alten's divison, a brigade of the Royal Artillery and a battery of the King's German Legion. At last he had numerical superiority over Ney and an equal number of guns. It was now that Ney learnt that d'Erlon was heading for Ligny. He fell into an understandable fury. In his order of the morning, Napoleon had detailed eight divisions to him, and he had now deprived him of five of them. Three divisions of Reille's corps were all the infantry he had with which to face Wellington's army,[1] and he had been requested not to make use of the cavalry of the Guard placed under his command. He realized now that he would have his work cut out even to contain the enemy, and could no longer hope to defeat him and drive him from his position.

As if this were not enough, Soult's order of 3.15 now reached the exasperated Marshal, instructing him to manœuvre immediately so as to fall on the rear of the Prussians. Charras is of the opinion that the officer bringing this despatch was the man responsible for the diversion of d'Erlon's corps. Catching up with it on his way from Fleurus to Frasnes, he would have taken it upon himself to order it across in the direction of Saint-Amand.[2] Ney perhaps suspected that this was the case, for he sent Delcambre off to make what haste he could along roads cluttered with wagons and wounded men, with orders that d'Erlon was to return immediately. Being one of the chief scapegoats of the campaign, Ney has been severely criticized for calling d'Erlon back, particularly on the grounds that d'Erlon could not now arrive in time to be useful. But this is a judgement made after the event, in the knowledge that d'Erlon did not, in fact, arrive back in time to take part in the battle. Ney could not foresee that his battle would end before d'Erlon reached the field; it was but 5.30 and the evenings were at their longest. Two days later, the battle of Wavre was not to finish until 11 p.m.[3]

Having sent off General Delcambre, Ney hastened back to direct operations as best he could.

[1] Girard's division having been called away the previous evening.

[2] Charras, *Histoire de la Campagne de 1815*, pp. 195-201.

[3] For a further discussion of d'Erlon's movements of the 16th see pp. 148-50ff. and Appendix C.

10

On the Ligny battlefield Frenchmen continued to assault the villages in heavy waves. Steinmetz was at last forced from Saint-Amand where he had lost over 2,000 men, and Blücher brought down reinforcements from the heights of Brye. The Prussian troops sustained heavy casualties as they came forward, for, as Wellington had seen, the site was defective; they were exposed to view and within range of the French guns which decimated them as they advanced. All the same, they swept down in vast numbers, almost driving Vandamme from Saint-Amand where, however, he managed to keep a foothold. Girard's division had taken La Haye but was driven out again; Girard himself was mortally wounded after rallying his troops and leading them back in a successful counter-attack. Hamlets and village streets were taken and re-taken hour after hour, but neither side could obtain the mastery. Blücher was anxious to hold this end of his line open for the arrival of help from Wellington, and he galloped about among his men, spurring them on with his cry; 'Forward, my children, forward!' No more was needed to make the soldiers return again and again to the attack.

Round Ligny the battle took on an even more violent character. Backwards and forwards the contending forces surged, driving each other alternately from end to end of the village. The afternoon was hot and oppressive; all nature was still and the atmosphere was charged with electricity. Fires were blazing throughout Ligny and smoke rolled voluminously overhead. Now General Gérard had the advantage and now General Jagow, but neither for very long. The French took possession of burning cottages and smouldering gardens, while the Prussians, gasping and choking, sought to drive them out again. Far behind, Napoleon, watching from the mill at Fleurus, drove battalion after battalion into the flaming village.

A combat of singular fury now developed in a very confined space.

Thousands of men had been driven against each other in this obscure village and they now had scarcely room to move. In and out of cottages they forced their way, now finding themselves crammed in humble kitchens or yards, now being felled by flaming beams. It can hardly be supposed that in such circumstances they knew any longer what they were doing, that Frenchmen killed only Prussians and Prussians only Frenchmen. Little could be distinguished in the smoke. Confusion reigned and everyone hit out blindly with bayonet, musket-butt or even bare fists. Blazing roofs fell in, screams tore the air, the gutters and the deep stream itself ran red with blood.

It would serve no purpose to linger on this atrocious scene. It was to continue hour after hour, while Napoleon trusted that Ney would throw back Wellington's forces and move across to Marbais, from there striking the rear of the Prussians. This was the ideal pattern of the battle; when in due course the Guard penetrated the centre, the left wing would break the Prussian right and prevent its union with the English by way of Wavre. Had this been achieved, Napoleon would again have won one of those colossal victories that struck terror into the hearts of Europeans. This outcome was a possibility until the early evening; but the chance presented to Napoleon was to be thrown away.

Wellington's army was still hastening from all directions to Quatre Bras. At four o'clock Captain Mercer and his troop reached Braine le Comte, 'almost ravenous with hunger,' he says, 'and roasted alive by the burning sun under which we had been marching all day'. An aide-de-camp rode past them in white satin breeches and embroidered jacket, 'having evidently mounted as he left the ballroom.' Sometimes the troop made their way with difficulty along encumbered roads, while at other times they journeyed through secluded woods. Eventually they joined the cavalry of Sir Hussey Vivian and with them approached Nivelles as the sun was sinking. A brisk cannonade could be heard and volumes of smoke hung over the trees. A castle was visible high up, bathed in golden light, while beneath it the country lay in purple obscurity.

In Nivelles the whole population was in the streets, standing in groups or 'hurrying along with the distracted air of people uncertain where they are going, or what they are doing'. Many wounded soldiers staggered about, bleeding to death as they dragged themselves painfully along, instinctively struggling away from the battlefield. Mercer writes:

One man we met was wounded in the head; pale and ghastly, with affrighted looks and uncertain step, he evidently knew little of where he was, or what passed about him, though still he staggered forward, the blood streaming down his face on to the greatcoat which he wore rolled over his left shoulder. An anxious crowd was collecting round him as we passed on. Then came others supported between two comrades, their faces deathly pale, and knees yielding at every step. At every step, in short, we met numbers more or less wounded, hurrying along in search of that assistance which many would never live to receive, and others receive too late.

Beyond the town the troop ran into crowds of panic-stricken deserters whom they assumed to be Belgians, since they were French-speaking. These men cried out that all was lost, the English were routed and destroyed. But a wounded private of the Gordon Highlanders, from whose knee the surgeon of G Troop paused to remove a musket ball, assured the troop that this was nonsense. The army was not shaken.

These deserters had left the field after a cavalry attack made by Ney about six o'clock. Wellington had been reinforced by the arrival of Alten with the brigades of Colin Halkett and Kielmansegge; and Ney, having no infantry to call on, ordered Kellermann to launch a cavalry attack. Kellermann, whose two divisions had been left in the region of Frasnes, brought up the brigade nearest to the battlefield, that of Guiton, and formed it for the attack. The charge was bold and vigorous, and it caused havoc in Halkett's brigade against which it was directed. Halkett's regiments formed into squares, but the 69th was ordered back into line by the Prince of Orange who was unaware that a charge was impending, with the result that, although the regiment stood firm, the French cavalry burst through their ranks, seized the regimental colours and swept right into Quatre Bras. It was this that had caused the deserters met by Mercer's troop to turn and and run. For a time the situation was dangerous for Wellington, since the French infantry was also gaining ground. But help arrived opportunely; a troop of horse artillery reached Quatre Bras and was able to fire at close range on the French horsemen. Kellermann had not the strength to keep his advantage; he had suffered heavy losses, and now his horse was shot from under him; unable to maintain his leadership, he saw his men fall into confusion, turn and retire. They raced off, in fact, as far as their original position at Frasnes. Reille's infantry came to a halt on seeing the flight of the cavalry, and by 6.30 p.m. the action was over and had failed. On foot, having had two horses killed under him, Marshal Ney rallied his soldiers, calling on them to hold on until the arrival of d'Erlon who could not fail to appear before long and give a new turn to the battle.

Towards seven o'clock, however, strong reinforcements reached Wellington, including Cooke's division of the Guards. The Duke now had about 36,000 men and seventy guns, and Ney was taxed to the utmost to save his forces from destruction.

D'Erlon's corps came within sight of the Ligny battlefield soon after 5 p.m. Arriving by way of Villers-Perwin, it was first seen by Vandamme's corps and mistaken for an enemy column. Girard's troops abandoned La Haye to meet the threat; there was panic among Vandamme's hard pressed forces who were in no state to face such an emergency, and the disorder was so great that General Lefol turned his guns on his own men to keep them from deserting.

At about five-thirty, Napoleon received an urgent message from Vandamme informing him that enemy troops were approaching, apparently on Fleurus, with the intention of turning the army. Vandamme said that he would be obliged to evacuate Saint-Amand and retreat unless the Emperor sent his reserve to meet and arrest the approaching column.

At this time Napoleon was preparing for an intensification of his attack on the Prussian centre. From his observation post he had seen with satisfaction that the Prussian reserves were rapidly diminishing, and that Blücher was reducing the strength of his centre to increase that of his right. On the French right, fighting had never become intensive, and Napoleon had a short time before taken Subervie's division from Grouchy and sent it to reinforce Vandamme; Blücher had also removed cavalry from this end of the line, sending it to his right. Napoleon believed that the time had come to strike a final blow at Ligny, and the Imperial Guard was already moving forward for this purpose, hidden from the enemy by the contours of the

MARIE LOUISE

Archiduchesse d'Autriche

IMPÉRATRICE REINE ET RÉGENTE

The Empress Marie-Louise, 1791–1847
Department of Prints and Drawings, British Museum

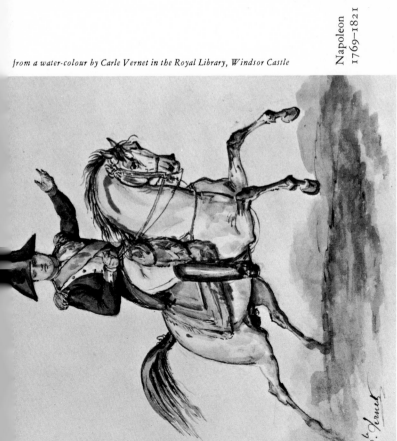

Napoleon
1769–1821

from a water-colour by Carle Vernet in the Royal Library, Windsor Castle

Cartoon by Cruikshank: 'General Nap turned Methodist Preacher'

British Cavalry Officers

Malmaison

Field-Marshal the
Duke of Wellington
1769–1852

from a miniature by Isabey
in the Wallace Collection

from the painting by Hippolyte
Le Comte at Apsley House

The Duke of Wellington
visiting the outposts at Soignies

La Belle Alliance

Department of Prints and Drawings, British Museum

(*From left to right*) Marshal Ney, Duke of Elchingen and Prince of the Moskowa, 1769–1815; Marshal Count de Grouchy, 1766–1847; Marshal Soult, Duke of Dalmatia, 1769–1851

The Battle of Waterloo

British Infantry in Squares

General Cavalié Mercer (1783–1868)
as a young man

Field-Marshal
Prince Blücher von
Wahlstadt, 1742–1819

Published and Sold July 1, 1814, by EDW.ᵈ ORME, Bond St. (corner of Brook St.) London.

PRINCE BLUCHER,
Field Marshal of the Prussian Forces.

A SKETCH FROM THE LIFE WHEN ON HIS VISIT TO LONDON, JUNE 1814.

BY MAJOR GENERAL BIRCH REYNARDSON.

Engraved by Freeman.

An officer of the Prussian Hussars

A private of the Prussian Uhlans

from water-colour drawings in the Royal Library, Windsor Castle

A French Cuirassier

An officer of the English Lifeguards

View of left centre of French position

from water-colours painted immediately after the battle by Dennis Dighton.
Royal Library, Windsor Castle

Farm of Hougoumont

land. Now, however, Vandamme's message arrived and Napoleon first ordered the Guard to halt and then brought it back to its original position before the mill at Fleurus. He sent the Young Guard under Duhesme to assist Vandamme, at the same time sending an aide-de-camp to reconnoitre the column approaching from Villers-Perwin. Although he had ordered Ney to march across to his aid, he was by no means certain that this was part of the left wing arriving. He realized from Blücher's efforts to force back the French at Saint-Amand that the Prussians were counting on help from Wellington to enable them to break through to the Fleurus road; and although he had a low opinion of the English army he had none the less to allow for the possibility, however remote, that they had prevailed at Quatre Bras and were coming across to strike him in the rear.

D'Erlon's column was two or three miles from Napoleon's headquarters, and it took the aide-de-camp about an hour to discover its identity and return with the information. Incredible as it may seem, Napoleon sent no orders to d'Erlon. He resumed his preparations for the final assault on Ligny, allowing d'Erlon to counter-march to Frasnes. In this way he threw away his chance of bringing the battle to its ideal conclusion. How he came to do this has remained a mystery. One theory is that he consented to d'Erlon's return to Frasnes in view of Ney's dangerous situation.[1] D'Erlon had been close enough to the battlefield at Quatre Bras to know that Ney was in serious difficulty, and he would presumably impart this information to the aide-de-camp sent by Napoleon; it is also likely that Delcambre had overtaken him by this time with Ney's order that he was to return to Frasnes, and in that case Napoleon would know from his aide that Ney had urgent need of d'Erlon. This could explain Napoleon's failure to make use of the corps he so urgently needed for the successful execution of his strategy.

Yet d'Erlon appears to have been in some uncertainty as to what he should do, perhaps because he was now within sight of Vandamme's section of the fighting and suspected that he was as much needed here as at Quatre Bras. By way of compromise, he left one of his divisions (that of Durutte) and his cavalry facing on Wagnelée for use on the right wing in case of need, and proceeded with the remainder of his corps towards Frasnes. It is difficult to see what better course he

[1] Charras, *Campagne de 1815*, pp. 198-9.

could have taken, though he has been bitterly reproached for not having second sight and foreseeing that the battle of Quatre Bras would have subsided by the time he neared that field, and that the battle of Ligny would fall short of being a decisive victory for Napoleon owing to his departure. All he knew was that his corps had been ordered across to Ligny by one of Napoleon's aides-de-camp and that now he had arrived it was apparent that Napoleon had not been expecting him. He had been misled by an excited and over zealous aide-de-camp.[1]

Had Napoleon, in addition to Soult's despatch of 3.15 p.m., sent new instructions ordering d'Erlon over to the Ligny battlefield, it is hardly imaginable that he would not have sent capable officers to lead this corps in the right direction for the action he had envisaged. In any case, whether ordered or not, the corps came in sight at an opportune moment, and it is surprising that no effort was made to use it at Ligny. Provided a total defeat could be inflicted on the Prussians it was not necessary for Ney to do more than contain the English at Quatre Bras. But Napoleon not only let d'Erlon go, but left Durutte inactive for the rest of the day, as he did Lobau who had now arrived on the scene. Thus Blücher escaped disaster.

It was now seven o'clock. During the past hour Vandamme, with the aid of the reinforcements sent by Napoleon, had recovered his lost positions. In Ligny, desperate fighting had continued without respite for four hours. The village blazed beneath heavy clouds of smoke, yet the fighting was not allowed to cease. The church and cemetery, encumbered with corpses, were endlessly contended for by men who must have wished themselves a thousand miles from both. Smouldering, burnt-out hovels repeatedly changed hands, and the combatants hounded each other in and out of flaming buildings where many wounded men were being burnt alive. On the right Grouchy was holding his own in an area where the fighting had never been intense. Lobau's corps, stationed on one of the roads to the east of Fleurus, remained idle.

Looking at the sloping ground behind Ligny and seeing it denuded of troops, Napoleon said to Gérard; 'They are lost; they have no reserve remaining.'

Blücher had received a message from Wellington, explaining

[1] See Appendix C.

that he was heavily engaged with the French at Quatre Bras and would be unable to join in the battle of Ligny. Suddenly it had grown so dark that he thought night had come and the battle was ending; Napoleon's reserve was concealed from his view, and he hoped to remain on the field overnight. But the sun still had some distance to travel and the obscurity was due to smoke and a great bank of thunderclouds which had gathered over Ligny. Heavy splashes of warm rain began to fall and a loud clap of thunder added to the roar of the guns.

The artillery of the Imperial Guard was now firing on Ligny. A tremendous bombardment from 200 guns began at half-past seven on this most tried section of the line. Napoleon was following a course so often successful in his battles; he had hammered for hours at a certain point, keeping in reserve his best troops who would sweep in at the end and break through the line as the enemy reached the last stages of weariness.

The Guard was assembled, full of confidence in victory. General Roguet called up the officers under him and proudly gave the command: 'Notify the Grenadiers that the first man who brings in a Prussian prisoner will be shot'.

It was 7.45 p.m. when the signal for the assault was given. The evening had grown still darker and a heavy shower now swept down accompanied by thunder and lightning. Napoleon, having descended from his mill, mounted his horse and placed himself on a hillock. Waving towards the swirling smoke and flames that marked the village of Ligny, he indicated the position to be attacked. The guns ceased firing but thunder still rolled as he took the salute from column after column of the Imperial Guard. 'Drunk with enthusiasm and fury,' as Charras puts it, the Guard rode down on Ligny, with loud cries of 'Long live the Emperor! No quarter!' They had little to fear. They knew that after all these hours of fighting they had only to seize the victory. The Prussians fought bravely, but Blücher had used his reserves recklessly during the afternoon and now had none to bring in. Napoleon had played his hand more skilfully.

Soon the Guard were surging through Ligny and up the slopes beyond. By 8 p.m. all was over. Blücher hastened up from his right to find the breach in his line rapidly widening and his troops in flight. Throwing himself energetically into the fighting, he led a cavalry charge against the Imperial Guard; but his horse was shot and in its fall it rolled on top of him and he could not free himself. His aide-de-camp, Count Nostitz, dismounted but was unable to help him, for the Prussian cavalry was now in flight before French cuirassiers. The cuirassiers raced past Blücher, while Nostitz stood at his side, both of them remaining unharmed. Presently the cuirassiers, in their turn, were put to flight by a body of Prussian Uhlans. Again, as they swept back, they surged round the fallen Blücher; but now Count Nostitz hailed the passing Uhlans who liberated their commander, though not without difficulty.

The Prussian army was obliged to retreat all along the line; yet, owing to Napoleon's failure to make use of d'Erlon's corps, there was no disorder except at the centre.

The thunderstorm had passed away, the sun had set and darkness fell. The French followed their defeated enemy but made slow progress. The Prussian infantry was now retreating in squares, their guns still firing at the attacking French cavalry. General Ziethen fell behind Brye, pursued by Vandamme; but his men went steadily, taking most of their guns with them. Further to the east, Thielemann retreated unscathed, leaving a strong detachment in Sombreffe.

The action died out at about half-past nine. The Prussians had been driven from the field, but they had not been routed. Their losses were 16,000 and twenty-one guns. The French lost over 11,000.

Blücher was taken to a cottage at Gentinnes, six miles to the rear, unconscious and severely bruised, although he had no broken bones. He was treated by a friction of brandy applied all over his body, and on regaining consciousness suggested that the remedy might be more effective if taken internally. This was not permitted, but he was allowed a bottle of champagne which went some way to restore his spirits. The command had temporarily been taken over by Gneisenau who ordered a retreat on Wavre, to begin at daylight. Wavre was to the north-east, on a level with Waterloo where Wellington would now make a stand. Since he could no longer hold his forward position now that the Prussians had been defeated, Wellington would retire northwards from Quatre Bras and the Prussians would retire on a parallel route. Three roads led to Wavre from Gembloux, and the retreat could therefore be made rapidly. Bülow's corps, still on its way, was also ordered to march to Wavre.

The struggle at Quatre Bras had ended at about the same time as the battle of Ligny. Wellington had finally become strong enough to take the offensive all along the line, and had driven the French back on Frasnes. The French had fallen back foot by foot, fighting with impeccable courage under their great leader and remaining to the end in good order. Round about 9 p.m., as the fighting was dying down, d'Erlon's corps had arrived on the field, weary and famished.

The battlefield was strewn with dead and wounded men. Wellington had lost 4,800, half of them British; the French had lost 4,000.

Behind Quatre Bras the British cavalry and Horse Artillery were now arriving. They had been stationed far off and Wellington had had to fight his battle without them. Captain Mercer, whose troop reached the scene as darkness fell, describes Quatre Bras:

> The firing began to grow slacker and even intermitting, as we entered the field of Quatre Bras – our horses stumbling from time to time over corpses of the slain, which they were too tired to step over. The shot and shells which flew over our line of march from time to time (some of the latter bursting beyond us) were sufficient to enable us to say we had been *in* the battle of Quatre Bras, for such was the name of the place where we now arrived, just too late to be useful. In all directions the busy hum of human voices was heard; the wood along the skirts of which we marched re-echoed clearly and loudly the tones of the bugle, which ever and anon were over-powered by the sullen roar of cannon, or the sharper rattle of musketry; dark crowds of men moved in the increasing obscurity of evening, and the whole scene seemed alive with them. What a moment of excitement and anxiety as we proceeded amongst all this tumult, and amidst the dead and dying, ignorant as yet how the affair had terminated! Arrived at a mass of buildings, where four roads met (*les quatre bras*), Major M'Donald again came up with orders for us to bivouac on an adjoining field, where, accordingly, we established ourselves amongst the remains of a wheat crop.

The men dismounted, the horses were tied to the wheels of the carriages, and water was brought from a well at Quatre Bras farm for soldiers and animals. A patch of wheat still standing was found and cut down to supplement the horses' ration of corn. 'Our animals cared for, the next consideration was ourselves. The men had provisions ready cooked in their haversacks, and therefore soon made themselves comfortable; but we had nothing, could procure nothing, and were likely to go supperless to bed.' The Company's doctor, however, presently turned up with the remnant of a meat pie which he shared with the five or six officers of the troop. The portions were small but welcome. 'The meal ended and cigars lighted, we sat enveloped in our cloaks, chatting and listening to the Babel-like confusion at the well, where crowds were still struggling for water, until, one by one, we sank on to the ground, overcome by sleep. . . .'

While Mercer and his friends dozed on the bare earth, Marshal Ney rested with Jérôme Bonaparte and other officers in some shelter he had found on the fringe of the battlefield. An aide-de-camp of Jérôme Bonaparte says:

> The wounded were attended to and bivouacs established. Unfortunately there were no supplies; the soldiers were spreading round the countryside, thieving in order not to starve. The Marshal invited Prince Jérôme to supper. The table was a plank resting on two empty barrels, and lighted by candles pushed into the necks of bottles.
> Night had fallen.
> We were beginning our frugal meal when Count Forbin-Jansen was brought in with the Emperor's order to march on Brye. . . .'[1]

This, presumably, was a copy of the order of 3.15 p.m., sent out by various routes. It would be interesting to know what Count Forbin-Jansen had been doing in the intervening time, but the subject of messengers remains obscure. Nor, unfortunately, is there any record of Ney's conversation with Jérôme Bonaparte. It may be that Ney was too exhausted to talk; or perhaps those present felt it wiser to keep what they heard to themselves. Ney certainly had cause for deep vexation of spirit. The instructions he had received so late in the day were confusing and out of keeping with the realities of the situation. Later, he had been deprived of troops on which he was counting, and had been sent impossible orders when engaged in battle. To terminate his own battle in order to take part in

---

[1] *Mémoires du Maréchal de Grouchy*. Vol. IV, pp. 103-4.

another was hardly possible. And if the decisive battle of the day was that against the Prussians, he had not been told so. On the contrary, it was easy for him to feel that it was he himself who had been fighting the decisive battle.[1] Although his words on this evening are lost, it is evident that his view of events, from the day's experiences, would be different from that of Napoleon, and also from that of history. His assessment of the situation is indicated in a letter which he wrote to Fouché ten days later.[2]

On the Ligny battlefield French soldiers sang and cheered as they sat round their bivouac fires, elated by their victory. At the centre, where the Guard had broken through, the rout of the enemy had appeared to be as decisive as at any of the renowned victories of the Empire, and those who had seen it believed the French triumph was complete.

The victory was, in fact, far from complete, Napoleon having kept with him insufficient numbers for the engagement with the Prussians. Yet he left the battlefield at 10 p.m. without giving orders for an organized pursuit of the enemy or for any reconnaissance.

Marshal Grouchy, expecting a pursuit of the Prussians to be ordered, was surprised to learn that Napoleon had gone without leaving instructions. He hastened after him and, catching up with him as he neared his headquarters, asked for orders. He was told that orders would be given to him the following morning.[3] Grouchy rode back to the battlefield where he sent out reconnaissances in the vicinity. At dawn or earlier he sent Generals Pajol and Exelmans with their cavalry to seek the enemy and obtain information,

---

[1] Houssaye takes seriously the claim of Colonel Baudus to have been sent by Napoleon to Ney with a duplicate of the supposed order calling d'Erlon to Ligny, and a verbal message that it was to be obeyed no matter what situation Marshal Ney was in. According to Baudus, Napoleon said: 'I do not attach great importance to what takes place today on his (Ney's) side. The affair is entirely where I am, for I wish to finish with the Prussian army. As for the Prince of the Moskowa, if he can do no better he must limit himself to containing the English.' This would have been useful information at mid-day, but since Baudus arrived at Quatre Bras with the message between 6.30 and 7 p.m., after Kellermann's attack, it was useless; for by now Marshal Ney had no choice of action remaining. What would have been the use of again ordering d'Erlon to countermarch? Moreover, d'Erlon was nearer to Napoleon than was Ney, and if Napoleon wanted the 1st Corps he had no need to plead with his marshal but might more usefully have sent Baudus with orders for d'Erlon. (Houssaye, *1815*, Vol. II. pp. 216-7).

[2] See appendix D.

[3] *Mémoires du Maréchal de Grouchy*, Vol. V. p. 115; Grouard, p. 266.

though whether he did so on his own initiative, or whether Napoleon had sent him instructions to this effect, is not certain. One account of the day's activities says that he called at headquarters at midnight,[1] but was unable to see Napoleon who had gone straight to bed; it may be that at this time he received orders to send out Pajol and Exelmans. He expected to receive at any moment orders for a far larger movement. He writes[2]:

> If Napoleon committed the fault, which indeed he did commit, of not pursuing the Prussians, of not immediately interposing his army between them and the English by manœuvring to his left, the two united enemy armies, taking a new line of operations from Quatre Bras to Brussels and Antwerp, would be able to face him with 200,000 men and 600 guns as early as the next day, 17 June. Such a plan was likely to be adopted by any general of reasonable intelligence; with a bold and active man like Blücher its adoption was certain. It was necessary, then, to prevent at any price, by means of a prompt, vigorous and relentless pursuit, a concentration of the beaten army allowing its reunion with the English.

Before sunrise, Grouchy was again at headquarters. But the order was that Napoleon was not to be disturbed. The Emperor, Grouchy was told, was not well.

The malady with which Napoleon was afflicted at this time was haemorrhoids. Lucien Bonaparte records that he was scarcely fit to mount his horse when he left Paris on the 12th; the trouble was becoming more serious, and he was now in the hands of his doctor, Larrey.[3] Opinion varies as to the effect this illness may have had on his conduct of the campaign. Grouard believes that the chief cause of the French defeat of 1815 lay in the weakening of Napoleon's faculties.[4] But most historians take the view that his mind was not affected by his illness. It is true that he had been ill before this and had not lost battles in consequence. He was an unhealthy man with a singularly detached and active brain; ill-health had perhaps acted as a spur to his ambitions throughout life, making him restless and dissatisfied with what he had. Many contemporaries, however,

---

[1] *Mémoires du Maréchal de Grouchy*, Vol. IV, pp. 145-6.   [2] Ibid., p. 35.
[3] James Kemble, in *Napoleon Immortal*, gives a most interesting and detailed account of Napoleon's health throughout his life, including his maladies during the hundred days.
[4] Grouard, *La Critique de la Campagne de 1815*, pp. 221, 225-6.

speak of the fits of irresistible drowsiness that would now overtake him at intervals, and this in itself denotes a general decline of his powers.

Grouchy waited, the rest of the army waited also. Marshal Ney had sent a report to Napoleon the previous evening at 10 p.m. in which he stated that the misunderstanding regarding d'Erlon's corps had deprived him of victory. But he himself had received no news of what had taken place on the Ligny battlefield. He could not leave his position with the English in strength before him, and could only await instructions. In the early hours of the morning he sent a further report to Soult, and at 6.30 he sent General Flahaut to Napoleon's headquarters to give an account of the previous day's events and ask for news of the battle against the Prussians.

There was nothing Ney could have done that morning without vigorous co-operation from the main army, although Thiers and other Bonapartists have criticized him harshly for not having attacked the English at an early hour and held them at Quatre Bras. Wellington's greatest danger had been an early, combined attack by the French, in which Ney might have attacked from the front and Napoleon borne down upon him from the Namur road, or cut off his retreat further north on the Brussels road. But Ney alone could not have held him at Quatre Bras; had Ney launched an early attack on him he would only have drawn off his troops behind a rearguard. Without assurance that Blücher had won the battle of Ligny (news he was not exactly expecting), the Duke would never have risked a stand at Quatre Bras.

Ney did the only thing that could reasonably be expected in the circumstances: he had his forces under arms at an early hour and waited for his orders.

Wellington received news of Blücher's defeat at about 7.30 a.m. He learnt that the Prussian army lay to the north of the Namur road and was withdrawing northwards on Wavre. He realized that the Namur road from Sombreffe to Quatre Bras was open to Napoleon and that he must retreat immediately. The question was, should he allow the soldiers time to have their breakfast? Baron Müffling was of the opinion that it would be safe to do so and remarked that, from what he had seen of the French army in Germany, it appeared they always prepared a meal in the morning and never moved before 10 a.m. Wellington much wished to avoid the dispiriting effects of a retreat combined with hunger, and the order was given that the troops were to have a hot meal. They would then retire on Mont St Jean, leaving the English cavalry and horse artillery behind as a rearguard.

The Prussians had, perforce, been alert and active throughout the night. The corps of Ziethen and Pirch I had rested for a time at Tilly and northwards, leaving their rearguard in possession of Brye; Thielemann's corps was at Sombreffe ready to cover the general retreat; and Bülow, who had come close to the battlefield by the evening, was directed to march to a village four miles east of Wavre. Ziethen and Pirch began their movement towards Wavre at dawn, quite unmolested by the French. Von Jagow quietly slipped out of Brye in their rear, and Thielemann left Sombreffe about the same time. Thus the Prussian army moved northwards, apart from a considerable stream of deserters who were hastening towards Namur.

These deserters, about 8,000 in number, were men who had broken at the centre after the Imperial Guard had breached the Prussian line at Ligny. Demoralized by the long ordeal in and around the blazing village, they could stand no more and had fled with one idea only in their heads: to escape from war, even though it meant starvation and wandering the earth as tramps. Pajol, instead of realizing that the disorderly stream of deserters represented the routed section of the army alone, wasted his time in pursuing them and capturing prisoners and guns which were of little use compared with the information regarding the movement on Wavre which he might have gathered. He sent a report to Grouchy in the early hours saying that he was following the enemy who was in full retreat on the road to Namur and Liège.

While Grouchy waited in Napoleon's antechamber, and Ney at Quatre Bras, Vandamme and Gérard waited on the Ligny battle-field. All were uneasy as the hours passed in inactivity. Napoleon had left the field the previous evening without communicating with the generals to whom he owed the victory. Vandamme and Gérard had spent themselves to the utmost. Vandamme on the left and Gérard at the centre had directed the severe battle; holding on hour after hour, outnumbered most of the time, they had shown impeccable courage, inspiring all beneath them and making possible the final victory. In such circumstances Napoleon had often bestowed the rank of marshal upon his triumphant though wearied generals on the field of battle, directly the victory had been gained. But neither Gérard nor Vandamme had received so much as a word of congratulation or thanks on this occasion. Napoleon had merely ridden off the field and all was silence and uncertainty.

On the Ligny battlefield the men were in their bivouacs still, and it is said that not only the generals but the private soldiers were becoming uneasy; they too felt that time was being lost. No one could relax on this field where the evidence of yesterday's slaughter was everywhere to be seen. All were anxious to pursue and destroy the enemy and to move on to Brussels, and men were asking one another why the Prussians were being given this long respite. Among the rank and file the rumour was going round that some treachery was on foot; but the higher officers openly criticized the Emperor. 'The Napoleon we used to know exists no longer,' said Vandamme; 'yesterday's success will lead to nothing.' Gérard, too, spoke of the delay as 'incomprehensible and irremediable'.[1]

At last, between seven and eight o'clock, orders came to the bivouacs: Napoleon was coming – to review the troops!

[1] Charras, *Histoire de la Campagne de 1815*, p. 212.

11

Napoleon's inactivity on the morning of the 17th; Grouchy sent after the Prussians; Wellington's retreat; The French pursuit

Marshal Grouchy, still waiting for his orders, was told at about half-past seven that Napoleon was up and was going to visit the battlefield. Grouchy was instructed to follow him there. There was still time to kill, however; Napoleon was having breakfast and had to consider Ney's report which had just been brought in by General Flahaut, and also the report from Pajol brought early in the morning by Grouchy.

Presently Napoleon, having studied Ney's report and listened to Flahaut's account of events at Quatre Bras and his request for news and orders, gave detailed instructions to Marshal Soult who replied to Ney as follows:

Monsieur le maréchal,

I learn from General Flahaut, who has just arrived, that you are unaware of yesterday's results. I believe, however, that I notified you of the victory gained by the Emperor. The Prussian army has been routed. General Pajol is pursuing it on the roads to Namur and Liège. Already we have taken several thousand prisoners and thirty guns. Our troops conducted themselves well: a charge of six battalions of the Guard, and the service squadrons of General Delort's cavalry division, pierced the enemy line, causing the greatest disorder in his ranks and carrying the position.

The Emperor is going to the mill at Brye, close to the high road running from Namur to Quatre Bras; it is therefore not possible for the English army to act on your front; if such a thing should happen, the Emperor would march directly upon them by the road to Quatre Bras while you attacked them from the front with your divisions, which must now be united, and they would be destroyed in an instant. Therefore, inform his Majesty of the exact position of the divisions, and of all that is going on in front of you.

His Majesty was grieved to learn that you did not succeed yesterday; the divisions acted in isolation, and you therefore sustained losses.

If the corps of Counts Reille and d'Erlon had been together, not a soldier of the English corps that came to attack you would have escaped; if Count d'Erlon had executed the movement on Saint-Amand ordered by the Emperor, the Prussian army would have been totally destroyed and we should perhaps have taken 30,000 prisoners.

The corps of Generals Vandamme and Gérard and the Imperial Guard were kept together all the time; one lays oneself open to reverses when detachments are jeopardized.

The Emperor hopes and desires that your seven divisions of infantry will be well formed and united, occupying as a whole less than a league of territory, so that they are well in hand for use if necessary.

It is his Majesty's intention that you should take position at Quatre Bras, according to the orders you have been given.[1] But if by some unlikely chance this cannot be done, report in detail immediately, and the Emperor will move across, as I have said. If, on the contrary, there is only a rearguard, attack it and take up your position.

The present day is needed for terminating this operation and replenishing munitions, rallying isolated soldiers and bringing in detachments. Give orders accordingly, and make sure all the wounded receive attention and are sent to the rear. Complaints have been made that the ambulances are not doing their duty.

The famous partisan, Lutzow, who has been taken, said that the Prussian army is lost, and that Blücher has for a second time imperilled the Prussian monarchy,

The Chief of Staff,
Duc de Dalmatie.

It would be difficult to reconcile this letter with the Napoleonic legend which has it that Ney ruined the situation that morning by his delays, hesitations and disregard of orders, and it is not surprising that it failed to stimulate him into any dramatic action. What, indeed, was he supposed to do? Apparently he was to attack Quatre Bras if it was only held by a rearguard; otherwise he was to inform Napoleon and await co-operation from Ligny. If Ney became hesitant, he perhaps took his tone from this vague and rambling letter which seemed to have no particular purpose and suggested no kind of urgency.

It is evident that, at the time this letter was sent, Napoleon believed

---

[1] Orders given in Napoleon's letter of the previous morning. (See p. 132.)

the Prussians were in full flight in the direction of Namur and Liège. As for Wellington's army, he seems to have discounted it altogether. Apparently it had fled even more precipitately than that of Blücher. The day was therefore to be spent in the replenishment of stores while the soldiers rested in their bivouacs.

Before leaving Fleurus for the Ligny battlefield, Napoleon sent a reconnoitring party to Quatre Bras and ordered one of Lobau's infantry divisions to join Pajol on the Namur road.

He entered his carriage, a heavy *berline*, shortly before nine o'clock, and as it rattled out of the paved courtyard a cavalcade of smart staff officers and other important persons fell in behind it. Marshal Grouchy, unable to approach Napoleon uninvited, could do no more than join them. The carriage took the road to Saint-Amand, but once fairly out in the country it swayed and rolled alarmingly over the ruts made by the military traffic of the previous day, and the Emperor abandoned it to mount a horse. Grouchy, taking advantage of the halt, now ventured to ask him for orders.

Napoleon was not pleased. 'I will give you my orders when I think fit,' he snapped.[1] And he rode on at leisure, talking to his suite and ignoring the presumptuous marshal.

On reaching Saint-Amand, he rode up and down the lanes and streets; gradually the wounded were being removed on carts. The dead and wounded lay piled up together on all sides, blood still flowing from them. The artillery had rolled over both dead and dying in the principal streets with appalling results. Napoleon lingered here though he had enemies to pursue, at one point waiting for fifteen minutes while a way was cleared for him to continue his tour. The village of Ligny was even more choked with the dead and the dying, and much of it was still in flames. Here in an area smaller than the Gardens of the Tuileries lay 4,000 dead men. Since the French wounded were being taken off first, large numbers of Prussians lay about. Napoleon spoke to some of them sympathetically enough, sometimes ordering brandy to be given to them; his command was that all should receive immediate attention and be cared for in the same way as the French; but the ambulances were inadequate, and there was little hope for the badly wounded.

Houssaye records that Napoleon noticed a Prussian officer who

---

[1] Grouchy, *Observations*, p. 11.

was terribly mutilated, lying where he had fallen the previous day. He called up a peasant who stood looking on and said in solemn tones: 'Do you believe in hell?' The alarmed peasant stammered an affirmative reply. 'Very well,' said Napoleon. 'If you don't want to go to hell, take care of this wounded man whom I entrust to you; otherwise God, who commands us to be charitable, will have you burnt.'

Without doubt this sprang from a desire to help a fallen man; yet one may wonder which of the two victims of Napoleon's gamble for power was the more unfortunate, the Prussian officer or the wretched peasant whose home was burnt out and whose family faced starvation. What could such a man do for a soldier dying of ghastly wounds, destitute as he was, helpless in the face of disaster and now held responsible?

Having visited the villages, Napoleon rode on to the *moulin de Bussy*, dismounted and reviewed his troops. Before each regiment he paused to say a few encouraging words to the officers, enquiring about the losses sustained and chatting with the soldiers. He was cheered in such resounding tones that the noise reached the rear of the retreating Prussians, still in Tilly.

The review over, Napoleon talked for some time with his staff officers and others accompanying him. Uppermost in his mind was not the threat from Blücher and Wellington, but the state of affairs at home. He examined the new form of government imposed upon him and discussed the intrigues of its members and the general prospects of French politics. Some of those present admired his powers of detachment at such a moment; others were merely worried as time passed by in inactivity. Grouchy still awaited his orders, but did not dare to suggest again that they should be given to him. In any case, it was now too late to pursue and disorganize the Prussians.

From time to time messages were brought to Napoleon. The first was the report which Ney had sent at 6.30 a.m.; it had reached headquarters after Napoleon had left and had been sent on by Soult. This brought the information that the English were still in position at Quatre Bras. Several columns of infantry and cavalry could be seen which seemed likely to take the offensive; if they did so, said Ney, he would hold on to the last and endeavour to repulse them until the Emperor sent orders.[1] Shortly after, the reconnoitring party sent out by Napoleon returned, also reporting that the English were at Quatre Bras. Information arrived from Pajol, still in pursuit of Prussian fugitives on the Namur road, and from Exelmans who reported that Prussians had been seen in masses at Gembloux.

The information from Quatre Bras suggested that Wellington's army still occupied that point, or had done so until recently. Napoleon therefore decided to move across to Ney's front, though even now he took his time. He ordered Lobau's corps (apart from the division sent to join Pajol), Subervie's light cavalry and the Imperial Guard to march as far as Marbais, where they were to await further orders. It was now about eleven o'clock, and a whole hour passed before he sent instructions to Ney.

About 9 a.m. the Duke of Wellington and Baron Müffling had received a message from Gneisenau reporting that the Prussians would be able to concentrate that night at Wavre. In reply the Duke told him he intended to fight a defensive battle on the plateau of Mont St. Jean, to the south of the forest of Soignies, provided Blücher could send him one of his army corps in support. A Prussian officer rode off with the message, to which the reply was to come during the night that Blücher would bring not one corps but his whole army to join in the battle.

Captain Mercer has described the morning scene at Quatre Bras. It was warm and fine after a clear sunrise. After waking very early he employed the time in watching the skirmishing that went on incessantly in and around the wood of Bossu. Then news came that a retreat had been ordered:

> At first everyone, exulting in the success of yesterday . . . anticipated, now our army was united, nothing less than an immediate attack on the French position. We were sadly knocked down, then, when the certainty of our retreat became known. It was in vain we were told the retreat was only a manœuvre of concentration; the most gloomy anticipations pervaded every breast.

Mercer received his orders for the day from Major McDonald, who first directed him to retire, but then added: 'Major Ramsay's

[1] Lachouque, Le Secret de Waterloo, p. 166.

troop will remain in the rear with the cavalry; but I will not conceal from you that it falls to your turn to do this if you choose it.'

The Major looked rather conscience-stricken as he made this avowal, so, to relieve him, I begged he would give the devil his due and me mine. Accordingly all the others marched off, and as nothing was likely to take place immediately, we amused ourselves by looking on at what was doing.

There was plenty of noise; the fire of skirmishers increased, and some infantry men were killing a pig from one of the farms with their bayonets, making sure of an evening meal.

All this time our retreat was going on very quietly. The corps at Quatre Bras had retired early in the morning and had been replaced by others from the left, and this continued constantly – every corps halting for a time on the ground near Quatre Bras until another from the left arrived, these moving off on the great road to Brussels, ceding the ground to the newcomers.'

The Duke remained with his rearguard, frequently raising his glass to scan the French bivouacs; for every half hour that passed by without an attack from the French he was most thankful.

After Napoleon had sent off troops to Marbais, he at last gave orders to Grouchy, telling him to pursue the Prussians with the right wing of the army. He would have under him the corps of Vandamme and Gérard, a division from Lobau's corps and the cavalry of Pajol and Exelmans, in all about 33,000 men. Napoleon told Grouchy that he himself was about to join Ney and deal with the English, and that his headquarters would be at Quatre Bras.

Thus the army was again to be divided, the two sections being widely separated. The instructions were that Grouchy was to proceed to Gembloux, reconnoitre towards Namur and Maestricht, directions which Napoleon believed the retreating army would be taking, and pursue the enemy. The report received during the morning from Exelmans regarding Prussian masses at Gembloux had thrown a new light on the situation and, although Napoleon persisted in his original expectation that the Prussians would retire on their base, he realized he must be prepared for an attempt on

Blücher's part to unite with Wellington. He told Grouchy to discover the intention of the enemy and to keep him informed. Grouchy was little pleased with his orders now that he had them. He had been impatient to pursue the Prussians at dawn, but he believed it was now too late and was convinced it would be better for Napoleon to keep his army together. By this time, indeed, Ziethen and Pirch had reached the environs of Wavre by way of Tilly and Mont St Guibert; in directing Grouchy on Gembloux, Napoleon was sending him far outside the line these two generals had taken. Grouchy's mission has the appearance of being no less hazardous than puzzling, for with his two army corps, wearied by the heavy fighting at Ligny, he was being sent in isolation to risk meeting the whole Prussian army. Thielemann's corps, which had been observed at Gembloux, had been let off lightly the previous day and was in good fighting order; Bülow's corps, which had not fought at all, was coming along the Roman road from Hannut and in itself was almost as large as Grouchy's entire force. About 100,000 Prussians were somewhere in the region; and Grouchy, who had first to discover their whereabouts, was expected also to unmask their plans and safeguard the main army from interference by them. He felt unequal to such a task and endeavoured, so he tells us, to persuade Napoleon to adopt another plan. He reminded him that many hours had now passed since the Prussians had begun their retreat, and that he could but follow their rearguard. His own forces were widely dispersed, and since they had not been warned to prepare for action some time must pass before the pursuit of the enemy could begin. He said that he did not believe it was possible to slow down Blücher's retreat at this stage, nor did he think that with his 33,000 men he could complete the defeat of the Prussian army. 'Furthermore,' he writes, 'I ventured to point out to the Emperor some of the strategical reasons for my thinking it undesirable that he should send me outside the circle of operations of the main body of the army with which he was going to fight the English. . . .'[1]

These observations were useless and Grouchy was ordered with severity to do as he was told. But events were soon to prove that he was right. If the Prussians were retreating on Namur as Napoleon

[1] *Mémoires du Maréchal de Grouchy*, Vol. IV, pp. 45-6.

felt persuaded was the case, what need was there to follow them since they would be well out of the way while he fought the English? Had Grouchy marched with the main army, keeping between it and the roads from the east, he could have fought off the Prussians from within if they made an offensive return, and this would have been far more useful than following them at a distance up to Wavre.

Having protested in vain, Grouchy prepared to obey his orders as quickly as possible.[1] Sending instructions to Vandamme by messenger, he rode to Gérard's headquarters to give him his orders personally. On his way, he ran into Soult who was about to rejoin Napoleon at the *moulin de Bussy*; he had a short conversation with him and Houssaye records that, after he had gone, Soult remarked to one of his aides-de-camp: 'It is a mistake to detach such a considerable force from the army when it is going to march against the English. The Prussians are in such a state after their defeat that it would have been enough to send a small body of infantry with the cavalry of Exelmans to follow and observe them.'

Soult evidently believed at this time that the Prussians had been routed (he had remained at Fleurus when Napoleon went to the battlefield, so would not yet know of Exelmans' report); but his criticism of the detachment of Grouchy's force shows that not all Napoleon's generals approved of his tendency to divide the army. Wellington's army had to be faced, yet Napoleon thought he could get the better of it with 74,000 men. This was the number he had reserved for the purpose. He had lost about 11,000 men on the 16th; Grouchy was taking rather more than 30,000, and he was leaving a reserve of another 8,000 behind in the Charleroi area.

When Soult reached Napoleon he was ordered to write the following despatch to Ney.

> Before Ligny,
> June 17th, Mid-day.

Monsieur le Maréchal,
    The Emperor has sent an infantry corps and the Imperial Guard to take position in front of Marbais. His Majesty instructs me to tell

---

[1] Grouchy, charged with wasting his time by the Bonapartists, was to reach Wavre, over twenty miles away, in twenty-four hours in exceptionally difficult conditions.

you that he desires you to attack the enemy at Quatre Bras so as to drive them from their position, while the corps at Marbais seconds your operations. His Majesty is about to leave for Marbais and urgently awaits your reports.

While Soult was thus occupied, the infantry of Wellington's rearguard began to retire; this was Alten's division which had been left at Quatre Bras in support of Uxbridge's cavalry. The Duke looked on with considerable relief. 'Well,' he said, 'there is the last of the infantry gone, and I don't care now.'

It was by this time very quiet at Quatre Bras. Captain Mercer noted the gradual cessation of gunfire as skirmishing ceased, and presently he found himself quite alone with his troop beside the farmhouse of Quatre Bras.

Thus solitary, as it were, I had ample leisure to contemplate the scene of desolation around me, so strangely at variance with the otherwise smiling landscape. Everywhere mementoes of yesterday's bloody struggle met the eye – the corn trampled down, and the ground, particularly in the plain, plentifully besprinkled with bodies of the slain. Just in front of the farm of Quatre Bras there was a fearful scene of slaughter – Highlanders and cuirassiers lying thickly strewn about; the latter appeared to have charged up the Charleroi road, on which, and immediately bordering it, they lay most numerously.

Some time later Captain Mercer rode into the surrounding woods and there came across a young man lying dead, close to his slain horse. Not a particle of clothing remained on him to indicate his nationality.

This victim of war was a youth of fair form . . . his countenance, even in death, was beautiful. . . . I know not why, but the rencontre with this solitary corpse had a wonderful effect on my spirits – far different from what I felt when gazing on the heaps that encumbered the field beyond. Seldom have I experienced such despondency – such heart-sinking – as when standing over this handsome form thus despoiled, neglected, and about to become a prey to wolves and carrion crows. . . .

All the senselessness of war was here symbolized, the ambitions of the mighty leading the humble in their train, the destruction of the young, the anguish of parents, the harsh, incredible indifference of those not immediately concerned, personified by some thieving peasant. The myriad dead and dying on the battlefield only stunned the senses; but this one youth lying peacefully on the warm earth raised the mind to the plain truth of what was taking place.

An aide-de-camp rode off with Napoleon's mid-day despatch to Ney; it cannot have arrived much before Napoleon himself reached Quatre Bras.[1]

Napoleon set out for Quatre Bras at about 12.15 p.m., travelling in his carriage. He reached Marbais shortly after one o'clock and paused there for some time, partly, no doubt, in order to take a meal. One important thing he failed to do: to reconnoitre the roads from this place up to Wavre. Tilly is less than a mile from Marbais so that even though such an essential reconnaissance had not been made early in the day, it might have been made now. He found waiting for him the troops he had sent off at eleven o'clock, and with them he eventually continued on his way. About two o'clock, being within a mile of Quatre Bras, he left his carriage to mount his horse, Désirée. All was quiet. Wellington's army, apart from the rearguard cavalry, was now far away. Napoleon is said to have waited impatiently for the sound of gunfire, astonished that Ney had not already joined battle with Wellington. This astonishment of Napoleon's haunts the annals of the legend and blame is heaped upon Ney.[2] But it was Napoleon himself who had lost time in inessential activities such as reviewing the troops; it was he who had miscalculated the situation, and now arrived to engage the English when only a small rearguard remained in the skilful hands of Lord Uxbridge.

Arranging his troops in order of battle, Napoleon now rode forward towards the crossroads. The cavalry of Milhaud led the way, followed by the 6th Corps and the Guard, with other cavalry regiments to the right and left. At the same time he sent Baron

[1] Speaking of the halt Napoleon made at Marbais, Houssaye says: 'Moreover, the halt was necessitated by the time it would take the officer carrying Soult's order (order sent at mid-day) to reach Ney at Frasnes, by way of the Roman road and Villers-Perwin. The Emperor had wished at first to second Ney's attack (see the order in question) and not to forestall it. . . . Houssaye, *1815*, Vol. II, p. 263, note 1.

[2] Houssaye speaks of Ney's apathy and negligence. Colonel Becke describes his inactivity on the morning of the 17th as a 'ruinous blunder.'

Marbot's hussars to Frasnes to establish contact with Ney. As a finishing touch to the whole unfortunate situation, the hussars, sweeping down on the Marshal's position, opened fire on some red-coated lancers on Ney's right, mistaking them for British troops. They found Ney's army in movement. Either Ney had now received his orders, or his scouts had reported the arrival of the main army along the Namur road. His forces were advancing on Quatre Bras in three or four bodies, and Lord Uxbridge awaited them.

Seeing that Wellington's army had gone, Napoleon fell into transports of anger and forthwith cast the blame upon Ney. 'On a perdu la France,' he said to d'Erlon.

He now ordered an attack on Wellington's rearguard, a futile measure indeed, but there was little else he could do. Cuirassiers, chasseurs and lancers rode off at a brisk trot and he himself galloped ahead to set them on their way.

Wellington's retreat had been conducted in a steady and orderly manner. His main concern had been to get his army beyond the village of Genappe through which the Brussels road wound steeply, and which was traversed by the river Dyle. This had long since been accomplished, and Wellington himself had recently ridden off and had paused for a meal at the village inn, Le Roi d'Espagne.[1]

Lord Uxbridge was sitting on the ground with Mercer and an aide-de-camp as Napoleon's army arrived from Marbais; he was watching the French position before Frasnes with the aid of his telescope and discussing with his companions the surprising inactivity of the French. Sir Ormsby Vandeleur's light dragoons were a short distance behind, and Sir Hussey Vivian's hussars were far away to the left. The morning had been hot and sunny; but great banks of cloud had been rising in the north-west during the previous hour or two and now the sky was overcast, although the high plain towards Marbais over which Napoleon's troops were marching was still in the sunlight. An aide-de-camp came up to report the arrival of cavalry from the direction of Gembloux, and Lord Uxbridge jumped on his horse and rushed down the valley to meet them, mistakenly believing they were Prussians. Mercer, left without

[1] Houssaye, 1815, Vol. II, p. 323.

orders and seeing the French advancing on two sides, decided to draw back to support Vandeleur by turning his guns on the Namur road and opening fire on the French cavalry as soon as they were close enough. 'I thought I could retire in sufficient time through his intervals to leave the ground free for him to charge,' he says. The movement was promptly executed; but scarcely had his men unlimbered the guns when Sir Ormsby Vandeleur dashed up indignantly and cried: 'What are you doing here, sir? You encumber my front, and we shall not be able to charge. Take your guns away, sir; instantly, I say – take them away.'

It was in vain that Captain Mercer tried to explain his intentions. Vandeleur wanted none of his assistance in meeting the enemy and continued to order him from the field. Mercer was preparing to obey when Lord Uxbridge returned, having discovered his mistake. At once the scene changed.

'Captain Mercer, are you loaded?' he called out.

'Yes, my lord.'

'Then give them a round as they rise the hill, and retire as quickly as possible. Light dragoons, threes right; at a trot, march!'

This last command was for Sir Ormsby who had to retire crestfallen. It was Sir Hussey Vivian who was called on to charge at the rear, and Mercer faced the hazards of firing on the advancing French before making his escape. He was to be well rewarded, as it happened, for the perils of his situation, for he was to see Napoleon in person.

'They are just coming up the hill,' Lord Uxbridge was saying. 'Let them get well up before you fire. Do you think you can retire quick enough afterwards?'

'I am sure of it, my lord.'

'Very well, then, keep a good look-out and point your guns well.'

Mercer describes his glimpse of Napoleon:

I had often longed to see Napoleon, that mighty man of war – that astonishing genius who had filled the world with his renown. Now I saw him, and there was a degree of sublimity in the interview rarely equalled. The sky had become overcast since the morning, and at this moment presented a most extraordinary appearance. Large isolated masses of thunder cloud, of the deepest, almost inky black, their lower edges hard and strongly defined, lagging down, as if momentarily about to burst, hung suspended over us, involving our position and everything on it in deep and gloomy obscurity; whilst the distant hill lately occupied by the French army still lay bathed in brilliant sunshine. Lord Uxbridge was yet speaking, when a single horseman, immediately followed by several others, mounted the plateau I had left at a gallop, their dark figures thrown forward in strong relief from the illuminated distance, making them appear much nearer to us than they really were. For an instant they pulled up and regarded us, when several squadrons, coming rapidly on the plateau, Lord Uxbridge cried out, 'Fire! – fire!' and, giving them a general discharge, we quickly limbered up to retire, as they dashed forward supported by some horse-artillery guns, which opened upon us ere we could complete the manœuvre, but without much effect, for the only one touched was the servant of Major Whinyates, who was wounded in the leg by the splinter of a howitzer shell.

The sudden clamour of gunfire, which had broken a tense silence, was followed by a violent clap of thunder immediately overhead, and simultaneously there came a blinding flash of lightning. Siborne describes it thus:

The concussion seemed instantly to rebound through the still atmosphere, and communicate, as an electric spark, with the heavily charged mass above. A most awfully loud thunder-clap burst forth, immediately succeeded by a rain which has never, probably, been exceeded in violence even within the tropics. In a very few minutes the ground became perfectly saturated, so much so that it was quite impracticable for any rapid movement of the cavalry.

The charge Vivian had been preparing was now impossible, and he followed Vandeleur with his hussars northwards towards Genappe while Captain Mercer raced off at the rear with men, guns and horses, closely pursued by Subervie and Domon. As often happens in moments of extreme danger, Mercer was sharply aware of his surroundings. He writes:

The sublimity of the scene was inconceivable. Flash succeeded flash, and the peals of thunder were long and tremendous; whilst, as if in mockery of the elements, the French guns still sent forth their feebler glare and now scarcely audible reports – their cavalry dashing on at a headlong pace, adding their shouts to the uproar. We galloped for our lives through the storm, striving to gain the enclosures about the houses of the hamlets, Lord Uxbridge urging us on, crying, 'Make haste! – make haste! for God's sake gallop, or you will be taken!'

Having begun the pursuit of Mercer and Vivian, Napoleon fell back to order d'Erlon to follow the French cavalry with all possible speed. The 2nd Corps under Reille was to follow that of d'Erlon, while Lobau fell in behind them and the Guard brought up the rear, flanked by the remaining cavalry.

Thus the whole of the French army, apart from that left in the region of Charleroi or sent off with Grouchy, was to be strung out in one interminable line on the Brussels road. Napoleon now galloped forward again with a cavalry escort and a battery of horse artillery to put himself at the head of the column. It was now about half-past three; the torrential rain was rapidly chilling the hot summer air and reducing visibility to a few yards.

At this time Grouchy, at the cross-roads near Sombreffe, watched the head of Vandamme's long column arriving through the storm. A despatch was brought to him from Exelmans confirming the presence of large numbers of Prussians at Gembloux; Pajol again reported that the Prussians were retreating towards Namur and Louvain. Grouchy ordered Vandamme's corps to march on to Gembloux; Gérard's corps was following. The road to Gembloux was poor at the best of times; now it was reduced to a slough of deep, heavy mud. The engineers struggled to keep the artillery moving; the infantry, ordered to cross fields, moved with painful slowness, soaked to the skin, stumbling, cursing, losing their shoes in the mud.

By the time Mercer and his troop reached Genappe they had thrown off the French; they crossed the bridge and slackened their pace as they ascended the narrow, winding street. The small town was deserted, and every shutter closed; but for the sound of the rain beating down and pouring in cascades from the roofs it was silent. The troop reached the top of the steep street and rode on beyond the town; but they soon came upon the cavalry drawn up in two lines across the road. The rearguard infantry were not far ahead and Lord Uxbridge had decided to make a stand while they gained ground. Captain Mercer was ordered to turn and make his way back to the bottom of the town with his guns and his men. Down there he found that the French had caught up; he placed his guns in a field and was soon exchanging shots with a French battery. French lancers poured into the town; the English hussars charged them but could not drive them back.

It was now that Napoleon reached the head of his column and threw himself into the fight with considerable vigour. Quickly establishing his horse artillery, he directed its fire himself upon Uxbridge's hussars. His voice loud with anger, he cried out: 'Fire! Fire! They're the English.' Like everyone else, he was soaked to the skin. Contemporary accounts stress his drenched condition which struck the imagination with its incongruity; for when men make an idol of a powerful man they tend to feel surprised that he cannot stop the tides or hold off the rain. Napoleon's costume, unique, unmistakable and seemingly inseparable from his personality, was now sadly awry. The famous greatcoat, made of a lightweight grey cloth for summer wear, flapped about his legs; his hat, that headgear curious even in military circles, now hung limply round his ears, and his leather boots, not unlike those we now call Wellingtons, were heavy with mud.

A stiff fight took place which lasted for some time, and there were casualties on both sides. Eventually Lord Uxbridge drew off the hussars, charged with his heavy cavalry and the Life Guards, and at last succeeded in driving the French back. The rearguard again hastened northwards, Captain Mercer's troop on the Brussels road and the cavalry regiments across the fields. On and on they went, now well in front of the French, and eventually they passed a few houses by the roadside, a pleasant inn with a garden being prominent among them. This inn was La Belle Alliance, soon to become famous. It had been so named by the local people because of the matrimonial adventures of the inn-keeper's wife, who in marrying for the fourth time had made herself mistress of the place. This group of houses was at the southern side of the field of Waterloo. Captain Mercer hurried by with his troop and crossed a broad, undulating plain. On the far side he came upon a gravel pit from which he decided to fire another round against the French. Taking possession of it, he loaded his guns and, as soon as French horsemen came in view, opened fire at a range of about 1,200 yards.

Greatly to his surprise, a heavy cannonade began in his rear at the same time, and he realized he had caught up with the main army. Sir Thomas Picton's brigade, hidden by a high hedge, was just behind the gravel pit. Wellington's army was in position, apart from a single brigade on its way from Ghent, and each regiment had gone to the place appointed for it in the action expected to take place the following day.

It was 6.30 p.m. and the rain had almost ceased, though heavy clouds hung overhead and a chilly mist shrouded the landscape. Napoleon had just reached La Belle Alliance and paused to reconnoitre the position. Mercer's guns were still firing and a shot fell near him. Anxious to discover the strength of the forces he discerned across the valley, Napoleon now opened a heavy fire on Wellington's line. Wellington at once replied with so many guns that Napoleon realized his enemy had halted for the night with his whole army. His question answered, he soon ceased firing and the English did the same.

Mercer's troop was ordered to bivouac for the night, and they retired to an adjacent farm where they established themselves in an orchard. It was a gloomy evening and at seven o'clock there was little light; the ground was waterlogged. There seemed no likelihood that the French would attack that night since their vanguard only had so far reached the scene and the weather hampered every movement. The French army was stretched out for miles on the Brussels road with the rear not yet past Quatre Bras. Many hours must pass before it could assemble. It may be thought surprising that Wellington did not attack and destroy the advance guard while it was thus vulnerable; but possibly the condition of the ground and the weariness of his troops prevented it. Whatever the reason, the whole army now sought rest as best it could.

The Duke retired behind his line for a few hours, his headquarters being at the village of Waterloo. His forces were disposed for the coming battle, 67,000 strong with 156 guns; another 17,000 men and thirty guns under Prince Frederick of the Netherlands were guarding the Mons road between Braine-le-Comte and Hal. Wellington was still of the opinion that Napoleon would manœuvre in that direction. Unaware that Napoleon had divided his army by detaching a large force under Grouchy, he supposed he would have the whole of the

Army of the North to fight and did not feel confident of victory without Prussian aid. The night was an anxious one as he awaited news from Blücher. If Blücher were unable to assist him he must continue his retreat, keeping clear of the French until he and Blücher were able to unite. And this would not be easy since Napoleon would advance at the least sign of a backward movement. Fortunately, at 2 a.m. a message came from the Prussian headquarters promising assistance the following day. Bülow's corps would march towards Mont St. Jean (the village immediately behind Wellington's line) at daybreak, followed by the corps of Pirch II, while the corps of Ziethen and Thielemann would he held ready to come in as needed. 'The exhaustion of the troops,' Blücher said, 'some of whom have not yet arrived, does not allow of my beginning my movement any earlier.' The question was settled. Wellington would hold his ground.

Napoleon made the farm of Le Caillou his headquarters. It was close to the Brussels road, and some distance to the rear of his line.

Wellington's troops had to bivouac on the ground where they would fight the following day, mostly in the open cornfields from which it was not safe to move them. Those French troops who had reached the area did the same. D'Erlon's corps had arrived, but Reille's men bivouacked round about Genappe, where Prince Jérôme and other generals dined at the *Roi d'Espagne*.

The bulk of Wellington's army had arrived before the storm broke and had been able to establish themselves and light their fires while the ground was dry; the Forest of Soignies being just to their rear, they had all the wood they needed and their fires blazed cheerfully. But the rearguard fared badly, for by the time they reached the field all the best positions were taken and the ground was like a bog. Captain Mercer and a few of his officers tried to sleep in a tent, rolled in wet blankets; they had eaten nothing since the previous evening and found nothing to eat now. For a time they lay in uncomplaining silence; it was raining heavily again and water poured through the tent in streams. Eventually, the misery of their situation being unendurable, they rose, one by one, and went outside. Some of the privates, they found, were very much better off, sitting round a couple of fires, 'smoking their short pipes in something like comfort'. They borrowed a few blazing sticks and made a fire for themselves; soon they were sitting before it, smoking cigars. 'Dear weed! what comfort, what consolation dost thou not impart to the wretched!' Mercer writes. 'With thee a hovel becomes a palace. What a stock of patience is there not enveloped in one of thy brown leaves! And thus we sat enjoying ourselves, puffing forth into the damp night our streams of fragrant smoke; being able now deliberately to converse on what had been, and probably would be.'

So the night passed in the English lines. A space of only 1,000 to 1,500 yards separated the foremost groups of the two armies. French troops bivouacked in a line stretching from the village of Plancenoit on the south-east of the field to the farm of *Mon Plaisir* on the south-west. The Guard bivouacked at Glabais, the only village between Genappe and the battlefield. Reille's corps, as has been said, was near Genappe.

Rarely can an army have been more miserable, although countless armies must have been equally miserable in their time. Contemporary descriptions of what some of the men endured make painful reading. Many of the infantry were bare-footed, having lost their boots in the deep and heavy mud they had been struggling through for hours. For the majority there was no food at all, and no possibility of making a fire. There was nowhere to lie down; some dozed standing in groups and leaning against each other; some of the cavalry remained on their horses and leaning forward slept. Those not too exhausted wandered about the flooded countryside, looking for dwellings to break into. Grouchy's men were at this time in much the same plight. Vandamme and Gérard reached Gembloux by 7 p.m. and prepared to halt there for the night. No one yet knew where the Prussians were, and Grouchy received conflicting reports in the early evening, though there were indications now that they were at Wavre.

12

Eve of the Battle of Waterloo; Wellington's troops in position; Napoleon's breakfast; Review of the French troops

Having given orders for the placing of his troops, Napoleon retired to the farm of Le Caillou where he dried himself before a good fire. The farmer and his family had fled. The Imperial servants prepared Napoleon's camp bed with its green satin draperies and gold tassels; the chef and his assistants were cooking a meal in the kitchen; upstairs rooms were being made ready for pages and staff officers, and bundles of straw arranged for others in the outhouses and barns.

After dinner Napoleon studied the messages which were continually arriving. A courier from Paris brought news of political events at home; to this he paid close attention, dictating letters to be taken back immediately to the capital. He paid less attention to information brought by General Milhaud at nine o'clock although, had he known it, it was of greater immediate importance. The General reported that, as he was marching from Marbais to Quatre Bras, a scouting party on his right had observed a column of Prussian cavalry going from Tilly to Wavre. Marshal Soult was so concerned by this news that he urged Napoleon to recall a part of Grouchy's force; but Napoleon would not listen.[1] He had given the Prussians a good beating the previous day, and felt that he had the military situation well in hand. He was far more concerned by the state of home politics. The despatches from Paris told him of a particularly stormy session in the Chamber of Deputies the previous day, and he was preoccupied by the need for humbling members of parliament rather than by impending battles. An added annoyance was that, in the midst of the despatches, was an anonymous letter threatening him with doom.[2]

At 10 p.m. Marshal Grouchy wrote to Napoleon:

Sire,

I have the honour to inform you that I have occupied Gembloux, with my cavalry at Sauvenière. The enemy, with

[1] Houssaye, *1815*, Vol. II, p. 278, note 1.   [2] Houssaye, Ibid., p. 283, note 3.

a strength of about 30,000 men, continue their retreat. . . . It appears from all reports that on arriving at Sauvenière they divided into three columns; one must have taken the road to Wavre, passing by Sart-à-Walhain, while another appears to be directed on Perwès. One may perhaps infer that one part is going to join Wellington, the centre under Blücher to retire on Liège, another column with artillery having retreated on Namur. General Exelmans has orders to send six cavalry squadrons on Sart-à-Walhain this evening and three on Perwès. Acting on their reports, if the mass of the Prussians is retiring on Wavre I will follow them to prevent their reaching Brussels and separate them from Wellington. If, on the other hand, my information proves that the main force has marched on Perwès, I will pursue them by way of that town. . . .'[1]

A cavalry officer set out in pouring rain to take the letter to Napoleon's headquarters, believed to be at Quatre Bras.[2] He had

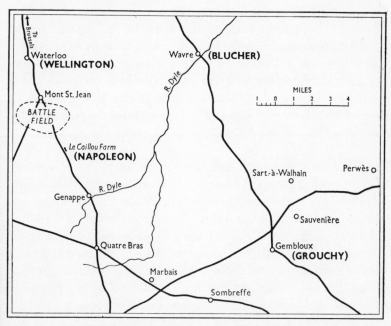

[1] Letter as quoted by Charras, *Histoire de la Campagne de 1815*, pp. 221-2. The version given in Grouchy's memoirs is rather differently worded but is identical in substance.

[2] Despite Napoleon's wish that Grouchy should keep in close touch with him, it appears that no attempt was made to inform Grouchy when the main army moved northwards up the Brussels road.

instructions not to return without a reply. It was midnight when he reached Quatre Bras to find a scene of desolation; corpses lay on all sides and wounded men called for help in vain. Finding that the Imperial headquarters had moved on, he took the road to Genappe along which groups of weary men were still marching, preferring to drive themselves along beneath the dripping trees rather than join those who were attempting to rest in the adjoining fields.

At this hour Blücher, at Wavre, had all his four army corps assembled close at hand. Discipline and organization had enabled the Prussians to accomplish that which Napoleon had dismissed as impossible. Thielemann's corps, which had reached Wavre at about 9 p.m., had been slowed down by the deluge to a pace of two kilometres an hour. There is little justice, therefore, in the charges levelled by historians against Grouchy of a reprehensible slowness of movement. Houssaye is outraged by the length of time Grouchy took to reach Gembloux and by the fact that he remained there overnight; but Grouchy was an able and conscientious soldier, and no doubt dealt competently with the problem of moving hungry and weary men with their equipment along bad roads and waterlogged fields under torrential rain. If at midnight he was considerably further from the field of Waterloo than Blücher was, this was the fault of Napoleon who had sent him in so belated a pursuit of the Prussian army.

After dining, Napoleon had slept for two or three hours. Now, at one o'clock, he rose and went on a tour of inspection with General Bertrand. The night was densely black, and although the storm had moved away some hours before, occasional flashes of lightning fitfully lit up the scene. Still the rain fell heavily. Going as far up the Brussels road as La Belle Alliance they could see from that point the bivouac fires of their enemy, an indication that Wellington had settled for the night and intended to accept battle. Napoleon expressed the greatest satisfaction, for his chief concern had been that Wellington might slip away under cover of darkness. He was perfectly confident of victory. Far from realizing that his adversary was a commander of genius, he had recently referred to him as a 'presumptuous, ignorant man, destined for great catastrophes'[1], and

[1] Charras, *Histoire de la Campagne de 1815*, p. 241.

he believed he would have little trouble in sweeping the English from the field.

Wellington, though he had the highest opinion of Napoleon's capacities, was reasonably confident also, despite his respect for the army before him. 'All will yet be well,' he said in one of the letters he wrote shortly before dawn. And to the Duc de Berry he wrote, 'I hope, and moreover I have reason to hope, that all will be well.' None the less, while Napoleon made not a single preparation for defeat, the Duke was prepared for the worst, and he urged the Duc de Berry to see that Louix XVIII left Ghent for Antwerp if he should learn for certain that Brussels had fallen to the French. It was still possible, he thought, that Napoleon would manœuvre to his right and attempt to reach Brussels by way of Hal. He was convinced that Napoleon's best chance of success lay in such a manœuvre, and he had therefore prepared for the possibility by leaving Prince Frederick of Orange on the Mons to Brussels road.

Wellington was in touch with Blücher throughout the night, and messages were exchanged regarding the movements of Prussian troops. Gneisenau, a suspicious man who personally disliked Wellington, was not enthusiastic about going to the aid of the English. He was exasperated by Wellington's failure to join in the battle of Ligny the previous day, and made no allowances for the circumstances. 'The English only consider their own interests,' he said. 'If they are beaten tomorrow the Prussian army will be in great danger.'

Blücher silenced him by replying: 'In order that they shall not be beaten, we must go to their assistance.'

Major Groben, who had been left in the rear to observe Grouchy's forces, reported that the French had not yet left Gembloux. He believed that Grouchy could be prevented by a single corps from crossing the river Dyle; the essential thing, he said, was to send as many troops as possible to Mont St Jean. Gneisenau still disapproved of the idea, but Blücher sent out orders that his army should march in two columns to the support of the Duke of Wellington. The 3rd Corps would be left to defend Wavre against Grouchy, but if not attacked would move over to Mont St Jean in its turn, leaving only a few battalions behind. Blücher, showing his habitual courage and will-power, was fully resolved to mount his horse the following day and lead his men to victory, although he had been confined to his camp bed since his fall on the 16th. In the early hours of the 18th, Gneisenau sent an officer to inspect the English and French positions at Mont St Jean. The English and Prussian armies, therefore, were fully co-operating, while Napoleon persisted in his belief that the Prussians were out of action.

On returning from his inspection of the front line, Napoleon dealt with matters awaiting his attention. An aide-de-camp brought in Grouchy's letter from Gembloux, which had arrived at about 2 a.m., and told him that the messenger was asking for a reply. No immediate reply, however, was given. Spies, Belgian deserters and his own staff officers had arrived for interviews, bringing small details of information, all tending to confirm his own conviction that Wellington was resolved to fight. Satisfied and confident, he saw no need to communicate with Grouchy.

Now was the time to weigh up the information from Grouchy and that received from General Milhaud some hours previously. He might safely assume from this information that Blücher was sending at least some of his army to the assistance of Wellington, and it was at this moment that he could have ordered Grouchy to rejoin the main army. He took no action, however, and Grouchy's messenger, after repeated attempts to obtain a reply, was eventually sent off empty-handed.[1]

Grouchy was not even informed that the English army was in position before the French.[2]

Between three and four o'clock in the morning Bülow began his march towards the field of Waterloo from Dion le Mont, three miles east of Wavre. Progress was exceedingly slow. Grouchy was struggling throughout this dark and difficult night to assess the situation. At 6 a.m. he wrote as follows to Napoleon:

Sire,
    All reports and information confirm that the enemy is retiring on Brussels in order to concentrate there or give battle after rejoining Wellington. The 1st and 2nd Corps of Blücher's army appear to be making for Corbais and Chaumont respectively. They must have

[1] *Mémoires du Maréchal Marmont, Duc de Raguse*, Vol. VII, pp. 124-5.
[2] Ropes, *The Campaign of Waterloo*, pp. 246, 279.

left Tourinnes yesterday evening at 8.30, marching all night; fortunately the weather was so bad that they cannot have made much progress. I am leaving at once for Sart-à-Walhain, and from there I shall go to Corbais and Wavre.

Instead of continuing to Wavre, Grouchy should, in the opinion of Jomini, Clausewitz, Charras and Houssaye, have made all haste this morning to cross the Dyle at Moustier and so place himself within the sphere of Napoleon's operations. He should have seen the need for this, these historians think, as soon as he was satisfied that Blücher was in fact joining Wellington. General Hamley, however, expresses a different view in his *Operations of War*. Grouchy could not know that Wellington and Blücher were to make a stand in the course of the day at Waterloo, but believed the Allies would unite at Brussels. Had this been their intention, Grouchy 'by marching to Wavre, would threaten decisively their communications with their base by Louvain, and so either prevent the execution of their project, or render it disastrous'.[1] It was indeed a mistake on Grouchy's part to believe that the Allies were making for Brussels, but not an unreasonable one. In any case, the question of whether Grouchy should have moved up the left of the Dyle or the right does not appear to be of great importance. One need but look at a map and note the positions and numbers of the contending forces to see that the French were by this time completely outmanœuvred by the Allies. Grouchy with his two army corps was almost twice as far from the field of Waterloo as the Prussians were and was therefore powerless to prevent their junction with the English. The chief mistake was not Grouchy's movement on Sart-à-Walhain, but Napoleon's decision to send the right wing of the army to operate in isolation, far from the main body.

The Duke of Wellington's army began to take up its position for battle at 6 a.m. In the early hours the rain had gradually ceased. Captain Mercer's troop, having received supplies of food, were preparing a meal. The men, after a ration of rum, made themselves a dish of porridge, but the officers preferred to wait for the beef that was cooking; in this way they were doomed to go hungry, for they

[1] Hamley, *The Operations of War*, pp. 196-7.

were called to duty before the meat was ready, although many hours were to pass before the battle opened.

The Duke of Wellington inspected his position. He visited the two outposts of Hougoumont and La Haye Sainte, and made sure the troops were well posted. In the distance, on the heights to the east, he could already see the cavalry of Bülow's corps, a reassuring sight.[1] His line at this eastern end was but thinly guarded, as it was here that the Prussians would arrive in due course to add their weight to the battle. But the centre and right were as strong as he could make them.

The army was extended along a ridge of low hills running nearly east and west. Along the southern edge of these hills ran a country lane, the *chemin d'Ohain*, which stretched from Braine-l'Alleud to the Ohain wood. Ohain was a village on the way to Wavre. The Brussels road cut through the lane at the centre, with high banks on either side. The lane marked Wellington's front line, though there were forward troops and advance posts at various places. Just behind the fortified position of Hougoumont the line left the lane and swept southwards. For defensive purposes the lane was excellent, being hedged and having a slope on its reverse side where the troops could shelter.

Forward of the lane the ground descended southwards in a long, gradual slope, then rose again to the French position opposite. At the foot of the slope on the English right, that is to say at the western end of the field, was Hougoumont, a substantial country mansion with a farm, a chapel and extensive grounds, including a dense wood. One of the advantages of the defensive position Wellington had chosen was that the upward slope by which the French must come if they made a frontal attack was steep enough to slow them down, especially as the ground was now waterlogged. The reserve troops could be well hidden behind the ridge, and the roads in the rear facilitated movement.

To the right of the Brussels road, just in front of the Allied centre, was the farm of La Haye Sainte, fortified and under the command of Major Baring with the 2nd Light Battalion of the King's German Legion. Hougoumont, more strongly held under the command of Colonel Macdonell, was so far forward as to jut right into the French

[1] Ellesmere, *Personal Reminiscences of the Duke of Wellington*, p. 232.

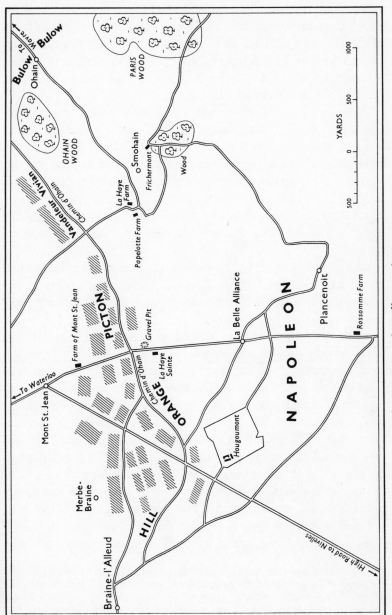

The position of Wellington's Army

position.[1] These two strongholds were to prove invaluable in the approaching struggle. Other advance posts were the gravel pit from which Captain Mercer had fired the previous evening (just in front of the centre of the line, on the opposite side of the road from La Haye Sainte) and the farms of Papelotte and La Haye, in front of the extreme left of the centre and held by the troops of Prince Bernard of Saxe-Weimar.

Wellington's front, three and a half miles long, was divided into three sections. To the left of the high road Sir Thomas Picton was in command, to the right the Prince of Orange. Further to the right, west of the high road from Nivelles to Mont St Jean, was the section under Lord Hill. Wellington placed the greatest reliance upon Lord Hill, and had posted him with large reserves of infantry where he most feared his line might be turned. Still further west were the troops at Hal, his other precaution against a turning movement to the west.

Wellington assessed the situation on the basis of what he himself would have done in Napoleon's place. The greatest quality of his well-trained British and German troops (upon whom he most relied) was their staying power in defence. The worst thing Napoleon could do would be to allow such soldiers to stand and defend themselves on their own chosen ground. In his place, Wellington would have manœuvred, and he made his plans assuming that this was what Napoleon would do. At the same time, he was well prepared for each of the three courses that his enemy might take in attacking him; and arrangements had been made for appropriate Prussian movements. If Napoleon attacked Wellington's right, the Prussians would march in force to Ohain to join in the battle; if he attacked the centre, the Prussians would send one column by way of Ohain to support Wellington's left, and another by St Lambert and Lasne to attack the French in the rear. If Napoleon advanced to St Lambert and tried to drive his army in between the Allies, the Prussians would stand and receive the attack while Wellington's army took the

---

[1] The mansion and farm buildings of Hougoumont were garrisoned by the light companies of the 2nd Guards Brigade, under Colonel Macdonell, and the orchards and wood by the light companies of the 1st Guards Brigade, under Lord Saltoun. The wood, which was very dense, and was at the southern end of the position, was occupied in addition by a regiment of Nassau troops and two companies of Hanoverian sharpshooters.

offensive and attacked the French left flank and rear. What had not been foreseen was the length of time that would be taken by the Prussians in reaching the battlefield. It had been decided that Bülow's corps should go into action first since it had not had to fight on the 16th; but on arriving in the region of Wavre it had been placed further to the east than the rest of the army so that much time was lost in waiting for it to pass ahead of the other corps. Although the cavalry had gone on in advance and were already to be seen on the heights of Ohain, the infantry was long delayed by flooded roads and fields, and the advance guard under Major-General Von Losthin did not reach Wavre until 7 a.m. Then, as the troops were marching through the town, a fire broke out by accident and spread so rapidly that all movement was brought to a halt. The bulk of the 4th Corps had to wait until the fire was extinguished, and they were thus delayed for more than two hours. In the meantime the corps of Pirch and Ziethen had to wait idle until Bülow had passed them, although they had bivouacked closer to the battlefield. This long delay and the fact that Wellington's forces at Hal were to be useless to him during the day did something to offset Napoleon's mistake in positioning Grouchy so far from the main army.

Wellington was ready in good time for the expected attack; but fortunately for him it was to be long before the battle was joined, so that the late arrival of the Prussian army was not to prove disasterous as might have been the case if Napoleon had been more prompt to begin. At eight o'clock much of the French army was still moving up the Brussels road from Genappe; but even had it been fully assembled, Napoleon would have been in no hurry for he considered the English were entirely at his mercy. 'I have them, then, these English!' he had exclaimed to those about him at dawn. There was also the question of the state of the ground. General Drouot was of the opinion that in two or three hours' time the wind would have dried the soil considerably and that it was worth while delaying the battle for this reason. Napoleon therefore decided to wait.

Between eight and nine o'clock he was seated at breakfast at Le Caillou Farm. The Imperial silver plate was used, and Soult, Bassano and Drouot were among the officers with him. When the meal ended maps were spread upon the table and Napoleon talked optimistically.

'The enemy outnumbers us by more than a quarter,' he said. 'All the same, we have not less than ninety chances in our favour, and not ten against.' In fact, Napoleon had available for the battle 74,000 men and 266 guns, and so outnumbered Wellington who had 67,661 men and 156 guns. Fortescue gives the odds at which Wellington engaged Napoleon as two against three. In this he takes the actual worth of the Duke's army in terms of men who could be trusted more or less.[1]

Marshal Ney now joined the generals round the breakfast table; he had been inspecting the advance posts and reported that there were signs that Wellington was retreating. But Napoleon had seen and heard enough to be sure Wellington intended to fight.

'Your observations have misled you,' he said. 'It is too late. Wellington would expose himself to certain defeat. The die is cast, and it is in our favour.'

Despite Napoleon's assurance, some of the generals present felt deep anxiety and wished that Grouchy and his forces were present. Those who had fought against the Duke of Wellington in Spain had the highest opinion of his ability, and others knew from hearsay that he was a formidable adversary. Only Marshal Soult spoke his mind; he had done so the previous evening and he returned to the subject now, urging Napoleon to send messengers calling Grouchy across to the battlefield.

'Because you have been beaten by Wellington,' Napoleon snapped at his Chief-of-Staff, 'you think he is a good general. I tell you Wellington is a bad general, and the English are bad troops. We shall make short work of them.'

'I hope it may be so,' said Soult.[2]

Shortly after, General Reille arrived with Jérôme Bonaparte; they had ridden in at the head of the 2nd Corps whose vanguard reached La Belle Alliance at about 9 a.m. Napoleon asked Reille his opinion of the English army. 'When the English infantry are well placed, as Wellington knows how to place them,' said Reille, 'I regard them as impregnable when subjected to a frontal attack; this is due to their calm tenacity and the superiority of their shooting. Before you can approach them with the bayonet you must wait

---

[1] Fortescue, *A History of the British Army*, Vol. X, p. 409.
[2] Houssaye, *1815*, Vol. II, p. 319.

until half your attacking force is destroyed. But the English army is less agile, less flexible, less easily manœuvred than ours.'

Napoleon broke off the discussion with an exclamation of incredulity.[1]

Jérôme Bonaparte brought Napoleon information to which he would have done well to pay attention. Jérôme had dined the previous evening at the *Roi d'Espagne* in Genappe where Wellington had taken a meal in the course of his retreat. An aide-de-camp of the Duke's had been thoughtless enough to talk openly of the decision of the Duke and Blücher to make a stand against the French south of the Forest of Soignies. The waiter who served Jérôme hastened to repeat all he had heard, telling him the Prussians would arrive by way of Wavre. But Napoleon dismissed this information as idle rumour. 'After such a battle as Fleurus,' he said, 'a junction of the English and Prussians is impossible within the next two days. Moreover, the Prussians have Grouchy on their heels.'[2]

There was no more to be said. He rose from the table and prepared to leave for La Belle Alliance. He already had his plan in mind. He rode up the road towards the battle front at about 9.30 a.m.

If his experienced generals were not over confident, the younger officers and servants left at Le Caillou felt as sure of the outcome of the battle as their Imperial master. It was understood that the Imperial headquarters would be established in Brussels that night; but Napoleon had ordered dinner for 6.30 p.m. at Le Caillou and had asked for a well-done shoulder of lamb; this meant that the arrival in Brussels would be late. But excitement was mounting; there was no doubt that all would take place as planned.

[1] Houssaye, saying that both Ségur and Thiers had this story from Reille himself, adds,'The Duc d'Aumale, who had also known Reille, described the incident to me differently. According to his version, Reille said nothing to Napoleon, but on leaving Le Caillou he talked to d'Erlon about the danger of attacking the English from the front. D'Erlon urged that they should go back and point this out to the Emperor; but Reille replied: "What's the use? He wouldn't listen to us." ' (Houssaye, *1815*, Vol. II, pp. 319-20.)

It may well be that this is the true version, since no one likes to lay himself open to such insults as Soult had just received. But however it may have been, there can be no doubt from the available evidence that the generals who had fought against Wellington in Spain felt that the utmost exertion was necessary. Napoleon, accustomed to regarding other military commanders as inferiors, disdained the Duke and his heterogeneous army.

[2] Houssaye, *1815*, Vol. II, p. 323.

With him as he rode to La Belle Alliance Napoleon took a local man as guide, a peasant named Decoster who owned a cabaret between Le Caillou and La Belle Alliance. Decoster rode between Napoleon and an aide-de-camp, his saddle tied to that of a trooper who rode behind him. Napoleon questioned him closely about the features of the land and kept him near throughout the day. It was Napoleon's habit to use local guides when he fought in foreign places, and he tried on this occasion to press a second peasant into service, a certain Joseph Bourgeois who shook with terror on being confronted with the Emperor. Asked afterwards to describe Napoleon, he gave the curious reply: 'His face is like the dial of a clock at which you would not dare to look at the time.'[1]

At La Belle Alliance Napoleon discussed the condition of the ground and the enemy's position with his engineers, and dictated orders for the placing of the troops which he intended to review as they marched into their battle positions. He then retired to the farm of Rossomme, mid-way between La Belle Alliance and Le Caillou; this farm stood on high ground and commanded an extensive view of Wellington's Line and the whole battle area. The hills and woods beyond Wellington's left were clearly to be seen; yet the French had not yet caught sight of Bülow's cavalry.

At this time Grouchy was at Sart-à-Walhain which he had reached at nine o'clock. His troops were marching on Wavre; those of Vandamme, in front, were nearing Nil St Vincent. A friendly notary living in the nearby village of Walhain, offered Grouchy hospitality and gave him useful information. Grouchy learnt that the Prussians had marched through or past the town in three columns, and that they were believed to be on their way to join Wellington at Brussels.

Napoleon's review of the troops began at 10 a.m. He watched from Rossomme while the army moved into place. It marched forward in eleven columns, spreading across the plain and revealing itself completely in all its strength. Very different were the tactics of Wellington who disguised the placing and numbers of his troops as much as possible; but Napoleon with his theatrical tastes tended

[1] Houssaye, *1815*, Vol. II, p. 322.

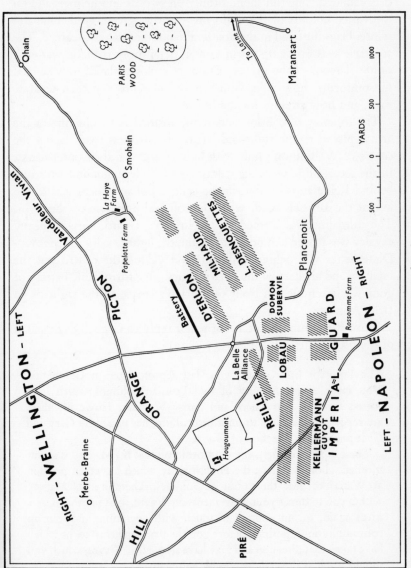

The position of Napoleon's Army

to rely upon display and probably hoped in the present instance to intimidate his foe. The bands were playing, drums rolled and trumpets sounded. The sun shone fitfully on swords and helmets and on the varied colours of the uniforms – scarlet, green, gold, blue and white. Flags fluttered in the breeze, the polished eagles gleamed. The spectacle was brilliant; yet in human detail how pathetic was each single element of the massive show; at a closer glance how stained the uniforms; how pale, famished and insecure was each separate man, and how anxious for the future.

The infantry of d'Erlon and Reille formed the front line of the army, placed to the right and left of the Brussels road, facing the centre of Wellington's line, with light cavalry on their outer flanks. In the second line were the cuirassiers of Kellermann and Milhaud, behind Reille and d'Erlon; in the centre, Lobau's corps was to the left of the Brussels road, with Domon and Subervie to the right. The third line was formed by the Imperial Guard. Guyot's heavy cavalry was placed behind Kellermann, the light cavalry of Lefebvre-Desnouettes was behind Milhaud; and behind the centre was the infantry and artillery of the Guard. Later on, a formidable battery of guns was assembled in front of d'Erlon's corps, to the right of La Belle Alliance.

From Rossomme Soult at last sent a reply to Grouchy's despatch of the previous evening:[1]

The Emperor has received your last report, dated at Gembloux. You speak to his Majesty of two Prussian columns which have passed through Sauvenière and Sart-à-Walhain. However, there are reports that a fairly strong third column has passed by Géry and Gentinnes in the direction of Wavre.

The Emperor requests me to inform you that his Majesty is at this moment about to attack the English army which has taken position at Waterloo, near the Forest of Soignies. Therefore his Majesty wishes you to direct your movements on Wavre, so as to draw nearer to us again, to put yourself in touch with operations and join up communications, pushing before you the Prussian army corps which have taken that direction and may have stopped at Wavre, which you should reach at the earliest possible moment.

Have those enemy columns which have taken a direction to your

[1] See pp. 178-9.

right followed by some of the light corps, so as to observe their movements and round up their stragglers.

Instruct me immediately regarding your arrangements and your march, as well as your information of the enemy, and do not fail to keep in close communication with us; the Emperor wishes to have news of you very frequently.

Thus Grouchy was ordered to continue on the road to Wavre. The letter to Grouchy was sent off; he was not to receive it until nearly 4 p.m. Napoleon now mounted his horse again and rode forth to take the salute from his troops. Moving from the left of his line to the right, he passed in front of all the regiments in turn. Standards were inclined before him and he was greeted with tremendous acclamations. The assembled army, in the words of Adolphe Thiers, 'was drunk with joy and hope.' To such lengths of imagination can historians go in the isolation of their studies.

Certainly the soldiers had received a double ration of brandy before being marched into place; but they were given no bread.

Napoleon now rode back to Rossomme where, according to Thiers, he snatched a brief sleep. It may be he needed sleep, but by leaving his soldiers to stand idle after the review he must have reduced their fighting power by giving them time to reflect on' their hunger and the danger they were in. 'This halt in the face of death,' says Captain Mauduit, 'was used by Wellington to sustain his men's energies by the distribution of food. As for the French army . . . it was reduced as always to fighting in a state of hunger. . . . All our supply wagons had remained at Charleroi where we were soon to find them again, heaped together, smashed – in a word, in the most frightful disorder.[1]

The Duke of Wellington was now riding up and down his line. Going down to Hougoumont, he remained some time in the wood, studying Reille's forces which were formed as though in readiness to attack the position. He found the Nassau troops somewhat nervous at the proximity of overwhelming enemy forces. He endeavoured to reassure them, but with no great success, for as he rode away some of them fired at him out of sheer bewilderment. The Duke rode

---

[1] Mauduit, *Les Derniers Jours de la Grande Armée*, Vol. II, p. 271. Grouchy's troops fared better, as they captured substantial Prussian supplies.

on, drily observing to his companions that he was expected to win a battle with men like these.

The British troops and German Legionaries gave him a hearty cheer as he rode past them; this was better, and it was a relief, too, to see the French army formed up for a frontal attack. Placed as it was, there was no chance that Napoleon intended to manœuvre. Wellington asked nothing better than to be able to stand and defend the position he had chosen. A message was sent off to the Prussians who, as agreed, would now attack the French in flank to the rear of La Belle Alliance, and also support the left of Wellington's line.

Napoleon, disregarding the views of his Peninsular generals, had indeed decided upon a frontal attack. Houssaye says; '*Il dédaigne de manoeuvrer*'. He might with advantage have attacked the left of Wellington's line, turning it and driving him away from the Prussians. But, as Houssaye implies, he did not deign to go to any great trouble on Wellington's account. One of the most curious features of the campaign is Napoleon's vast assurance before the battle of Waterloo. It is true that everything had the appearance of being in his favour. He had a great advantage in guns, in weight as well as numbers. He was well informed regarding the composition of the Duke's ill-assorted army, and may even have heard of the Duke's own opinion of it; it might be expected that such an army would not long stand before his own with its national spirit and enthusiasm for his cause. The best British troops, too, had been seriously reduced by their losses at Quatre Bras. Had Napoleon's assessment of Wellington been accurate, there would indeed have been no need for tactical *finesse* in the coming battle. What he failed to realize was that Wellington could direct a battle as no other general living and was likely to overcome all difficulties. Refusing to listen to his generals, who could have warned him of his danger, and believing Wellington was a nonentity, it is understandable that he should see no need for recalling Grouchy. He could strike in his own time; the result was not in doubt. An hour or two pounding at Wellington's centre with a massive concentration of artillery, cavalry and infantry, and he would break through and surge up the Brussels road, throwing the remnant of the Anglo-Belgian army back to the Channel.

'Damn the fellow, he is a mere pounder after all!' Wellington was to say during the action, as though disappointed that some of the much vaunted military genius of his adversary was not being exhibited.[1]

Napoleon was so certain of success that he had brought up the Imperial treasury to the farm of Le Caillou with his robes of state and other trappings for the morrow when he would address his loyal Belgian subjects from their capital. And the Old Guard had been ordered to carry their parade dress in their haversacks ready for a triumphal march through Brussels. The weight these men had to carry was 65 lbs.[2] They were being kept to the rear, and presumably Napoleon did not anticipate having to bring them into the fight except, perhaps, to hasten the English collapse at the end.

It was now 11 a.m. Blücher, surpassing himself, mounted his horse and rode forth from Wavre with Bülow's column. The soldiers plodded along ankle-deep in mud, hauling their gun-carriages with the greatest difficulty over the ruts. Blücher, riding up and down, genially encouraged his men and their spirits rose wherever he showed himself. It was while he was thus making his way towards the battlefield that he received news that the French were about to attack Wellington's centre; orders were thereupon given for the manœuvre agreed upon in the circumstances.

Marshal Grouchy, at Walhain, was writing another report to Napoleon, informing him of all the details of Prussian movements he had now gathered. He would be massed at Wavre that evening, he said, and he asked for further instructions.

Having sent off the report by a well-mounted messenger, Grouchy sat down to lunch with his attentive host, the notary, in a pleasant summer-house in the garden.

Napoleon was now seated in a heavy, old-fashioned chair at a large table, outside the farm of Rossomme. The furniture had been placed on a thick layer of straw. Taking frequent pinches of snuff, he studied his maps and from time to time glanced at the square plain extended before him where the armies faced each other in lines like the pieces on a great chess-board. Presently he dictated his

---

[1] Ellesmere, *Personal Reminiscences os the Duke of Wellington*, p. 179.
[2] Houssaye, *1815*, Vol. II. p. 328.

orders to Marshal Soult: 'As soon as the whole army is drawn up for battle, round about 1 p.m., the Emperor will give the order to Marshal Ney and the attack will be launched for the seizure of the village of Mont St Jean where the roads intersect. . . .'

A battery of guns was to bombard the English, and Count d'Erlon would begin the attack, followed by Count Reille. Engineers were to be ready to barricade the village immediately it was taken.

About this time Grouchy's report of 6 a.m. was brought to Napoleon: 'Sire, all reports and information confirm that the enemy is retiring on Brussels in order to concentrate there or give battle after rejoining Wellington. . . .' Whether or not this suggested to Napoleon that he might have to fight the Prussians during the day one cannot tell; he did not appear to attach much importance to the message and no reply was sent until one o'clock.

Although the assault on the centre of Wellington's line was planned for one o'clock, an attack on Hougoumont was to begin almost at once. At 11.15 a.m. Reille was ordered to clear the wood before that stronghold, and the first shots of the battle of Waterloo were fired at 11.30 a.m.

13

First phase of the battle; Grouchy at Walhain; Second phase; Unsuccessful attack on Wellington's left centre

The first phase of the battle, the attack on Hougoumont, is usually regarded as a feint of which the object was to induce Wellington to move troops from his centre to his right. Wellington did not move a single man from his centre, however; and if the attack was intended as a diversion this was soon lost sight of by the generals in command, for a ferocious struggle was to go on round Hougoumont throughout the day, proving far more costly to the French than to the English.

Reille's three divisions were extended before Hougoumont (the fourth having been left at Fleurus) under Generals Jérôme Bonaparte, Foy and Bachelu. One of his batteries now opened fire on the English position, and Jérôme began the attack on the south-east end of the wood. Skirmishers ran forward, followed by supporting columns in echelon. English batteries opened fire, and musket fire broke out from the fringe of the wood; but the French pressed on and soon had a foothold among the trees. The Nassau troops, who had lost their heads in Wellington's presence a short time earlier, now fought bravely side by side with the Hanoverians; they were driven back but contested their ground foot by foot. Jérôme's men were followed by those of Foy and Bachelu; the air was filled with smoke and the noise of battle.

The sound reached Walhain where Marshal Grouchy was peacefully at lunch. He had reached his dessert, a plate of strawberries, when he was interrupted by one of his colonels who came into the summer-house to say that firing could be heard from the garden. He jumped up to listen and, indeed, a low rumbling was audible far off in the west. The garden was filled with officers, some gazing westwards, some kneeling with an ear to the ground, others talking in groups. A few peasants had wandered in and were anxiously listening. General Gérard demanded insistently that Grouchy should march at once towards the firing. But Grouchy replied that what they heard was probably a rearguard action as Wellington retreated on Brussels. Seeing the peasants, he asked them where they thought the firing would be, and they replied that it must be at Mont St Jean. Grouchy discussed the matter with the officers about him, but could see no reason to change his course.

On the battlefield the French had now gained possession of most of the wood of Hougoumont; but the defenders, well supported by the guns of Major Bull and Captain Sandham, presently drove them out again, though only momentarily. Jérôme made renewed efforts and eventually succeeded in capturing the entire wood, though he was brought to a halt by the strong walls surrounding the gardens and courtyard of the château. The Duke of Wellington had been watching the fighting and directing it from the road behind. He now withdrew the Hanoverian and Nassau troops from the grounds and sent down six companies of Guards to reinforce the garrison within the walls. Then, satisfied that they would hold their own, he rode on to the centre which he could see was about to be attacked. Ney, indeed, was massing guns in the great battery at La Belle Alliance for a bombardment.

Reille's orders had been merely that the approaches of Hougoumont should be occupied, and now that the wood was securely held General Guilleminot, Jérôme's Chief-of-Staff, recommended that the engagement should be broken off. Reille sent orders to that effect more than once[1]; but Jérôme ignored the instructions and made every possible effort to break through the walls and capture the château. In this way the action at Hougoumont went entirely in favour of the English; the French had enormous losses, and the English kept them at bay with a small garrison.

On Napoleon's orders, Kellermann's two horse artillery batteries joined in the firing; Piré's horse battery also came into action and enfiladed the guns firing from Wellington's line. Captain Mercer felt the effect of Piré's guns. He had been brought down to the right of Wellington's second line from the farm of Mont St Jean where he had been placed in reserve, and he had orders to observe Piré's lancers stationed to the west of Hougoumont, but on no

[1] Houssaye, *1815*, Vol. II, p. 336, note 1; p. 338, note 4.

account to fire on them unless they advanced. Piré's batteries, however, began firing on Mercer's troop and although most of the shot fell short some came very close, howitzer shells in particular.

In front of him Mercer could see light dragoons of the German Legion, from which detachments moved forward from time to time; further away, almost concealed in tall corn, French riflemen were moving about. To his left were masses of British infantry in squares, and on his right was fine, open country, peaceful and undisturbed. The sky was now overcast and rain was falling. As far as the battle was concerned, he had no way of telling what was taking place. He writes:

About this time, being impatient of standing idle, and annoyed by the batteries on the Nivelle road, I ventured to commit a folly for which I should have paid dearly had our Duke chanced to be in our part of the field. I ventured to disobey orders, and open a slow deliberate fire at the battery, thinking with my 9-pounders soon to silence his 4-pounders. My astonishment was great, however, when our very first gun was responded to by at least half-a-dozen gentlemen of very superior calibre, whose presence I had not even suspected, and whose superiority we immediately recognized by their rushing noise and long reach, for they flew far beyond us. I instantly saw my folly, and ceased firing, and they did the same – the 4-pounders alone continuing the cannonade as before. But this was not all. The first man of my troop was touched by one of these confounded long shot. I shall never forget the scream the poor lad gave when struck. It was one of the last they fired, and shattered his left arm to pieces as he stood between the wagons. The scream went to my very soul, for I accused myself as having caused his misfortune. I was, however, obliged to conceal my emotion from the men, who had turned to look at him; so, bidding them 'stand to their front', I continued my walk up and down, whilst Hitchins (the surgeon) ran to his assistance.

The Duke, as it happened, had observed this act of disobedience from a distance, but thought the culprit was Captain Sandham, the commander of a near-by battery. Seeing one of the French four-pounders struck by a British shell, he promptly sent orders that Captain Sandham should be placed under arrest. Fortunately Captain Sandham was able to extricate himself by offering some kind of explanation, and Captain Mercer was not discovered.[1]

[1] Becke, *Napoleon and Waterloo*, pp. 189-90.

Captain Mercer and his men resumed their rôle as passive spectators, while Piré's guns continued to fire upon them. Patience and endurance were much demaded by the Duke on this day, and he himself set the tone. In their trying situation, however, the artillery captain and his men could still find amusement in what went on. Two or three officers strolled up to speak to them, and one of them, a surgeon, was holding up an umbrella. A shower of projectiles from the French guns happened to come at that time and sent the visitors hurrying off again; the surgeon was so alarmed that he dropped to his knees and shuffled off on all fours, still carefully sheltering himself from the rain with his umbrella. 'Our fellows,' says Mercer, 'made the field resound with their shouts of laughter.'

The increased firing at Hougoumont was noticed by Grouchy and his companions at Walhain. The battlefield was about fourteen miles away as the crow flies, and clouds of smoke could be seen rising above the horizon. It was evident that a major action was taking place between the armies of Napoleon and Wellington. Gérard, supported by General Valazé of the Engineers, still urged Grouchy to march towards the firing. But General Baltus, in command of the artillery, said that it would be impossible to get the guns along the flooded lanes leading to Mont St Jean. An argument ensued in which Valazé insisted that his engineers could very well move the guns, Baltus refused to be persuaded, and Gérard grew angry with Grouchy who was perplexed but hesitated to change his direction.

'*Monsieur le maréchal*, it is your duty to march towards the guns!' Gérard cried.

'The Emperor told me yesterday that it was his intention to attack the English army if Wellington would accept battle,' said Grouchy. 'Therefore I am in no way surprised by the engagement now taking place. If the Emperor had wished me to take part in it, he would not have sent me off at a distance at the very moment he was moving against the English.'

Grouchy's answer was quite reasonable, and had Napoleon been more ready to admit his own mistakes, we should have heard little of this episode at Walhain. The emphasis would not have been on Grouchy's refusal to march towards the guns, but on the fact that

Napoleon had sent him too far away to be of use in the battle of Waterloo.

The falsifications of St Helena have made it possible to turn Grouchy into a scapegoat: the incompetent, apathetic marshal who could have saved the day had he only heeded Gérard's promptings. The battlefield, according to the legend, is not so far from Walhain; the roads not too bad, and the Prussians none too vigilant. Napoleon, as always, is presented as irreproachable; he has given his marshal the clearest instructions; he is counting on his arrival to take part in the battle. We are even assured that Grouchy had been informed during the night of the impending battle and instructed how to co-operate.[1]

The actual situation was far more complicated than that of the legend. The battlefield was very far away; the troops could not reach it as the crow flies but would have to follow meandering lanes which were in an atrocious condition after the exceptional rainfall of the previous day. It has since been found that a man walking quickly can cover the distance from Walhain to Plancenoit in five and a half hours[2]; this, in fact, is about the time that the messenger bringing Napoleon's despatch of 10 a.m. took to reach Grouchy,[3] an indication, perhaps, of the difficulty of the roads. A well mounted man with nothing to carry but a letter would have been able to get along more quickly than an army corps, so that one may suppose that Grouchy could not have reached the battlefield, even if he had been able to march there unmolested, before eight or nine in the evening. Bülow marched on a similar line to Plancenoit that day, the operation taking eight and a half hours (not including the two hours' delay at Wavre). Grouchy had two or three miles further to move. But the point to be remembered is that the Prussians were watching Grouchy's movements; it is not to be supposed that they would have allowed him to join Napoleon at his ease.

It was now mid-day. Bülow's advance guard was at Chapelle-Saint-Lambert, his other divisions were between that place and

[1] Gourgaud, *Campagne de 1815*, p. 70; Napoleon, *Mémoires*, 1830, Vol. IX, p. 102. Houssaye gives conclusive reasons for disbelieving this assertion (*1815*, Vol. II, p. 278, note 1.) See also Chesney, *Waterloo Lectures*, pp. 166-7.

[2] Chesney, *Waterloo Lectures*, pp. 199-200.

[3] Houssaye, *1815*, Vol. II, p. 461.

Wavre. Prussian troops faced Exelmans, who was at the head of Grouchy's advancing column at La Baraque. Ziethen was on his way from Wavre to Ohain, having left troops in observation at Limal. The two first divisions of Pirch I had crossed the Dyle and were advancing on Chapelle-Saint-Lambert in the wake of Bülow, and the remaining two were following; Thielemann, having left a strong rearguard in Wavre, was moving on Couture in the direction of Plancenoit. Later, when it was seen that Vandamme was moving on Wavre, Thielemann's corps and the two last divisions of Pirch I suspended their march; these forces, nearly 35,000 in number, would have contested Grouchy's march to Mont St Jean. 'Moreover,' says Charras, 'one must not forget that these 35,000 Prussians, whom Grouchy would have found on his route in marching towards Napoleon in accordance with Gérard's advice, took no part, absolutely none, in the battle of Waterloo.'[1]

Though it was clear from information he now received from Exelmans that the Prussians were marching to join Wellington, Grouchy decided against turning westwards. It seemed to him safer to attack the Prussians nearest to him, those at Wavre, rather than risk a hazardous cross-march which might be against the Emperor's wishes. The hazards of the march probably counted much less with him than his fear of disobeying Napoleon, for he regarded himself first and foremost as under orders, and his orders had been to pursue the Prussians. He therefore continued on the way to Wavre. Calling for his horses, he rode up the road to join the head of the column. At 1 p.m. he reached Nil St Vincent where Vandamme was awaiting orders, and directed him to continue the march to Wavre. A little before 2 p.m. Vandamme's infantry, preceded by the cavalry of Exelmans, reached Baraque, two miles south of Wavre, and engaged the rearguard of Pirch I.

At one o'clock Napoleon, at Rossomme, was dictating a reply to Grouchy's letter of 6 a.m.:

Monsieur le maréchal,
    You wrote to the Emperor at 6 o'clock to say you were marching on Sart-à-Walhain, your project then being to move on to Corbaix and Wavre. Such a move is in accordance with the arrangements of

[1] Charras, *Histoire de la Campagne de 1815*, pp. 337-8.

his Majesty, which have been communicated to you. However, the Emperor orders me to say that you must continually manœuvre in our direction, approaching the army so as to join us before any corps can get between us. I am not indicating the direction. It is for you to discover our whereabouts and make your plans accordingly, keeping in communication so as to be prepared at any time to fall on and destroy enemy troops if they attempt to interfere with our right.

At this moment we are engaged in battle on the line at Waterloo.

Maréchal duc de Dalmatie.

All was ready for the main attack on Wellington's line, and one of Ney's aides-de-camp awaited Napoleon's order to open fire. Before giving this order, Napoleon looked searchingly over the battlefield and the countryside stretched about him. Immediately below him was the farm of Rossomme with the Brussels road running northwards. Beyond was the shallow valley, traversed by this highroad, and then rising ground up to the English line, overhung on its right by clouds of smoke. Near by, on his own right, was the village of Plancenoit, surrounded by woods; and across to the north-east were the green heights of Ohain and Chapelle-Saint-Lambert. Looking in this direction, he at last caught sight of some of those Prussian troops that had long been observed from Wellington's side of the field. What he could see was a column of Bülow's infantry emerging from the wood of Chapelle-Saint-Lambert; from such a distance it appeared only as a dark patch, but on looking through his glass he seemed to recognize men on the march.

He drew the attention of his staff officers to the point, and all their glasses were at once raised. Soult said he could perfectly well distinguish a large army corps which had piled its arms; others disagreed with him and said they could see nothing but a copse, or the shadow of a cloud; still others saw a marching column but said the uniforms were French. A cavalry detachment was sent off at a gallop to obtain information, but before it could return a Prussian officer had been captured and brought before Napoleon; on him was a letter from Bülow to Wellington, and he confirmed that the troops visible on the hills were indeed Prussian. 'The whole of our army was at Wavre during the night,' he said. 'We saw nothing of the French, and concluded they had marched on Plancenoit.'

Napoleon's letter to Grouchy had not yet been sent off. Soult added a few words to the last sentence to indicate more precisely the position of the battlefield, and wrote the following postscript: 'A letter which has just been intercepted shows that General Bülow is to attack our right flank. We believe we can see this corps on the heights of St Lambert. Therefore do not lose an instant in coming over to join us and destroying Bülow whom you will take *flagrante delicto*.'

It is easy to believe that Wellington would have retreated in such circumstances as those in which Napoleon now found himself. The Duke had patience to manœuvre in the eighteenth-century manner, for days and weeks on end, saving his men to the utmost, and taking every care not to be drawn into any clash in which victory was unlikely. But Napoleon was determined to have his gamble. According to Gourgaud, he did for a moment consider carrying his line of operations on to the Nivelles road and outflanking Wellington's right; but he rejected the idea, partly because it would facilitate the junction of the Prussians and English, and partly because he could see that Wellington's right would be most difficult to break.[1]

He professed to be hardly less confident than before. 'This morning there were ninety chances in our favour,' he said to Soult. 'We still have sixty against forty.' He gave orders that the light cavalry of Domon and Subervie should move in the direction of Chapelle-Saint-Lambert in order to observe the Prussian advance; and soon afterwards he sent Lobau with the 6th Corps over to the right. Thus, having diminished his forces by some 10,000 men, Napoleon faced Wellington's 67,661 with 64,000. Everything now depended on his striking hard and rapidly against the English centre and breaking through before the Prussians arrived. He had before him, although he could not know it, two clear hours; for although they were so near, the Prussians still had to cross the most difficult country of all their march.

Napoleon now gave orders that the battery facing Wellington's left centre should open fire; and with this cannonade, at about 1.30 p.m., the second phase of the battle opened. Eighty French guns were firing, and Wellington's artillery replied at once.

The centre of Wellington's line was strongly guarded. The section

[1] Gourgaud, *The Campaign of 1815*, pp. 118-19.

now being bombarded, to the left of the Brussels road, was commanded by Sir Thomas Picton who had under him the brigades of Sir James Kempt, Sir Dennis Pack, Colonel Best and Colonel von Wincke. Sir James Kempt was nearest to the highroad, and three companies of the 95th Rifles had been thrown forward from his brigade to occupy the gravel pit and adjacent ground. In the interval between Kempt and Pack, well down the slope in front of the Ohain lane, was a Dutch-Belgian brigade commanded by Major-General Bylandt, placed in a most vulnerable position and there for no apparent purpose. This unfortunate brigade had to face the bombardment helpless and unsheltered, with terrible results. Behind Kempt was Sir William Ponsonby with the Union Brigade. On Picton's left, Prince Bernard of Saxe-Weimar was in command with some of his forces in reserve and others occupying La Haye, Papelotte and the hamlet of Smohain. Still further left were the cavalry squadrons of Vandeleur and Vivian holding the end of the line, Vivian having patrols as far out as Ohain.

The French bombardment lasted for half an hour. The intention had been so to exhaust the enemy that they would be unable to withstand the infantry attack which would follow. Yet, apart from the terrible effect it had on Bylandt's exposed brigade, it achieved very little. The guns were a considerable distance from Wellington's line, and the shells did not fall far beyond the Ohain lane. Sir Thomas Picton's men, lying on the ground on the reverse slopes of the lane, remained unshaken and casualties were not serious.

At about two o'clock Ney was given the signal to launch the main attack, and at the same time Napoleon moved forward, establishing himself on a height just outside Decoster's house, a short distance behind La Belle Alliance. Here he had a view of the whole battlefield, only the lowest part of the valley before him being hidden from sight.

The French guns now suspended their fire while d'Erlon's corps moved forward. 16,000 men advanced under Generals Quiot,[1] Donzelot, Marcognet and Durutte. They moved in echelon, the left being furthest forward with the outpost of La Haye Sainte as its objective, while Durutte, on the right, faced the farm of Papelotte,

[1] In Allix's absence, General Quiot, one of his brigade commanders, had been put in charge of his division.

held by Prince Bernard of Saxe-Weimar. Apart from Durutte who, on his own initiative, had ordered a more readily deployable formation, the generals moved their men forward in divisional columns, so closely massed that only the men at the front were in a position to fire on the enemy. 'One can hardly understand how such a formation came to be used by men who had been making war for twenty years,' says Grouard. The formation, we are told, belonged to the classical world and so was considerably out of date; but it was not unknown in Napoleon's battles. Some historians take the view that the order must have been misinterpreted, and that the intention was for the battalions to move forward at deploying intervals so as to be mobile and ready to form quickly into squares if charged by cavalry. But since Napoleon himself was looking on and sent no one forward to prevent the formation used, it may be that it was indeed part of the massive, solid type of attack he had decided upon. He meant to drive through by sheer weight, and he might have succeeded had the defence been less skilful.

Allix's division, on the left and commanded by Quiot, descended the valley, then climbed the opposite slope under heavy fire; Ney and d'Erlon were at its head. The divisions of Donzelot, Marconget and Durutte followed in turn, making their way through the uncut rye covering the slopes. The English skirmishers fell back; the defenders of the orchards and gardens of La Haye Sainte retreated into the building as the French surged upon them in overwhelming numbers. Quiot's own brigade now attempted to take the farm building; but like Hougoumont La Haye Sainte was enclosed by solid walls against which small arms were useless, and no guns had been brought up the Brussels road to fire on the outpost at close range. The defenders fired effectively from their concealed positions, and the 95th Rifles were firing from the gravel pit.

The Duke of Wellington had taken up his position beneath a large elm which stood at the juncture of the Brussels road and the Ohain lane, a short distance behind La Haye Sainte.[1] Seeing that the French now surrounded La Haye Sainte, he ordered a battalion of the German Legion to go to the assistance of Major Baring. The

[1] The Wellington tree, as it came to be called owing to the Duke's having stood beneath it during the greater part of the battle, was later to be uprooted and removed to England where it was made into thousands of souvenirs, such as walking-sticks, snuff-boxes, etc., for the Duke's grateful and admiring fellow-countrymen.

Germans ran down the slope, driving the French from part of the grounds, but were now attacked by a brigade of cuirassiers under General Travers, sent across by Napoleon himself in support of the action. These horsemen inflicted heavy losses on the Germans and, riding roughshod over them, continued up the slope towards Alten's division. Allix's second brigade, on the right, the brigade of Bourgeois, had by this time reached the gravel pit and overwhelmed the three forward companies of the 95th, forcing them to retire and following them right up to the Ohain lane. Donzelot's division now came into action and with ringing cries of *'Vive l'Empereur!'* fell upon the right of Bylandt's brigade while Marcognet neared its left. On the extreme right of d'Erlon's advancing corps, Durutte was approaching Prince Bernard's position.

Bylandt's brigade, severely shaken by the heavy cannonade from La Belle Alliance, had reached breaking point; as Marcognet's great column of men assailed their left, the survivors turned and fled in a disorderly rout. This was the state to which Napoleon hoped he had reduced the entire section of the line he had been firing on; but it was not so. The whole of Sir Thomas Picton's division, hidden behind the banks to the rear of the Ohain lane, was calm and collected. Behind them, Ponsonby's heavy cavalry was ready for action.

The Duke of Wellington now had to withdraw from under the elm. With him went his staff officers and the diplomatic representatives of the Allied nations who had been observing the action at his side. Several of the company were slightly wounded but were unwilling to leave the field without seeing the outcome of the great drama unfolding before them. Donzelot and Marcognet pursued the fleeing Dutch-Belgian brigade and were very close to the Ohain lane; on their right, Durutte was now well up the slope and was driving Prince Bernard out of the farm of Papelotte. To the west of the Brussels road Count Alten awaited the onslaught of the French.

It was an exciting moment for those watching with Napoleon from Decoster's garden. Bylandt's brigade could be seen in headlong flight; the 95th Rifles were retreating with the French on their heels; the cuirassiers of Travers had reached the crest of the ridge, west of the Brussels road. All the visible forces of the enemy were falling back; from this distance Wellington's front line appeared to be collapsing and d'Erlon to be in possession of the ridge. It was only necessary now for the reserve cavalry to sweep in and strike the final blow. Victory appeared certain. Ever since Wellington had made a stand before him, Napoleon had envisaged defeating him with just such a massive, sledge-hammer blow.

All along the line, however, the tide was about to turn.

On the left, Travers was now engaged with a brigade of Alten's division, the Hanoverians of Kielmansegge, who, on his approach, had formed into squares and were putting up a strong fight.

East of the Brussels road, Bourgeois' brigade and Donzelot's division halted about thirty paces short of the Ohain lane in order to deploy. But this could not be done with any speed or precision owing to their unwieldy formation. Even as those watching from La Belle Alliance exulted, Picton brought Kempt's brigade up to the hedges of the lane and ordered them to fire. Caught by the volley and taken by surprise, the French could make no organized resistance and began to move away. Picton now ordered a bayonet charge and fell while leading the attack. By sheer weight of numbers Donzelot's men repulsed their assailants several times; but the British returned to the charge again and again and the fighting became increasingly bitter and confused.

On Donzelot's right, Marcognet had not attempted to deploy his division but had gone further than Donzelot, plunging right through the hedges into the fields beyond the lane. Suddenly, however, the brigades of Best and Pack appeared. Hitherto concealed in the tall corn, they now leapt to their feet to discharge a deadly volley at the French. The attackers recoiled before this heavy fire which they were unable to answer effectively because of their formation.

The fourth column, under Durutte, met with more success than the other three. Durutte had cleared Papelotte and La Haye of Prince Bernard's troops, reached the lane in good order, and forced his way through the hedges, driving back the Hanoverians of Best and Wincke.

It was at this point in the battle that the British cavalry came into action.

The Earl of Uxbridge had prepared two brigades for action, those of Somerset and Ponsonby, both of them heavy cavalry. They were now ordered to charge on their respective fronts.

West of the Brussels road it was English versus French heavy cavalry. Somerset's brigade (1st and 2nd Life Guards, 1st Dragoon Guards and the Blues) charged Travers' cuirassiers who had twice been repulsed while attacking the squares of Kielmansegge. The opponents were well matched and the encounter impressive, and those not otherwise occupied looked on from both sides of the field in admiration, as if watching a joust. 'It was a fair meeting of two bodies of heavy cavalry, each in perfect order,' says Shaw-Kennedy, who was present. But this action, chivalrous and ceremonial, was an exception; the subsequent contests, he says, were either between heavy cavalry in which one side had previously been wrecked upon squares of infantry, or between light and heavy cavalry. After a short struggle, the cuirassiers were driven off.[1] The English cavalry were unable to follow up this initial success, however, as the battalions of Quiot and Bachelu's division (which Ney had called in somewhat late to reinforce d'Erlon's attack) came to Travers' rescue.

On the other side of the Brussels road it was a case of cavalry versus infantry. Here, Uxbridge had ordered Ponsonby's regiments (Royals and Inniskillings with the Greys in support) to charge through the intervals of the English infantry and fall on d'Erlon's divisions, at this moment still reeling under the deadly effect of the English massed volleys and bayonet charges. The densely formed masses of French infantry struggled in vain, so pressed together that they could hardly aim at the horsemen plunging into their confused ranks or even use their side-arms. All who could now fled, though many were mown down as they attempted to escape, and some 3,000 prisoners were taken. On the French right, Durutte, who had so far been successful, was obliged to fall back with the rest of the 1st Corps, his division being the only one to retire in good order.

From La Haye Sainte to Papelotte the French were now falling back. In the eagerness of the pursuit, Ponsonby's brigade was unfortunately carried away by excitement and went much too close to the enemy's line. Siborne writes:

The Brigade, after overthrowing the French Infantry, lost nearly all

[1] *Waterloo Letters*, p. 44.

regularity, and galloped madly up to the French Position, notwith-
standing all the efforts of the Officers to prevent it, and began
sabring the Gunners and stabbing the horses of the Enemy's Batteries.
But they were now attacked by a body of French Lancers, and their
horses being blown and exhausted, they suffered severely in their
confused retreat to the British Position.[1]

Sir William Ponsonby was unhorsed and gave himself up as a
prisoner to a French lancer named Urban; seeing this, a few of the
Scots Greys returned in an attempt to rescue him, whereupon Urban,
fearing to lose his prisoner, struck him through the heart with his
lance.

It was Travers' cuirassiers and Colonel Bro's lancers who fell
upon Ponsonby's cavalry. Vandeleur now moved down to save the
remnant of the brigade with the 12th and 16th Dragoons; he charged
the French successfully from two directions, forcing them to turn
back to their own side of the valley. As Vandeleur turned to his
position, a sudden silence fell upon the field which the lesser sounds
of the fighting at Hougoumont scarcely seemed to disturb. Prince
Bernard's troops returned to the farm of Papelotte; the 95th Rifles
returned to the gravel pit and Wellington to his elm tree. D'Erlon's
infantry, having lost about 5,000 men, took up its original position.
Wellington had lost a quarter of his cavalry. The French had left
3,000 prisoners behind them and two of their batteries had been
put out of action. In addition they had lost two of their eagles.

The second phase of the battle had ended indecisively. The
question of whether Napoleon was to rule France was still to be
fought out; and yet the scene already resembled the aftermath of a
major battle. The field was strewn with the dead and dying, with
fallen horses, knapsacks, arms and accoutrements. A Scottish officer
who took part in the defence of La Haye Sainte writes:

> The ground was literally covered with French killed and wounded,
> even to the astonishment of my oldest soldiers, who said they had
> never witnessed such a sight.[2]

Riderless horses were grazing, and from time to time a wounded
Frenchman could be heard calling '*Vive l'Empereur!*' The weather at
this time was still dull and wet.[3]

[1] *Waterloo Letters*, pp. 58-9.   [2] Ibid., p. 406.   [3] Ibid., p. 199.

At Hougoumont the fighting increased in ferocity. Napoleon had now withdrawn his brother Jérôme from action and kept him at his side, presumably in order to spare him. He had ordered howitzers to open fire on the buildings and barns had been set alight. Here the wounded had been carried and it proved impossible to rescue them; they perished in the rapidly spreading flames. Soon the large Hougoumont mansion and the adjacent farmhouse were blazing; but the defenders retreated into the chapel and the gardener's house, both of which remained intact, and continued their fusillade while the French tried in vain to dislodge them.

Baron Müffling was on the left flank of Wellington's army, where Prussian officers arrived from time to time to give him news of Blücher's approach. The Prussians were most eagerly awaited by their Allies in the field, but they would be unable to enter into action for some time yet and the Duke was anxious about the next phase of the battle; for he was aware that his inferiority to the French in cavalry and guns was dangerous, although his artillery was serving him most brilliantly.

Blücher had reached Chapelle-Saint-Lambert at about one o'clock; but before risking a difficult descent into the gorges of the river Lasnes which separated him from Wellington's army he had had the whole region reconnoitred to make sure Grouchy's troops were not coming that way. Three-quarters of an hour later, being assured that the area was clear of the enemy he set his troops in motion towards Plancenoit. They had to descend steep swampy ground to the stream below, then climb the opposite bank, hauling their guns and wagons inch by inch. No meal had been provided for the men since the previous evening; they were famished and exhausted. Yet they struggled on, heartened by the presence of Blücher. 'Come along, comrades,' the old Marshal called to the gunners, who were desperately striving to move wheels sunk deep in heavy mud, 'you wouldn't let me break my word to Wellington!'

Grouchy was at last in contact with the enemy and was very near to Wavre. Just before two o'clock, Exelmans' dragoons had been attacked at La Baraque by a detachment of Prussian Hussars under Colonel Ledebur. It was only a minor affray, and Ledebur soon withdrew to Wavre. He was followed by Vandamme's corps while

Grouchy, not altogether certain that he was acting wisely, rode off to reconnoitre in person in the direction of Limalette. It was between half-past three and four o'clock when he returned to the Wavre road to receive the message sent by Napoleon at 10 a.m. '. . . his Majesty is at this moment about to attack the English army which has taken position at Waterloo. . . . Therefore his Majesty wishes you to direct your movements on Wavre so as to draw nearer to us again . . . pushing before you the army corps which have taken that direction and may have stopped at Wavre, which you should reach at the earliest possible moment'. He was much relieved. This message confirmed that he was doing exactly as ordered by the Emperor. In answer to Napoleon's subsidiary order that he should keep in touch with the main operations and establish communications, he instructed Pajol to take his forces to Limal where he was to seize the bridge and cross the Dyle. Satisfied that he had done everything possible to conform to Napoleon's wishes, Grouchy now rode on to Wavre to command the battle against the Prussians. He found Vandamme already in action against Thielemann's corps. Thielemann had placed his men well, and the battle now opening was to be long and exceedingly violent.

The second phase of the battle of Waterloo had ended shortly after three o'clock. A curious lull lasting about half an hour now hung over the field.

Wellington employed the time in preparing for the next assault. He moved Sir John Lambert's infantry brigade up into line with Picton's division. Picton was replaced by Sir James Kempt as divisional commander. La Haye Sainte was reinforced. The infantry drew together, Best closing on Kempt, and Wincke on Best. Bylandt's men, who had fled from the French, were re-formed and stood to the rear of Pack. Lambert's brigade was placed behind Kempt. What remained of Ponsonby's brigade retired to re-form at the rear.

Wellington judged that Napoleon would not attempt to force his left again but, if he made another frontal attack, would assail the centre and right. This part of his line, behind La Haye Sainte and westwards, was held by Count Alten's division; troops of the King's German Legion were nearest to the highroad, under Baron von Ompteda; on their right was the Hanoverian brigade under Count Kielmansegge which had been attacked by Travers, and beyond Kielmansegge was Sir Colin Halkett's brigade. Behind Hougoumont were the British Guards of Sir George Cooke's division, the brigade commanders being Maitland and Byng. To the right and rear of the Guards were the regiments of Colonel Mitchell's brigade, some of whom were now brought into the front line. The Brunswick battalions were posted between Maitland and Halkett. The divisions of Chassé and Clinton were held in reserve. The artillery remained stationed along the crest, in front of the infantry.

If Wellington felt anxious as he considered the price his army must pay in holding out until the Prussians arrived, he could also feel thankful that the great infantry assault on his left centre had so completely failed. Napoleon, who stood between two hostile armies, had far more reason to feel uneasy. He had underestimated both Wellington and Blücher and his situation at 3 p.m. was hazardous. He might, indeed, have chosen to draw out of the contest at this time. Although he had made no provision for a retreat, it would still have been possible for him to withdraw and save his army, leaving Ney to fight a rearguard action.

The smoke in the valley was clearing. Looking across from Wellington's line at La Belle Alliance, the professional soldiers, those who considered warfare as an art and took pride in being tested against the Emperor Napoleon, passed the lull in speculation. What would the next move be? Would Napoleon manœuvre so as to force Wellington to leave his carefully chosen ground? Was the Imperial Guard to come into action?

On sending Lobau to his right to face the Prussians, Napoleon had brought up the Imperial Guard from Rossomme to occupy the ground thus vacated. They now stood massed on both sides of the Brussels road, just to the rear of La Belle Alliance. To his opponents, Napoleon's difficulties must have been less apparent than the obvious strength of the Grand Army which, despite the defeat inflicted upon d'Erlon's corps, was impressive. With his magnificent cavalry and his superiority in guns, Napoleon indeed commanded a tremendous striking force. To those who had so recently been amazed by the brilliant exploit of his return from Elba, it must have seemed that he had good chances still of winning the day.

14

Third phase of the battle; The great cavalry attacks; Entry of the Prussians into the combat

During the lull, Napoleon was to be seen walking up and down at his headquarters, tense and pale, gazing downwards with his hands joined behind his back, lost in thought. A group of staff officers respectfully and silently followed him at a short distance, to hand in case he had a sudden command to give. His generals, never in his confidence, had nothing to do but await the workings of his genius, hoping it would now shine at its brightest since never before had so much depended upon it.

In the past, his mind had ever been fertile with flashes of inspiration which would reveal a way out of difficulties. Now, however, his orders, when at last they were given, showed no change of plan. They were merely that Marshal Ney should seize La Haye Sainte which was to be used as a base from which to make a new assault on Wellington's line. His mind was still fixed upon his original objective, the capture of Brussels.

For his task, Ney was given no other infantry but that of Reille and d'Erlon; but he was to be allowed to call upon the cavalry of Milhaud and Lefebvre-Desnouettes. The artillery remained under Napoleon's command. Additional guns were now taken to the grand battery on the ridge before La Belle Alliance, and were directed on the centre and right of Wellington's line. D'Erlon's infantry had been re-forming since their defeat, but were far from being completely rallied. Famished, exhausted by lack of sleep, many of them barefooted, they had lost heart when repulsed and were not to be capable of another determined effort until after six o'clock. A quick break through the English line would have encouraged them and given them a new access of strength; but they had no reserve of energy with which to take reverses. Yet Napoleon, remaining aloof from the battle, could not see that his front-line infantry were weary and disheartened. He expected d'Erlon's troops to go forward to the new attack with the efficiency of strong and vigorous men, and he expected Reille's troops to join them. Seeing flames shooting up from Hougoumont, he assumed the position could not be held much longer by his enemy and that Reille's corps would therefore be free to surge up the slope beyond it. But the garrison at Hougoumont showed no sign of weakening. The outpost was not to fall at all, and its gallant defenders did splendid service to their side in keeping Reille's infantry engaged throughout the day.

Not even now, when this third phase of the battle was opening, did Napoleon make plans for a retreat. No guides were appointed to direct the men along alternative routes to the frontier; no provision was made to get them across the Dyle by other means than struggling in thousands through the narrow main street of Genappe; no messengers were sent to Charleroi to ensure that at least a few preparations were made for the orderly passage of a defeated army back to France. Just as Napoleon drove his devoted soldiers to fight without food, so he was ready to abandon them in defeat.

Marshal Ney prepared for the assault on La Haye Sainte, the preliminary to the new effort to breach Wellington's line. At the same time, a diversion was made with Piré's light cavalry against the English right, which had the effect of causing Uxbridge to remove Grant's cavalry from the position the French were soon to attack. There seemed little chance of seizing La Haye Sainte since the previous attack had failed and Ney now had fewer instead of more infantry. However, he made the attempt with d'Erlon's infantry and was presently to be seen leading Quiot's brigade to the attack. One of Donzelot's brigades in skirmishing formation swarmed up the slope in support. It was not long before Quiot's troops were forced to retire, having been decimated by the well-directed fire of Major Baring's company; and the skirmishers were driven back before they reached the top of the slope.

The great cannonade was now resumed and was directed against the English line between the Brussels and Nivelles highroads. It far surpassed in violence the bombardment which had heralded d'Erlon's attack. The earth shook beneath the concussion of the guns; even the oldest soldiers on the field had never before experienced such heavy firing. Wellington withdrew the infantry most endangered; the wounded were carried from the front as rapidly as possible. The only arm now visible from the French side was the artillery, still in its forward positions, returning the fire of the battery at La Belle Alliance. Major Baring, anticipating further assaults on his outpost, sent for new supplies of ammunition. Unfortunately, owing to some oversight, no ammunition was available for La Haye Sainte, and this created a dangerous situation at the centre of Wellington's line.

It was four o'clock. The leading brigades of Bülow's column, under von Hiller and von Losthin, and part of Prince William of Prussia's cavalry, had crossed the deep ravine of the Lasne and were approaching the Wood of Paris which Prussian patrols had found unoccupied. Lobau awaited them at Frischermont.

In this new phase of the battle, Napoleon had only one chance of success. He would have to make a well co-ordinated assault of all arms on Wellington's line and strike quickly, breaking through before the Prussians could assemble in strength to attack him. If he could face the Prussians with victorious troops, all might still be well. But Wellington's position was so strong, and his nucleus of first-rate troops, the salt of his army, so trustworthy, that the assault must be vigorous indeed. Napoleon would have to risk leaving his right flank unguarded except by such troops as he had already sent to meet the Prussians, while he threw the whole weight of his army at Wellington's line.

This supreme effort was not made. Instead of directing the assault personally, Napoleon relied on Ney. Remaining in the rear, he could not see from moment to moment what was required. Ney could see, but Ney had not the command of the army but only of a limited number of troops. Napoleon cast on his Marshal a responsibility too heavy for the means allowed him, and when he failed made him one of his principal scapegoats.

At Wavre, Vandamme's corps was engaged in attacking Thielemann's corps, which held a strong position in the town. The Prussians were being driven back from the suburbs, but the French were unable to pass the barricaded bridges leading into the town itself.

Although in weight of fire Napoleon had increased his pressure on Wellington's line, his guns were not so placed as to be fully effective; they did harm and the bombardment was hard to endure, but the result was not devastating. At Hougoumont the French still wasted their efforts, while fighting on a small scale continued at La Haye Sainte where some of Quiot's brigade had remained in the orchard. It might have been expected that at this point the infantry of the Guard, supported by cavalry, would come into action. Instead, however, a grand assault of cavalry alone was ordered. Normally, unsupported cavalry was not used against a defensive line in good order. Why it was now so used has remained an unsolved problem.

According to Charras, when Wellington moved back his front-line infantry to the shelter of the reverse slopes, Napoleon was misled into thinking that his adversary was about to retreat.[1] The impression of a general movement of withdrawal was increased by the flight of many deserters, unnerved by the cannonade, and by the movement of prisoners and wagonloads of wounded men in the direction of Brussels. From the French line all this was imperfectly seen through clouds of smoke, and Napoleon, it was said, ordered a cavalry charge with the intention of turning the supposed retreat into a rout.

The cavalry attack was to fail, and in the writings of St Helena Napoleon disclaims all responsibility for it. In his first account of the manœuvre, dictated to Baron Gourgaud, he casts the blame on Ney, while in his second account he makes no mention of Ney but appears to blame Milhaud.[2] His supporters accuse Ney of having ordered the charge against the wishes and intentions of Napoleon, and Houssaye asserts that it was the Marshal and not Napoleon who made the mistake of believing Wellington to be in retreat.

It is, in fact, hard to believe that either Napoleon or Ney would have thought that Wellington was retreating. What reason could Wellington have had for retreating at this moment? He had success-fully resisted every assault of the French, and the Prussian army was to hand. One must suppose either that Napoleon ordered the cavalry attack, believing it would succeed against the English position, or that Ney, having been instructed in general terms to break through

---

[1] Charras, *Histoire de la Campagne de 1815*, pp. 277-8; 334. Houssaye, *1815*, Vol. II, pp. 364-5.

[2] Gourgaud, *Campagne de 1815*, pp. 85-7, 93, 97-8. Napoléon, *Mémoires*, 1830, Vol. IX, pp. 131-3.

the enemy line, now ordered the cavalry up because he had no other unwearied troops with which to attack.

The charge was to be made with the cuirassiers of Milhaud and the light cavalry of the Guard under Lefebvre-Desnouettes, the command to move forward being sent to the generals concerned by Marshal Ney. General Delort, in command of one of Milhaud's divisions, protested; but Ney informed him that he had had his instructions from the Emperor. This suggests that Napoleon himself ordered the cavalry attack; but even if Ney meant only that Napoleon had given him authority to use Milhaud's forces it is evident that Napoleon, as Commander-in-Chief, could have countermanded the action. According to Bonapartist tradition, Napoleon was unaware of what was going on because he was obliged to leave his post at this time in order to direct the battle against the Prussians on his right. But the cavalry attack was mounted soon after four o'clock, and at that time von Hiller and von Losthin had only just reached the Wood of Paris and Napoleon was at La Belle Alliance.

The preparations for the cavalry attack were viewed with interest from the other side of the field. Shaw-Kennedy writes:

> No one in the Anglo-Allied line could imagine what the next move would be – that is, how the third act of the drama would begin; and when it did open it was certainly in a manner quite unexpected.... At about four o'clock the cannonade became violent in the extreme.... This was evidently the prelude to some serious attack. To our surprise we soon saw that it was the prelude to an attack of cavalry upon a grand scale. Such an attack we had fully anticipated would take place at some period of the day; but we had no idea that it would be made upon our line standing in its regular order of battle, and that line as yet unshaken by any previous attack of infantry.[1]

The cavalry, 5,000 strong, now moved down to the valley where they were formed up by Ney who placed himself at their head. As trumpets rang out, they moved to the attack, the British looking on admiringly. Shaw-Kennedy says:

> This was effected in beautiful order, and the formation and advance of that magnificent and highly disciplined cavalry had, as a spectacle, a very grand effect. These splendid horsemen were enthusiastic in the

[1] Shaw-Kennedy, *Notes on the Battle of Waterloo*, pp. 115-6.

cause of Napoleon – full of confidence in him and in themselves –
thirsting to revenge the reverses which had been suffered by the
French armies – led by most experienced and able cavalry commanders and they submitted to a rigid discipline. Their advance to
the attack was splendid and interesting in the extreme.[1]

The commanders of Wellington's army braced themselves to the
assault with confidence, the more so as they saw it was an injudicious
move on Napoleon's part.

Our surprise at being so soon attacked by this great and magnificent
force of cavalry was accompanied with the opinion that the attack
was premature, and that we were perfectly prepared and secure
against its effects, so far as any military operation can be calculated
upon.[1]

The infantry waited in squares, or oblongs, in a chequered formation. The batteries were in action on the edge of the plateau, and the
Duke's order was that, after firing their last round at the oncoming
cavalry, the officers and men were to abandon the guns and run
for the squares within which they would shelter, sallying forth
again as the cavalry withdrew.

The French cavalry advanced up the slope in echelon, moving
diagonally to their left and approaching Wellington's line at a slow
trot. The battery at La Belle Alliance ceased firing, while the fire of
the English guns was intensified. The batteries of Lloyd and Cleeves,
in front of Halkett's brigade which the oncoming cavalry faced,
discharged their last salvoes when the horsemen were only forty
paces off, bringing down half the leading squadrons. For a moment
the cuirassiers paused, then the cry went up '*Vive l'Empereur!*' and
they pressed forward among fallen men and horses, while the
English gunners ran back to the squares.

The infantry were now at the mercy of the great wave of horsemen which surged upon them, but they stood firmly. With the
front ranks on one knee, the butts of their rifles on the ground,
their bayonets projecting outwards, while the inner ranks fired
over them, the squares proved to be invincible. The cavalry charged
them, but the horses swerved on meeting the bayonets while their
riders slashed out with sabres and lances to no great effect. Moreover,

[1] Shaw-Kennedy, *Notes on the Battle of Waterloo*, pp. 115-6.

since the squares were in chequered formation, the cavalry were unable to attack any one of them except under a flanking fire from others; exceedingly vulnerable themselves, they inflicted comparatively little damage. The irruption of this mass of cavalry into the English line presented an alarming spectacle, however, for cuirassiers and lancers were racing about freely between the squares, covering the ridge between La Haye Sainte and the rear of Hougoumont. The abandoned front line batteries were in their hands, and it was fortunate for Wellington that they had not the means to put them out of action. Houssaye points out that the guns could have been spiked quickly if only some of the horsemen had had on them a few headless nails and a hammer.[1]

The Earl of Uxbridge had formed up a body of heavy cavalry for a counter-attack. When the French cavalry had become sufficiently disorganized he led his men against them and had not much difficulty in putting them to flight. The gunners left the squares and ran back to their pieces, while French skirmishers crept up to fire on the infantry.

Driven down into the valley, the cuirassiers and lancers quickly re-formed and Ney now led them up the slopes for a renewed attack. It was now after half-past four and gunfire could be heard some distance east of the French line. The Prussians were coming into action.

Although Blücher had had half of Bülow's infantry and much of his cavalry close to the Wood of Paris by four o'clock, he would have liked to have awaited the arrival of the rest of the corps before attacking the French. But an urgent message from Wellington, the thunder of the French cannonade and the sight of Milhaud's cuirassiers going into action (visible to him at a distance) had made him decide to enter the battle immediately. He had accordingly made his preparations, and his men were now emerging from the wood, Losthin's infantry on one side of the Plancenoit road and Hiller's on the other, their front covered by two cavalry regiments and three light batteries. These batteries fired on the cavalry of Domon and Subervie which slowly retreated, exposing the infantry of Lobau which now prepared to attack. The Prussians fired their cannonade partly to announce to their allies that they were in action, and great

---

[1] Houssaye, *1815*, Vol. II, p. 372, and note 2.

was the relief all along Wellington's line when it was realized that help had come at last.

Ney's cavalry had again reached the crest of the slope and the English gunners had retreated into the squares. As before, the horsemen surged about the groups of infantrymen, going beyond the first line and appearing to be in possession of the crest from La Haye Sainte to Hougoumont. Captain Mercer, still posted on the extreme right of the second line, near the Nivelles road, describes his impressions at this time:

> . . . Such shoals of Lancers and others came sweeping down the slope that the whole interval between the lines was covered with them, a mixed and various multitude, all scattered and riding in different directions.
>
> The 14th Regiment immediately stood to their arms and closed their Square, whilst we made a disposition to support them with the left division of our Battery.
>
> Of the first line we could see only the deserted Guns still in position on the ridge, but of the Infantry Squares nothing! Every living soul seemed to have been swept away by this terrible burst, and so dismal was the appearance of things that an Officer of rank who happened to be standing with me at the time expressed his serious apprehension that all was over.[1]

The Earl of Uxbridge, however, watching with a critical eye as he awaited his moment to strike, was not greatly impressed by the performance of the French cavalry. He writes:

> In the afternoon a very heavy attack was made upon the whole of our line to the right of the road, and connecting itself with the troops attacking Hougoumont. It was chiefly made and frequently repeated by masses of Cuirassiers, but never in one connected line, and after the first grand attack of the morning they never came on with the degree of vigour which could give them a hope of penetrating into our immovable Squares of Infantry.[2]

Napoleon was watching from Decoster's garden. Cries of victory rang out about him, for the English guns were seen to be abandoned

---

[1] *Waterloo Letters*, pp. 216-7. Mercer gives the time as 'perhaps about 2 p.m.' but this is a mistake as it was soon after the event he describes that he was brought into the firing line where he was at once charged by Guyot's Grenadiers whose attack was made after 5 p.m.

[2] Ibid., p. 10.

and the attacking cavalry to be well over the ridge. But the Emperor, according to some accounts, was worried and displeased. Houssaye quotes the remarks he is said to have exchanged with Soult: 'Here we have a premature movement which might have fatal results.' To this Marshal Soult replied: 'He (Ney) is endangering us as he did at Iéna.' Napoleon now took a searching look round the battlefield, says Houssaye, reflected a moment or two, and then said: 'It is an hour too soon, but we must stand by what is done.' And he sent General Flahaut with orders to Generals Kellermann and Guyot to advance with their cavalry in support of Ney. This meant that the whole of his cavalry was now to go into action, a most unexpected and hazardous development. Charras says merely that Napoleon sent Kellermann's cavalry into action at this time, and that the division of grenadiers and dragoons, under Guyot, followed. Napoleon has it that Guyot joined the charge without instructions, while Flahaut, on the contrary, states that the orders he carried were that all the cavalry was to join the action. What actually happened has never been made clear, though it seems reasonable to infer, as Siborne does, that 'the French Emperor was not altogether displeased with the grand experiment which was about to be made.'[1]

General Kellermann protested against the order. But even as he turned to give his reasons to General Flahaut, General Lheritier, commander of his first division, led his men off at a trot without awaiting his confirmation. Kellermann accepted the situation and ordered the second division to advance, leaving one regiment, however, in a hollow near Hougoumont and giving the commander, General Blancard, instructions that he was on no account to move without his written order. Blancard's 800 horsemen were, indeed, the sole cavalry reserve left to the army. Guyot followed Kellermann into the valley where preparations went forward for the attack.

While all this was taking place, fighting developed on the French right between the Wood of Paris and the hamlet of Plancenoit. Lobau had made an energetic assault upon the Prussians; he had under him excellent troops, and although they were hungry they had at least been inactive throughout the day and were sufficiently rested to fight well. The Prussians, on the other hand, were not only hungry but had been on the march for twelve hours in appalling

[1] Siborne, *History of the War in France and Belgium in 1815*, Vol. II, p. 77.

conditions; they were a famished, white-faced, red-eyed company. They fought doggedly but could not withstand the French assault and had to fall back. This was only for a time, however, for the remaining brigades of Bülow's corps now emerged from the wood, and Blücher could muster 30,000 men against Lobau's 10,000. He manœuvred to Lobau's right in order to gain Plancenoit, and Lobau fell back to the level of that village which he occupied with one of his brigades.

Before Wavre, Grouchy had just received Napoleon's despatch of 1.30 p.m. with its urgent postscript ordering him to move over at once to Mont St Jean where Bülow threatened the French right flank. Heavily engaged as he now was in fighting Thielemann in Wavre, and with no troops on the left of the Dyle, there was nothing he could now do in time to be of help. However, he prepared to obey his orders to what extent he could; troops were sent to seize the bridge at Limale, held by the Prussians, and he instructed the two divisions of the 4th Corps which had not yet come into action at Wavre to march to Limale in readiness to take the road to Waterloo. Hours were to pass, however, before he could open a way westwards.

Thielemann, greatly outnumbered by the French (since one of his brigades had left for Waterloo before it was realized that Grouchy was moving on Wavre), was making a determined stand. He had sent an urgent despatch to Blücher, announcing that he was being attacked by superior forces which he feared he would be unable to vanquish. This message reached Blücher between 5.30 and 6 p.m. It received scant attention from the old marshal and his Chief-of-Staff, occupied as they were by their own immediate problems. 'Let General Thielemann defend himself as best he may,' said Gneisenau to the aide-de-camp who had brought the message. 'No matter if he is overwhelmed at Wavre if we have a victory here.'

The Earl of Uxbridge had again driven the cavalry of Milhaud and Lefebvre-Desnouettes down into the valley where Ney, in a high state of excitement, set about reforming them with the order that they were to follow Kellermann and Guyot, who were now ready to go into action. Sixty squadrons were assembled, some nine thousand strong. Seeing the formidable company of horsemen gathered before them, the men of Wellington's first line realized with amazement that they were to be subjected to an even larger cavalry assault than before. Once more they were under heavy bombardment, and skirmishers were swarming up the slope and firing on them. The infantry squares steeled themselves; the gunners were at their posts. The Duke of Wellington gave orders for the strengthening of the line and looked askance at two squares of Brunswickers, placed in front of Maitland's Guards, who were nearly out of their wits with fear and appeared likely to break up at any moment. He ordered Sir Augustus Frazer, who commanded the horse artillery, to bring Mercer's battery forward and place it between them.

The new assault upon the line now began. Slowly the French cavalry moved up from the valley: cuirassiers, lancers, chasseurs and dragoons. It was a fine spectacle, and many professional soldiers watched admiringly. Shaw-Kennedy writes:

> This third attack of cavalry consisted of seventy-seven squadrons, and was one of the most powerful efforts ever made by cavalry against infantry in the history of war. When it is considered that about 12,000 men were employed in this attack, and that only 1,000 horsemen could stand in line in the thousand yards which separated the enclosures of La Haye Sainte and Hougoumont – that, therefore twelve different ranks, two deep, could assail in succession the allied force opposed to it – and when, further, the composition of this force is considered, and the reputation of its leaders, its imposing character becomes evident. It will be recollected that these horsemen could advance only on a front of 500 yards, as they were obliged to keep at some distance from the enclosures both of Hougoumont and La Haye Sainte; and it will also be recollected that the fire of artillery, under the protection of which this vast force of cavalry advanced to make its attack, was of the most formidable character. Nearly the whole of the ground between La Haye Sainte and Hougoumont was covered with this splendid array of horsemen; their advance to the attack, made in a manner that showed the highest discipline, was majestic and imposing.[1]

Sir Augustus Frazer had galloped up to G Troop to bring them

[1] Shaw-Kennedy, *Notes on the Battle of Waterloo*, pp. 117-8. Shaw-Kennedy speaks of 12,000 cavalry. The figure given by Fortescue is 9,000 or thereabouts.

into the firing line, 'Left limber up, and as fast as you can!' he called out. Mercer writes:

The words were scarcely uttered when my gallant troop stood as desired in columns of subdivisions, left in front, pointing towards the main ridge. 'At a gallop, march!' and away we flew, as steadily and as compactly as if at a review. I rode with Frazer, whose face was as black as a chimney sweep's from the smoke, and the jacket-sleeve of his right arm torn open by a musket-ball or case shot, which had merely grazed his flesh. As we went along, he told me that the enemy had assembled an enormous mass of heavy cavalry in front of the point to which he was leading us (about one-third of the distance between Hougoumont and the Charleroi road), and that in all probability we should be immediately charged on gaining our position.

The Duke of Wellington, who had waited to see the troop arrive, remarked: 'Ah! That's the way I like to see horse artillery move'. The English field batteries were far superior to those of the French; they were considerably more mobile, and their personnel were thoroughly trained and severely disciplined. Napoleon's guns could only be moved with much difficulty on the boggy ground, but Wellington's batteries could be moved rapidly to threatened points on his line.[1] This technical superiority did much to compensate for the fact that the French had many more guns on the field than had the English.

The position which Mercer's troop now approached was immediately between the Brunswick squares. Whereas the batteries for the most part were stationed along the crest of the position in front of the infantry, with the lane behind them, G Troop was on the reverse slope, though only two or three feet below the level of the lane, which ran immediately in front of it. Beyond the lane was a plateau of fairly level ground extending for forty or fifty yards; then the ground descended to the valley dividing the two armies.[2]

By now the Brunswick squares were considerably thinned out; they were under heavy fire and were falling fast. Every moment the shot was making great gaps which, Mercer says, 'the officers and sergeants were actively employed in filling up by pushing their

[1] Naylor, *Waterloo*, pp. 32-3.
[2] *Waterloo Letters*, maps facing pages 186 and 214, and pp. 217-8.

men together, and sometimes thumping them ere they would move'.
These Brunswick troops were very young and were both frightened
and bewildered. Mercer refers to them as mere children, none of the
privates appearing to be above eighteen years of age.[1]

As G Troop ascended the reverse slope to its position, Sir Augustus
Frazer instructed Mercer not to expose his men but to retire into
the infantry squares if the cavalry charged home. The Duke's orders
were positive, he said. And he then rode away. Mercer writes:

> We breathed a new atmosphere – the air was suffocatingly hot,
> resembling that issuing from an oven. We were enveloped in thick
> smoke, and *malgré* the incessant roar of cannon and musketry could
> distinctly hear around us a mysterious humming noise, like that which
> one hears of a summer's evening proceeding from myriads of black
> beetles; cannon-shot, too, ploughed the ground in all directions,
> and so thick was the hail of balls and bullets that it seemed dangerous
> to extend the arm lest it should be torn off.

The leading subdivision had scarcely gained the interval between
the two squares when Mercer caught sight of the advancing enemy.
He writes:

> ... A heavy column of Cavalry, composed of Grenadiers à Cheval
> and Cuirassiers, had just ascended the plateau and was advancing
> upon us at a rapid pace, so that there scarcely appeared time even to
> get into action, and, if caught in column, of course we were lost.
> However, the order was given to deploy, and each gun as it came
> up immediately opened its fire; the two Infantry Squares at the same
> time commencing a feeble and desultory fire; for they were in such
> a state that I momentarily expected to see them disband.[1]

A glance at the squares showed him that he would be obliged to
disobey the Duke's orders. It would be madness to seek refuge
among those demoralized young soldiers. The moment they saw
his men running from the guns they would turn and run themselves.

> We had better, then, fall at our posts than in such a situation. Our
> coming up seemed to reanimate them, and all their eyes were directed
> to us – indeed, it was providential, for, had we not arrived as we did,
> I scarcely think there is a doubt of what would have been their fate.

[1] *Waterloo Letters*, p. 218.

All the cavalry of Napoleon's army was approaching the first line with their battle cry of '*Vive l'Empereur!*' There was the dull thudding of thousands of horses' hoofs and the English guns roared. G Troop faced a massive column of horse grenadiers and cuirassiers, and it seemed nothing could save them from being overrun. When their guns came into action there was great slaughter, but the advance of the French continued steadily until they were separated from the troop by little more than the width of the lane. Each round, however, encumbered the ground increasingly, and the horsemen were beginnning to have difficulty in making their way forward. The guns, firing at such close range, wrought havoc, and suddenly, as if miraculously, the horsemen, instead of surging round the gunners and putting them to the sword, fell into disorder and turned to escape. The scene that followed, Mercer says, is scarcely to be described.

> Several minutes elapsed ere they succeeded in quitting the plateau, during which our fire was incessant, and the consequent carnage frightful, for each Gun (9 Prs.) was loaded with a round and case shot, all of which, from the shortness of the distance, and elevation of the ground on which they stood, *must* have taken effect.
>
> Many, instead of seeking safety in retreat, wisely dashed through the intervals between our Guns, and made their way as we had seen others do; but the greater part, rendered desperate at finding themselves held, as it were, in front of the Battery, actually fought their way through their own ranks, and in the struggle we saw *blows* exchanged on all sides. At last the wreck of this formidable Column gained protection under the slope of the hill, leaving the plateau encumbered with their killed and wounded, and we then ceased firing, that our men, who were much fatigued with their exertions, might rest themselves and be fresh against the next attack, which we saw preparing; for they had not retired so far down the hill but that the tall caps of the Grenadiers of the leading Squadrons were visible above the brow.[1]

Thus Mercer's troop gained the distinction of repelling by its own unaided fire a heavy cavalry charge of the Imperial Guard.

Elsewhere the batteries had fired with telling effect until the last moment, and then the gunners had run back to the infantry squares

---

[1] *Waterloo Letters*, pp. 218-9.

as ordered, though here and there a man had merely thrown himself beneath his gun while the storm passed over his head. Again the squares had stood firmly as the horsemen came over the crest. Bristling with bayonets, they drove off their assailants with steady volleys of musket fire, while the cavalry, as before, surged unavailingly round them and eventually retired to re-form.

The retreat of the cavalry was succeeded by a shower of shots and shells, and Mercer says that he and his men must have been annihilated but for the little bank which gave them some degree of cover. Presently skirmishers crept up to fire on them at close range with carbines and pistols; this was the prelude to a new assault by the cavalry and the intention was to draw the fire of the guns. The gunners, while waiting for the renewal of the cavalry charge, had to stand with lighted portfires in their hands, and the temptation to fire on the skirmishers was so great that Mercer had difficulty in restraining them. Finally, to make sure they did not fire, he urged his horse up the little bank and rode up and down in front of his own guns; he was within speaking distance of the skirmishers who immediately made a target of him. Their shooting was not very accurate, but he describes an encounter with one of them who only narrowly missed him.

. . . I shook my finger at him, and called him *coquin*, etc. The rogue grinned as he reloaded, and again took aim. I certainly felt rather foolish at that moment, but was ashamed, after such bravado, to let him see it, and therefore continued my promenade. As if to prolong my torment, he was a terrible time about it. To me it seemed an age. Whenever I turned, the muzzle of his infernal carbine still followed me. At length, bang it went, and whiz came the ball close to the back of my neck, and at the same instant down dropped the leading driver of one of my guns (Miller), into whose forehead the cursed missile had penetrated.

The cavalry column once more mounted the plateau and the skirmishers wheeled off to the right and left, leaving the ground clear for their charge. The horsemen came on in compact squadrons at a steady trot.

None of your furious but galloping charges was this, but a deliberate advance, at a deliberate pace, as of men resolved to carry their point. They moved in profound silence, and the only sound that could be heard from them amidst the incessant roar of battle was the low thunderlike reverberation of the ground beneath the simultaneous tread of so many horses. On our part was equal deliberation. Every man stood steadily at his post, the guns ready, loaded with a round shot first and a case over it; the tubes were in the vents; the portfires glared and sputtered behind the wheels; and my word alone was wanting to hurl destruction on that goodly show of gallant men and noble horses. I delayed this, for experience had given me confidence. The Brunswickers partook of this feeling, and with their squares, much reduced in point of size – well closed, stood firmly, with arms at the recover, and eyes fixed on us, ready to commence their fire at our first discharge. It was indeed a grand and imposing spectacle!

Mercer waited until the head of the column was within fifty or sixty yards, then gave the order, 'Fire!' The effect, he says, was terrible. Nearly the whole leading rank fell at once, and the round shot penetrated deep into the column. 'The ground, already encumbered with victims of the first struggle, became now almost impassable.' The column still came on, but progress was increasingly difficult. The gunners worked with amazing speed and accuracy, while the Brunswickers, transformed by the example before them, kept up a spirited running fire. Pushing their way among heaps of carcasses, the head of the cavalry advanced only to fall and further impede those who came after. 'The discharge of every gun was followed by a fall of men and horses like that of grass before the mower's scythe.'

All fell into disorder. There was such a vast barrier of dead and dying men and horses on the plateau that the column was brought to a standstill. The general who had led the horsemen into action, and whom Mercer had particularly noticed as being clad in a rich uniform and loaded with decorations, was still unharmed. His gesticulations and volubility were in striking contrast to the restrained and serious demeanour of the men under him whom he was now ordering 'with loud and rapid vociferations' to press forward. Some of them devotedly endeavoured to obey him; but the horses could not be urged any further onwards and the column had to retire.

Of course the same confusion, struggle amongst themselves, and slaughter prevailed as before, until gradually they disappeared over the brow of the hill. We ceased firing, glad to take breath. Their retreat exposed us, as before, to a shower of shot and shells: these last, falling amongst us with very long fuses, kept burning and hissing a long time before they burst, and were a considerable annoyance to man and horse. The bank in front, however, again stood our friend, and sent many over us innocuous.

All along the line the squares were being assailed and were resisting as before, though with diminishing numbers. A private of the 95th Rifle Regiment describes his experiences during the cavalry attacks:

Boney's Imperial Horse Guards, all clothed in armour, made a charge at us; we saw them coming and we all closed in and formed a square just as they came within ten yards of us, and they found that they could do no good with us; they fired with their carbines on us, and came to the right about directly, and at that moment the man on my right hand was shot through the body.... We kept up a constant fire at the Imperial Guards as they retreated, but they often came to the right about and fired; and as I was loading my rifle, one of their shots came and struck my rifle, not two inches above my left hand, and broke the stock, and bent the barrel in such a manner that I could not get the ball down; just at that time we extended again, and my rifle was no use to me; a nine-pound shot came and cut the sergeant of our company right in two; he was not above three file from me, so I threw down my rifle and went and took his rifle as it was not hurt at this time. We had lost both our colonels, major, and two eldest captains, and only a young captain to take command of us.... Seeing we had lost so many men and all our commanding officers, my heart began to fail, and Boney's Guards made another charge on us; but we made them retreat as before, and while we was in square, the Duke of Wellington and his staff came up to us in all the fire, and saw we had lost all our commanding officers; he, himself, gave the word of command; the words he said to our regiment were this, – '95th, unfix your swords, left face, and extend yourselves once more; we shall soon have them over the other hill'; and then he rode away on our right, and how he escaped being shot God only knows, for all that time the shot was flying like hailstones.[1]

At times Wellington would retire into one of the squares; when the cavalry drew off to re-form he would emerge to see what

[1] Anon., *The Battle of Waterloo 1815*, p. 200.

damage had been done and bring up reserves to fill the gaps. The enemy charged again and again while the squares shrank and the men grew increasingly weary. Casualties, however, were inflicted not so much by the cavalry as by the French skirmishers who were employed in great force and poured a galling fire on the squares whenever the horsemen withdrew. Trip's Netherlandish cavalry brigade deserted at this time, and the Cumberland Hussars, a Hanoverian regiment, untrained and badly led, also left the field and galloped back to Brussels, spreading panic as they went. But the infantry squares did not move. Even the young Brunswickers stood their ground to the end.[1]

The vast concourse of French cavalry became increasingly confused. They were far too dense a body for the field. They had come up from the valley packed so closely together that they could not manœuvre; and now as they rode about among the twenty or so attenuated squares the men of different regiments became commingled, and they were continually breaking one another's charges. General Lheritier led his cuirassiers to the rear of the second line and came under the fire of Wellington's reserve batteries. An entire French regiment moved to its left, swept up the Nivelles road, then turned off towards Braine l'Alleud behind Mitchell's position, coming down again past Hougoumont to re-form in the valley. But such forays gained them nothing.

The charges became less rapid, less vigorous. The atmosphere had grown stiflingly hot under clouds of sulphurous smoke. Most of the French generals were wounded. Marshal Ney, his third horse having been shot under him, was on foot. The great attack was failing, was becoming incoherent. And now the Duke of Wellington came out of the square of the 73rd Regiment to order his cavalry into action. Soon the English squadrons fell upon the great company of French horsemen and succeeded in driving them down into the valley, broken and defeated.

Even now Marshal Ney would not give in. Seeing Blancard's carabiniers, left in reserve by Kellermann, he seized a horse and rode across to them. General Blancard did his best to save this small

[1] The French claim to have broken a few of the squares and taken two colours (Houssaye, *1815*, Vol. II, p. 383), but this is evidently incorrect (see Fortescue, *A History of the British Army*, Vol. X, pp. 375-6).

reserve, but Ney insisted upon leading them at the head of a new attack. There was no possibility of success. The carabiniers reached some of the squares but were impeded by the bodies of the slain which formed impassable barriers and were soon driven back by Grant, who had returned to his original position after discovering that Piré's movements were merely a demonstration. Yet again the main body renewed its attack, gallantly but wearily. The horses could not move with any speed; they had not been cared for during the night, and the many which had had to stand in the rain loaded with their riders were obviously much the worse for it. A stream of dismounted men continually poured to the rear; then horses began to retire with their riders, and soon the whole wavered and turned, discouraged and broken, riding back to the centre of the valley, followed at a distance rather than driven off by the English cavalry, themselves exhausted.

On the French right flank, Bülow's corps had now succeeded in driving out the brigade placed by Lobau in Plancenoit; taking possession of the village, they opened fire on Lobau's troops, their round-shot reaching the Charleroi road, behind Napoleon. In danger now of having his line of retreat cut off, Napoleon sent Duhesme with the Young Guard and twenty-four guns to recapture the village. The cavalry of Durutte, in the region of Papelotte and La Haye, was obliged to turn and face the Prussians.

Forced to retire with his men who could make no further effort, Ney now threw in six infantry regiments from Reille's corps against the British line, supporting them with a few remnants of cavalry which he had gathered together. But the force was not strong enough; the English gunners opened fire and 1,500 were shot down in a few moments; the rest were beaten off by the brigades of Duplat and Halkett. The cavalry could not even pass the English batteries and soon returned down the hill.

Ney had lost a third of his men and horses, and many commanding officers had fallen. The losses on Wellington's side were no less severe; although the Duke was unhurt, many of his Staff officers had been killed at his side. The heavy cavalry on both sides was too exhausted for further effort.

The British line had been contracted and the front reinforced during the cavalry charges. Chassé's division was now on the march from Braine- l'Alleud, the Duke being by this time persuaded that Napoleon would not manœuvre to his right. Adam's brigade (of Clinton's division), which had been in reserve, was moved towards the right centre and formed up behind the ridge north of Hougoumont. But the Hal detachment was not brought into the fight, although it might have been expected that the Duke would make use of it. D'Erlon's infantry, although the attempt to take La Haye Sainte had been so promptly repulsed, continued fighting intermittently about that stronghold whose defenders were now running short of ammunition and could not be supplied with more.

On the French right flank, Duhesme had succeeded in driving the Prussians out of Plancenoit. But the corps of Pirch I was nearing the Wood of Paris and Ziethen's advance guard had reached Ohain.

Such was the position at 6 p.m. at the end of the third phase of the battle.

15

Fourth phase of the battle; La Haye Sainte captured; Fifth phase; The attack of the Imperial Guard; Ziethen's arrival; Rout of the French army

Rain had ceased during the afternoon and the evening was to be fine. Napoleon was now seen riding forward to inspect the battlefield, considerably heartened by the success of the Young Guard who were in possession of Plancenoit. One or two of the generals accompanying him were wounded at this time, for he had moved within range of the enemy's fire. Decoster, the peasant guide who had been forced to follow the Imperial party, showed signs of panic and made repeated attempts to turn his horse and get away. 'My friend,' Napoleon is reported to have said, 'a bullet will hit you behind just as certainly as in front and it will not look so well.' Of late, Napoleon had often been morose and silent, but he was now in excellent form; he talked encouragingly to the soldiers and assured his companions that they would reach Brussels that night in time for supper. Despite Wellington's determined resistance, he did not admit the possibility that the English could withstand the prolonged pounding of the Grand Army; he imagined they must by now be on the point of collapse, and he gave Ney the order to take La Haye Sainte at all costs.

Napoleon still had a chance of breaching Wellington's line; but now that the whole of his cavalry was wrecked he could not hope to do more than inflict a reverse upon his enemy. A retreat at this point would no doubt have been preferable to remaining on the field; but the Imperial mind was clouded by delusion.

Ney was now approaching La Haye Sainte at the head of Donzelot's division and a detachment of engineers. At the same time, on the right, Durutte advanced on the farm of Papelotte.

La Haye Sainte had recently been reinforced, but Major Baring's repeated requests for more ammunition had remained unanswered. For some reason or other, the place had not been adequately prepared for defence. 'The most important mistake which the Duke of Wellington committed as to the actual fighting of the battle of

Waterloo,' says Shaw-Kennedy, 'was the overlooking the vast importance of retaining possession at any cost of the farm and enclosures of La Haye Sainte,'[1] Not only had an inadequate supply of ammunition been provided, but all tools and implements with which the defence could have been strengthened had been removed. Taking stock at this time, the defenders found they had only three or four rounds of ammunition each. There was some question of withdrawing to the main position, but the men were so willing to fight to the end that Major Baring decided to hold out as long as he could. The French now assailed the position with resolution; many fell, but gradually the fire of the defenders died down. Their ammunition was spent. Ney's engineers were able to batter down the gates and doors of the farm with their axes and enter the buildings. Stubborn hand-to-hand fighting continued until the heroic garrison was almost wiped out. At last, having delayed the French occupation until the last possible moment, Major Baring struggled up the Brussels road with forty-two of his men, all who remained of the original garrison of 378.

In capturing La Haye Sainte, Ney had gained a great advantage for the French and he followed up his success promptly, bringing up a battery to fire from the position at the Allied troops on the Ohain lane, and placing a French regiment in the gravel pit which the 95th had been forced to abandon. The whole front was in action once more; Reille's infantry were engaged at Hougoumont; a group of cuirassiers had rallied and was forming in the valley, not far from La Haye Sainte; Durutte had driven Prince Bernard's forces out of Papelotte, and the divisions of Quiot and Marcognet, stimulated by Donzelot's success, began to assail Wellington's line anew.

Wellington now faced a critical situation. His centre was subjected to a steady fire from the French troops sheltered in the gravel pit, while the battery brought up by Ney bombarded it at close range. D'Erlon's infantry surged upon the Ohain lane, moving up on both sides of the farm, while the cuirassiers who had been forming in the valley came forward in support. It was now that the Prince of Orange made a disastrous mistake. A battalion of the King's German Legion was in square, awaiting the attack, and he ordered it to

---

[1] Shaw-Kennedy, *Notes on the Battle of Waterloo*, p. 174.

deploy and drive off the French infantry despite the urgent appeal of its commander, Colonel von Ompteda. The battalion succeeded in driving off the enemy infantry, but was inevitably charged and destroyed by the cuirassiers. Fewer than twenty of the battalion survived, and Ompteda himself was killed. The 3rd German Hussars charged and drove off the French cavalry, but there was now a dangerous gap at the centre, and Kielmansegge's brigade, which adjoined that of Ompteda, was already very thin. Between Halkett's and Kempt's right the line was open.

Shaw-Kennedy galloped across to the Duke, who had again had to withdraw from the elm and was with the Guards, and informed him of the situation. He writes:

> This very startling information he received with a degree of coolness and replied to in an instant with such precision and energy, as to prove the most complete self-possession; and left on my mind the impression that his Grace's mind remained perfectly calm during every phase, however serious, of the action; that he felt confident of his own powers of being able to guide the storm which raged about him; and from the determined manner in which he then spoke, it was evident that he had resolved to defend to the last extremity every inch of the position which he then held. His Grace's answer to my representation was in the following words, or nearly so: 'I shall order the Brunswick troops to the spot, and other troops besides; go you and get all the German troops of the division to the spot that you can, and all the guns that you can find.'[1]

There were other gaps along the line. The 73rd Regiment of Sir Colin Halkett's brigade had not a single officer remaining; Major Kelly, sent by the Duke, took charge; so precarious did the situation seem that he had the colours, which were riddled with shot, removed from the staff and sent to the rear, rolled round the body of a sergeant. Officers were hurrying to the Duke from all sides to ask for instructions, telling him that their situation was growing desperate; but they received no other order than to stand firm to the last man. Deserters streamed away to the rear; a Belgian regiment began firing their muskets in the air, meaning to move off under cover of the smoke; they were only prevented by the intervention of the Duke

[1] Shaw-Kennedy, *Notes on the Battle of Waterloo*, p. 125.

and an officer of Vandeleur's dragoons who placed his squadron in their rear.

As a finishing touch to the situation in which Wellington was now placed, General Ziethen, instead of joining the battle on the left of the English line, was marching down from Ohain to reinforce Blücher at Plancenoit.

Ziethen had arrived at Ohain at six o'clock with his advance guard and had been met by Colonel Freemantle, an aide-de-camp of Wellington's. Freemantle explained to him that help was urgently needed and asked if he could send reinforcements immediately, even if few in number. But Ziethen would not risk·throwing his corps into action in small sections, and would do no more than promise to help directly he had the bulk of his corps assembled. While waiting for his forces to come up, he had sent an aide-de-camp towards Mont St Jean to find out what was taking place; but this officer, finding great confusion on Wellington's rear and misled by the stream of deserters, had returned to report that Wellington's army was in retreat. Fearing to become involved in a rout, Ziethen decided to join Blücher and the main army.

Fortunately Wellington had a loyal colleague in Baron Müffling who was on the look-out for the arrival of Ziethen's corps. From his post just above Papelotte he saw the Prussians moving southwards, and he galloped after them at full speed, determined to bring them back.

It was equally fortunate that Ney was unable to press home his advantage. The infantry at his disposal, though they had rallied sufficiently to take La Haye Sainte and advance to the Ohain lane, were too weak from hunger and exposure to make the culminating effort now required. Though Wellington's line was so dangerously thinned out by casualties and desertion, the men who remained were still formidable. Men like Mercer and his troop could not be routed; they had to be killed where they stood. Wellington's trained infantry were true to their tradition; as their comrades fell they closed their ranks and stood firm. The artillery continued their fire although many guns were now out of action and hundreds of gunners lay dead. In many places, the dead were piled high in front of the line. Ney's troops, though they had the advantage at the centre and although Ney himself ordered them forward, urging them to seize their chance of victory, recoiled at the sight of the barrier before them and would go no further. A body of unwearied troops from the reserve was urgently needed to breach the line. Ney now sent Colonel Heymès galloping back to La Belle Alliance with a request that Napoleon should at once send him the necessary infantry from the Imperial Guard. The Colonel was not well received. 'Troops!' the Emperor snapped. 'Where do you expect me to find them? Am I to make them?'

Napoleon still had in reserve fourteen infantry battalions of the Imperial Guard. But the request came at a moment of crisis. On his right flank the Prussians had rallied after being driven out of Plancenoit and had returned to the attack. Lobau fell back; the Young Guard, after a desperate struggle, were forced out of the village. Bülow was in possession of Plancenoit and was bombarding La Belle Alliance. Napoleon was threatened with an irruption of Prussian troops to his rear and, ignoring Ney's appeal, he turned his full attention to the second conflict now developing. Yet the first necessity was to break through the English line, for Wellington had reserves to bring up and if allowed a short respite would save himself. Napoleon's Empire was lost unless he put the English out of action at this moment.

Two battalions of the Old Guard, under General Morand, were now sent to retake Plancenoit. At the same time, Napoleon ordered eleven battalions of the Guard to be formed in squares and positioned alongside the Brussels road between La Belle Alliance and Rossomme Farm, facing Plancenoit. A battalion of chasseurs, which had been at Le Caillou farm all day guarding the Imperial coaches and treasury, turned to face the Prussians who were already surging into the Wood of Chantelet. Thus Napoleon used the Guard to protect his rear while Ney, completely frustrated, could do no more than keep his forces engaged along the fringe of Wellington's line.

General Morand's force, with a bayonet charge on Plancenoit, succeeded in driving the Prussians 600 yards to the east of the village. This action, bold and successful, took twenty minutes. It was now seven o'clock. For the time being Plancenoit was firmly held, and Napoleon prepared to strike at Wellington with the Guard.

By this time Wellington had filled in the dangerous gaps and strengthened his line. He had not only ordered the Brunswick troops to the centre, but had placed himself at their head. Part of Kruse's Nassau contingent were to their rear, Chassé's division had arrived from Braine l'Alleud, and the cavalry of Vandeleur and Vivian now came up at a quick trot from the left of the line. Baron Müffling had overtaken General Ziethen and had explained the true state of affairs to him. 'The battle is lost,' he said, 'if the 1st Corps does not go to the Duke's rescue.' Ziethen thereupon countermarched his men, allowing Müffling to direct the advance. And as soon as they were assured of the approach of the Prussians, Vandeleur and Vivian had left for the centre of the line. Thus Wellington was prepared for the assault of the Imperial Guard.

Ziethen's cavalry was visible above the farm of Papelotte, and the infantry was moving down on Smohain. Pirch I was emerging from the Wood of Paris with his corps, ready to join Bülow and aid him in a renewed assault on the rear of the French.

Blücher was now coming into action with three infantry corps and a strong force of artillery and cavalry; already he had in the region just under 52,000 men. 104 guns with their wagons of ammunition had been successfully brought across the difficult tract of country from Wavre. Wellington's line stood firm; the men, though weary and becoming short of ammunition, were in good heart now that Ziethen's corps was in sight. The guns of Grouchy and Thielemann could be heard in the distance, firing at Limale and Wavre.

Count Drouot was bringing up nine battalions of the Imperial Guard from their positions on the Brussels road to La Belle Alliance. Ney had been ordered to prepare d'Erlon's corps to support the new attack, and to make ready what he could of the cavalry. As the squares of the Guard moved forward, a French deserter galloped across the field to the right of Wellington's line; he gave information of the impending attack, even saying at which point it would be directed.

The sun was falling towards the horizon. After being hidden most of the day it now shone forth brilliantly, casting long shadows over the field of Waterloo. Hours ago, when it rose, Napoleon had declared that it was destined to illumine the ruin of England before it set. Raising his glass, he looked across the field at Wellington's line; on his left, fighting raged round flaming Hougoumont which the

English still held. At the centre, the infantry of Quiot, Donzelot and Marcognet were skirmishing on the slope before the Ohain lane, while Durutte, though in possession of La Haye and Papelotte, was threatened by the arrival of Ziethen's troops which were approaching him from Smohain. Already Durutte's men were recoiling at the sight of the unknown column now to be seen on their flank. In the valley, the weary and dispirited cavalry were inactive.

Napoleon's situation had become catastrophic, and the only reasonable thing he could now do was to attempt to save as much of his army as he could, using the Imperial Guard to cover a retreat. At Le Caillou, indeed, the commander of the chasseurs had already made the decision to send the entire train of carriages and wagons left in his charge to the rear. He had given orders that the Imperial travelling carriage should be halted at the lower end of Genappe while most of the other vehicles were to continue down the road to Charleroi. But Napoleon resolved to play his last stake.

Firing had much diminished on both sides of the field as ammunition was running low, but the French batteries now increased their fire. Napoleon came forward to speak to the soldiers of d'Erlon's corps, now being re-formed by Ney, and urged them to surpass themselves and carve out for him a way to Brussels. Six battalions of the Middle Guard now arrived at La Belle Alliance and he hastened their formation. Addressing them in their turn, he used all his eloquence to arouse their ardour, promising them victory, and for good measure announcing that Grouchy was just arriving on the field to take the enemy in the rear. This last piece of news was also carried to all parts of the field by officers whom Napoleon sent off in urgent haste. Grouchy was arriving with 30,000 men! The Guard was coming into action and the day was won! Even general officers were not spared the deception. 'Reille, d'Erlon and the generals under their orders,' says Charras, 'received it from Labédoyère, aide-de-camp of Napoleon.'[1] The fraudulent message produced its momentary effect; hope returned as the troops prepared for the final effort demanded of them. Yet, willing though they now were to fight on, they were not capable of the vigorous action Napoleon was ordering. Reille's infantry increased their efforts at

[1] Charras, *Histoire de la Campagne de 1815*, pp. 295-6.

Hougoumont, but unavailingly; d'Erlon's men forced their way once more to the Ohain lane, but were kept at bay by the Brunswick and Nassau troops under Wellington. As for the cavalry, with the exception of a detachment of cuirassiers which was re-forming, they were too broken to make any further effort.

The Guard were moving forward. 'A black mass of the grenadiers of the Imperial Guard, with music playing and the great Napoleon at their head, came rolling onward from the farm of La Belle Alliance,' as an English observer put it.[1] Posting one battalion on high ground between La Haye Sainte and Hougoumont, Napoleon led the other five onwards towards the English line and appeared to be about to command the assault in person. He had ended his stirring address with the cry: '*Tout le monde en arrière!*' which suggested that he intended to place himself in front. For a time he did, indeed, march at the head of the troops; but as they reached La Haye Sainte he relinquished his place to Marshal Ney and took shelter in the gravel-pit. An eye-witness says:

> This fine and terrible column which he had sometime headed, found him here as it passed and defiled before him in order to advance, taking a demi-tour to the bottom of the hillock, and directly in front of the enemy's squares, which Buonaparte himself could not see from the lateral point which he occupied, although it is very true that he was close enough to the enemy's batteries. As the corps passed him, he smiled and addressed to them expressions of confidence and encouragement. The march of these old warriors was very firm, and there was something solemn in it. Their appearance was very fierce. A kind of savage silence reigned among them. There was in their looks a mixture of surprise and discontent, occasioned by their unexpected meeting with Buonaparte who, as they thought, was at their head.[2]

Marshal Ney led the Guard into action. Their front being covered by d'Erlon's troops, which were engaged immediately to the west of La Haye Sainte, they turned obliquely to the north-west, aiming at Wellington's right centre. The five battalions advanced in echelon. The 1st battalion of the 3rd Grenadiers took the lead with Marshal Ney and General Friant riding at their head; they were followed on

[1] Sidney, *The Life of Lord Hill, G.C.B.*, p. 309.
[2] Anon., *The Battle of Waterloo 1815*, p. 117.

their left by the 4th Grenadiers, then by the 1st and 2nd battalions of the 3rd Chasseurs, who gradually merged into one group, and finally by the 4th Chasseurs who were on the extreme left. The generals rode slowly at the head of their battalions, and the whole body of men moved with admirable precision.

Smoke hung in sulphurous clouds over the field; the light of the declining sun pierced it in gold shafts. Fighting continued above La Haye Sainte where the Duke was directing the Brunswick, Nassau and Hanoverian troops as they fought off d'Erlon's infantry. British Horse Artillery and Field Brigades waited in a concave line along the ridge which ran down from the Ohain lane to the rear of Hougoumont. They now opened fire on the leading battalion of the Guard, taking them in the flank with a double salvo of grape-shot from over thirty guns. Marshal Ney fell from his fifth horse, rose and continued to lead the column on foot. Closing their ranks, the grenadiers moved on, reaching the Ohain lane, driving back some Brunswickers and seizing guns temporarily abandoned. Then, deviating slightly, they attacked Halkett's brigade, and the 30th and 73rd Regiments retired before them. General Friant fell wounded from his horse and was taken to the rear. Pausing at La Haye Sainte, he talked to Napoleon, assuring him that the Guard were breaking through Wellington's line and that victory had been achieved. Napoleon, still in the gravel-pit, awaited the arrival of the three battalions of the Old Guard, due to follow the Middle Guard into action. From time to time, says a contemporary French account, he made as if to go towards the front line, whereupon Bertrand or one of the others would urgently restrain him, telling him that the safety of France and the army depended upon his life. He was easily dissuaded from any rash action, and it was noticed that when any message had to be taken it was sent by one of those who had remained silent, not by one who had reminded him of the value of his life.

On the left of Sir Colin Halkett's position, a battery was now brought up by General Chassé which opened fire on the French grenadiers; then Ditmers' brigade, 3,000 strong, was ordered forward in a bayonet charge against the left flank of the French, driving them down the slope. By this time the second battalion of the Guard, the 4th Grenadiers, had arrived on the scene. Supported by artillery, it attacked the right-hand square of Halkett's brigade, the 33rd and 69th Regiments. These regiments, terribly reduced by the great cavalry attacks, showed signs of breaking; but Sir Colin Halkett seized the standard of the 33rd and stood firm, waving it above his head. He fell, wounded, but his courage had inspired his men. They held their ground and succeeded in throwing off the attackers.

The 1st and 2nd battalions of the 3rd Chasseurs were now on their way to strike at the point held by Maitland's brigade. The Duke of Wellington, seeing their approach, rode across and instructed Bolton's Field Brigade to keep a good look out.

There was movement everywhere. The grenadiers were still retiring into the valley; the last battalion of Ney's column was moving forward with cavalry in support. Napoleon was riding down into the valley from La Haye Sainte to meet the three battalions of the Old Guard who were just leaving La Belle Alliance to form for the attack.

The gunfire from the English line had slackened owing to shortage of ammunition; but as the chasseurs approached Maitland's position Bolton's brigade opened point-blank fire, inflicting heavy casualties. The chasseurs came on firmly, reaching the summit of the position. Maitland's Guards awaited them, lying concealed in the corn behind the lane, and, on a command from the Duke of Wellington, 'Up, Guards, and make ready!' they sprang to their feet and opened fire on the chasseurs, who were taken completely by surprise. 300 of the French fell, and while they halted in confusion Wellington ordered a charge. The British Guards rushed forward with a cheer, and the chasseurs broke and fled down the slope. But now the 4th Chasseurs were coming into action and the British Guards returned to their line to await the new assault.

The 4th Chasseurs, the last of Ney's assault column, now reached Wellington's line. Maitland's Guards and Halkett's brigade awaited them, and William Halkett's Hanoverian brigade emerged from Hougoumont to fire on their rear. The 52nd Light Infantry of Adam's brigade was concealed on the reverse slope of the Allied line, to the right of the Guards. Sir John Colborne, their commanding officer, watched the chasseurs moving forward to the summit of the slope. On his own initiative, and choosing his moment well, he wheeled the 52nd upon its left company, bringing it out nearly parallel with the left flank of the attacking column on which he opened fire. Taken by surprise, the French turned towards the new foe and began firing from the flank. But Maitland's Guards and the 95th Rifles were firing on them from the front and, caught on two sides, they first gave ground and then broke and fled in confusion. The 52nd, who had moved with great coolness and precision, were now ordered to charge with the bayonet, an order they received with a resounding cheer as they pressed forward, led by Sir John Colborne. Followed by the 71st Regiment and the 95th Rifles, (i.e. the rest of Adam's brigade) they moved obliquely across the field, making their way forward steadily in the direction of the southern end of the orchard of La Haye Sainte, and by so doing forcing the 4th Chasseurs to carry back with them in retreat all the troops on their right. Colborne's movement was a brilliant one, in striking contrast to the movements made throughout the day on the French side which had all been obvious and visible to the enemy. The Duke now ordered Vivian's cavalry forward, and these horsemen, still unshaken by battle, wheeled on to the field through the space left by Adam's brigade.

It was 8 p.m. The sun was sinking below the horizon and a heavy mist was rising from the sodden ground. Reille's infantry still fought round Hougoumont, but the brigades of Donzelot and Quiot and the inactive French cavalry saw the rout of the Middle Guard and themselves fell back. Along the length of the French army the cry was heard, 'La Garde recule!' On the extreme right, panic had seized Durutte's infantry as they realized that the great body of cavalry and infantry arriving from the heights of Ohain was not the promised army of Grouchy but the corps of Ziethen. Driven out of Papelotte and La Haye by the Prussians, they fled to the rear with cries of 'Nous sommes trahis!' and 'Sauve qui peut!'

The Duke of Wellington, watching the French retiring all along the line, saw that the time had come when his army, having withstood the charges of the enemy for over eight hours, could take the offensive in its turn. Standing on the crest of the slope by Maitland's position and silhouetted against the bright sunset, he raised his hat and waved it. His officers all along the front recognized the signal. Drums beat, trumpets sounded for a charge, the bagpipes played, and the surviving men of the army swept forward over the plain in pursuit of the enemy.

Movement was difficult. Mercer had just seen the Duke pass by 'apparently much fatigued' and now watched a line of infantry advancing from the rear, 'slowly, with ported arms and uttering a kind of feeble, suppressed "Hurrah!", ankle-deep in a thick, tenacious mud. And threading their way or stepping over the numerous carcasses . . . out of breath from their exertions and hardly preserving a line'. Riding across the field himself, the Duke caught up the 52nd. 'Go on. Colborne, go on!' he shouted. 'Give them no time to rally!' And the 52nd, sweeping from right to left across the field, moved on without a pause until it reached the Brussels road in advance of the orchard of La Haye Sainte, 800 yards from the starting point of the charge. In places the fields were so waterlogged that men sank in up to their knees.[1] This was the ground which had helped to exhaust the French all day as they repeatedly moved across it to the attack.

The 52nd had forced the French Guards to withdraw without a halt. 'It is perhaps impossible to point out in history,' says Shaw-Kennedy, 'any other instance in which so small a force as that with which Colborne acted had so powerful an influence on the result of a great battle.'[2] Everywhere the French were pouring back to their line; La Haye Sainte and Hougoumont were abandoned; the battalion of grenadiers which Napoleon had posted in reserve near Hougoumont was retreating in square; east of the Brussels road Durutte's division was in disorderly flight before the Prussians, with the exception of Brigadier Brue's brigade which was retreating in order.

Ziethen's corps was now pouring over the battlefield. Some of his men had joined Blücher in the region of Plancenoit, some had crossed the Brussels road and were near Hougoumont. In the dusk there was much confusion, and one Prussian battery had settled down about 400 yeards from Mercer's troop and proceeded to rake it from end to end with a heavy and incessant fire. Not knowing who was firing on them, the exhausted gunners of G Troop slowly swung round their two left flank guns and fired back. A Brunswick

[1] Becke, *Napoleon and Waterloo*, p. 227
[2] Shaw-Kennedy, *Notes on the Battle of Waterloo*, p. 147.

officer soon arrived in agitation to protest that Mercer was firing on his Prussian allies, whereupon Mercer ordered his men to cease firing. The officer retired, but the Prussians continued their fire and soon reduced the troop, which had so bravely withstood the day, to wreckage. Those who survived owed their lives to the timely arrival of a Belgian battery, all of whose personnel were drunk, which settled down on Mercer's left and in its turn opened fire on the Prussians who thereupon retired. Meantime the British artillery was ordered forward and an aide-de-camp galloped up to Mercer with instructions. 'Forward, Sir, forward!' he shouted. 'How, Sir?' Mercer replied, pointing to the shattered remains of his once splendid troop; his guns were smashed, the ground was strewn with dead and dying men and horses. The aide-de-camp rode off in silence. Mercer writes:

> My poor men, such at least as were untouched, fairly worn out, their clothes, faces, etc., blackened by the smoke and spattered over with mud and blood, had seated themselves on the trails of the carriages, or had thrown themselves on the wet and polluted soil, too fatigued to think of anything but gaining a little rest. . . . For myself, I was also excessively tired – hoarse, to make speech painful, and deaf from the infernal uproar of the last eleven hours. Moreover, I was devoured by a burning thirst, not a drop of liquid having passed my lips since the evening of the 16th. . . .

Napoleon had been engaged in forming the Old Guard in the valley when the rout of his army became apparent. Hastily he ordered the three battalions into squares, with their right on the Brussels road, about 100 yards from La Haye Sainte. Vivian's cavalry surged round them but were driven off; Allied infantry and artillery soon followed, however, and against these the squares could do little: Napoleon therefore ordered them to retreat. He then galloped down the Brussels road with Bertrand and other members of his suite, keeping with him the guide, Decoster. He had left two battalions of grenadiers in position at Rossomme, and these he now joined, taking refuge within one of the squares and hoping to stem the rout from this position. But he had driven the Grand Army beyond endurance, and nothing could now be done.

D'Erlon was trying in vain to control the flood of panic-stricken fugitives pouring down the slope from La Haye Sainte. As he was irresistibly carried back in their midst, Marshal Ney called out to him: 'D'Erlon, if you and I get out of this we know what awaits us – we shall be hanged!' Then Ney caught sight of Brue's brigade, greatly reduced yet keeping admirable order in the midst of the general chaos. Animated by desperation, he rushed towards them and ordered them to halt and turn. Bareheaded, his face black with powder, his uniform torn and bloodstained, he waved a sword broken to the hilt and placed himself at the head of the small band of men. 'Follow me!' he roared, 'and I will show you how a marshal of France dies on the battlefield.' Dutifully the men followed, once more driving themselves up the muddy slope to face the enemy. But the marshal might have spared them this useless action, for they had nothing to fear from the Bourbons. Most of them perished, while Ney escaped the death he sought and found his way into one of the retiring squares. Durutte, his right hand severed, his forehead gaping, was carried backward on his horse in the midst of a charge of the English cavalry which swept him to La Belle Alliance, and thence he escaped down the Brussels road.

The Young Guard, under Duhesme, and two battalions of the Old Guard, under General Pelet, fought valiantly to hold Plancenoit. The village was mostly in flames, but they held on until they fell, thus preventing the Prussians surging over the Brussels road and cutting off Napoleon's retreat.

The three squares of the Old Guard left by Napoleon below La Haye Sainte fought their way slowly back to La Belle Alliance. Reduced by incessant attacks, they could no longer form squares three deep and so changed to triangles, two deep; with their bayonets fixed they kept their formation though continually harassed. English officers, coming close, entreated them to save their lives by surrendering, but received only General Cambronne's famous reply, '*Merde!*' A few moments later this valiant soldier, struck in the forehead by a bullet, fell senseless to the ground. Later in the evening, unconscious and stripped by the peasants even of his underwear, he was carried off the field a prisoner.[1]

Cambronne fell just as the remnant of his battalion reached the heights of La Belle Alliance. Unable to hold together, the men were

[1] The bold Cambronne was later to be compensated for present horrors; he recovered, married an Englishwoman, and was created a viscount by Louis XVIII, while his somewhat startling exclamation on the battlefield was transformed in the salons of Paris into the more gentlemanly phrase: '*La garde meurt, elle ne se rend pas!*'

now merged with the general wave of fugitives where everyone was for himself. Only three battalions of the Old Guard were now in order; they were the two battalions of grenadiers which Napoleon had joined at Rossomme, and the 1st Chasseurs which had been left all day at Le Caillou. Napoleon was within one of the squares at Rossomme; a battery had been brought up at his orders, and trumpets sounded to rally the fugitives. In spite of enemy attacks, the squares of grenadiers did not move, except to close up over those who fell.

Eventually the Prussians broke through in masses upon Rossomme, driving before them those troops on the right – Count Lobau's infantry, the cavalry of Domon and Subervie, the Young Guard in Plancenoit – who had been covering the retreat of the army. These French fugitives were attacked by British cavalry as they reached the heights of Rossomme; seeking refuge in the squares of the Old Guard, they were shot down with others trying to break in. General Duhesme fell severely wounded. His aide-de-camp, assisted by one or two privates, lifted him from the ground, and they carried him with them as they endeavoured to escape.

Between La Belle Alliance and Rossomme there was the most murderous chaos. Cuirassiers who had lost their horses threw down their heavy armour in order to run more quickly, thus adding to the debris that littered the ground. Drivers of vehicles cut the traces of the harness and galloped off; in this way, hundreds of wounded men were abandoned to their fate. Cannon and overturned wagons blocked the way; dead horses, dead men, were strewn on roads and fields; the Allied pursuers sabred and bayoneted the French as fast as they could, and no doubt each other as well as the light failed and the universal madness increased.

In the midst of the débâcle the two squares of grenadiers stood firm and beat off all assailants; never was the courage and self-control of the Imperial Guard better displayed. But Napoleon now ordered them to retreat. He himself galloped back with Soult, Drouot, Lobau and about half a dozen mounted chasseurs. Reaching Le Caillou, he found the personal escort he had posted there, the 1st Chasseurs, and ordered them to proceed with him to Genappe. 'I count on you,' he said. Keeping to the side of the column, while the two battalions of grenadiers, commanded by General Petit, covered his retreat, Napoleon rode on.

16

Prussian pursuit of the French; Napoleon in flight; His carriage and other possessions captured; His journey to Paris

Slowly the two squares of grenadiers retreated from Rossomme, always keeping their formation and successfully blocking the route to Genappe so that the Prussians, now alone in pursuit, were unable to pass them.

Soon after nine o'clock, at the time when the French were at last being driven out of Plancenoit, Blücher and Wellington had met by chance at La Belle Alliance.[1] It was their first meeting since the day of Ligny. La Belle Alliance was the name Blücher would have liked to give to the battle, in honour of the loyal co-operation of the two armies. The Marshals had embraced, Prussian bands had played 'God save the King', and there was general rejoicing. It had been decided at this meeting that the French must be pursued so that they could not rally; but as Wellington's troops had reached the last extremity of weariness the task was left to the Prussians. From any normal standpoint, the Prussians were exhausted too; but there were many on the field who had not had to fight, and they were more able to continue in action than were their allies. The men of Wellington's army, therefore, were released, and most of them sank to the damp, chilly ground and slept where they were.

The Duke rode back at a walk to his headquarters, followed silently by the remnant of his staff. The wounded were now being carried to Waterloo for medical attention, and the Duke, who had left the field in tears, spent some time at the side of the many dead and wounded personal friends who were lying in the village. 'I have never fought such a battle,' he was to say to Lord Fitzroy Somerset, 'and I. trust I shall never fight such another.' Later he remarked that there was only one thing sadder than a battle lost, and that was a battle won.

He sat down to write his despatch, and in due course the first

[1] According to one or two accounts the meeting took place further south on the Brussels road.

casualty lists were brought in; he wept again as name after name was read aloud. When all the figures became known, they were to show that, in killed, wounded and missing, Wellington had lost nearly 15,000 men. The Prussians had lost about 7,000. The French are estimated to have lost 25,000 killed and wounded.

The Allied troops bivouacked on the battlefield that night, and all about them, in an area of three square miles, lay 43,000 killed and wounded, and thousands of dead and wounded horses. The moon cast its chilling light on the desolate scene, while crafty peasants stole about, removing every stitch of clothing from the dead and the helpless and harness from the horses. The wounded tried to help each other. Occasionally a fanatical Bonapartist would hit out and curse his adversaries, even in his agony. Early the following day, Captain Mercer had a glass of water that he was offering to such a man thrown in his face; but such instances were rare. Throughout the battle, indeed, the soldiers on both sides had often paused to help the fallen, regardless of nationality. Colonel Frederick Ponsonby, who had to lie many hours on the field with seven severe wounds, said afterwards that he considered he had only survived because a French officer stopped to give him a drink of brandy.

On the battlefield, the most severe trial for the wounded and those too exhausted to move was lack of water. Captain Mercer, having dozed fitfully for a time, rose and looked about him. In the moonlight, in the cold, indifferent silence which had fallen on the plain of Waterloo, the scene was more horrifying than the battle itself where the excitement of uncertainty, the noise and confusion, kept the mind occupied. In places the dead and dying, men and horses, were piled high; now and then he saw a man manage to raise himself from the ground and stagger a few paces before stumbling and falling again. Stricken with grief he wandered about, unable to rest. Help came slowly and was wholly inadequate to the immense scale of the disaster.

The Prussian cavalry, led by Gneisenau, pursued the French down the Charleroi road, but were unable to break the two squares of grenadiers, and eventually fell back out of range of their fire. There were plenty of fugitives in the rear to occupy them, and they chased across the fields, striking terror everywhere by the beating of their drums. Behind Gneisenau and his cavalry came Blücher on the main road with the infantry of Bülow's corps. Those French soldiers who had not managed to escape in front of the grenadiers were in a grim situation. Many of the right wing of the army had had their line of retreat cut off when Plancenoit fell, and the majority were struck down or taken prisoner. Five or six thousand of Reille's infantry had rallied and retired over the open fields, a mile or so to the west of the main road. But the Prussians bore down on them, putting many of them to the sword; the survivors threw down their arms and ran. Only the troops on the extreme French left were able to save themselve. Piré's lancers, and many cuirassiers who still had horses, took the road to Malplaquet and reached the frontier unmolested. The artillery fell into the hands of the Allies.

General Petit, finding that the Prussians had now fallen well to the rear, changed the formation of the two squares of grenadiers and allowed them to march on in columns. They were now about half a league from Genappe. At the same time, since there was no immediate threat from the Prussians, Napoleon left his escort of chasseurs and galloped ahead with his personal attendants towards Genappe where, according to Houssaye, he hoped to halt the enemy and rally the remnant of his army. In fact, as will be seen, he made no attempt to do so.

Finding the main road choked with fugitives, he continued the journey along adjacent lanes. Decoster was still one of his party and must have known that there was an alternative route across the river Dyle, by the bridge of Ways, a village only a quarter of a mile from Genappe; but Napoleon did not cross at Ways, perhaps because his travelling carriage had been sent to Genappe and he hoped to continue his journey in it.

Reaching Genappe in due course, he found the narrow street leading down to the bridge thronged by men demented with hunger and panic, and blocked with vehicles whose drivers had unharnessed the horses and fled. The bridge was wide enough for only six men abreast, and while those in its vicinity fought madly to reach it, the street to their rear became more and more crowded with shouting, demoralized soldiers. Yet Ways was deserted all that evening; and the river was so shallow that it was easily fordable.[1]

[1] Houssaye, *1815*, Vol. II, p. 433, note 1.

When the three battalions of the Old Guard (the chasseurs who had escorted Napoleon, and the grenadiers under General Petit) reached the entrance to Genappe they did not attempt to push their way through the struggling mass of soldiers but by-passed the town to the east and reached Charleroi without further trouble.

In Genappe, a handful of men who had kept their heads were erecting a barricade against the approaching Prussians. But there is no mention of Napoleon's having endeavoured to organize the retreat in any way. It would appear that he passed through the town without making himself known, though it is said that it took him an hour to do so. He found his travelling carriage with its six grey horses near the bridge, and he took his place in it.

At this moment, however, the Prussian drums were heard approaching, and panic in the town reached its height as uhlans and hussars arrived. The barricade was quickly overthrown and its defenders slain. The cavalry of General von Röder entered Genappe; Blücher was not far behind with his infantry. Napoleon, on hearing the alarm, leapt from his carriage and mounted his horse. With his personal escort he made his way to the bridge and managed to cross just in time. Once on the highroad at the other side, he galloped off into the night.[1]

As the Prussians made their way down the street, a nightmarish scene met their eyes. The approaches to the bridge were cluttered with abandoned vehicles of all kinds, including the Imperial coach and baggage wagons. A dense mass of French soldiers, out of their minds with fear, were fighting for a foothold on the bridge. Many hacked about them with sabres and bayonets, trying to clear a way through to safety. The living were entangled with the slain; those who retained their reason were imprisoned in the surging mob and were helpless. A general officer had no more influence than a private. The only distinction left was whether a man was alive or dead. The great crowd struggled to move in one direction only; it was not until the Prussians, slashing out with their sabres, were fully

---

[1] He shared the general panic, according to the Duc de Raguse who writes: 'During the disorder, terror took possession of Napoleon's mind. He retired at a gallop for several leagues, and at every moment thought he saw enemy cavalry on the road or on his flank, and sent someone to reconnoitre. I have these details from officers attached to the Emperor and with him at the time.' (*Mémoires du Maréchal Marmont, Duc de Raguse*, Vol. VII, pp. 121-2.)

upon them that they turned to the right and left of the bridge and began at long last to wade the shallow river.

Beyond Genappe the pursuit continued down the Charleroi road and all the lanes and tracks running southwards. The moon was up, and fleeing soldiers were everywhere visible, cavalry men on their worn-out horses, and infantrymen who had thrown away their arms and haversacks in order to move more quickly. Panic and terror were such that even the badly wounded from the abandoned ambulances found the strength to run. Generals, colonels, captains, their authority gone, were overtaken by the mass emotion of terror. Yet the Prussian pursuit was now being carried out by no more than 4,000 men. Bülow's infantry had been halted at Genappe, and the troops of Pirch and Ziethen had gone no further than Le Caillou Farm. Before Gneisenau and two battalions of cavalry, mounted on weary horses, 30,000 to 40,000 Frenchmen were in full flight. Such was the end of the Grand Army.

At Genappe, Marshal Blücher settled down for the night at *Le Roi d'Espagne*. Here he learnt that the wounded General Duhesme had arrived among the prisoners. The devoted band of soldiers who had carried him had succeeded in reaching Genappe but there had fallen into Prussian hands. Blücher showed a consideration reminiscent of eighteenth-century warfare; he had Duhesme taken to a bedroom at the inn, attended by a French aide-de-camp; he sent his own surgeon to look after him and visited him himself. But Duhesme, who had fought so bravely throughout the campaign, died within a few hours.

In keeping with the dramatic nature of the night was the capture of the French artillery, of Napoleon's personal possessions, and of a fortune in gold, silver and diamonds brought to cover the expenses of his intended triumphs in Brussels. When the Prussian troops in Genappe began to clear the street of obstructions, they found not only a considerable assortment of war material but much else besides. By far the most attractive prize was Napoleon's great travelling *berline*, the last word in comfortable transport in its day. Napoleon had had it made by the firm of Symonds in Brussels for his Russian campaign, and for part of his travelling in 1812 its body had been placed on a sledge.[1] It was fitted out with the greatest

[1] Anon., *The Battle of Waterloo 1815*, p. 75, note.

opulence, as suited the master of Europe who was planning to travel in it on his way to becoming the master of Asia also. It contained a bedstead in steel with a merino mattress, drawers fitted with toilet articles and a table service of massive gold. In it was found clothing ready for Napoleon's appearance in Brussels: a state mantle and diamond tiara, a sword, a hat and spurs. There were changes of linen and a velvet cap. Most interesting of all was a uniform, in the lining of which were sewn unmounted diamonds worth a million gold francs. These diamonds, according to Houssaye, had been given to Napoleon by his brother Joseph.[1] Napoleon's baggage wagon was also in Genappe, containing yet more diamonds as well as silver services engraved with the Imperial arms. His travelling library was there, consisting of some 800 volumes, and so were the bales of proclamations already referred to.

Major von Keller's fusiliers captured this extraordinary booty; everything of outstanding interest was taken to Blücher; the finest diamonds were singled out to be presented to the King of Prussia. But there were diamonds, gold and silver for all comers; an immense number of diamonds were found concealed in powder wagons. A Prussian officer wrote just after the event: 'Besides his (Napoleon's) hat and sword, his seal-ring was also taken and now blazes on the hand of the Hero Gneisenau. . . . The Fusiliers sold four or five diamonds as large as a pea, or even larger, for a few francs. . . . The subaltern officers of this battalion dine now upon silver.'[2] The soldiers' haversacks were filled with their finds, which included gold coins and portraits of Napoleon. Blücher wrote on the 19th: 'Napoleon escaped in the night without either hat or sword. I send both sword and hat today to the King. His most magnificently embroidered state mantle and his carriage are in my hands, as also his perspective glass, with which he observed me during the battle. His jewels and all his valuables are the booty of our troops. Of his equipage he has nothing left.'[3]

Napoleon reached Quatre Bras at 1 a.m. The dead lay as he had left them on the 16th and 17th, unburied and naked. Marauding peasants had dragged from them the last rag of clothing.

[1] Houssaye, *1815*, Vol. II, p. 434, note 1.
[2] Anon., *The Battle of Waterloo, 1815*, p. 73, note.   [3] Ibid., pp. 71-5.

Some of the soldiers who had formed his escort lit a fire in the Bois de Bossu, and the small company paused to warm themselves. Napoleon ordered Soult to send a message to Grouchy, instructing him to retire across the frontier immediately. For a time he waited for Girard's division (which had remained behind at Fleurus), for he had sent an order to its commander earlier in the day, instructing him to take his forces to Quatre Bras. But there was no sign of these troops; so, after sending a messenger to seek them and notify them of the retreat, he and his party continued on their way to Charleroi, passing through Gosselies and Lodelinsart. They were now well out of the way of the Prussians. Gneisenau's company had diminished rapidly as they rode down the road from Genappe, for his men were exhausted and were rapidly falling out. Gneisenau could see that the French were incapable of rallying; further pursuit was therefore unnecessary, and just beyond Frasnes he called a halt. He passed the night at an inn suitably named *A l'Empereur*.

It was five o'clock in the morning when Napoleon reached Charleroi. At this time Wellington was writing his despatch at the inn at Waterloo, and most of the soldiers of the Allied armies were sleeping. The French had Charleroi to themselves, and there was nothing to prevent their evacuating it in an orderly manner. Yet panic prevailed even here and all was in utter confusion.

When the French army invaded Belgium on the 15th, it was followed by trains of wagons carrying equipment, ammunition and food, which were left in Charleroi in reserve. On the 17th, the wounded from Ligny and Prussian prisoners were brought into the town, as well as captured guns and equipment. The streets, squares and outskirts were therefore heavily encumbered. On the 18th, a messenger was sent off to Charleroi from the battlefield as soon as the retreat began, with orders that all vehicles were to be taken across the frontier immediately; but it was past one o'clock in the morning when he arrived and he had the utmost difficulty in rousing anyone to action. The commander of the place was dead drunk, and the messenger had to seek out the *chefs de service* one by one before any movement could be made. In the meantime, wounded soldiers and deserters had been pouring through the town in increasing numbers, crossing the bridge throughout the night and hastening back to the frontier. Eventually those who had been routed on the field began arriving, and soon the town was thronged with panic-stricken men.

Horses were now being harnessed to the supply wagons and gun carriages, and gradually the vehicles were moving in the direction of the bridge. Suddenly a disorderly group of cuirassiers galloped down the street, and, as they plunged on to the bridge, the wooden parapet gave way. Several of the horsemen fell into the river and a sentry box was sent flying, causing a service wagon to overturn; this wagon was part of a convoy of vehicles carrying provisions, and from it fell hundreds of loaves. The wagons following were unable to pull up in time; there was a further collision and a number of men were injured, while sacks of rice and flour fell to the ground and casks of brandy and wine thumped downhill towards the bridge. The steep street behind was now blocked with wagons, with struggling, fallen horses and a wealth of that food which had been denied to the soldiers in action. The bridge itself was effectively blocked while soldiers leapt over the obstructions, spearing loaves on their bayonets as they ran by. The great tuns of wine and brandy were soon noticed; holes were made with rifle butts, and the gutters flowed with liquor.

Some way up the street, following the provision wagons, was a well-guarded coach, drawn by six horses, carrying Napoleon's personal treasury. It had been in Le Caillou and had been sent off the previous evening with the rest of the Emperor's belongings. Loaded with gold and silver coins to the value of 1,600,000 francs, it was a weighty responsibility for the official in charge. Seeing that no orderly attempt was being made to clear the road, that the whole town was in a state of anarchy and that the halted provision wagons were being pillaged, he decided to unload the bags of money and send them over the bridge with the soldiers of his escort, trusted men to whom he gave instructions as to where they were to assemble on the other side of the Sambre. But now shots were heard. Soldiers down the road were firing into casks of wine in order to break into them more quickly. At once the cry went up, 'The Prussians! The Prussians! We have been turned!' In the sudden renewal of panic, a crowd of townspeople who had been gazing at the coach fell upon the men who were unloading the money bags and a fierce fight ensued. Sacks were snatched and money spilled to the ground; fleeing soldiers, halted by the sight of gold, joined in the struggle. The guardians of the treasure were soon overpowered; and a wild mob of townspeople and soldiers fought for the Emperor's wealth, maddened by the thought that here was an end to all their troubles, if only they could seize enough of the gold before their eyes. In a short time, the whole of it had been pillaged.

Not a vehicle could move in the town. Further back the Duc de Bassano, in a coach carrying documents, was hurriedly destroying important papers. The vehicles had to be abandoned, and were later seized by the Prussians.

Napoleon and his escort made their way with difficulty to the bridge. Having crossed the Sambre, they paused to rest for an hour in a field. According to Decoster's account, a tent was pitched and a fire lit. Napoleon dictated orders, while all round, in the fields and lanes, the army continued its flight.

It was now that Decoster was set free, there being no further need of his guidance. Betrand gave him a gold Napoleon, his reward for services during the past twenty-four hours. It was scant compensation, perhaps, for a wrecked home, particularly as the Imperial party requisitioned his horse in dismissing him; but Bertrand was feeling too apprehensive to be in a generous mood. These were the fortunes of war, and, as he made his way back on foot to La Belle Alliance, Decoster might well reflect that had the French prevailed, Napoleon and his companions, in their joy, would not have been able to do enough for him.[1]

Napoleon now rode on, and before long was safely across the frontier. Thousands of men were spreading alarm in the villages. While some indulged in plunder, others struggled courageously along, guarding their standards in small groups and helping the wounded, or those more seriously wounded than themselves. General Durutte, blinded by blood from a wound in his forehead, was led by a sergeant of the cuirassiers across the frontier to safety. Marshal Ney was on foot, lost in the crowd and so exhausted and dazed that he could scarcely remain upright. A corporal supported him and helped him along until at last a major of the lancers recognized him, jumped from his horse and helped him to mount, himself continuing the journey on foot.

At 9 a.m. Napoleon reached Philippeville, a fortified town. Finding the gates locked, he had to await admittance until the governor

[1] Decoster eventually did very well for himself as a guide to the battlefield.

came out and recognized him. Here he was joined by the Duc de Bassano and other officers. After taking a rest, plans were made and messages sent out. The generals who had remained in France were given instructions, the commanders of fortified places on the frontiers were told to prepare for attack. The fleeing soldiers were directed to reassemble at Laon, Soissons and elsewhere. Although he had clearly lost his gamble, Napoleon's overwhelming desire was to keep the war going at all costs. The alternative now to his retiring from power was to make the whole of France a battlefield. Let the nation now fight for his survival. If time could be gained, the unexpected must eventually take place and give him the advantage. The essential thing was to hold on in this world of incessant change, so that in altered circumstances he could renew the power which alone made his life worth having. But for that it was necessary that all France should identify itself with him, and instead of saying 'Napoleon is in danger' say 'France is in danger.'

He sent off two letters to his brother Joseph from Philippeville. One was intended to be read to the council of which Joseph was president, giving a misleading account of the lost battle; the other was a personal letter in which he admitted that the army was routed, but spoke with confidence of the resources of France upon which he now meant to draw, and showed that he intended to carry on the war to the last extremity. 'Everything can be repaired,' he wrote. 'Let me know what effect this horrible affray has produced in the Chamber. I think the deputies will be convinced that their duty in this time of crisis is to unite with me to save France. Prepare them to support me with dignity.'[1]

While Napoleon was employed with his correspondence at Philippeville, his messenger sent from Quatre Bras reached Grouchy near Wavre. Grouchy and his wing of the army had fought the previous evening until 11 p.m., and the battle with Thielemann had ended indecisively. Outnumbered by two to one, the Prussians, excellently led, had managed to hold the French at bay. Both sides had bivouacked for the night where they had fought, and fighting was resumed in the morning. The Prussians were much heartened by news of the victory on the plain of Mont St Jean, which came with the added information that Pirch I was drawing near to cut off

[1] Napoléon, *Lettres Inédites*, Vol. II, p. 357.

Grouchy's line of retreat. Despite the stimulating effect of this news, however, they had to give way at last before superior numbers, and Thielemann ordered a general retreat up the Brussels road. The fighting came to an end at about 10.30 a.m., and Grouchy, who had as yet had no news of the main battle, assumed that Napoleon would have scored a victory and therefore prepared to march on Brussels himself. But now Napoleon's messenger arrived from Quatre Bras.

He was brought before Grouchy who thought him either drunk or mad, for he gabbled incoherently with a wild and distracted air; for some time no one could understand him, but eventually, by dint of close questioning, Grouchy and his generals learnt that disaster had overtaken their ruler, that they themselves were in the greatest danger and must retreat with all haste. The news was catastrophic. Blücher's victorious army was close and was free to bring its full strength against them. At least Grouchy was now his own master, unhampered by the fear of going against Napoleon's wishes. Napoleon, it was clear, was finished. Acting with the greatest energy, Grouchy now manœuvred with skill and rapidity, aided by Vandamme who showed his finest qualities of courage and resolution. Between them they were to save the right wing of the Grand Army,[1] retreat in good order before the pursuing enemy, fight their way out of some exceedingly difficult places, and not only save their equipment but throughout take good care of the wounded. Grouchy's able handling of this most difficult retreat belies the blame cast on him for the loss of the battle of Waterloo.

While Napoleon was at Philippeville and Grouchy was receiving the news of defeat, Wellington was in Brussels engaged upon the admirable report of the battle which he had begun to write at Waterloo. Mr Thomas Creevey called on him while he was at his task and congratulated him upon his victory. Creevey writes:

> He made a variety of observations in his short, natural, blunt way, but with the greatest gravity all the time, and without the least approach to anything like triumph or joy. 'It has been a damned serious business,' he said. 'Blücher and I have lost 30,000 men. It has been a damned nice thing – the nearest run thing you ever saw in your life. . .' Then as he walked about, he praised greatly those Guards who kept

[3] Gérard had been severely wounded during the fighting of the previous afternoon.

the farm (meaning Hougoumont) against the repeated attacks of the French; and then he praised all our troops, uttering repeated expressions of astonishment at the men's courage. He repeated so often its being *so nice a thing – so nearly run a thing*, that I asked him if the French had fought better than he had ever seen them do before. – 'No,' he said, 'they have always fought the same since I first saw them at Vimeira.' Then he said: 'By God! I don't think it would have done if I had not been there.'

Brussels had been through three agitating days, and all but the partisans of Napoleon were now rejoicing. Even so, the magnitude of the victory was not yet suspected. Although it had been learnt during the night of the 18th that the French were defeated, rumours had circulated for some hours that after retreating they had turned Wellington's army and would capture Brussels the following morning. Fanny Burney had tried to leave for Antwerp with friends on the 18th, but they had failed to obtain transport. On the 19th her friends set off at the crack of dawn, despite the news of victory, for they did not suspect that the war was virtually over. Fanny Burney remained in Brussels. But it was not until Tuesday, the 20th, she writes, that she had certain and satisfactory assurances of 'the matchless triumph of the matchless Wellington'. Her record continues:

> I met at the Embassade an old English officer who gave me most interesting and curious information, assuring me that in the carriage of Bonaparte, which had been seized, there were proclamations ready printed and even dated from the palace of Lachen, announcing the downfall of the Allies and the triumph of Bonaparte! But no satisfaction could make me hear without deadly dismay and shuddering his description of the field of battle. Piles of dead! Heaps, masses, hills of dead bestrewed the plains!

Leaving Marshal Soult in Philippeville to collect together and rally as much of the army as possible, and borrowing his carriage, Napoleon continued his journey to Paris. He rode alone. Two carriages followed him in which sat Bassano, Bertrand, Drouot, Gourgaud, Flahaut and Labédoyère. An indirect route was taken. Late at night (it being Monday the 19th) they reached Mezières and had difficulty in changing horses owing to the requisitioning for the army. While they waited, the Governor of the town, the commander of the fortress and a group of staff officers stood respectfully beside the carriages. Little was said, and that in low tones; weighed down by the disaster, the men behaved as if at a funeral. At midnight, now supplied with horses, the carriages drove off. The next stop was at Maubert-Fontaine on the way to Laon. Here, at a very early hour on Tuesday morning, Napoleon and his companions took breakfast at the *Hôtel du Grand Turc*, and it is recorded that Napoleon ate a couple of eggs.[1] Rooms were taken, and they all slept for some hours. The journey was then resumed, and the party reached Laon between six and seven in the evening. They alighted on the outskirts at the *Hôtel de la Poste*, and while some of his attendants went to notify the authorities of the town of his arrival, Napoleon paced the courtyard, gazing at the ground; he was thus observed by a crowd of local people who did not dare to raise their voices to acclaim him.

A guard of honour presently arrived, followed by the Commander, the Prefect of the department with the municipal councillors, and various generals. Napoleon greeted them and a conference was held. But he paused only for a few hours at Laon. Having given instructions for the military measures to be taken in the region, he turned to the official bulletin for the *Moniteur* by means of which the nation would be notified of the defeat at Waterloo. He had begun to dictate it at Philippeville, and he finished it here. It is a sorry piece of work, mere self-excusing with no truth in it. He would have done better to have given the plain facts, atrocious though they were, for this would in no way have made his situation worse, and an honest avowal of failure would have won him some respect. Instead, presenting himself as blameless, he trumped up a curious tale of a battle all but won, then thrown away by the folly of the soldiers who fell into a panic when there was not the least need for it.

At ten or eleven in the evening he and his companions re-entered their carriages and continued the journey. Travelling through the night, they reached Paris at 8 a.m. on the morning of Wednesday, 21 June. Napoleon had been absent just nine days.

By this time, Grouchy and his army were safely across the river at Namur and were to cross the frontier during the day and concen-

[1] Houssaye, *1815*, Vol. II, pp. 450-1, note 3.

trate at Givet. Further westwards, Blücher and Wellington had already entered France.

Napoleon drove straight to the Elysée palace. His letters to Joseph, sent from Philippeville, had arrived the previous afternoon; but as far as the general public was concerned he had travelled more quickly than the bad news. On Sunday morning, as the soldiers on the field of Waterloo had waited for the battle to begin, Parisians had been roused by a salute of guns at the Invalides, fired in honour of the victory at Ligny, and yesterday the papers had still been filled with glowing accounts of the successes of French arms. Few but the Ministers knew of the disaster, and they were not fully informed; Joseph had read aloud to them the letter sent by Napoleon for that purpose, and they knew no more.

Caulaincourt, the Minister for Foreign Affairs, greeted Napoleon at the Elysée, loyal and devoted as ever, but exceedingly anxious. A meeting of Ministers had been arranged to take place during the morning.

White-faced and haggard, Napoleon spoke breathlessly. 'The army had done wonders,' he said. 'It was overtaken by panic. Everything has been lost. Ney behaved like a madman – made me butcher all my cavalry – I can do no more – I must have two hours' rest before I get down to business.' He paused to order a bath, and then continued his explanations. Destiny had three times robbed him of victory. But all was not lost. He counted on the two Chambers rallying to him and according him the means of saving the country; when once this was assured he would return to Laon.

Caulaincourt did not hide the fact that the deputies were in a hostile mood; he feared the Emperor would not find the support he was hoping for, and he much regretted he had not remained in the midst of his army, which was his strength and his safeguard.

'I no longer have an army,' said Napoleon, 'I have only deserters. But I shall find both men and guns. All can be restored. The deputies will second me; I think you misjudge them. The majority are good Frenchmen. I only have La Fayette and a few others against me. I am in their way; they want to work for their own ends. But my presence here will keep them in check.'

Napoleon retired to his bath. But the relaxation he desired was hardly possible at such an hour as this, and he was scarcely in the steaming water when his Minister for War was announced. Admitted to the Imperial presence, Davout came forward in the highest state of anxiety, bowing low. Napoleon greeted him with the words: '*Eh bien, Davout, eh bien!*' And with his meridional habit of expressive gesture and unfailing lack of consideration, he raised his short but heavy arms in the air and brought them down smartly so that a shower of bath water shot out over Davout's fine uniform.[1] There followed a description of the disaster, marked by bitter complaints against Ney. Davout, after trying to put in a good word for Ney and finding that Napoleon would not listen, urged his sovereign to act with energy. The most pressing need, according to Davout, was to prorogue the two Chambers, otherwise they would paralyse every measure Napoleon might wish to take.

Davout was followed by Cambacérès, President of the Chamber of Peers, and Peyrousse, the Treasurer. Then, when Napoleon was out of his bath, Comte Lavalette arrived. Napoleon, says Lavalette in his memoirs, received him in his cabinet and came forward to greet him 'with a frightful epileptic laugh'.

Thus began the nightmarish midsummer day.

[1] Chénier, *Davout*, Vol. II, p. 556

17

Napoleon and his Ministers; La Fayette's action; Napoleon forced to abdicate; He leaves Paris for Malmaison; Napoleon's surrender; End of hostilities

While Napoleon was having his bath, taking a bowl of soup and receiving in private those Ministers with whom it was essential to confer quickly, the Elysée was filling with men avid for news. The Ministers who had been called to the meeting shortly to be held were arriving, and with them a crowd of other functionaries and officers of high rank. All who had some kind of claim to enter the palace crowded in; those who were near enough listened eagerly, though with mounting alarm, to the tale told by the officers who had followed Napoleon back to the capital. Those who could not hear what was said had only to look at the soldiers from Waterloo to realize that the disaster was great. Torn and bloodstained clothing, pale faces and eyes red with weeping, spoke of a bitter ordeal and the loss of all hope.

Joseph and Lucien Bonaparte now arrived and were admitted to the presence of their brother. For some time the three were closeted together; then, at length, they showed themselves and at ten o'clock the meeting of Ministers opened. Napoleon, reanimated by his bath and in possession once again of his authority and confidence, spoke with his habitual disarming ease. After a brief outline of military events, he said that he had returned to call the country to a great and noble task. If France rose to the occasion, the enemy would be crushed. The resources were there. The army could soon be rallied. In a few days' time he would have 65,000 men at Laon; by July 1st he would have 90,000. The corps of Rapp and Lamarque, recalled from Alsace and the Vendée, would enter into line before the 10th, and he would then have at his disposal well over 100,000 men and artillery in abundance. The 1815 conscripts were about to come into service and there would be new levies. 'In two months I levied 180,000 National Guards; can I not find 100,000 more? Can I not be provided with 100,000 conscripts? We should then have good patriots behind us to fill in the gaps in our ranks, and a few months of this struggle would be enough to tire the patience of the Coalition. . . .'[1]

Thus he proposed to enforce upon Europe that totality in war which was one of the attributes of his system. He was ready to order every young man from his home to face renewed scenes such as those he had watched at Ligny and Waterloo.

'In order to save the country,' he now told his audience, 'I need to be invested with great power, with a temporary dictatorship. In the public interest I could seize that power; but it would be better for it to be given to me by the Chambers.'

Here in the Council of Ministers he had many of his personal friends about him and obtained a sympathetic hearing. But although Carnot spoke warmly in favour of a continuance of the war and appeared to believe the Chambers would consent to any measure the Emperor desired, the other Ministers were under no illusions but knew that the deputies would on no account willingly subject themselves to a renewal of Napoleon's dictatorship. Caulaincourt, Bassano and Cambacérès spoke guardedly of the need for Napoleon to act in concert with his parliament, while Davout, on the other hand, urged that the Chambers should be prorogued at once. Regnaud de St Jean d'Angély gave a warning that the Chambers might demand Napoleon's abdication, and Lucien angrily declared that in that case his brother would dispense with the Chambers and would save France as dictator. Lucien, indeed, was ready to re-enact his role of the 18th Brumaire when he had so effectively aided his brother to seize power. Napoleon himself remained undecided although he alarmed Fouché by the vigour of his speaking. Was he about to take bold measures? No. Had he felt within himself the old capacity to domineer he would not have been closeted here in conference, he would have been in action. 'That devil of a man frightened me this morning!' Fouché exclaimed later in the day to a royalist friend. 'I thought he was going to begin all over again! Luckily, one doesn't begin again.'[2]

If Napoleon and his friends were uncertain as to how to act, Fouché, his leading enemy, was taking well measured steps to

[1] Charras, *Histoire de la Campagne de 1815*, pp. 398-9. Houssaye, *1815*, Vol. III, p. 16.
[2] Houssaye, *1815*, Vol. III, p. 22.

ensure the Emperor's downfall. Fouché more than anyone else was to be responsible for Napoleon's second abdication. He had prepared his instruments in the Chamber of Deputies (La Fayette, the President Lanjuinais, Manuel, Jay and Lacoste) and they had no difficulty in leading the House in the direction they wished it to go. He was in contact with both royalists and liberals. After the meeting of Ministers called by Joseph the previous afternoon, he had told La Fayette that Napoleon had lost his army, was on his way to Paris to raise a new one, and suggested that his first action would be to get rid of the two Chambers. This was more than enough to stimulate a man such as La Fayette to action. Fouché had even made use of such a loyal Bonapartist as Regnaud de St Jean d'Angély in the course of his complicated intrigues, persuading him that the Bonaparte dynasty could only be saved by a Regency in favour of the King of Rome, and encouraging him to press for Napoleon's abdication as the best means of bringing this about.

While Napoleon was unfolding to the Council of Ministers his plans for a defensive campaign against the Allies, the Chamber of Deputies was moving towards decisive action. The desire to get rid of Napoleon, now that he had failed, was uppermost in the minds of the elected representatives. The rumours Fouché had spread regarding Napoleon's intentions had had their effect, and while the Ministerial meeting was in progress at the Elysée he saw to it that messengers were sent to the Palais Bourbon to inform the deputies that Davout and Lucien were pressing the Emperor to dissolve both Houses.

Proceedings at the Palais Bourbon opened at 12.15 p.m. instead of at the normal hour of two in the afternoon. But for hours before that time urgent and excited discussions had been going on in the corridors and passage-ways. Reports coming in from the Elysée were exaggerated and distorted. The 18th Brumaire, when Napoleon had overthrown the Directory, was much in mind, especially as Lucien, who had played such an indispensable role in that *coup d'état*, was now heard to be advocating the suppression of parliament by force. Everything was tending to increase the alarm of the deputies and to incite them to quick action.

And now Regnaud, who with various other Ministers had left the session at the Elysée to be present at that of the Chamber of Deputies, informed La Fayette of all that had taken place so far at the cabinet meeting. La Fayette, in consultation with Lanjuinais, President of the Chamber, decided to act at once. Mounting the tribune, he addressed an audience which listened to him with rapt attention:

Gentlemen, if after many years I raise a voice which I believe all the old friends of liberty here will recognize, it is because I feel it my duty to draw your attention to the dangers threatening our country which you alone can save. Sinister rumours have been circulating, and now they are unhappily confirmed. The moment has come to rally round the old tri-colour standard, the standard of '89, of liberty, equality and public order. It is this cause alone that we must defend, both against foreign pretensions and internal threats. Gentlemen, may a veteran of this sacred cause, who was never drawn into any faction, submit certain preliminary resolutions, of which you will, I hope, see the necessity?

There followed the celebrated resolution which placed the Chamber of Deputies in a state of defence against any attempt to usurp its powers:

. . . The Chamber declares itself in permanent session. Any attempt to dissolve it is high treason, and any person who makes such an attempt is a traitor to his country and will be treated as such. '
. . . The Ministers for War, Foreign Relations, the Interior and the Police are invited to attend at once in the House of Representatives.

The motion was passed unanimously. It was a *coup d'état*, in favour of parliamentary institutions. According to the *Acte Additionnel*, Napoleon was entitled to prorogue the Houses if he chose to do so; but now the deputies were fighting for the right to be consulted in every move he made. Napoleon had been outwitted and would be unable now to close down the Chambers except by force, and force would lead to civil war.

When the debate ended, messengers were sent to inform both the Chamber of Peers and Napoleon of the motion adopted. But long before they left, Regnaud had hurried to the Elysée to give the news to the Emperor who was still deliberating with his Council of Ministers.

Napoleon saw defeat more clearly now than on the field of Waterloo. 'I ought to have dismissed these men before my departure,' he said. 'It is the end. They will destroy France.'

All about him grew uncertain in the face of this new blow. Only Lucien remained firm and advocated the use of force. Lucien, who had shown the greatest good sense a month previously in urging his brother to abdicate, now took the opposite view. He used all his eloquence to call Napoleon to stern measures. The truth was that Napoleon had had some excellent cards to play the previous month and could have hoped to abdicate with a good grace on reasonable terms. Now he had no cards at all, and with nothing to lose he might as well take a risk. Lucien, very ambitious in his way, although he had never sought royal status, now had visions of the Bonaparte family brought crashing to earth, perhaps even exiled from Europe, and he felt the time had come for extraordinary exertions. He begged Napoleon to stand firm, to resume absolute power. But Davout, a bold man who earlier in the meeting had been in favour of violent measures, now said that all was over. As Minister for War, he was not prepared to take action that would lead to civil strife when all Europe was moving on France. 'The moment for action is past,' he said.

Though remaining doubtful, Napoleon could not but be impressed by Davout's opinion. He would abdicate in case of need, he said, but he would make no decision for the moment. He refused to allow his Ministers to appear before the deputies, being angered that they should be supposed to be at the beck and call of men of lesser importance. But he sent Regnaud to the House of Representatives and Carnot to the House of Peers, with a conciliatory message to the effect that the Emperor, in consultation with his Ministers, was drawing up proposals for meeting the perilous situation in which the country found itself. These proposals would shortly be made available.

By now the Chamber of Peers was beginning its session at the Palais du Luxembourg. Between one-thirty and two o'clock the message was read in the two Houses. In neither did it create a favourable impression. Carnot reached the House of Peers before the members had heard of La Fayette's motion. When he had finished reading Napoleon's message an uneasy silence fell on the assembly. No one rose to speak in reply. The moments passed, and presently the message containing La Fayette's motion arrived from the Chamber of Deputies. Animation returned. There was a general sense of relief. 'The Chamber of Representatives has set us a fine example', someone called out, and after this the resolution was quickly voted upon and adopted by the peers in their turn. The peers then adjourned their sitting.

Napoleon, still with his Ministers – though the official meeting of the Ministers seems to have come to a close by the early afternoon – was being kept informed of the latest developments from moment to moment. The disaffection of the Upper House was an additional blow. Now that the Chamber of Peers was echoing the call of the deputies for the immediate attendance of his Ministers it became increasingly hard not to acknowledge parliamentary supremacy by acceding to this request. He was reluctant to do this, but was now even less able than he had been earlier to bring himself to seize the initiative by force. He therefore temporized. While permitting certain of his Ministers[1] to appear before the Houses, he appointed Lucien to lead them and look after his interests in the capacity of *commissaire extraordinaire*, in this exercising a right given him by the *Acte Additionnel*. Furthermore, he made the Ministers the bearers of a second message which let it be known that negotiations for a peace settlement were to be opened; that his representatives were ready to impart any information asked of them; and which ended with a plea for unity between the three constituent parts of the State.

At six o'clock Lucien and the Ministers arrived at the Palais Bourbon. After the House had gone into secret session at his request, Lucien read the message, to be followed by Davout, Caulaincourt and Carnot who talked with an attempt at optimism of the military resources of the country and the diplomatic outlook. It was useless. Jay now rose and challenged the Ministers to say whether they really believed that France could resist the combined armies of the rest of Europe, and whether the presence of Napoleon on the throne was not the main obstacle to the conclusion of peace. He went on to propose that the House should send a deputation to Napoleon asking him to abdicate and warning him that in the event of his refusing he would be declared deposed.

Lucien mounted the tribune to defend his brother's position. It was entirely untrue, he cried, that the Allies fought only to remove Napoleon. They were fighting so that they could invade France

[1] These were Carnot, Caulaincourt, Davout and Fouché.

and divide her provinces among themselves. 'It is not Napoleon who is being attacked by Europe, but the French nation. And yet it is suggested that France should abandon her Emperor!' His speech was impassioned and well delivered, and only the most clear-headed remembered that the Allies had been quite free to loot France the previous year had that been their desire. He was, in fact, pleading for the continued grandeur of his family, and with mounting emotion he threatened the deputies with responsibility for destroying the State and with perpetual dishonour if they should fail in their duty towards Napoleon.

La Fayette replied with words that undid the effect of Lucien's eloquence. 'You accuse us,' he said, 'of failing in duty and honour towards Napoleon. Have you forgotten what we have done for him? Have you forgotten that the bones of our children, our brothers, everywhere attest our fidelity? In ten years three million Frenchmen have perished for a man who again desires to struggle against Europe. We have done enough for him. It is our duty now to save the country.'

Reminded of the grievous losses the country had sustained while dominated by Napoleon, the deputies felt anew that their hope lay in ridding themselves of him. But Jay's motion was not in the end put to the vote. It was decided instead that a commission consisting of five members from each House should take part in the deliberations of the Council of Ministers to agree upon measures of national safety. It was clear, however, that the members would not rest until they had assured themselves of Napoleon's downfall. The remainder of the Chamber's time was taken up with the appointment of its representatives, while Lucien and the four Ministers paid a brief visit to the Chamber of Peers where Napoleon's message was read and the House asked to nominate members to take part in the combined cabinet-parliamentary discussions shortly to be held.

Lucien now returned to the Elysée to report on what had taken place at the Palais Bourbon and the Palais du Luxembourg.

Napoleon had dined with Hortense who, as usual, urged him to get in touch with the Tsar, Alexander. Hortense always had faith that Alexander, who had been on very friendly terms with her mother and herself at the time of the first abdication, would manage to patch up any situation in favour of her stepfather if rightly appealed to, and her mind was closed to the idea that anyone could reasonably wish to be rid of the Bonapartes and all their works.

Lucien told Napoleon that he must either dissolve the Chamber of Representatives or abdicate; there was no hope of temporizing with these men. But he was alone in urging his brother to assert himself; even Bassano and Caulaincourt were recommending abdication as the only course now open to him.

Napoleon retired to bed without having come to any conclusion; he was by now too exhausted for further thought and the confidence with which he had addressed the Ministers some twelve hours previously had long since ebbed away in the face of repeated blows.

This long day, 21 June, had been marked by some disturbances in the streets and popular demonstrations in Napoleon's favour. More significant, perhaps, were the general calm and rising prices on the Bourse which indicated the business community's confidence that the return of Louis XVIII was imminent and would bring with it peace and a renewal of normal conditions.

Yet even now the day was not over. At eleven o'clock, while Napoleon slept, his Ministers opened their meeting with the commissioners of the two Chambers in the Palace of the Tuileries. Throughout a night of debates the Ministers tried to keep all discussion fixed entirely upon measures of national defence. But the commissioners, with La Fayette at their head, made it clear that they would not tolerate a continuation of the war if it could be ended by the removal of Napoleon. The talks were inconclusive, but, when they finally ended at three o'clock in the morning, it had been agreed that Napoleon should be requested to allow the Chambers to nominate plenipotentiaries with a view to negotiating for peace.

When Napoleon rose on the morning of the 22nd, friends, Ministers and family waited anxiously to see what his resolve might be. He appeared most of all to want time to think over his situation; but time was not available, for his enemies were fully determined to bring him down before the day was out. Some of his closest associates now most earnestly begged him to abdicate, seeing that this was at least better than that he should be thrown down from his position by force. Adolphe Thiers writes:

Napoleon took in good part the advice of those who, like the Duc de Rovigo, Comte Lavalette and the Duc de Bassano, told him that he should abandon people who did not deserve that he should save them, and take himself and his imperishable glory to the vast and free wilds of America, there to end his life in profound repose, to the admiration of a world which rendered him justice after his fall. But he took very ill this same advice when offered by those who seemed to hope either to gain something themselves from his sacrifice or to see in it the prospect of public gain.[1]

The resolution of the committee which had sat all night was put before him: that the Chambers should nominate plenipotentiaries to negotiate with the Coalition for peace. By nine o'clock the Chamber of Deputies was assembled and awaited his reply in an angry mood. Their presumption enraged him; yet he was powerless to refuse them what they asked unless he forcibly closed the two Chambers. The concession, a further admission of his diminishing authority, was wrung from him by his Ministers with difficulty; but at last a messenger set off to inform the deputies that he agreed to their request, and that he was ready for every sacrifice if he were an insuperable obstacle to peace. Even this conciliatory message did not satisfy the deputies who had hoped to hear that the Emperor had already abdicated. This abdication was now loudly demanded in a stormy session; then the sitting was suspended for half an hour and Lucien, who had been present, returned to the Elysée to report. He could only tell his brother that the deputies were determined to dethrone him forthwith if he did not voluntarily abdicate. And shortly afterwards a deputation arrived which, in an urgent though respectful manner, begged Napoleon to sacrifice himself for the sake of the country. In reply, Napoleon said that he would shortly send them his decision.

After the deputation had retired, Napoleon conferred with his brothers, Joseph and Lucien, and his Ministers. All were reconciled to his abdication except Lucien whose pride was stung by the presumption of the deputies. Yet again Lucien pressed his brother to call out the army and finish with the Chambers. But Napoleon now looked within himself in vain for the spark of will, daring and optimism that would fire his soul, as so often in the past, with confidence and reveal the way to success. The last thing he wished for was the loss of his great position; nothing was so hateful to him

[1] Thiers, *Histoire de l'Empire*, Vol. IV, p. 600.

as to be obliged to submit to the will of other men. But the spark he sought flickered only fitfully, and was very faint. Catching sight of it for a moment, he jumped to his feet and cried in a voice which shook the room that he would not renounce his position . . . it was not too late. . . . He strode up and down, looking like the dictator of old. Even now, it seemed, he might see his way with dazzling clarity, might call out all the military forces in Paris and dissolve his parliament. He would be seen on horseback in the streets of Paris, smiling and genial, while the people cheered him and trades-men retired crestfallen behind their shutters. Grouchy, so it had been learnt that morning, was safely in France with his army; Soult had sent word that 3,000 men of the Old Guard were assembled under him. With a handful of men, the incomparable General Bonaparte would harass the enemy, while his fiery eloquence incited the whole nation to resist to the death.

But the old brilliance and decision were gone for ever, and Napoleon could no more dominate the political scene in Paris than he had been able to control and dominate the battlefield at Waterloo. The spark of ambition, energy and will power died out, and a thick blanket of doubts, fatigue and pessimism smothered his mind. Instead of giving sharp, clear orders right and left, he was now talking to himself in broken, unintelligible words. He was a man fallen from power, needing to be helped to sort out his confused thoughts. Regnaud de St Jean d'Angély said to him: 'Sire, I beg you not to struggle any longer against the overwhelming force of circumstances. Time is flying and the enemy draws near. Do not give the Chamber, and the nation, grounds for accusing you of preventing peace. . . .'

The fiery rage and energy of a few minutes before were now replaced by irritation. 'I will see,' he said shortly, 'It has not been my intention to refuse to abdicate. But I want to be left to think it over quietly. Tell them to wait.'[1]

Soon after, however, he ordered Lucien to take pen and paper and dictated to him a proclamation of abdication. His mind was at last made up; the abdication was in favour of his son, and he requested that a Regency should be formed at once. Copies were made of the proclamation and taken to both Houses where they were read

[1] Houssaye, *1815*, Vol. III, p. 58.

simultaneously at two o'clock. It was Fouché who gave the welcome news to the Chamber of Representatives. The main business of a long day of debates, which only closed at nine o'clock in the evening, was the setting up of a Provisional Government. The upshot was that power was transferred from Napoleon and his Council of Ministers to an Executive Commission of five members – three of whom (Carnot, Fouché and General Grenier) were chosen by the Lower House, and two others (Quinette and Caulaincourt) who were nominated by the Chamber of Peers.

One of the most striking events of the day occurred after Carnot had read the notice of abdication to the Upper House. He was then proceeding to read a reassuring message from the Minister of War on the military situation when his soothing words were rudely interrupted.

'It is not true!' someone cried in loud tones. Silence fell on the assembly and everyone turned to see who had spoken. It was Marshal Ney; he had reached Paris a few hours previously and had come, as a peer, to take his part in the debates of this terrible hour. He continued to speak. 'The news the Minister of the Interior has given you is false, false in every respect. The enemy is the victor on all points. I have seen the disorder, since I was in command under the Emperor.'

Briefly the Marshal gave his account of the Waterloo campaign. Throughout, the men had done their duty, he said. But there had been terrible faults of command, leading to a disaster unequalled and beyond repair. 'In six or seven days the enemy can be in the heart of the capital. There is no means of saving the country but that of opening negotiations.'

The peers listened in stupefaction. Until now, no one had suggested to them that the situation was hopeless. They were not ready for such stark realities. The faults Ney spoke of were evidently Napoleon's, and they were not willing to accept this either. Paris was full of rumours as to the blunders of the marshals in Belgium, and Ney above all was being blamed for the loss of the campaign. Napoleon blamed him, and what Napoleon said was being repeated. It was easy to make a plausible case against Ney; but who was to know of the difficulties under which Ney had acted? Ney had seen and endured the faults of command. They were Napoleon's faults, glaring, inexcusable faults, including dangerous delays, lack of attention at vital moments, a persistent underestimation of the enemy, and vague instructions. But the peers looked suspiciously at the Prince of the Moskowa, and, remembering his betrayal of Louis XVIII, were ready to think that he was now a traitor to Napoleon. And, indeed, Ney would have done better to remain silent, for he had paved the way for Napoleon's return, even though he had been tricked into doing so, and was therefore not without responsibility for the terrible *débâcle* into which France had been led.

The capital was open to the enemy as Ney had said. And yet the dominating concern among the politicians was that of power. Commissions and delegations were being formed, and men strove for place. Lucien, having failed to incite his brother to resort to force in dealing with the Chambers, now made surpassing efforts to retrieve the family fortunes by raising his nephew, the King of Rome, to the vacated throne. Much eloquence was expended in vain upon the Chamber of Peers in the course of the day in an attempt to rouse enthusiasm for the young prince.

Throughout this day, 22 June, there were demonstrations in the streets in Napoleon's favour; these often took a most exaggerated form, and in the Place Vendôme two or three hundred people knelt in front of the column erected to the glory of their hero. These devotees were in a dangerous mood, and anyone who ventured to smile or express a doubt was likely to be attacked forthwith. There were many fights in the course of the evening between Bonapartists and royalists. Yet the price of shares had risen sharply with news of the abdication, and this was the measure of a widespread relief.

On the 23rd, Fouché was elected President of the Provisional Government; but Napoleon remained at the Elysée as if not knowing what to do next. Throughout the day his adherents endeavoured to promote the cause of Napoleon II, but without success. Fouché was seeking to establish relations with Louis XVIII, and the royalists were gaining an increased following from hour to hour.

Between 18 June and the signing of the Capitulation of Paris on 3 July, military operations were carried on sporadically, the Allies advancing into France while Grouchy (now Commander-in-Chief in place of Soult) fell back before them. Little serious resistance was offered to the invaders, though severe fighting occurred in one or two places, notably at Villers-Cotterets where Vandamme and Pirch II came into collision on 28 June.

Mercer's diary presents a picture of what had been taking place at Waterloo since the battle ended and gives some insight into the mood of both victors and vanquished. When light came on the morning of the 19th, he and his men had discovered a well at Hougoumont and had set about taking water to the wounded on the field. He writes:

> Nothing could exceed their gratitude, or the fervent blessings they implored on us for this momentary relief. The French were in general particularly grateful; and those who were strong enough entered into conversation with us on the events of yesterday, and the probable fate awaiting themselves. All the non-commissioned officers and privates agreed in asserting that they had been deceived by their officers and betrayed; and, to my surprise, almost all of them reviled Buonaparte as the cause of their misery. Many begged me to kill them at once, since they would a thousand times rather die by the hand of a soldier than be left at the mercy of those villainous Belgic peasants.

Everywhere the French wounded implored the English soldiers to remain with them: 'They looked on us as brother soldiers, and knew we were too honourable to harm them. "But the moment you go, those vile peasants will first insult, and then cruelly murder us." This alas! I knew was but too true.'

One young Frenchman Mercer had contrived to rescue soon after dawn. He was a grenadier who had fallen close to G Troop's position and had lain groaning throughout the night only a few paces away.

> He was a most interesting person – tall, handsome and a perfect gentleman in manners and speech; yet his costume was that of a private soldier. We conversed with him for some time, and were exceedingly pleased with his mild and amiable address. . . . We all felt deeply interested for our unfortunate prisoner, and did all in our power for him, which consisted in kind words and sending two careful men to lead him to the village – a most painful undertaking, for we now found that, besides one ball in the forehead, he had received another in his right thigh, which, together with his being

barefooted, could not but render his journey both tedious and painful.

Another interesting encounter was with an elderly lancer of the Old Guard who, with magnificent fortitude, had risen above his own torments to help and encourage his wounded companions. Mercer found him delivering an oration on the need for courage and detachment in life; he was sitting on the ground; with one hand he gesticulated, while the other lay severed at his side. A ball, probably case-shot, had entered his body, another had broken his leg. Mercer gave him the only help he could, which was a drink of cold water and assurances that wagons would soon be sent round to collect the wounded.

He thanked me with a grace peculiar to Frenchmen and eagerly enquired the fate of their army. . . . After a very interesting conversation, I begged his lance as a keepsake. . . . The old man's eyes kindled as I spoke, and he emphatically assured me that it would delight him to see it in the hands of a brave soldier, instead of being torn from him, as he had feared, by those vile peasants.[1]

On the evening of the 19th G Troop had bivouacked a mile from the field in an orchard 'with a turf like velvet and perfectly dry'. Mercer washed in a bucket of water and changed his clothes. 'This was the first time I had undressed since leaving Strytem – four whole days and three whole nights. It may be imagined with what joy I got rid of my bloody garments.' There was abundant food – ham and cheese, eggs, milk and cider. 'Hilarity reigned at our board – if we may so term the fresh turf at the foot of an apple tree; and over our grog and cigars we managed to pass a most pleasant evening.' They were the happy victors to whom a square meal and a night's sleep on the ground was bliss.

Moving southwards with the army, Mercer's troops crossed the frontier into France on the 21st.[2] The event was taken calmly by

---

[1] The French soldier's name was Clément, of the 7th Company of the Lancers of the Imperial Guard. His lance was honoured throughout Mercer's long life and every June 18th stood on the lawn of Cowley Cottage, Mercer's home, dressed with laurels and roses. (Leathes, *Reminiscences of Waterloo*, pp. 14, 15, 28, 29, 32.)

[2] It may seem surprising that a sufficient number had survived for the troop still to be active. But at the time of the Prussian incident, many had been despatched to the rear with the wounded, and before the close of the action others had been sent off to bring up a fresh supply of ammunition.

the French. 'From what I have seen of these people,' Mercer writes, 'it appears very doubtful whether they care a farthing who rules over them. Be that as it may, we undoubtedly entered France amidst cheers and greetings of the populace.'

Having spent the 23rd at Montay, the troop moved the next day to a neighbouring village, Forêt. Here too the populace seemed cheerful enough, and women and girls soon arrived at the bivouac selling cherries and seeming quite at their ease. A manifesto had been posted up by order of the Duke of Wellington, with which the villagers were well pleased since, as Mercer puts it, 'it assures them they shall be treated like gentlemen and not get the punishment which France, as a nation, so richly deserves'. Moreover, the people were promised that the strictest discipline would be maintained by the Allied army and that everything needed by the troops would be paid for at the full value. The English soldiers, therefore, paid a high price for their cherries.

Louis XVIII was also on French soil, returning after an absence mercifully and surprisingly short, to take possession of his palaces and throne. He was to pass through Forêt during the evening on his way to Catou, and as a mark of respect Mercer and one of his officers rode out of the village to meet him.

The cortège consisted of several Berlines, escorted by about two squadrons of the Royal Garde de Corps – fine young men (all gentlemen), dressed in a very becoming uniform, blue turned up with red, and silver lace tastefully disposed, with Grecian helmets, silver, with a golden sun on the front, the most elegant I ever saw. The King was in the last carriage, on each side of which rode the Duc de Berri and the General whose acquaintance I made on the drill-ground near Alost. We had drawn up on the roadside as the cortège passed. The moment the Duc de Berri and the General saw us, they came up, and, offering us their hands, poured forth such a torrent of compliments and congratulations as made even our horses blush. His Royal Highness could never sufficiently testify his gratitude to the English nation, etc., etc.; was impatient to see us in Paris, for then and there indeed, etc., etc. The General was equally profuse in compliments and promises, so that, forgetting the adage, 'Put not your trust in princes,' Leathes and I have ever since been feeling the Croix de St Louis dangling at our breasts – *nous verrons!* The monarch was detained from his dinner more than half an hour by my worthy friend Mons. le Curé, who, in full pontificals, and followed by his congregation *en habits de dimanche*, met him at the entrance of the village, and, standing on a little bank at the coach door, delivered a long harangue, set off by mandarin-like bobs of the head at the end of every period, and a most profound bow at the conclusion, all which were received and returned by his Majesty with exemplary patience and punctuality.

By the evening of the 29th the wreckage of the Army of the North had reached Paris; Blücher had his headquarters at St Denis on the outskirts of the capital; and Wellington was at Senlis.

This same night Mercer had reached Pont St Maxence on the Oise. On approaching the river, he had thought with some uneasiness that it was at such a place that the French would make a stand; he wondered why it was that the cavalry had been allowed to advance alone into this country, for the infantry were far behind. He says,

> Of course the Duke knew there would be no opposition; and yet it was difficult to imagine what had become of the French force, which we knew was retiring before us. . . . No opposition was there. Instead of finding the banks of the Oise garnished with cannon and bristling with bayonets – instead of broken-up roads and inundated fields, woods full of riflemen and the town of grenadiers – instead of all this, we found a peaceable population in a lovely country, labourers in their fields and fishermen on the rivers, whilst flocks and herds pastured in quiet security on the verdant carpet which overspread the plain.

With the Allies advancing on Paris, Fouché made every effort to negotiate a peace settlement on the best possible terms, as he was determined to remain in power under yet another régime. And although he and the Executive Commission made some show of preparing the country for a war of national defence, their emergency measures travelled little further than the legislature. Diplomatic contact was made with the Allies at Laon as early as 24 June; and on the 27th, at a meeting of Ministers and leading parliamentarians convened by Fouché, commissioners were chosen to treat with the enemy. By the 30th it had become clear that there was no question of the Allies being content with an armistice: they wanted surrender.

And since even the most obstinate generals had to accept that Paris could not be defended, the Capitulation of Paris was signed on 3 July in the Palace of St Cloud. Under the terms of the Convention, which was purely a military agreement, the capital surrendered and the army agreed to take up positions behind the Loire.[1] Within a few days Louis XVIII was re-established and, through the influence of Talleyrand, Fouché had been made his Minister of Police.

During these days one of the chief difficulties of the government was the presence of Napoleon near the centre of affairs. On the one hand, it was hard to convince the Allies that the abdication was not a mere feint, and on the other, the very fact that he was to be seen was the cause of frequent civil disorder in the capital. At the Elysée, Napoleon was not averse to showing himself in the gardens and saluting the crowds, while enraged royalists looked on and prophesied new disasters for the country. It was for this reason that, on 25 June, at Fouché's request, he left Paris, going first to Malmaison and subsequently to Rochefort.

While at Malmaison, Napoleon was obsessed by the idea that some opportunity would suddenly present itself, enabling him to maintain a hold on events. It seemed to him that the army would take action on his behalf and force the government to send for him.

In hot and beautiful weather he waited for news, spending much time in the resplendent gardens, talking to Hortense who was again his hostess. His mind went much to Joséphine, and again he asked for the portrait which Hortense had promised to copy for him. As on his visit to this house in May, he appeared oppressed by a realization that all had gone wrong in his life when he parted with Joséphine to further his ambitions.

Marie Louise, the instrument of his nemesis, was taking a holiday in Baden, and had received news of the great victory at Waterloo with a well controlled lack of emotion. But one of her ladies-in-waiting had danced and sung for joy, and this, no doubt, expressed the feelings of the household.[2] Marie Louise now needed one thing only to complete her happiness, and that was the return of Count Neipperg, who had become deeply involved in military and political

[1] The actual peace treaty between France and the four Powers (the Second Treaty of Paris) was not signed until 20 November. This bound France to carry out the new arrangements imposed on her as a result of Napoleon's return from Elba.

[2] Bertaut, *Marie Louise*, pp. 247-9.

affairs since being called upon to lead the campaign against Murat.[1]

One of Napoleon's preoccupations at this time was the choice of a place of exile in case the worst should happen and nothing saved him from this fate. M. de Caulaincourt had recommended Russia where he had spent some delightful years as French ambassador. But Russia did not appeal to him; he felt he would prefer England. 'England,' he said, 'will be pleased to find me asking her for shelter, for she is generous. There I will taste the only consolation permitted to a man who once governed the world, that of associating with enlightened minds.' It was put to him by his friends, however, that the English had long been in the highest state of exasperation with him and that he could not count on the proverbial political generosity, at least for the moment. They urged him rather to turn his thoughts to America. Napoleon resigned himself. America still had idyllic associations for Europeans. 'Since I am refused the society of men,' he said, 'I will take refuge in the heart of nature, and there I will live in that solitude so appropriate to my last thoughts.' If he did not actually use these words, which are recorded by Thiers, they are at least such as any educated man of the time might have spoken over his glass of brandy after dinner.

Having come to this decision, he sent a message to Paris, requesting that two armed frigates, then in the Rochefort roads, should be reserved for him. In reply, Fouché placed the two frigates at Napoleon's disposal and sent an application to the Allies for safe-conducts. By the 28th, however, it had emerged that the Allies wished to decide Napoleon's future themselves, and that there was no chance of his being given the freedom of the seas. Fouché therefore became anxious that he should leave the Paris area where he was in danger of being taken by the Prussians. He sent emissaries to Malmaison during the night of the 28th, recommending Napoleon to leave immediately for Rochefort where the frigates would weigh anchor without waiting for permits.

Napoleon did not leave, however, without making one final effort to persuade the government to put him at the head of the army for the purpose of striking a blow at the invading enemy. Early on the morning of the 29th, dressed in his military uniform, he

---

[1] Murat was to be executed at Pizzo on the coast of southern Italy on 13th October 1815 while making a foolhardy attempt to regain power in Naples.

explained his plan of action to General Becker whom he then sent to Paris at a gallop with his proposals. As General Bonaparte, he would fight a battle before Paris, relinquishing his command the moment he had scored a victory. The Executive Commission refused the offer coldly, and Fouché's last words were: 'Napoleon would not change the state of affairs in any way. His appearance at the head of the army would only cost us one disaster the more and the ruin of Paris. Let him depart, for we are being asked to deliver him to the enemy and we cannot answer for his safety for more than a few hours.'

Returning to Malmaison, General Becker found Napoleon and his aides-de-camp prepared to jump on their horses, all of them fully assured that they had the Prussians at their mercy. Now, however, they had to resign themselves to failure. Napoleon saw that all was at an end and he must leave. Prussian cavalry were at St Germain and he was no longer safe. Going to his study he laid down his sword, then changed from his uniform into a plain, dark-coloured civilian suit. He asked to have Joséphine's room opened, and remained in it alone for some time. Carriages were now drawn up for his departure, and he took leave of Hortense, his brothers and the many officers who were assembled. All were in tears, from the Bonapartes themselves to the soldiers on guard who are said to have wept as he drove off. Napoleon, that versatile character who gave himself fully to every moment as it came, wore a pale and tragic air. Leaning back in his carriage he remained silent throughout the journey to Rambouillet where he spent the night.[1] Much drawn to actors, and devoted to classical tragedy, he was himself a great actor on the stage of life, entering every role with vigour and taking care to be suitably dressed for it. One may wonder, indeed, if it had not been the sight of his friend Talma strutting on the boards of the *Théâtre Français* which had originally caused him to set his heart on Imperial power. With his superabundant energy and his thirst for experience, he was able to act many roles, each one impressive and convincing while it lasted; but of inward unity we see no sign. He could be Charlemagne, he could be Augustus; he could equally well be Werther or Hamlet. He presented a wonderful spectacle of human personality, with qualities the most brilliant, with virtues and faults and diversified capacities and powers, not merged but

Houssaye, *1815*, Vol. III, pp. 229-30, 349.

alternately taking control with dramatic and often explosive effect.

He was accompanied on his journey by a few chosen friends, including Bertrand who rode beside him in his carriage. Members of his suite and a number of servants followed, and the party arrived at Rochefort on 3 July. Here Napoleon remained for five days, seeking a means of leaving the country. His situation was exceedingly difficult. The Provisional Government had done their best to assist him to escape, but they had been able to do no more than give him a sporting chance of slipping away unobserved by sea. The two armed frigates awaited him, but outside the harbour an English cruiser, the *Bellerophon*, was keeping watch. Loyal military and naval men crowded round with suggestions, and there seemed to be a reasonable chance of getting away on a neutral ship. But Napoleon could not reach a decision, and seemed unwilling to take a risk at sea. The army had now been marched off to the Loire valley, according to the terms of the armistice. Joseph Bonaparte, who was himself on the way to exile, had been in touch with some of the generals and arrived at Rochefort with urgent messages. Napoleon was begged to go to the Loire, to take command and prolong the war. But he realized that it was too late and spoke regretfully of the opportunity he had lost in Paris.

On the 8th, positive orders arrived from Paris that he must leave the country. The Provisional Government had only a few hours to live and was to be replaced by the government of his most Christian Majesty. Scant mercy might be expected from the royalist government. The frigates were authorized to take Napoleon anywhere he chose, apart from the coast of France. Napoleon, therefore, allowed himself to be rowed out to the *Saale*; that very time Paris was celebrating the entry of Louis XVIII. Adverse winds and the presence of British men-of-war kept the frigates from sailing, and thus another week passed by. It was the alarming intelligence from Paris that the royalists were planning to seize him which forced him to choose between attempting to escape out to sea and surrendering to the English. He decided upon the latter course.

On the morning of the 15th, his companions having made the necessary arrangements with the captain, Napoleon was rowed out to the *Bellerophon* where he was received with the honours accorded to a reigning sovereign. At the same time, Gourgaud was at his

request provided with a light naval vessel in which to sail immediately for England carrying a letter to the Prince Regent. This letter
read:

> Your Highness,
>
> Exposed to the factions which divide my country and to the
> enmity of the great European Powers, I have ended my political
> career. I come like Themistocles to seat myself at the hearth of the
> British people. I place myself under the protection of its laws,
> asking this of your Royal Highness as the most powerful, the most
> constant and the most generous of my enemies.
>
> Napoleon.

The request was to be refused, not by England acting alone, but
by all the Powers. The statesmen of the Coalition decided it was
not safe to leave him free in Europe. When this decision was made
known to him later on, Napoleon behaved as though the question
concerned himself and England alone, and he tried his best to
brand England as for ever infamous. He wrote a protestation which
ran as follows:

> I hereby protest solemnly in the face of heaven and mankind against
> the violation of my most sacred rights. I am not a prisoner, I am the
> guest of England. . . . If this act be consummated it would be vain
> for the English to talk of their good faith, of their laws, of their
> liberty. British faith would be lost in the hospitality of the *Bellerophon*.
> I appeal to history. She will tell how an enemy, who warred for
> twenty years against the English people, came of his own free
> will, in the day of his ill fortune, to seek an asylum beneath her laws.
> What greater proof could he give of his esteem and trust? But what
> answer did England make to such magnanimity? She pretended to
> stretch out a hospitable hand to this enemy, and, when he delivered
> himself up in good faith, she sacrificed him!

These inconsequential though high-sounding protests were to
leave a widespread and lasting impression that England, in not
welcoming him as a free citizen, was lacking in honourable feeling
towards him. This impression has been shared by not a few of the
English themselves. In this respect it is perhaps regrettable that
Captain Maitland of the *Bellerophon* did not make it perfectly clear
that, if Napoleon came aboard his ship, he came as a prisoner of war;
Napoleon would still have come, for he knew that he would be far

safer with the English than with the French royalists, who desired his execution. Captain Maitland appears to have carried deference to excess. Descending the steps to receive Napoleon and helping him on board, he treated him as if he were still at the height of his power; the officers were presented to him, and not long after Admiral Hotham came on board from the *Superb* and showed himself equally assiduous, carrying Napoleon back to his ship, there to dine with him. Thus Napoleon was given some grounds for calling himself the guest of England, and England and Europe in general were done much harm; for the Napoleonic legend, which in due course brought Napoleon III to power and thus inaugurated a decline towards militarism, could be said to stem from this grievance. It was a grievance the Whigs were very ready to echo for Napoleon in order to embarrass the Tories. The great legend was given a flying start by Englishmen.

Napoleon appears to have benefited from the days at sea, for all who have recorded meetings with him at this time speak of his energy and good spirits. He spent much time on deck, chatting with the sailors and asking many questions; once more he was the alert man who had made the daring journey from Elba. Everyone was charmed by him. Seeing England for the first time, he admired the beauty of the Devon coast and said that it resembled places he knew in Italy. With his companions he dined off the Imperial gold plate, which had been brought, and kept up a dignity suitable to a visiting monarch. Gourgaud had rejoined the party, however, with news that the Prince Regent had refused to receive the letter sent to him. It was realized that this was an ominous sign.

The weather continued to be perfect; the sky vied with the sea in its brilliant depth of blue; the harbour was filled with small craft and coloured sails were vividly reflected in the water. In all England there was but one emotion, astonishment. For twenty years Napoleon had been an almost legendary bogey, scarcely thought of as a being who could be taken into captivity and brought within sight. To hear that the Royal Navy had Belial on board would hardly have caused more surprise; and, since the fine summer days were inviting, the roads leading to the West Country rang with horses' hooves as all who had the means and the leisure hastened off to see for themselves.

In Torbay he was indeed to be seen. Every day he strolled on deck and bowed to the innumerable Englishmen who raised their hats to him from yachts and rowing boats. Many a young girl, brought up with nursery threats of being carried off by Boney if she misbehaved herself, was really surprised to see that he was a normal man, much like others, and that he even appeared quite calm and affable. There was something about his expression and his silhouette that appealed to people and even made them feel they would like to oblige him in some way. Devon gentlemen sent him baskets of fruit from their gardens, and he received many marks of respect.[1]

As the days passed, more and more sightseers arrived; small boats jostled one another in the vicinity of the *Bellerophon* and it became difficult to draw near. In their eagerness to catch sight of the illustrious captive, many people fell in the water and some were even drowned. It eventually became necessary to forbid the public to approach the vessel.

Napoleon had been hoping to land. But he now learnt that he was not to be permitted the life of a citizen of England which he sought. It was decreed by the victors that he should be sent into exile and closely watched to prevent his escaping. It fell to England, as the possessor of remote islands and of a fleet which could guard them adequately, to be his custodian. The place of confinement chosen was St Helena.

He made his protest, but could do no more and had to submit to being conveyed towards Plymouth where he was transferred to the *Northumberland*. Surrounded by the devoted friends who had chosen to accompany him, he now set sail for a very tolerable captivity which he was to employ in fabricating his own history. It was on 7 August that the great sails of the *Northumberland* vanished into the mists as Napoleon left England's shores, carried far from that Europe whose old, easy-going traditions of limited warfare had been destroyed for ever by a military gigantism of which his power was the product and which his ambitions had served to promote.

[1] For a description of the immense power of fascination which Napoleon could exert, see Caulaincourt, *Mémoires*, Vol. I, pp. 314, 315. He writes, for instance, '*Il avait, quand il voulait, dans la voix, dans la physionomie, comme dans les manières, quelque chose de séduisant, de persuasif qui lui donnait autant d'advantages sur la personne avec laquelle il causait que la supériorité et la flexibilité de son esprit. Jamais homme ne fut plus séduisant quand il le voulait, et il fallait pour lui resister avoir fait, comme moi, l'épreuve de tout de que cet art cachait d'erreurs politiques.*'

APPENDIX A

THE ANGLO-ALLIED ARMY

COMMANDER-IN-CHIEF
Field-Marshal the Duke of Wellington

CHIEF OF THE STAFF
Colonel Sir William Howe de Lancey, K.B.

ADJUTANT-GENERAL
Major-General Sir E. Barnes, K.B.

COMMANDING ROYAL ARTILLERY
Colonel Sir G. A. Wood

COMMANDING ENGINEER
Lieut.-Colonel Smyth

PRUSSIAN ATTACHÉ AT BRITISH HEADQUARTERS
Major-General Baron von Müffling

FIRST CORPS

Commander, the Prince of Orange
1st Division, commanded by Major-General Cooke

BRIGADES
Major-General Maitland (B):[1] *2/1st and 3/1st Guards*
Major-General Sir John Byng (B): *2/2nd and 2/3rd Guards*
ARTILLERY
Lieut.-Colonel Adye
Captain Sandham's Field Brigade, R.A.;
Major Kühlmann's Horse Artillery Troop, K.G.L.
TOTAL: 4,061 men[2]

3rd Division, commanded by Lieut.-General Count Sir Charles Alten
BRIGADES
Major-General Sir Colin Halkett (B): *2/30th, 33rd, 2/69th, 2/73rd*
Colonel Baron von Ompteda (K.G.L.): *1st and 2nd Light Battalions, and 5th and 8th Line Battalions*
Major-General Count Kielmansegge (H); (6 battalions)

---

[1] B denotes British; H, Hanoverian; K.G.L., King's German Legion.
[2] This and the subsequent divisional totals do not include the numbers of men in artillery units. The artillery is treated separately on p. 291.

ARTILLERY
Lieut.-Colonel Williamson
Major Lloyd's Field Brigade, R.A.;
Captain Cleeves' Field Brigade, K.G.L.
TOTAL: 6,970 men

2nd Dutch-Belgian Division, commanded by Lieut.-General Baron
de Perponcher
BRIGADES
Major-General Count de Bylandt: *5 Dutch-Belgian battalions*
Prince Bernard of Saxe-Weimar: *5 Nassau battalions*
ARTILLERY
Major-Van Opstal
Bijleveld's Horse-Battery and 1 Field Battery
TOTAL: 7,533 men

3rd Dutch-Belgian Division, commanded by Lieut.-General
Baron Chassé
BRIGADES
Major-General Ditmers: *6 Dutch-Belgian battalions*
Major-General d'Aubremé: *6 Dutch-Belgian battalions*
ARTILLERY
Major van der Smissen: *1 Horse and 1 Field Battery*
TOTAL: 6,669 men
Total First Corps: 25,233 men, 56 guns

SECOND CORPS

Commander, Lieut.-General Lord Hill
2nd Division, commanded by Lieut.-General Sir Henry Clinton
BRIGADES
Major-General Adam (B): *1/52nd, 1/71st, 2/95th and 3/95th*
Colonel du Plat (K.G.L.): *1st, 2nd, 3rd, and 4th Line Battalions*
Colonel W. Halkett (H): *4 Landwehr battalions*
ARTILLERY
Lieut.-Colonel Gold
Captain Bolton's Field Brigade, R.A.;
Major Sympher's Horse Artillery Troops, K.G.L.
TOTAL: 6,833 men

4th Division, commanded by Lieut.-General Sir Charles Colville
BRIGADES
Colonel Mitchell (B): *3/14th, 1/23rd and 51st*

Major-General Johnstone (B): *2/35th, 1/54th, 2/59th and 1/91st*
Major-General Sir James Lyon (H): *5 battalions*
ARTILLERY
Lieut.-Colonel Hawker
Major Brome's Field Brigade, R.A.;
Captain von Rettberg's Hanoverian Field Battery
TOTAL: 7,212 men

Corps of Prince Frederick of the Netherlands

1st Dutch-Belgian Division, commanded by Lieut.-General Stedman
BRIGADES
Major-General d'Hauw: *6 battalions*
Major-General d'Eerens: *5 battalions*
TOTAL: 6,389 men
Lieut.-General Anthing's Netherland Indian Brigade: *5 battalions and 1 field battery*
TOTAL: 3,583 men
16 men detached from other regiments.
Total Second Corps: 24,033 men, 40 guns.

RESERVE
Commander, Field-Marshal the Duke of Wellington
5th Division, commanded by Lieut.-General Sir Thomas Picton
BRIGADES
Major-General Sir James Kempt (B): *1/28th, 1/32nd, 1/79th and 1/95th*
Major-General Sir Denis Pack (B): *3/1st, 1/42nd, 2/44th, and 1/92nd*
Colonel von Wincke (H): *4 Landwehr battalions*
ARTILLERY
Major Heisse:
Major Rogers' Field Brigade, R.A.;
Captain Braun's Hanoverian Field Battery.
TOTAL: 7,158 men

6th Division, commanded by Lieut.-General the Hon. Sir Lowry Cole
BRIGADES
Major-General Sir John Lambert (B): *1/4th, 1/27th, 1/40th and 2/81st*
Colonel Best (H): *4 Landwehr battalions*
ARTILLERY
Lieut.-Colonel Brückmann:
Major Unett's Field Brigade, R.A.;
Captain Sinclair's Field Brigade, R.A.
TOTAL: 5,149 men

British Reserve Artillery, commanded by Major Drummond
Lieut.-Colonel Sir H. Ross's Horse Artillery Troop
Major Bean's Horse Artillery Troop
Major Morrison's Company, R.A.
Captain Hutchesson's Company, R.A.
Captain Ilbert's Company, R.A.

Brunswick Corps, commanded by the Duke of Brunswick
Advanced Guard, 4 companies infantry and 1 cavalry detachment;
2 brigades (each 3 battalions) and 2 batteries
TOTAL: 5,376 men
Nassau Contingent, commanded by General von Kruse
3 battalions
TOTAL: 2,880 men

Total Reserve: 20,563 men, 64 guns

GARRISONS
7th Division
7th British Brigade: *2/25th, 2/37th and 2/78th*
3 British Garrison battalions
TOTAL: 3,233 men
Hanoverian Reserve Corps *12 Landwehr battalions in 4 brigades*
TOTAL: 9,000 men

Total Garrison: 12,233 men

CAVALRY
Commander, Lieut.-General the Earl of Uxbridge
BRIGADES
Major-General Lord Edward Somerset (B): *1st and 2nd Life Guards,
Royal Horse Guards Blues, 1st Dragoon Guards*
Major-General Sir William Ponsonby (B): *1st Royal Dragoons, 2nd
Dragoons Greys, 6th Inniskilling Dragoons*
Major-General Sir William Dörnberg (B and K.G.L.): *1st and 2nd Light
Dragoons, K.G.L., and 23rd Light Dragoons*
Major-General Sir John Vandeleur (B): *11th 12th and 16th Light Dragoons*
Major-General Sir Colquhoun Grant (B and K.G.L.): *7th and 15th
Hussars, and 2nd Hussars, K.G.L*
Major-General Sir Hussey Vivian (B and K.G.L.): *10th and 18th Hussars
and 1st Hussars, K.G.L.*
Colonel Baron F. von Arentschildt (B and K.G.L.): *13th Light Dragoons,
and 3rd Hussars, K.G.L.*
TOTAL: 8,473 men

British Horse Artillery Troops attached to the Cavalry:
Commander, Lieut.-Colonel Sir Augustus Frazer.
Major Bull's Troop (howitzers)
Lieut.-Colonel Webber-Smith's Troop
Lieut.-Colonel Sir R. Gardiner's Troop
Major E. C. Whinyates' Troop (with Rockets)
Major Norman Ramsay's Troop
Captain Mercer's Troop

1st Hanoverian Cavalry Brigade: Colonel von Estorff
3 regiments: *Prince Regent's Hussars, Bremen and Verden Hussars, Cumberland Hussars*
TOTAL: 1,682 men

Brunswick Cavalry
1 regiment of Hussars, 1 squadron of Uhlans
TOTAL: 922 men

Dutch-Belgian Cavalry Division: Lieut.-General Baron de Collaert
3 brigades under Major-General Trip; Major-General de Ghigny; Major-General van Merlen
Artillery: 2 half-horse batteries
TOTAL: 3,405 men

Total Cavalry: 14,482 men, 44 guns

ARTILLERY

	Guns	Men
BRITISH		
7 Field Batteries of 6 guns each	42	
3 ,, ,, ,, 4 ,, ,, (18 prs.)	12	
8 Horse ,, ,, 6 ,, ,,	48	5,030
K.G.L.		
1 Field ,, ,, 6 ,, ,,	6	
2 Horse ,, ,, 6 ,, ,,	12	526
HANOVERIAN		
2 Field ,, ,, 6 ,, ,,	12	465
BRUNSWICK		
1 Field ,, ,, 8 ,, ,,	8	
1 Horse ,, ,, 8 ,, ,,	8	510
DUTCH-BELGIAN		
4 Field ,, ,, 8 ,, ,,	32	
3 Horse ,, ,, 8 ,, ,,	24	1,635
	204	8,166

MISCELLANEOUS

Engineers, Sappers and Miners, Wagon Train and Staff Corps   1,240

TOTAL STRENGTH

Infantry	82,062
Cavalry	14,482
Artillery	8,166
Miscellaneous	1,240

Grand total 105,950 men
204 guns

Adapted from Siborne's tables

PRUSSIAN ARMY

COMMANDER-IN-CHIEF
Field-Marshal Prince Blücher von Wahlstadt

QUARTERMASTER GENERAL AND CHIEF OF THE STAFF
General Count von Gneisenau

CHIEF OF THE GENERAL STAFF
General von Grölmann.

FIRST CORPS
Commander, Lieut.-General von Ziethen

BRIGADES[1]
Major-General von Steinmetz
Major-General von Pirch II
Major-General von Jagow
Major-General Count von Henckel Donnersmarck
    Cavalry Corps commanded by Lieut.-General von Röder
Major-General von Treskow
Lieut.-Colonel von Lützow
    Artillery, commanded by Colonel von Lehmann
3 horse artilley, 3 12 pdr. and 5 6 pdr. field batteries, 1 howitzer battery
    Total First Corps: 31,129 men, 80 guns

---

[1] There was no divisional organization in the Prussian army of 1815, though the brigades were each about the strength of a French division.

SECOND CORPS

Commanded by Major-General von Pirch I

BRIGADES

Major-General von Tippelskirch
Major-General von Kraft
Major-General von Brause
Major-General von Bose
   Cavalry Corps, commanded by Major General von Wahlen-Jurgass
Colonel von Thümen
Colonel Count von Schulenburg
Lieut.-Colonel von Sohr
      Artillery, commanded by Colonel von Röhl
3 horse artillery; 2 12-pdr. and 5 6-pdr. field batteries.
    Total Second Corps: 31,529 men, 80 guns

THIRD CORPS

Commanded by Lieut.-General von Thielemann

BRIGADES

Major-General von Borcke
Colonel von Kämpfen
Colonel von Luck
Colonel von Stülpnägel
   Cavalry Corps, commanded by General von Hobe
Colonel Von der Marwitz
Colonel Count von Lottum
   Artillery, commanded by Colonel von Mohnhaupt
3 horse artillery; 1 12-pdr. and 2 6-pdr. field batteries
    Total Third Corps: 24,141 men, 48 guns

FOURTH CORPS

Commanded by General Count Bülow von Dennewitz

BRIGADES

Lieut.-General von Hacke
General von Ryssel
General von Losthin
Colonel von Hiller
   Cavalry Corps, commanded by General Prince William of Prussia
General von Sidow
Colonel Count von Schwerin
Lieut.-Colonel von Watsdorf
   Artillery, commanded by Lieut.-Colonel von Bardeleben

3 horse batteries; 3 12-pdr. and 5 6-pdr. field batteries.

Total Fourth Corps: 30,862 men, 88 guns

Total Strength, 117,661 men, 296 guns

Adapted from the tables of De Bas. The figures do not include officers or musicians; with these last added, the grand total, with train, etc., is approximately 124,000

THE FRENCH ARMY

COMMANDER-IN-CHIEF
the Emperor Napoleon

CHIEF OF THE STAFF
Marshal Soult, Duke of Dalmatia

CHIEF COMMANDER OF ARTILLERY
Lieut.-General Ruty

CHIEF COMMANDER OF ENGINEERS
Lieut.-General Baron Rogniat

FIRST CORPS
Commanded by Lieut.-General Count Drouet d'Erlon

1st Division, commanded by Lieut.-General Allix (in Allix's absence Baron Quiot commanded the division)
BRIGADES: Quiot, Bourgeois
2nd Division, commanded by Lieut.-General Baron Donzelot
BRIGADES: Schmidt, Aulard
3rd Division, commanded by Lieut.-General Baron Marcognet
BRIGADES: Noguez, Grenier
4th Division, commanded by Lieut.-General Count Durutte
BRIGADES: Pégot, Brue
Cavalry Division, commanded by Lieut.-General Baron Jacquinot
BRIGADES: Bruno, Gobrecht
Artillery, commanded by Baron de Salles (6 batteries)
Engineers
5 companies

Total First Corps: 20,731 men, 46 guns

SECOND CORPS
Commanded Lieut.-General Count Reille
5th Division, commanded by Lieut.-General Baron Bachelu

BRIGADES: Husson, Campy

  6th Division, commanded by Lieut.-General Prince Jérôme Bonaparte

BRIGADES: Baudouin, Soye

    7th Division, commanded by Lieut.-General Count Girard

BRIGADES: Devilliers, Piat

    9th Division, commanded by Lieut.-General Count Foy

BRIGADES: Gauthier, B. Jamin

  2nd Cavalry Division, commanded by Lieut.-General Baron Piré

BRIGADES: Hubert, Wathiez

       Artillery, commanded by Baron Pelletier

6 batteries

Engineers

5 companies

    Total Second Corps: 25,179 men, 46 guns

THIRD CORPS

Commanded by Lieut.-General Count Vandamme

  8th Division, commanded by Lieut.-General Baron Lefol

BRIGADES: Billard, Corsin

  10th Division, commanded by Lieut.-General Baron Habert

BRIGADES: Gengoult Dupeyroux

  11th Division, commanded by Lieut.-General Baron Berthézène

BRIGADES: Dufour, Lagarde

  3rd Cavalry Division, commanded by Lieut.-General Baron Domon

BRIGADES: Dommanget, Vinot

    Artillery, commanded by General Doguereau

5 batteries

Engineers

3 companies

    Total Third Corps: 18,105 men, 38 guns

FOURTH CORPS

Commanded by Lieut.-General Count Gérard

  12th Division, commanded by Lieut.-General Baron Pécheux

BRIGADES: Rome, Schoeffer

  13th Division, commanded by Lieut.-General Baron Vichery

BRIGADES: Le Capitaine, Desprez

  14th Division, commanded by Lieut.-General de Bourmont (afterwards
by General Hulot)

BRIGADES: Hulot, Toussaint

  7th Cavalry Division, commanded by Lieut.-General Maurin

BRIGADES: Vallin, Berruyer

Artillery, commanded by General Baron Baltus

5 batteries

Engineers

4 companies

Total Fourth Corps: 15,404 men, 38 guns

SIXTH CORPS

Commanded by Lieut.-General Count Lobau

19th Division, commanded by Lieut.-General Baron Simmer

BRIGADES: Bellair, M. Jamin

20th Division, commanded by Lieut.-General Baron Jeannin

BRIGADES: Bony, Tromelin

21st Division, commanded by Lieut.-General Baron Teste

BRIGADES: Laffitte, Penne

Artillery commanded by Lieut.-General Baron Noury

4 batteries

Engineers

3 companies

Total Sixth Corps: 10,821 men, 38 guns

RESERVE CAVALRY

Commanded by Marshal Count de Grouchy

FIRST CORPS

Command by Lieut.-General Count Pajol

4th Division, commanded by Lieut.-General Baron Soult

BRIGADES: St Laurent, Ameil

5th Division, commanded by Lieut.-General Baron Subervie

BRIGADES: A. de Colbert, Merlin

Artillery

2 horse batteries

SECOND CORPS

Commanded by Lieut.-General Count Exelmans

9th Division, commanded by Lieut.-General Baron Strolz

BRIGADES: Barthe, Vincent

10th Division, commanded by Lieut.-General Baron Chastel

BRIGADES: Bonnemains, Berton

Artillery

2 horse batteries

THIRD CORPS

Commanded by Lieut.-General Kellermann, Count Valmy
11th Division, commanded by Lieut.-General Baron Lheritier
BRIGADES: Picquet, Guiton
12th Division, commanded by Lieut.-General Roussel d'Hurbal
BRIGADES: Blancard, Donop

Artillery

2 horse batteries

FOURTH CORPS

Commanded by Lieut.-General Count Milhaud
13th Division, commanded by Lieut.-General Wathier de St Alphonse
BRIGADES: Dubois, Travers
14th Division, commanded by Lieut.-General Baron Delort
BRIGADES: Farine, Vial

Artillery

2 horse batteries
Total Reserve Cavalry: 13,144 men, 48 guns

THE IMPERIAL GUARD

Commanded by Marshal Mortier, Duke of Treviso[1]
Aide-Major-Général de la Garde, Lieut.-General Count Drouot
Infantry, Lieut.-General Count Friant

General Petit, *1st Grenadiers*
General Christiani, *2nd Grenadiers*
General Poret de Morvan, *3rd Grenadiers*
General Harlet, *4th Grenadiers*
Lieut.-General Count Morand

General Cambronne, *1st Chasseurs*
General Pelet, *2nd Chasseurs*
Colonel Malet, *3rd Chasseurs*
General Henrion, *4th Chasseurs*[2]
Lieut.-General Count Duhesme

Colonel Secrétan, *1st Voltigeurs*
Colonel Trappier, *1st Tirailleurs*

[1] Mortier did not take part in the campaign, but had to remain behind at Beaumont on account of ill-health.

[2] The 3rd and 4th Grenadiers and the 3rd and 4th Chasseurs were popularly known as the 'Middle Guard' although officially they formed part of the 'Old Guard.'

Colonel Hurel, *3rd Voltigeurs*
Colonel Pailhès, *3rd Tirailleurs*
   Light Cavalry, Lieut.-General Lefebvre-Desnouettes
General Colbert, *Lancers*
General F. A. Lallemand, *Chasseurs*
   Reserve Cavalry (heavy) Lieut.-General Count Guyot
General Dubois, *Grenadiers*
General Letort, (in place of Ornano, who remained in Paris) *Dragoons*
  Colonel d'Autancourt (heavy cavalry) Gendarmerie d'Elite
   Artillery, Lieut.-General Desvaux de St Maurice
13 Foot and 3 Horse Batteries
   Total, Imperial Guard, 20,755 men, 96 guns

TOTAL STRENGTH: 124,139 men, 350 guns

Figures of men are taken from Houssaye, guns from Siborne

EFFECTIVE STRENGTH OF THE ARMIES ON THE FIELD OF WATERLOO[1]

ANGLO-ALLIED ARMY

Infantry	49,608
Cavalry	12,408
Artillery	5,645
Total	67,661 and 156 guns

PRUSSIAN ARMY (7 P.M.)

Infantry	41,283
Cavalry	8,858
Artillery	1,803
Total	51,944 and 104 guns

FRENCH ARMY

Infantry	47,579
Cavalry	13,792
Artillery	7,529
Total	68,900 and 246 guns

[1] Taken from Siborne. Houssaye has a higher figure for the French Army (p. 188).

APPENDIX B

Marshal Ney and Quatre Bras

Napoleon not only claims to have ordered Ney to seize Quatre Bras on the afternoon of the 15th, but provides the very conversation that took place. We read in *The Campaign of 1815* by Gourgaud:

'Marshal, you are well acquainted with the position of Quatre Bras?' said Napoleon.

'Yes, Sire,' replied Ney, 'how can it be otherwise? Twenty years ago I served in this country; the position of Quatre Bras is the key to all the rest.'

'Well,' said the Emperor, 'rally your two corps, and, if necessary, throw up some redoubts; hasten the march of d'Erlon, and let him call up all the detachments he has left on the bridges of the Sambre; all must be assembled before midnight.'

Ney instantly replied, 'Depend upon it, in two hours we shall be at Quatre Bras, unless all the enemy's army be there!'

It seems unlikely that Ney would think of Quatre Bras as the key to all the rest, since he had no information about the positions of the various bodies of troops constituting the armies of the enemy. Moreover, if he had felt it was a vital point to be seized at all costs, no doubt he would have made efforts to seize it, and no doubt, also, Napoleon would have made some attempt during the evening to verify that it had been taken. Napoleon made no such attempt and, in fact, in all his written commands of the 15th and 16th there is not a word to suggest he had given instructions either on the afternoon of the 15th, or during the night following, that Quatre Bras was to be taken. The following order was sent to Drouet d'Erlon shortly before Ney arrived in Charleroi and was given his command:

En avant de Charleroi, à 3 heures du soir,
15 juin, 1815

Monsieur le comte d'Erlon, l'Empereur ordonne à M. le comte Reille de marcher sur Gosselies, et d'y attaquer un corps ennemi qui paraissait s'y arrêter. L'intention de l'Empereur est que vous marchiez aussi sur Gosselies, pour appuyer le comte Reille et le seconder dans ses opérations. Cependant, vous devrez toujours faire garder Marchiennes, et vous enverrez une brigade sur les routes de Mons, lui recommandant de se garder très militairement.'

The following order was also sent to d'Erlon; the date is given, but no time; but it is obvious from the wording that it was sent after Ney had been given the command. There is still no mention of Quatre Bras, but only of Gosselies.

Charleroi, le 15 juin, 1815.

Monsieur le Comte, l'intention de l'Empereur est que vous ralliez votre corps sur la rive gauche de la Sambre, pour joindre le 2e corps à Gosselies, d'après les ordres que vous donnera à ce sujet M le maréchal prince de la Moskowa.

Ainsi, vous rappellerez les troupes que vous avez laissées à Thuin, Solre et environs; vous devrez cependant avoir toujours de nombreux partis sur votre gauche pour éclairer la route de Mons.

Le maréchal d'empire, major général,
Duc de Dalmatie.

Marshal Soult and Colonel Heymès alone were within hearing when Napoleon gave Ney his orders. When one of Marshal Ney's sons, seeking to redeem his father's reputation, called on Soult in 1829 and asked him if Napoleon had in fact ordered Ney on the afternoon of the 15th to take Quatre Bras, he was told that Napoleon had had no thought of occupying Quatre Bras at the time, and had not given the order. Colonel Heymès was emphatic in denying the order was given. But the word of men given long after the event is never entirely satisfying, and the historians who believe that Napoleon must inevitably have desired to take Quatre Bras at once, merely dismiss this evidence as useless. Houssaye, who believes Napoleon gave the order, produces as final proof the fact that the French bulletin sent to Paris that evening contains these words: 'The Emperor has given the command of the left to the Prince of Moskowa, who had his headquarters this evening at Quatre Bras on the road to Brussels.' It appears to Houssaye evident from this that Napoleon had ordered Ney to take Quatre Bras and assumed when the bulletin was sent out that he had done so. However, in Baron Fain's letter to Joseph Bonaparte, sent the same evening, we read that the advance guards were placed half-way along the roads from Charleroi to Brussels and Charleroi to Namur; this was neither true, nor did it signify that Napoleon had ordered troops to be so placed; it was the kind of misleading and over-optimistic account of events that was inclined to be sent back to the capital in official bulletins.   The assertion of the bulletin regarding Quatre Bras cannot, therefore, be taken as reliable evidence.

APPENDIX C

d'Erlon's Movements on the 16th

The fact that d'Erlon's corps was called over to the right and then not used is one of the unsolved mysteries of the campaign. D'Erlon himself describes how he rode ahead of his troops on the way up to Quatre Bras and was overtaken by one of Napeoleon's aides-de-camp. He writes:

> Beyond Frasnes I paused among the Generals of the Guard where I was joined by General Labédoyère who showed me a pencilled note which he was taking to Marshal Ney and which called on that Marshal to direct my army corps on Ligny. General Labédoyère informed me that he had already given the order for the movement, changing the direction of my column, and he told me where I could rejoin it. I followed the route indicated straight away, and sent my Chief-of-Staff, General Delcambre, to the Marshal, to inform him of my new destination.

Could this note shown to d'Erlon have been the despatch sent by Soult at 3.15, or a duplicate of the despatch of 2 p.m.? Could the messenger have talked so much and so speciously that the actual content of the despatch was not properly noted? It hardly seems possible. D'Erlon would surely read any order presented to him with attention, and would realize on looking at either of Soult's despatches that nothing in them justified the diversion of his corps without Ney's consent. The general he had left at the head of his column had even more reason to read the note carefully before diverting the whole corps in the absence of his chief, for he was being asked to take a most serious step. By the time d'Erlon himself read the order he was close to the battlefield of Quatre Bras; if he read that Ney was to manœuvre to his right and realized that the messenger had taken it upon himself to direct the manœuvre in person, he would scarcely tolerate such interference. Ney was engaged with the enemy, and he alone could direct the manœuvre according to the circumstances in which the order found him. It appears certain that d'Erlon must have read a message specifically ordering his own corps across to Ligny, or else have taken the word of the messenger that Napoleon had authorized him to send the corps across if he came upon it on his way to Ney with the message. In that case, the pencilled note was either a forgery, or was in fact sent by Napoleon.

No such order appears on Soult's register, however, and Napoleon says nothing in his memoirs about d'Erlon's movement except that it was inexplicable. He appears to know nothing whatever about it. One does not get the impression from his behaviour on the battle-field that he had sent for d'Erlon, and the letter to Ney written by Soult the following day seems to settle the matter, for Ney is taken to task for not keeping his two army corps compactly together. The relevant passages are as follows:

> His Majesty was grieved to learn that you did not succeed yesterday; the divisions acted in isolation, and you therefore sustained losses.
>
> If the corps of Counts Reille and d'Erlon had been together, not a soldier of the English corps that came to attack you would have escaped; if Count d'Erlon had executed the movement on Saint-Amand ordered by the Emperor, the Prussian army would have been totally destroyed and we should perhaps have taken 30,000 prisoners.
>
> The corps of Generals Vandamme and Gérard and the Imperial Guard were kept together all the time; one lays oneself open to reverses when detachments are jeopardized.
>
> The Emperor hopes and desires that your seven divisions of infantry and cavalry will be well formed and united, occupying as a whole less than a league of territory, so that they are well in hand for use if necessary.

Houssaye, who believes that Napoleon wrote the note ordering d'Erlon to the right, quotes out of their context the words 'if Count d'Erlon had executed the movement on Saint-Amand ordered by the Emperor. . . .' (1815, Vol. II, p. 206, note), which taken in isolation seem to prove his case. But when the sentence is read as a whole it can be seen that Soult is simply discussing two possibilities. In speaking of the movement on Saint-Amand which was not executed, he is referring to the order in his despatch of 3.15, not to the mysterious note supposed to have been sent by Napoleon as an afterthought.

Napoleon could not understand the arrival of d'Erlon, nor Ney his departure, and each thought the other responsible. The solution of the riddle seems to be, therefore, that the messenger, seeing his opportunity to speed things up, gave a false order.

Did not this mysterious messenger, variously given as Labédoyère, Laurent, Forbin-Jansen and an unnamed sergeant of the Guard, do Napoleon a great deal more harm than Soult, Ney, Grouchy, or d'Erlon, the popular scapegoats of the legened?

Drouet d'Erlon says, 'Had General Labédoyère been given the mission of changing the direction of my column without first seeing Marshal Ney? I do not think so. But in any case, this circumstance alone was the cause of all the marches and countermarches that paralysed my army corps during the day of the 16th.'

There does not seem to be any particular reason for doubting that the impetuous Labédoyère was the messenger in question. Houssaye dismisses d'Erlon's assertion that Labédoyère was the messenger with these words: 'impossible, since we know from Petiet that at five o'clock Labédoyère was near the Emperor.' And then, only two pages further on, he gives us the following: 'Forbin-Jansen was the bearer, not of Soult's despatch but, of the pencilled order of the Emperor, and after having communicated the order to d'Erlon he returned directly to Fleurus. . . . *Back at Fleurus at about five o'clock*, he was again sent to Ney by the Emperor . . ., etc.' (*1815*, Vol. II, 1899 ed., p. 204, note 1; p. 206, note 1).

Whoever the messenger may have been, his feelings on learning that his bold ruse had misfired cannot have been enviable.

APPENDIX D

Marshal Ney's account of the Battle of Quatre Bras

We advanced towards the enemy with an enthusiasm difficult to be described. Nothing resisted our impetuosity. The battle became general, and victory was no longer doubtful, when, at the moment that I intended to order up the first corps of infantry, which had been left by me in reserve at Frasnes, I learned that the Emperor had disposed of it without advising me of the circumstance, as well as of the division of Girard of the second corps, on purpose to direct them upon St Amand to strengthen his left wing, which was vigorously engaged with the Prussians. The shock which this intelligence gave me confounded me. Having no longer under me more than three divisions, instead of the eight upon which I calculated, I was obliged to renounce hopes of victory, and, in spite of all my efforts, in spite of the intrepidity and devotion of my troops, my utmost endeavours could thenceforth only maintain me in my position till the close of the day. . . .

By what fatality did the Emperor, instead of leading all his forces against Lord Wellington, who would have been attacked unawares, and could not have resisted, consider this attack as secondary? How did the Emperor, after the passage of the Sambre, conceive it possible to fight two battles on the same day? It was to oppose forces double ours, and to do what military men who were witnesses of it can scarcely yet comprehend. Instead of this, had he left a corps of observation to watch the Prussians, and marched with his most powerful masses to support me, the English army had undoubtedly been destroyed between Quatre Bras and Genappes; and, this position, which separated the two allied armies, being once in our power, would have opened for the Emperor an opportunity of advancing to the right of the Prussians, and of crushing them in their turn. . . .

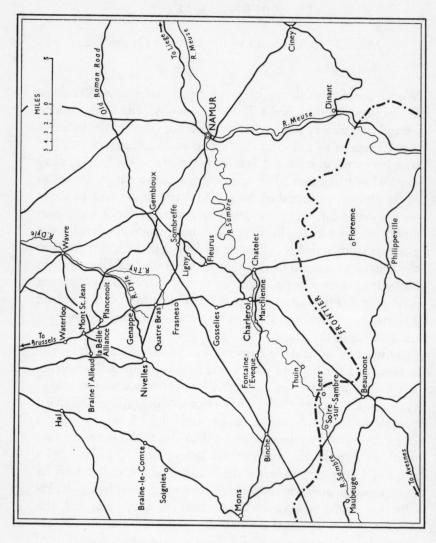

General map of the
Campaign of 1815

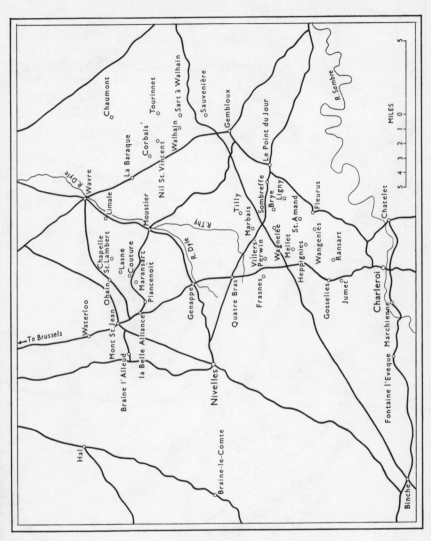

The country of the
Campaign

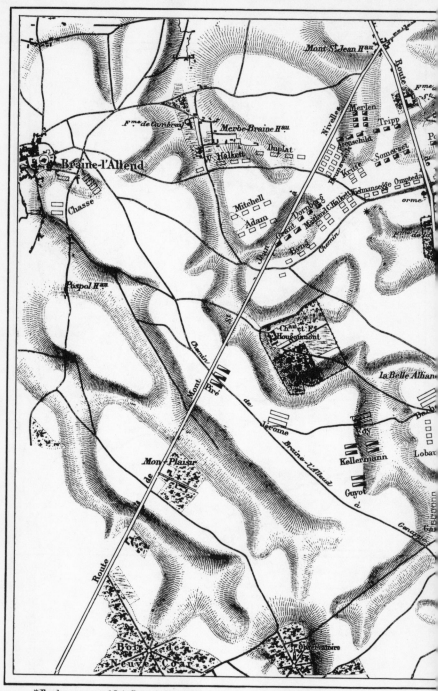

Mont St Jean H^{au}

Braine-l'Allend

F^{me} de Cambrai

Merbe-Braine H^{au}

Duplat

Halkett

Merlen

Tripp

Somerset

Ompteda

Mitchell

Adam

Maitland Halkett

Chasse

Pospol H^{au}

Chan et F^{te}
Hougoumont

la Belle Alliance

Pré

de Jérôme

Kellermann

Lobau

Mont

Mon-Plaisir

Guyot

Route

Bois de
Neuve Cour

Observatoire

✻ Emplacement actuel de la Butte du Lion belge.
♦ ■ Maison Decoster.

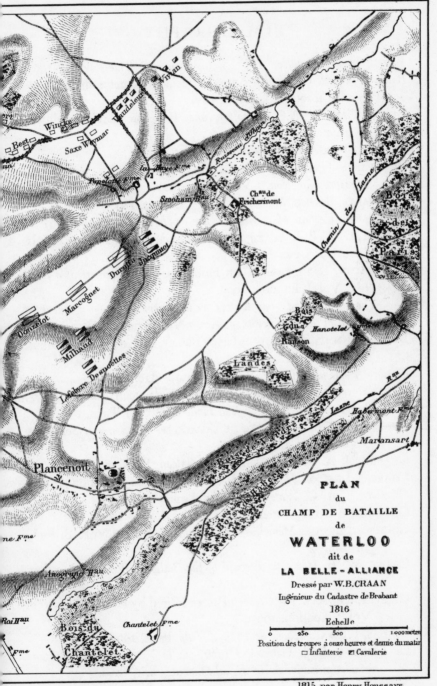

PLAN
du
CHAMP DE BATAILLE
de
WATERLOO
dit de
LA BELLE - ALLIANCE
Dressé par W.B. CRAAN
Ingénieur du Cadastre de Brabant
1816
Echelle

0   250   500   1.000 mètre

Position des troupes à onze heures et demie du matin
□ Infanterie   ▨ Cavalerie

1815 _ par Henry Houssaye

BIBLIOGRAPHY

BARNI, JULES. *Napoléon I et son historien, M. Thiers.* Paris, 1869.

Battle of Waterloo 1815, the (Anon.) Official documents and contemporary accounts. London, 1852.

BECKE, CAPTAIN A.F. *Napoleon and Waterloo.* Revised edition, London, 1936.

BERTAUT, JULES. *Marie Louise.* Paris, 1940.

BONAPARTE, HORTENSE. *Mémoires de la reine Hortense, publiées par le prince Napoléon.* 3 Vols. Paris, 1927.

BONAPARTE, JÉRÔME. *Mémoires.* Vol. VII. Paris, 1866.

BONAPARTE, JOSEPH. *Mémoires et Correspondance.* Vol. X. Paris, 1854.

BONNAL, G. A. B. E. H. *La Vie Militaire du Maréchal Ney.* 3 Vols. Paris, 1910, etc.

BROUGHTON, LORD. (John Cam Hobhouse). *Recollections of a Long Life.* Vol. I. London, 1909.

—— *The substance of some Letters written from Paris during the Last Reign of the Emperor Napoleon.* 2 Vols. London, 1817.

BURNEY, FANNY. *The Diary of Fanny Burney.* Edited by Lewis Gibbs. London, 1940.

Cambridge Modern History. Vol. IX. Cambridge, 1906.

CAULAINCOURT. *Mémoires du Général de Caulaincourt, Duc de Vicence.* Introduction et Notes de Jean Hanotau. Vol. 1. Paris, 1933.

CHAMANS, A. M. J., COMTE DE LAVALETTE. *Mémoires et Souvenirs.* 2 Vols. Paris, 1831.

CHAPTAL, J. A. *Mes Souvenirs sur Napoléon.* Paris 1893.

CHARRAS, LT.-COL. *Histoire de la Campagne de 1815.* London. 1857.

CHESNEY, COL. C. *Waterloo Lectures.* London, 1869.

CHUQUET, ARTHUR. *Lettres de 1815. Première Série.* Paris, 1911.

COCHELET, LOUISE. *Mémoires sur la Reine Hortense.* 4 Vols. Brussels, 1837-8.

CRAAN, W. B. *Historical Account of the Battle of Waterloo.* London, 1817.

CREEVEY, THOMAS. *The Creevey Papers.* Edited by Herbert Maxwell. Vol. I. London, 1903.

DE BAS, F. *La Campagne de 1815.* 4 Vols. Paris, 1908-9.

DE CHENIER, L. J. Gabriel. *Histoire de la Vie Politique, Militaire et administrative du Maréchal Davout.* Paris, 1866.

DECOSTER, J. B. *Relation de ce que Napoléon Buonaparte a fait . . .* Brussels (?), 1816.

DE GROUCHY, E. *Le Maréchal Grouchy de 16 au 19 Juin.* Paris, 1864.

DE GROUCHY, George. *Mémoires du Maréchal de Grouchy.* Paris, 1873.

DE LA FAYETTE, MARQUIS. *Mémoires.* 6 Vols. Paris, 1837-8.

DE MAUDUIT, HIPPOLYTE. *Les derniers jours de la Grande Armée.* 2 Vols. Paris, 1847-8.

DE MENEVAL, BARON C. F. *Marie-Louise et la Cour d'Autriche.* Paris, 1909.

DE VAULABELLE, ACHILLE. *Histoire de deux Restaurations.* Vol. II. Paris, 1847.

DE VIEL-CASTEL, LOUIS. *Histoire de la Restauration.* Vol III. Paris, 1861.

DROUET, J. B. *Le Maréchal Drouet, Comte d'Erlon.* Paris, 1844.

DU CASSE, A. *Le Général Vandamme et sa Correspondance.* 2 Vols. Paris, 1870.

ELLESMERE, FRANCIS, EARL OF. *Personal Reminiscences of the Duke of Wellington.* London, 1903.

FANTIN DES ODOARDS, L. G. *Journal.* Paris, 1895.

FLEISCHMANN, HECTOR. *Étapes Napoléoniennes. 1. Le Quartier General à Waterloo.* Paris, 1912.

FORTESCUE, THE HON. J. W. *A History of the British Army.* Vol. X. London, 1920.

FULLER, MAJOR-GENERAL J. F. C. *The Decisive Battles of the Western World.* Vols. II and III. London, 1956.

GEYL, PIETER. *Napoleon – For and Against.* London, 1949.

GONNARD, PHILIPPE. *Les Origines de la Légende Napoléonienne.* Paris, 1906.

GOURGAUD, GENERAL. *The Campaign of 1815.* London, 1818.

GROUARD, A. *La Critique de la Campagne de 1815.* Paris, 1904.

GUEDALLA, PHILIP. *The Hundred Days.* London, 1934.

HAMLEY, GENERAL SIR EDWARD. *The Operations of War.* Edinburgh and London, 1900.

HENDERSON, E. F. *Blücher and the Uprising of Prussia against Napoleon.* New York and London, 1911.

HOBHOUSE, JOHN CAM. *See* BROUGHTON, LORD.

HOOPER, GEORGE. *Waterloo, the Downfall of the First Napoleon.* London, 1904.

HOUSSAYE, HENRY. *1815.* 3 Vols. 1. *La Première Restauration – Le Retour de L'Isle d'Elbe – Les Cent Jours.* Paris, 1911; 2. *Waterloo.* Paris, 1910; 3. *La Seconde Abdication – La Terreur Blanche.* Paris, 1905.

JAMES, LT.-COL. W. H. *The Campaign of 1815.* Edinburgh and London, 1908.

JOMINI, GENERAL BARON. *The Campaign of Waterloo.* Translated by S. V. Benet. New York, 1853.

JUNG, T. *Lucien Bonaparte et ses Mémoires. 1775-1840.* 3 Vols. Paris, 1882-3.

KELLY, CHRISTOPHER. *A . . . Circumstantial Account of the Battle of Waterloo.* London, 1828.

KEMBLE, JAMES. *Napoleon Immortal.* London, 1959.

LABRETONNIÈRE, E. *Souvenirs du Quartier Latin.* Paris, 1863.

LACHOUQUE, COMMANDANT HENRY. *Le Secret de Waterloo.* Paris, 1952.

LACOUR-GAYET, G. *Talleyrand 1784-1838.* 4 Vols. Paris, 1930-4.

LEATHES. H. M. *Reminiscences of Waterloo.*

LE GROS, H. N. P. *Le Maréchal Grouchy.* Paris, 1912.

LENIENT, E. *La Solution des Enigmes de Waterloo.* Paris, 1915.

LEROY, ANDRÉ. *Les Roses de Redouté et de l'Impératrice Joséphine.* Paris, 1950.

McGRIGOR, SIR JAMES. *Autobiography.* London, 1861.

MAHAN, ALEXANDRE. *Marie Louise.* Paris, 1933.

MARIE-LOUISE. *Marie-Louise et Napoleon, 1813-14.* Edited by C. F. Palmstierna. Paris, 1955.

MARMONT, MARÉCHAL, DUC DE RAGUSE. *Mémoires.* Vol. VII. Paris, 1857.

MAXWELL, SIR HERBERT. *The Life of Wellington.* 2 Vols. London, 1899.

MENEVAL, BARON. *Napoléon et Marie-Louise. Souvenirs Historiques.* 3 Vols. Paris, 1844-5. New edition entitled *Mémoires.* 3 Vols. Paris, 1894.

MERCER, GENERAL CAVALIÉ. *Journal of the Waterloo Campaign.* London, 1927.

METTERNICH, PRINCE CLEMENT. *Mémoires.* Vol. I. Paris, 1880.

MOLLIEN, COMTE, *Memoires d'un Ministre du Trésor Public.* 3 Vols. Paris, 1898.

NAPOLEON, *Correspondance.* Vol. XXVIII. Paris, 1869.

—— *Lettres Inédites de Napoléon Ier.* Vol. II, Paris 1897.

—— *Mémoires pour servir à l'histoire de France.* Vol. IX. Paris, 1830.

—— *The Portfolio of Bonaparte.* Paris, 1815.

NAYLOR, JOHN. *Waterloo.* London, 1960.

NEY, J. N., DUC D'ELCHINGEN. *Documents Inédits sur la Campagne de 1815.* 1840.

NICOLSON, SIR HAROLD. *The Congress of Vienna.* London, 1946.

OMAN, SIR CHARLES. *Studies in the Napoleonic Wars.* London, 1929.

PASQUIER, E. *Histoire de Mon Temps. Mémoires du Chancelier Pasquier.* Vol. III. Paris, 1894.

PETIET, AUGUSTE. *Souvenirs Militaires de l'Histoire Contemporaine.* Paris, 1844.

PEYRUSSE, J. G. R. *Mémorial et Archives de M. le baron Peyrusse.* Carcassonne, 1869.

PIÉTRI, FRANÇOIS. *Lucien Bonaparte.* Paris, 1939.

PION DE LOCHES, A. A. F. *Mes Campagnes, 1792-1815.* Paris, 1889.

RATCLIFFE, B. *Marshal Grouchy and the Guns of Waterloo.* London, 1942.

ROPES, J. C. *The Campaign of Waterloo.* London, 1903.

ROSE, J. H. *Napoleonic Studies.* London, 1904.

SCOTT, JOHN. *Paris Revisited in 1815.* London, 1816.

SHAW-KENNEDY, GENERAL SIR JOHN. *Notes on the Battle of Waterloo.* London, 1869.

SIBORNE, MAJOR-GENERAL H. T. *Waterloo Letters.* London, 1891.

—— CAPTAIN W. *History of the War in France and Belgium in 1815.* 2 Vols. London, 1844.

SIDNEY, THE REV. EDWIN. *The Life of Lord Hill, G.C.B.* London, 1845.

STANHOPE, EARL OF. *Notes of Conversations with the Duke of Wellington, 1831-51.* London, 1888.

TALLEYRAND. *Correspondance inédite du Prince Talleyrand et du Roi Louis XVIII pendant le Congrès de Vienne.* Paris, 1881.

THIÉBAULT, BARON. *Mémoires.* Vol. V. Paris, 1895.

THIERS, ADOLPHE. *Histoire du Consulat et de l'Empire.* 20 Vols. Paris, 1845-62.

'UBIQUE'. *Famous Batteries of the Royal Artillery.* Portsmouth, 1930.

VILLEMAIN, A. F. *Souvenirs Contemporains d'Histoire et de Littérature.* Paris, 1854.

WELLINGTON. *The Dispatches of Field Marshal the Duke of Wellington,* Compiled by Lieut.-Colonel Gurwood. Vol. XII. London. 1838.

—— *Supplementary Despatches, Correspondence and Memoranda of Field Marshal Arthur, Duke of Wellington, K. G.* Edited by his son, the Duke of Wellington, K. G. Vol. X. London, 1863.

INDEX

THE HUNDRED DAYS

Soult—*cont.*
131, 138, 141, 161, 167-8, 192-3, 196, 203, 248, 255, 273, 294
Stassart, Baron de, 71-2
Steinmetz, Major-General von, 115, 117, 119, 140, 145, 292
Subervie, Lieut.-General Baron, 148, 164, 172, 192, 204, 220, 248, 296

Talleyrand-Périgord, Charles Maurice de, Prince of Benevento (1754-1838), 3, 5, 51, 52, 72, 280
Thiébault, Baron de, 56
Thielemann, Lieut.-General von, 111, 121, 128, 136, 152, 158, 166, 176, 180, 202, 216, 223, 239, 293
Tolentino, battle of. *See* Battle of Tolentino
Travers, General, 207, 208, 209, 210, 213
Treaty of Chaumont (1 March 1814, renewed 18 March 1815), 43, 48
Treaty of Paris, the Second (20 November 1815), 280n
Treaty, secret, of 3 Jan. 1815, 3, 49

Uxbridge, Lieut.-General the Earl of, 106, 168, 169, 171, 172, 173, 174, 208, 209, 215, 220, 221, 223, 290

Vandamme, Lieut.-General Comte, 41, 70, 101, 107, 113, 114, 115, 117, 121, 122-3, 124, 128, 130, 139, 140, 145, 148, 149, 150, 158, 159, 161, 165, 167, 173, 177, 202, 211, 212, 216, 259, 276, 295
Vandeleur, Major-General Sir Ormsby, 170, 171, 172, 205, 210, 237, 239, 290
Villers-Cotterets, battle of. *See* Battle of Villers-Cotterets
Vivian, Major-General Sir Hussey, 146, 170, 171, 172, 173, 205, 239, 244, 290

Waterloo, battle of. *See* Battle of Waterloo
Wavre, battle of. *See* Battle of Wavre
Wellington, Arthur Wellesley, Duke of (1769-1852): arrives in Vienna, 3; leaves Vienna for the Low Countries, 56-7; criticized in Parliament on 7 April, 58; plans for the war, 65; builds up his army in Low Countries, 83-4; strength of English army, 99; well informed as to military movements in France prior to invasion of Belgium, 100; receives reports of French movements, 104; his secret intelligence, 105-6; position of his troops on 15 June, 106; Napoleon's contempt for, 110, 139; Napoleon's expectation as to his movements on 15 June, 116; first contact of his troops with French, 120; well served by his forward officers on 15 June, 121; hears of French invasion, 126; hesitation in ordering troops to Charleroi area, 126-7; at Duchess of Richmond's ball, 126-7; his views as to Napoleon's best plan of action, 126-7; orders army to Quatre Bras, 127; leaves Brussels, 128; arrives at Quatre Bras, 134; confers with Blücher at Brye, 136, 137; at Quatre Bras, 137; his strength at Quatre Bras, 142; receives reinforcements, 143; gains the advantage at Quatre Bras, 148; Prussians await his help at Ligny, 149; obliged to retire as result of battle of Ligny, 152; drives back French on Frasnes, 153; losses at Quatre Bras, 153; receives news of Ligny and orders retreat on Mont St Jean, 157; informed that Prussians will concentrate at Wavre, 164; lets Gneisenau know he will make stand at Mont St Jean, 164; infantry of rearguard retires from Quatre Bras, 168; success of his retreat, 170; lunches at *Le Roi d'Espagne*, 170; army positioned at Mont St Jean, 175; strength of forces available for battle, 175, 298; Prussians promise assistance on 18th, 176; his confidence on eve of battle, 181; believes Napoleon might manœuvre to the right, 181; prepares for retreat, 181; in touch with Blücher on night of 17th, 181-2; Gneisenau's dislike of him, 181; his army begins to take up its position for battle, 183-4; inspects his position, 184; catches sight of Bülow's cavalry, 184; advantages of his position on battlefield, 184; he expects Napoleon to manœuvre, 186-7; plans for various contingencies, 186-7; strength of forces available at Waterloo, 188; inspects his front-line, 193-4; not induced to move troops to his right by attack on Hougoumont, 197; reinforces garrison in Hougoumont, 198; the cannonade of 1.30 p.m., 204-5; reinforces troops in La Haye

322